Digital Depression

THE GEOPOLITICS OF INFORMATION

Edited by Dan Schiller, Pradip Thomas, and Yuezhi Zhao

Digital Depression

Information Technology and Economic Crisis

DAN SCHILLER

UNIVERSITY OF ILLINOIS PRESS

Urbana, Chicago, and Springfield

Chapter 4 is a modified version of Dan Schiller, "The
Militarization of U.S. Communications," *Communication,
Culture and Critique* 1, no. 1 (March 2008): 126–38.

Library of Congress Cataloging-in-Publication Data
Schiller, Dan, 1951-
Digital depression : information technology and
economic crisis / Dan Schiller.
pages   cm. — (The geopolitics of information)
Includes bibliographical references and index.
ISBN 978-0-252-08032-6 (paperback : alk. paper)
ISBN 978-0-252-03876-1 (cloth : alk. paper)
ISBN 978-0-252-09671-6 (ebook)
1. Information technology. 2. Economic policy.
3. Economic development—Technological innovations.
4. Global Financial Crisis, 2008–2009.
I. Title.
HD30.2.S325   2014
338.9'26—dc23   2014012439

To Sunie

Contents

Acknowledgments

A book is a collective labor. This one grew out of conversations with those who are not present, as well as with a worldwide community of contemporary scholars, journalists, and activists.

Great thanks to Susan Davis, Richard Hill, Richard Maxwell, Robert McChesney, Vincent Mosco, ShinJoung Yeo, and Yuezhi Zhao for reading and criticizing drafts of this work, for supplying me with citations, and for sharing their own work. Thanks to Serge Halimi and his colleagues, for creating continued opportunities for me to engage with the readers of *Le Monde diplomatique*. These individuals may, or may not, agree with my formulations—for which I am solely responsible.

Research projects undertaken by a group of talented students helped germinate fruitful lines of argument. Thanks to Matt Crain, ShinJoung Yeo, Shen Hong, Katrina Fenlon, Tang Min, and Sindha Agha. At the University of Illinois, a formative intellectual role was played by my undergraduate seminars on "The Communications Industry and the Economic Crisis," commencing in 2009, and my doctoral seminars on "Information in Society" and "The Social History of U.S. Telecommunications." I am fortunate to enjoy the camaraderie of my colleagues at the Graduate School of Library and Information Science, especially Alistair Black and Bonnie Mak. Thanks also to Linda Smith for making room for me to pursue this work. Zach Schiller and Anita Schiller sent ideas and documents. The Help Desk and the Technical Staff at GSLIS saved me from various possible catastrophes.

Conferences and presentations gave me the benefit of critical responses to early forms of argument. I thank the organizers of these far-flung events: Yuezhi Zhao for "Communication and Global Power Shifts," Communication University of China, and for "Communication and Global Power Shifts," Simon Fraser University; Lu Xinyu and Yuezhi Zhao for "Conference on Critical Communications," Fudan University; Janet Wasko for the "Television Studies Conference," University of Oregon; Nick Dyer-Witheford for a presentation at University of Western Ontario; Mari Castañeda for a presentation at the University of Massachusetts; Larry Gross for a presentation at the University of Southern California; Susan Davis and Inger Stole for a presentation at the University of Illinois; Rod Stoneman for a presentation at the National University of Ireland at Galway; Sarita Albagli and Maria Lucia Maciel for "IBICT and UFRJ Seminar on Information, Power and Politics," Federal University of Rio de Janeiro; and Rodrigo Gómez García for "XXI National Congress," Mexican Association for Mass Communication Research, Puebla.

Thanks to the University of Illinois Press for initiating "The Geopolitics of Information" series, to which this book contributes; to my co-editors in this venture, Pradip Thomas and Yuezhi Zhao; and to Willis Regier, Danny Nasset, Jennifer Clark, and Julie Gay for their expert advice and editorial guidance.

Thanks to Lucy Schiller and Ethan Schiller, and to Susan G. Davis—to whom I dedicate this book—for their generosity of spirit and loving support.

I acknowledge the International Communication Association for permission to draw on excerpts from Dan Schiller, "The Militarization of U.S. Communications," *Communication, Culture and Critique* 1, no. 1 (March 2008): 126–38.

Digital Depression

Introduction

A Contradictory Moment

Today's financial and economic crisis originated, paradoxically, in the heartland of advanced information and communications technology (ICT): the United States. California, home to both Silicon Valley and Hollywood, was perhaps the hardest-hit U.S. state.[1] Late in 2013, San Jose, California—at the center of Silicon Valley—was cutting social services, leaving potholes in disrepair, and planning to strip city workers of health benefits.[2]

It was not supposed to turn out this way. For decades we were told that ICTs constitute a source of general economic uplift. From the theory of postindustrial society, first advanced during the 1960s, to "new economy" boosters during the 1990s, to their successors today, public discourse has ordained the regenerative benefits of ICTs. A benign future would be borne to us, as we became an information society anchored by networks; the forecast was endlessly bright. Instead, the United States, the historical driver of digital systems and services, led the world into the deepest and most prolonged slump since the 1930s.

Commencing in December 2007, a recession turned into a full-scale panic. At the nadir of the financial collapse, in September and October 2008, twelve of the thirteen largest U.S. financial institutions were at risk of collapsing within two weeks. The crisis, however, was global in scale, as central banks from the Bank of England to Brazil and from the European Central Bank to South Korea became desperate for dollar liquidity.[3] Federal Reserve Bank Chairman Ben Bernanke told the Financial Crisis Inquiry Commission that this period "was the worst financial crisis in global history, including the Great Depression."[4]

The U.S. government intervened on an unprecedented scale, making commitments worth an estimated $23.7 trillion through thirty-five separate programs to backstop the reeling financial system.[5] The emergency was arrested, but not before the turmoil carried over to the economy—both domestically and internationally. Output, trade, and investment plunged. As the economy staggered into 2009, the language employed by sober analysts was only somewhat more subdued: a "Great Recession," a "Second Great Contraction," even a "Lesser Depression."[6]

A recovery was officially declared in June 2009 by the National Bureau of Economic Research.[7] Talk of depression faded, but the syndrome of financial turmoil and economic stagnation did not dissipate. In 2010, 15.1 percent of Americans—46.2 million, a greater number than at any time since records began to be compiled more than half a century ago—were officially living in poverty.[8] The crisis's financial and economic ramifications continued to spool across the world. "Technically, there is no depression," stated the *Financial Times* in 2011, "as there has not been a large and sustained drop in economic activity"; yet, this influential voice of transnational business followed Keynes in singling out "another sort of depression: a prolonged period of suboptimal activity, in spite of aggressive fiscal and monetary policy . . . a toxic mix of below-peak production, negative real policy interest rates, high unemployment and government deficit."[9] This syndrome only persisted, miring the global economy in what two critical analysts call an "endless crisis."[10]

If, as it enters its seventh year, the underlying condition is clear, then it is noteworthy that the word "depression" figures only occasionally in public discourse. A few intrepid economists—notably, Paul Krugman—insist on using it.[11] And, in comparing the "ongoing crisis to the Great Depression," economist J. Bradford DeLong has concluded that "there is hardly anything 'lesser' about it."[12] These, however, constitute exceptions. The drumbeat of economic reports during winter 2013–14 signaled "stagnation," a higher "jobless rate," "flat" household incomes, "sluggish" trade, "tepid growth,"[13] "deflation,"[14] "slow" U.S. capital spending,[15] a possible "tech bubble,"[16] an "emerging markets sell-off,"[17] and a "new" financial crisis[18]—yet the persistence of the slump has not yet resulted in a shared awareness that we are indeed living through a depression. Nor have this depression's profound longer-term ramifications really yet begun to register.

Crises are characterized by financial stress and economic stagnation. As existing structural relationships strain and crack apart, economic policy acquires urgency. But what if the political economy is not only battered and languishing? What if it is also undergoing a far-reaching structural transformation? What if, behind momentary initiatives aimed at restoring normalcy, we are amid a metamorphosis that is actually altering what may be considered normal? The Great Depression of the 1930s provides a portentous illustration.

In the United States, the political mobilizations of the 1930s brought forth an unprecedented governmental response to the Depression, and the results were to reconstruct U.S. capitalism and, for a time, to vitalize democratic practices. In contrast, in Germany and Japan, overarching responses to the Depression arrived in the form of fascist state mobilizations and expansionist militarism. Domestically and especially internationally, the Great Depression saw fierce conflicts, as rival states and social classes vied to restructure the global political economy.

A less familiar historical feature also merits emphasis: that the Depression harbored sites of regenerative productive activity. Michael A. Bernstein shows that, in the United States, economic dynamism actually carried forward throughout the 1930s in industries such as chemicals, building materials, petroleum, tobacco, food products, and nonelectrical machinery.[19] Although profit-making investment began to channel into these and other emerging industries,[20] this nascent pole of growth began to power the wider economy only following years of violent social change. Between the financial crash of 1929 and the end of World War II, states took emergency measures to rebalance domestic class relations; cooperated and clashed in reweaving the institutional fabric of the global political economy; and contended with rising postcolonial actors and socialist adversaries. Irresistible momentum built behind decolonization and national liberation as European and Japanese empires fell.

Is the present crisis comparable? Are new poles of growth—of profitable accumulation—forming? Are rival states contending to steer the global capitalist political economy in divergent directions? What sort of a restructuring is underway: What are the chief contour lines traced by programs for political-economic reorganization? Is regeneration in prospect?

A bright thread of digital technology runs through all these questions. To trace this thread, we need a theory of the current crisis. Bookstores fortunate enough to have survived are chockablock with volumes analyzing the meltdown. Before turning to develop my own account, I will briefly inventory those that are on offer.

An official postmortem concludes that the crisis required time to gestate and that it testifies to a recurrent tendency. "[T]he vulnerabilities that created the potential for crisis were years in the making," declared the National Commission on the Causes of the Financial and Economist Crisis in the United States: "In the decade preceding the collapse, there were many signs that . . . risks to the financial system were growing unchecked." The commission went on to contrast the U.S. housing bubble with "tulip bulbs in Holland in the 1600s, South Sea stocks in the 1700s, Internet stocks in the late 1990s."[21] Influential academics and policymakers belatedly conceded that financial booms and busts are not exceptional but are recurrent and structural traits; one leading account offers a complex typology of financial blowouts down through the centuries.[22]

Another group of studies exhibits disparate objectives and invites us to consider not cyclical financial trends but exposures of individual self-interestedness and wrongdoing and institutional corruption. These accounts are grounded in outrage at the greed, malfeasance, and willful lack of accountability that contributed to the financial crisis and, tellingly, also pervaded its management.[23]

Quite a different set of inquiries emphasizes structural tendencies beyond the financial boom-and-bust cycle: escalating economic inequality, financial deregulation, and increased consumer indebtedness. These trends, each of which deepened beginning in the 1970s, introduced vulnerabilities that rendered the political economy more likely to undergo a crisis.[24] Radical analysts may link these trends to a far-reaching conception of "monopoly capital" and portray economic stagnation as endemic.[25] Disparate variants of this thesis have been offered, and some aptly underline that even chronic stagnation need not necessarily curb corporate profitability. Doug Henwood thus points to "the great upsurge in corporate profitability from 1982 through 1997."[26] During the first nine quarters of the "recovery" announced in June 2009, real corporate profits again spiked, both in absolute terms and as a proportion of national income growth.[27]

Whatever the merits of these diverse accounts—and there are many—none of them pinpoints the contradictory matrix of technological revolution and stagnation that constitutes capitalism today. Liberal and radical political economists situate the slump in capitalism's contemporary history, but they neglect, belittle, or simply abstract away from ICTs' economic role. Doug Henwood, for example, has been an explicit critic of the economic importance of information and communications, linking this sector only to a deeply coded tendency toward uncontrolled financial speculation. One looks in vain for more than peripheral discussions of ICTs and the internet in recent works by liberal economists such as Paul Krugman, Joseph Stiglitz, and Robert Kuttner. They uniformly evacuate information and communications from their analyses; in turn, the relationship between the two constituent features—ICTs and the slump—remains uncharted.

The supposed contributions of information technology are of course much vaunted elsewhere. However, the oracles of the information society refrain from connecting ICTs to capitalism's historical development. For a period of decades, their reticence to forge this link betrayed a particular ideological alignment. Postindustrial and information society theories originated, during the 1960s and 1970s, in the notion that the growth of the services sector and of information occupations, alongside society's incorporation of "intellectual technologies," amounted to a historic transcendence of capitalist property relations.[28] Arguments that abstract away from the persistent social relationships of capitalism have continued to win influence, even as they shed some of postindustrial theory's other problematic features. One example is the idea of "network society" offered by sociologist Manuel Castells. In order to engage the heterogeneous global social formations of the contemporary world, Castells eschews capitalism as a totalizing conception. The contrast between Castells's approach and that of Raymond Williams is instructive, as Williams holds that "no mode of production and therefore no dominant social order and therefore no dominant culture ever in reality includes or exhausts all human practice, human energy, and human intention."[29] Yet modes of production and dominant social orders persist. From time to time, Castells does posit that "network society" continues to be a kind of capitalism[30]; but his account withdraws from the idea that capitalism constitutes a central presence and a general shaping force. Castells indeed establishes a fundamental analytical distance from capitalism on the very first page of his magnum opus, where he introduces "network society" as incarnating "a new form of relationship between economy, state, and society."[31]

The theory of digital capitalism, in contrast, is distinctive for foregrounding communications and information as an emerging pivot of the ever-mutating capitalist political economy.[32] I developed this conception during the late 1990s, as a corrective to the "New Economy" boosterism that fed the internet bubble as it inflated. I showed that U.S. capital and the U.S. capitalist state remained paramount determinants of political-economic change all the way through this metamorphosis, whereby capitalism was made over to accept a more ICT-intensive orientation.

How, then, may the concept of digital capitalism be applied today? How may it be modified to assimilate and to track the profoundly reworked and still unfinished history of the early twenty-first century? For there is no doubt that such a revision is needed. Our epoch is marked not by expansion but by contraction, not by stasis but by dizzying structural change. The conception of digital capitalism needs to be altered and expanded so as to underline the continuing societal appropriation of network capacities. Today, a technological revolution is wrapped up inside an economic collapse: Whence came this digital depression? The same edition of the *Financial Times* that headlined "deflation fears" in November 2013 also carried a front-page story heralding the good fortune of Twitter's founders, when they became overnight billionaires following the company's initial public offering.[33] What accounts for the emergence of this pole of relative growth, which is so evident, even amid the slump? What are the historical dynamics that animate this digital depression, and where may they lead?

It is the thesis of this book that the role of information and communications needs to be sought *within* the political economy's chief developmental processes. In part I, I single out three of these: capital's reorganization of the system of production, through fresh cycles of labor restructuring and spiking foreign direct investment; capital's concurrent ingress into finance; and escalating military procurement spending. In part II, I turn to examine a fourth trend, the sprawling recomposition of the information and communications sector.[34] Embedded deep within these complex trends have been digital systems, devices, services, and applications. Investment in ICTs arrived as a part of capitalist development, rather than from outside.

Capitalism's developmental processes are, however, contradictory. "Capital is an infernal machine," writes Fredric Jameson, "constantly breaking down, and repairing itself only by the laborious convulsions of expansion."[35] As regeneration takes hold, the seeds of a subsequent crisis are planted deep in the political economy. On one hand, then, an emergent digital capitalism imparted a powerful impulse to renewed accumulation; on the other hand, it introduced its own world-shaking tensions. As David Harvey puts it, "The crisis tendencies are not resolved but merely moved around."[36] The outcome of a prior contested restructuring, today's slump is marked by escalating conflict over the nature of any prospective resolution. What are the sources and character of this contention? This forms the subject of discussion in part III.

The through-line of this book traces an arc from the causes of the crash of digital capitalism in 2007–08 to the raggedly uneven character of its leading growth pole—communications and information—and through to today's fierce political-economic struggles to capture whatever growth still may follow.

Commodity Chains

To set out on this journey I draw on a concept borrowed from world-system theory: the "commodity chain." Developed by Terence Hopkins and Immanuel Wallerstein during the 1970s, the concept's purpose is "to show that most production within the capitalist world-economy that placed items for consumption on the market was the result of a long chain that in fact crossed frontiers, and that this had been so throughout the entire history of the capitalist world-economy from the long sixteenth century to today."[37]

It is useful to contrast the commodity chain concept with the more familiar notion of the "value chain" formulated by business professor Michael Porter in the 1980s and widely circulated ever since. Although both constructs highlight links between and among industries, as Jennifer Bair underlines, they differ sharply in their orientations. "Value chain" pivots neither on labor nor on prof-itability, but instead on industrial organization and the so-called "value-added" at successive stages of an industry's operations. "Commodity chain" focuses attention, in contrast, on how a global division of labor evolves and mutates in the historical context of an ever-reconfiguring process of capital accumula-tion.[38] "Value chain" internalizes the thinking of the executive suite, from which "commodity chain" grants us much-needed analytical distance.

Commodity chains bring together diverse labor systems to effect globally distributed production processes. Analysts have used this construct to study several commodities, from grain and other agricultural and extractive products to manufactured capital goods such as ships and, more recently, automobiles, electronics, services, and even cocaine. The direction and constitutive features of a specific commodity chain are neither predetermined nor mechanically implanted,[39] though top-down planning by units of capital, and protection by agencies of the state, have been regular concomitants.

The analytical power of the commodity-chain construct stems from its out-ward-looking inclusiveness, its insistence that the social relationships through which production occurs are both dispersed and multifaceted. Commencing with the labor needed to produce sustenance for the workers whose own labor then forms a basis, via "sub-chains," for making components, the chain extends to the production processes in which these intermediate products are then put to use as inputs in still other forms of production, culminating in the assembly of a final commodity and its distribution for consumption. For world-system theo-rists, as Jennifer Bair helpfully suggests, the commodity chain concept permits seemingly disparate, far-flung mobilizations of labor power to be related as the essential substrate of capitalist production.[40] The analytical motivation is that, "by tracing the networks of these commodity chains, one can track the ongoing division and integration of labor processes and thus monitor the constant devel-opment and transformation of the world-economy's production system."[41]

Adherents go on to assert that the structural relations that link differently situated regions and industries, and the spatial distribution of more- and less-profitable production processes, divulge an underlying pattern. More profitable processes are seen to be located in, and monopolized by, capital in the wealthy "core" regions, while less-profitable processes are based disproportionately in the "periphery"—denoted successively by colonized territories, less-developed countries, or emerging markets. In this perspective, "the major direction of interzonal movements along the commodity chains is from a peripheral product to a core product."[42] Although "the chains are scarcely static for a moment,"[43] thus, the logic of their ongoing elaboration discloses an obdurate structural inequality. As Hopkins and Wallerstein put this, "The capitalist world-economy reveals itself via this kind of radiography as a fast-moving network of relations that nonetheless constantly reproduces a basic order . . . or at least has thus far reproduced this basic order."[44]

In part III, I place this theoretical claim in question. The core-periphery model—the deep structure posited by world system theory—seems more contingent today, in light of the profoundly transformative capitalist development of China and, in lesser measure, of some other once-peripheral countries. Still crucial, nevertheless, is the world system analysts' goal of piercing the opaque developmental rhythms of the capitalist world-economy by scrutinizing how alternating cycles of growth and depression are connected to the reorganization of labor systems within far-flung commodity chains. Taking note of Hopkins and Wallerstein's insight that "the work on so-called leading industries could be reformulated in terms of such a network of chains,"[45] the pivotal question becomes how to assimilate networks and ICTs more broadly into our consideration of commodity chains.

This concern has not been merely academic. How to bring network systems into commodity chains in fact has proved to be a pervasive strategic preoccupation for big capital. Commodity chains enfolding local-to-transnational production processes have been incessantly disaggregated and reassembled, I will argue, in light of capital's continued appropriations of network capacities.[46]

Digital capitalism offers a name for the historical watershed we are traversing and a conceptual framework for understanding this progression. The concept points to a new phase change in a five-hundred-year history that has been marked by abiding tendencies: capital's continually extended use of wage labor, its search for new and often contested sites of commodification, and its episodic crises, wherein rampant financial speculation triggers a fall into depression and economic stagnation. Digital capitalism, therefore, is comparable to "industrial capitalism," a conception that began to be used in the nineteenth century to describe the far-reaching political-economic mutations that were being introduced around new forms of machinery in England and, increasingly, elsewhere. The specificity of digital capitalism needs, again, to be set *within* abiding structural trends and historical crisis tendencies rather than in a putative break with them or an evolution out of them.

Drawing on my own continued research, and borrowing liberally from the thinking of other analysts, this book tries to deepen the conception of digital capitalism by integrating it with an account of the political economy's return to crisis. The financial panic of 2008 only kicked off this new phase, as the wider economy fell into stagnation and the syndrome that resulted, as became evident by 2012–13, became a continuing crisis. Considerable indeterminacy remained, of course, but two chief contentions are warranted: that the economic contributions made by information and communications to contemporary—digital— capitalism rendered the digital a fundamental pole of growth, akin to the nascent consumer industries of the 1930s; and that, when it arrived, the crisis could be traced not only to financial speculation but to capital's multifaceted integration of digital systems into the political economy.

recovering profitability and improving competitiveness."[11] What followed was no mere mechanical exercise, but a many-sided and contingent mutation. Vijay Prashad underlines that "the U.S. government authorized a major assault on its own economy, to reshape it, to follow the axiom of the German sociologist Werner Sombart, so that 'from destruction a new spirit of creation arises.'"[12] At the center of this destructive creativity were information and communications, which animated wrenching changes in production.

A basement-to-attic redesign touched everything from the content of specific jobs to the technical division of labor within companies and entire industries, to the location of discrete and now increasingly isolable production processes. This "great transformation," as Kim Moody (recalling Karl Polanyi) calls it,[13] encompassed both the location and character of capital expenditures and the types and quantities of labor mobilized by that investment. "Lean production,"[14] followed by "total quality management" and "re-engineering," were catchphrases that lent an unjustified aura of thoughtfulness to savage attacks on existing practice; "just-in-time inventory," "teamwork," "outsourcing," and "downsizing"[15] fell into the same category. Behind the jargon, long-familiar processes of cost cutting and transformation ripped through communities of wage earners in the United States and Western Europe. In the global south, meanwhile, the reorganization of production concurrently brought millions of peasants and rural producers into the circuits of wage labor.

I will study this "Great Transformation" from two vantage points. The first concerns the labor process,[16] the second, the wider commodity chains within which labor has been mobilized.

■ ■ ■

This, of course, was not the first time that production was restructured. From its historical origins in English agriculture, capital had fixated continually on a need to wring out inefficiencies, increase profits, and reassert control over refractory workers. This was not a straight-line rational progress. Misplaced priorities, fantasies of managerial control, ignorance of the workaday processes of production, and worker resistance prevented capital from any wholesale realization of its programs to change work and to bend workers to its wishes. Cycles of revision, pushback, and adjustment were continual. Within these limits, however, the labor processes on which production relied were recurrently revolutionized.

A tripartite conception of the history of the labor process was developed by Marx, through his reading of English factory inspectors' reports and parliamentary papers[17] in an effort to comprehend the high-tech labor process of his own day—in Britain's factory system. The process of capitalist development had set in motion within the labor process, Marx found, a long-term progression: from handicraft, to manufacture, to what he called large-scale industry.

On the skilled handiwork of the artisan rested craft production of every sort, from printing to blacksmithing; craft labor, in which a single artisan often produced an entire commodity, placed stringent limits not only on productivity but also on the inroads which capital might make in assuming control over the labor process. A subsequent stage, which Marx called manufacture, he detected in portions of sixteenth-through-eighteenth-century Europe; manufacture bespoke capital's success in establishing a more productive technical division of labor. Over time, jobs, once the preserve of a single individual, were broken up into components, so that the repetition of each of a number of activities could be assigned to separate workers. What characterized this division of labor in manufacture, Marx related, was that previously independent workers became subjected to the discipline of capital, so that a "hierarchic gradation" beyond ad hoc cooperation characterized the transformed labor process.[18] He was respectful toward this phase: manufacture ultimately "towered up as an economic work of art, on the broad foundation of the town handicrafts, and of the rural domestic industries."[19] Dozens of separate trades, each with its own skills and practices, supplied the "associated labour" needed to realize productivity that remained unattainable for artisans laboring in small workshops. The age of manufacture coincided with the world of labor memorably chronicled by Adam Smith, in which the making of a seemingly simple pin rested on dozens of distinct operations.

Only the historical appearance of a third form, however—"large-scale industry"—transformed the labor process "to its very core."[20] Under renewed pressure to increase the productiveness of labor, capital moved unevenly and incompletely beyond the subordination of labor "on the basis of the technical conditions in which it historically finds it."[21] Through the application of science and the related introduction of specialized machinery powered by inanimate energy, the skills of individual craft workers were progressively eclipsed "as the regulating principle of social production": "Along with the tool," Marx asserted, "the skill of the workman in handling it passes over to the machine. The capabilities of the tool are emancipated from the restraints that are inseparable from human labour-power. Thereby the technical foundation on which is based the division of labour in Manufacture, is swept away."[22]

The tools of production, as they shifted from the artisan's workbench to complex and interlinked machines, compelling labor from dozens, hundreds, and eventually thousands of coordinated workers, signified a fundamental vector of labor-process analysis. Large-scale industry progressively transformed "the instruments of labour into instruments of labour only usable in common"—which, not coincidentally, enabled "the economizing of all means of production by their use as the means of production of combined, socialized labour."[23]

The archetype of "instruments of labour only usable in common" was the nineteenth-century English factory. Cooperation and division of labor had become widely used practices during the late eighteenth century; but subsequent innovation of machines powered by steam and then by fossil fuels spelled unprecedented increases in output and productivity. Eric Hobsbawm, a historian not given to hyperbole, states: "The Industrial Revolution marks the most fundamental transformation of human life in the history of the world recorded in written documents."[24] The labor process lay at the center of this sweeping shift. With machine technology, as David Harvey sums it up, "the speed and the continuity are determined internally to the machine system, and workers have to conform to the movement of, say, the assembly line."[25] Symptomatic of the widespread application of machines in Britain during the first half of the nineteenth century were, Marx showed, both an extended workday so that the costly plant could hum without interruption, and intensified work.[26]

The Industrial Revolution was not an event but a complex, drawn-out process. Commencing with the application by British capital of the steam engine and the cotton mill, emergent forms of machine-structured production extended and ramified from this base: the process of change grew by twists and turns from industry to industry, labor process to labor process, and region to region.[27] A spiral of innovation generated a cascade of new consumer commodities and capital goods: sewing machines, woodworking products, reapers, bicycles, and automobiles. Carrying forward from Britain, Glenn Porter writes about the U.S. experience of industrialization during the later nineteenth and early twentieth centuries: "Factory organization, specialized machines, precision manufacture, interchangeable parts, carefully coordinated work sequences and materials flows, and new methods for stamping and welding metal" became sites of sustained analysis, experiment, and reorganization.[28] Manufacturing technology continually burst through prior limits on the scale of commodity production.

Achieved gains in manufacturing output depended on a trio of emerging network industries—in transportation, power, and telecommunications; these helped manufacturers to generate nationwide product markets. These great infrastructures likewise enabled a profound reorganization of manufacturing labor processes.[29] Introduced into American industry between 1885 and 1890, electricity came to the forefront of industrial reorganization after the introduction of centralized power generation by electric utilities after 1900.

The supplanting of coal and steam by electricity, however, went far beyond substituting one power source for another. When compared with the possibilities provided by electrical power delivery, Richard DuBoff showed, earlier methods, practices, and organizational designs suddenly stood out as "almost visibly redundant." Electrification thus became the pivot of a widening "reorganization in manufacturing techniques." "Cost cutting became possible over much larger ranges of output than under steam," DuBoff explains: "Subdivision and mobility of power units offered a wider array of labor, material, and capital equipment combinations."[30] Electricity established a newfound ability to fractionalize power requirements, to diffuse power equipment throughout plants, and to decentralize and intensify individual operations.

An important concomitant was continuing growth in the information processing labor force itself. When we think of the Industrial Revolution, we may picture grimy smokestacks, a clattering din of machinery, and "unskilled" factory "hands." Even at its outset, however, the process of industrialization also gripped information generation, processing, and management. Corporate information processing bulked up to process the sales orders, support the accounting and financial initiatives, and—beginning in the late nineteenth century—develop the systematic marketing and technology research plans that were all predicates of national capital. Nonproduction employees as a fraction of U.S. total manufacturing employment had already reached around 19 percent by 1919 and hovered around this proportion throughout the crisis decades that followed; but the figure climbed after World War II, to 28 percent by 1979.[31] In the science-based industries of electrical and electronic equipment, instruments, chemicals and petrochemicals, and machinery, the proportion was especially high, and industry leaders such as General Electric employed more nonproduction workers than did smaller firms.[32] Symptomatic was the increase in the number of engineers in the United States, from 77,000 in 1910 to 1.2 million in 1970.[33] But the occupational shift was much wider. Corporate managers, as well as skilled services workers in everything from accounting and advertising to telecommunications—professional, scientific-technical, clerical, and management occupations—all expanded.

As early as the 1920s,[34] these multiplying information workers posed an identifiable cost problem for U.S. capital. In an insightful article published sixty years ago, Seymour Melman addressed the rise of what he called "administrative overhead" in U.S. manufacturing. Between 1899 and 1947, he found, administration personnel increased by 485 percent in U.S. manufacturing, to 2,672,000; production personnel increased by only 160 percent, to 12,010,000. Melman located the cause of this increase in the relative proportion of administrative employees not in declining efficiency but in "the addition of *new functions* carried out by the administration personnel." He explained that the substance of the shift lay in the "growing variety of business activities which are being subjected to controls," as management "attempted to control, in ever greater detail, production costs, intensity of work, market demands for products, and other aspects of firm operation."[35] Other research confirmed and updated this trend in the occupational structure.[36] And the buildup of U.S. foreign direct investment during the decades after World War II only further swelled the ranks of technical, managerial, and clerical labor, within and around transnational corporations. How could executives and owners improve their grip on this expansive—and expensive—cost category?

Radical thinkers from late-nineteenth-century Germany to the mid-twentieth-century United States grappled with the implications of this question. It was the achievement of Harry Braverman to show that this labor—whether called "administrative" or "white-collar" or "brainwork" (the term employed in the late-nineteenth-century German debate that kick-started theorizing about this metamorphosis)—had drawn capital's insistent scrutiny. As clerical, professional, managerial, and technical work became prominent, Braverman demonstrated, corporate executives scrambled to identify and apply means of rendering this work more efficient. A rationalizing impulse toward cost cutting and reorganization took a pervasive hold. It brought more women into the waged labor force and induced continual changes in the division of labor and the content of jobs, and it centered more and more on new office technologies.

Geoffrey D. Austrian showed that efforts to restructure labor processes relied extensively on "accurate and timely cost accounting," so that the application of punched-card machines for electromechanical data processing "depended on the prior rationalization of work."[37] Often, as a result, corporate executives realized benefits that went beyond increased labor productivity. The New York Central railroad substituted punched cards for each of the nearly four million freight waybills it generated each year by 1895; as a result, the carrier could chart freight movements and revenues on a weekly rather than monthly basis and route freight more efficiently across its intricate rail network.[38] All told, at least one hundred new office machines were placed on the market in the United States after World War I, as managers became "convinced of the need for a systematic approach" to office work; by the late 1940s the number had grown to around three thousand.[39] Generations of mechanical and electromechanical office machinery, from typewriters and vertical files to adding machines and calculators and punched card data processors, continually altered the labor process; however, sweeping and measurable productivity gains still proved elusive.[40]

While the deployment of machines therefore allowed labor to qualitatively increase the output of many commodities, by the 1950s no technological revolution had transformed the work performed by the diversifying information processing labor force itself. While growing capital intensity bespoke an increasingly routine reliance on tools for common use throughout factory assembly, handicraft principles—supplemented by division of labor, cooperation, and electromechanical equipment—still predominated throughout the sphere of information processing. Architects designed and drafted by hand. Secretaries typed letters, memos, and reports—sixty words a minute was the hoped-for standard—and posted or placed these documents in vertical files. Clericals and low-level managers "kept tabs" on corporate operations, drafted and consulted memos and other documents, and with higher management conducted telephone conversations and, endlessly, face-to-face meetings. In advertising, so-called "creatives" brainstormed over campaigns, exhibiting a Don Draperish mix of glibness, theatricality, and topical awareness, while gesturing toward consumer- and media-research findings. Head tellers and bookkeepers performed complicated statistical operations manually or using simple machinery; as late as the 1930s, the calculation of some of the most elaborate arithmetic operations demanded by government and corporate bureaucracies was being performed by cadres of female "computers."[41] Could the relatively high labor content necessitated by a swelling apparatus of administration, management, office work, science, and engineering—all the "white collar" labor that fed into the giant corporation—be rationalized?

The impulse that had generated a collective labor process—"instruments of labour only usable in common"—within English factories thus carried over as a shaping force, and for much the same reason, into computer-networked labor processes. During the final decades of the twentieth century and into the twenty-first, a Herculean reorganization of work tore through corporate production in factories and fields, offices and laboratories. It could never have taken place without ever-more versatile and far-ranging computer-communications.

Networks—including, when it emerged as a general foundation for networking projects of every kind, the internet—constitute toolkits. Network-enabled tools are distinctive for enabling production throughout the swelling information-processing occupations to overcome restrictions tied to existing handicraft skills. Artisanal techniques of information work, from copying or writing by hand to typewriting, and from architectural drafting to product design, were transformed through the innovation of shared tools and data via networks. Capital investment per office worker sharply increased, relative to capital investment per factory hand.[42] Networks thus conveyed the longstanding historical tendency for tools to be transformed into "instruments of labour only usable in common" into fresh fields of practice and previously exempt segments of the division of labor—from Google's Search function and Gmail to standardized software packages for word processing or tax preparation, to specialized enterprise software for managing corporate databases. Across an ever-widening front of systems and applications, what was sometimes called "information resource sharing" catalyzed qualitative changes in labor processes, as capital redefined skill requirements across innumerable industries and occupations.[43] I am not arguing that these network tools transcended human skill as such; of course they could be implemented only by cultivating new skills. Corporate IT technical staffs and outside suppliers developed skills and identified still additional skill requirements as technical advance proceeded.

Even as the response to the 1970s downturn commenced, in a brilliant pioneering work, Harry Braverman charted how, "in office and service processes, the recently swollen mass of employment has not as yet been subjected to the same extremes of rationalization and mechanization as in the factories, although this is underway."[44] Ursula Huws subsequently drew on Braverman in order to explain the steps involved. Business organizations were parsed analytically into constituent parts. Within each part or function, study proceeded to examine "particular skills and tasks," and there ensued "a progressive codification of knowledge exercised by workers, including tacit knowledge." Tasks were reduced to component elements, "setting explicit standards for their performance and, often, introducing an elaborated division of labour whereby the more routine tasks are transferred to less-skilled workers." Externally dictated forms of control and management were devised and implemented, along with output measures.[45]

Networks participated in this triply: by enabling productivity increases, through shared use of resources and automation of tasks; by enhancing administrative oversight of and intervention into labor processes that had escaped this previously; and by forging linkages between hitherto isolated production processes. The labor mobilized within offices, classrooms, studios, and laboratories, as Nick Dyer-Witheford explains, often could be brought into direct relation, for the first time, not only with labor on the factory floor but also on the part of the final consumer.[46] Computer networks qualitatively extended the reach of the labor process to which Marx had assigned significance in reference to the factory system. Networked tools built exclusively for collaborative use incarnated standardized routines and stitched together multifarious skills and diversely situated workers, enabling them to apply shared knowledge to powerful effect.

The prospect of developing such collaborative potentials supplied a chief motive for computer-network development. In planning for the experimental Arpanet, an ancestor of the internet, Joseph Licklider and Robert Taylor emphasized in 1968 that "a well-programmed computer can provide direct access both to informational resources and to the *processes* for making use of the resources." The "revolutionary" impact of multi-access computers linked by telecommunications, they declared, stemmed from these systems' ability to support "sharing" of "distributed intellectual resources" in support of "cooperative modeling"—that is, "cooperation in the construction, maintenance, and use of a model."[47] The U.S. Defense Advanced Research Projects Agency (DARPA) program grant to develop the Arpanet, initiated in 1969, in fact bore the title "Resource Sharing Computer Networks."[48]

The fact that computers were then very large and costly instruments, as Janet Abbate suggests,[49] functioned as a motivation for developing networks as a means of sharing both processing power and software programs—though Licklider and Taylor seemed, even in 1968, to be pointing to a capability that was more overarching than this. The prime contractor for the Arpanet was a company called BBN; and BBN's review of the project in 1981—a decade before the World Wide Web altered and enlarged the internet—certainly highlighted resource sharing. The volume of messages traversing the Arpanet had increased by orders of magnitude, from around six thousand in 1971 to ten million by 1977.[50] BBN found that as this growth had occurred, Arpanet had accomplished two leading objectives. First, it had enabled the development of techniques and knowledge for interconnecting computers "in such a way that a very broad class of interactions [were] possible." Second, it had allowed its users "to improve and increase computer research productivity through resource sharing."[51] Computer networks enabled effective connections between previously incompatible computers incarnating disparate technical standards, permitting any user or program on any of the computers that were to be linked "to utilize any program or subsystem available on any other computer without having to modify the remote program."[52] The import of this interaction was understood in terms that already carried far beyond this particular Defense Department research program—to "society at large."[53] By 1981, BBN explicitly envisioned "a significant eventual impact on the use of computers in both the public and private sectors."[54]

During the 1960s, some of the first publicly accessible electronic databases had enabled remote access to shared machine-readable bibliographic and data files. By the 1970s, as Licklider and Taylor seem to have forecast, email—which denotes sharing of expressed human thought rather than of software or processing power—was beginning to allow computer scientists, working in universities and military industry, to collaborate from dispersed locations. During the 1980s, local area networks widened the tendency toward shared use, in this case, of arrays of software utilities and office resources such as printers; while, directly in manufacturing production, so-called electronic data interchange enabled information flows between newly equipped machines on the factory floor and between factories and suppliers. Wide-area networks were by now also permitting a great range of database resources and applications to be migrated to proprietary or special-purpose online systems. The progression to mini- and desktop workstations only carried forward the trend of using networks for resource sharing—which has been continually reincarnated in and around computer networking projects.

Technologists—executives as well as computer scientists and engineers—now turned to examine a higher-order problem: how to interconnect entire computer networks, rather than merely discrete mainframe computers. Multiple pathways to this objective were identified, and rival approaches to networking innovated. Indeed, it remained uncertain until the early 1990s which of several data communications technologies might predominate. A spasmodically growing capacity for shared use, however, constituted a decisive element, so that the outcome of the competition between different systems rested in part on this key feature. The protocols used to build out what began to be called the "internet" (using TCP/IP protocols) by the early 1980s stressed interoperability over other design objectives. With release of the software that constructed the World Wide Web, this advantageous trait of internet systems—the ease with which it enabled dispersed users to connect to shared databases and applications tools—became spectacularly greater. A tipping point had been reached. The internet both enlarged the scope of connectivity-enabled functions and widened access to these networked tools far beyond the bounds of any proprietary data communications system—indeed, sometimes, seemingly uncontrollably.

Capital's determination to appropriate network connectivity imported or, better, actually reinvented the labor process of large-scale industry. It accomplished this by using networks to incubate combined, socialized production within previously exempted segments of the division of labor, and to bring these into direct relations with already advanced labor processes. Patterns of adoption, as James Cortada emphasizes, varied unevenly by industry sector and by individual company.[55] "Because businesses began using telecommunications networks long before the wide availability of the Internet," innovating systems "worth trillions of dollars in prior investments," he underlines, "much structural change had already occurred that the Internet has, even now, yet to alter."[56] The management choices opened up by networks spanned across a nearly infinite horizon for reprogrammable and expansible networks are among the most versatile tools ever created.

By the 1980s, it was widely understood that networks granted room for giant companies to "create and sell to others information that is a byproduct of their operations" and, more generally, to "capitaliz[e] on corporate knowledge."[57] Scores of U.S. companies, trumpeted *Business Week*, "are discovering that they possess valuable information resources that can be used as potent strategic weapons." "By using this information in a variety of new ways," the magazine added, "these companies are finding that they can better support their basic businesses, offer services that extend their markets, and create new products and businesses that distinguish them from their rivals."[58] This focus became a fixation through subsequent decades.

Not only did administrative controls come to be applied across a great range of clerical, professional, managerial, and technical work, big companies' strategic applications of networks also faced in other directions. First, they used networks to outsource to specialized suppliers, such as SAP and Oracle and IBM, applications that were becoming standardized. Second, they used networks to develop structured forms of market advantage. A spate of management gurus emphasized how computer systems could be deployed to erect barriers to market entry (by getting customers to rely on their software and support, thereby raising the cost of switching); to alter the balance of power in relationships with suppliers (by allowing giant firms like GE or GM to offload their own inventory costs by instituting online access to suppliers' stocks of parts); and to change the basis of intra-industry competition by developing new products and services.[59] Bloomberg stole a march on existing vendors of financial data by establishing a proprietary system and locking in corporate customers.[60] Third, companies used networks to offload labor costs. Building, as Michael Palm shows, on the self-service idea that had been showcased by telephone networks built around automatic (electromechanical) switches after the early twentieth century, computer networks enabled companies to offload huge quantities of unpaid labor to consumers.[61]

Many applications cost more or simply did not work out as promised. Nevertheless, business came to revolve ever more extensively around deployments of computer-network connectivity. IBM's chief scientist estimated in 1980 that across the U.S. workforce in its entirety, there existed one computer terminal for every forty-eight employees; among IBM customers, one terminal for every twenty-five employees; and within IBM—at that point an unrivaled titan of high tech and a beacon for corporate America—one terminal for every five employees. He projected that "terminals" would continue to proliferate rapidly.[62] His forecast, of course, proved correct. "[I]t is not uncommon," according to a 2012 study, "for 100 percent of the people involved in a supply chain to use IT routinely every working day in the most advanced economies."[63]

However, this Olympian view obscures the changes networks were inducing in work itself. "Few processes have been as totally revolutionized by computer technology as design," claimed Harley Shaiken, an expert on auto-industry reorganization, in 1984. He identified four fundamental benefits to management in computer-assisted design (CAD): to enlarge design alternatives, enhance opportunities for revision, integrate design more closely with manufacturing processes, and remove some limits of time and geography.[64] CAD permitted designers to experiment with how different materials and different parts would react to stress, heat, and other variable conditions without always building expensive and time-consuming clay prototypes. Designers could also model the structure and shape of materials in an effort to trim weight, reduce corrosion, and sculpt eye-catching styles.[65] Rapid reductions were achieved in the product development cycle as the speed of the design process was increased.[66] Advances were made in geometric modeling, particularly the innovation of three-dimensional modeling techniques, partially preprogrammed engineering analysis to appraise structural features, examination of how parts would move with one another by means of "kinematics," and automated drafting.[67]

By 1984, two-fifths of GM's drafting work was performed on computers, up from less than one-fifth just a few years before; mathematicians at the automaker drew on computer models to predict whether a specific metal or alloy could be shaped into a particular design. Rapid migration to computer-assisted design continued with GM's Saturn project, which was to be the first auto designed completely on computers.[68] CAD and its cousin, computer-assisted engineering, or CAE, were refined and extended throughout the next thirty years, as they were welded into vehicle development practices. Caution must be exercised in evaluating this progression, as it introduced cascading difficulties even as existing blockages also might be superseded: Toyota's recalls of around eleven million vehicles during 2010 was traced, for example, to its "heavy reliance on virtual testing of its cars and prototypes."[69] Corporate efforts to control production introduced their own irrationalities.

Mechanization and automation nevertheless diffused through previously exempted labor processes, to the point that, as the Marxist theoretician Ernest Mandel declared early in the 1970s, "all branches of the economy are fully industrialized for the first time."[70] Before he shifted over to a thesis emphasizing societal discontinuity—the so-called "Third Wave"—the futurist management consultant

Alvin Toffler referred to the emerging system in similar terms, as "super-industrial capitalism."[71] This did not signify that networked cooperation—the typifying labor process of large-scale industry—was being universalized across the length and breadth of all commodity chains, but only that existing limits on its adoption were being overcome. Disparate labor systems survived; new occupations developed and expanded. All the while, computer network support for collaborative practice was continually enhanced and enlarged.

Collaboration via computer networks began to be posited as an intrinsic, totalizing feature, separated from any connection with capitalist production. So abstracted, it then verged on becoming a deus ex machina. Frequent claims that the "Arab Spring" of 2011 was a reflex of internet and mobile-phone access comprise a recent example.[72] The internet's enablement of emerging forms of collaboration—of "peer-production,"[73] as Benkler calls it—was not rooted, however, in a commons. Who appropriated this capability for resource sharing and common labor was a question engaged by differentially placed social actors, some demonstrating greater power than others. If a capacity for dispersed cooperation was key to computer networks' significance, then this feature was layered into societies marked by exploitive relations and divisions, some of which were forged at work. The crucial questions were, once more, which actors dominated in appropriating networks' capacity for dispersed cooperation, and for which purposes?[74]

In practice, corporate profit-making initiatives repeatedly advanced while other, disparate networking projects mostly occupied the margins. Starting in the 1970s in the developed capitalist economies, managers and executives rapidly widened their embrace of a long-familiar tenet: "that the vast majority of work should be viewed as collections of processes," and that "collecting data . . . about work flows" could be made "a routine part of everyone's work."[74] This insight engendered spasms of change throughout a metastasizing production system. How to remake the corporation—and its workforce—in light of the availability of network tools became a basic reference point during the epoch of capitalist globalization. Networks thus played a fundamental role in the "Great Transformation," through which capital sought to reorganize not only the content of the labor process but also—as we now will see—the sequencing, spatial arrangement, and management of production within reconstructed commodity chains.

CHAPTER 2

Networked Production and Reconstructed Commodity Chains

We must learn to set the growth of digital networks within the lengthy and complex process of capitalist globalization. The roots of transnational corporations (TNCs) reach back to the seventeenth century, but TNCs became capital's dominant expression during the twentieth. One spur was that the productive capacity of manufacturing industry was bursting through its previous limits. There were others: readier access to cheap labor and natural resources, and an improved ability to administer distribution and marketing in tempting foreign markets. National restrictions, such as patent laws, quotas, tariffs, and other barriers to exports, also motivated big U.S. companies to establish factories and sales offices, mines, and plantations outside their own domestic bases.[1] Reduced transportation costs and, following World War II, the strength of the U.S. dollar were also inducements.[2] Already between 1958 and 1965, economic historian Judith Stein observes, "U.S. companies increased their investment in foreign countries at a rate 50 percent faster than their investment in the United States." In 1965, new foreign direct investment (FDI) composed 34 percent of overall net U.S. investment in rubber manufacturing; 25 percent in manufacturing of transportation equipment; 25 percent in chemicals; and 21 percent in electrical machinery.[3]

Capital based in the United States was far and away the most important source of transnational investment at this time, as U.S. leaders maneuvered for advantage against and between European imperialists and anticolonial liberation movements in the decades after World War II. U.S. foreign direct investment (FDI) was uneven, to be sure, and was unevenly concentrated in just a few regions. Latin America, which already had been in the U.S. orbit for a century, garnered a modest but significant share; oil resources in the Middle East also drew foreign investment. Africa, where European interests still predominated, saw negligible U.S. FDI. Japan's carefully structured industrial policy placed sharp limits on incoming foreign investment, as did India's during the decades until the 1990s, during which the Jawaharlal Nehru government and its successors embraced principles of import substitution. Though there were exceptions, for the most part, neither the Soviet Union nor the People's Republic of China accepted capitalist investment. Transnational capital headquartered in the United States incorporated natural resources drawn from Asia, Africa, and Latin America into its commodity chains; but at this time U.S. FDI surged outward to only some parts of the world, including, above all, Western Europe. The two sides of the North Atlantic formed the primary axis of postwar capitalist globalization, and manufactured products, capital equipment, and financial flows streamed between and across these regions. During the 1970s, however, this pattern of FDI, and the commodity chains to which it was linked, began to undergo dramatic revision.

Renewed intercapitalist competition, as Japan and Germany were rebuilt, as well as exchange-rate fluctuations and national policies to placate strong industrial working classes and to protect domestic capital, fed a new phase of capitalist globalization. This phase also was conditioned by another far-reaching trend: ever-deepening excess capacity and the disproportion that ensued from it between enlarged output and constrained demand. The necessity of reorganization seemed, to capital, increasingly inexorable. During the four years of the Carter administration in the United States—1977 to 1980—U.S. FDI accelerated[4] and, after the U.S. election of 1980 that brought Ronald Reagan the presidency, the process only gathered additional force. The U.S. government and the multilateral institutions that it largely dominated rammed through policies to enable more unrestricted capital investment.

The spatial restructuring of commodity chains was a fraught historical process, replete with contradictory elements and complex historical consequences. As U.S. foreign investments in manufacturing relocated increasingly to low-wage East Asian countries, local suppliers of components established themselves. Hong Kong, South Korea, Taiwan, and Singapore became centers of manufacturing industry—and came to see themselves as possessing interests that divided them from other poor countries. As well, and crucially, a growing share of their production returned to the United States. A 1985 account underlined that "volume manufacture in foreign locations for re-export to the home market or other export markets is a qualitatively new feature of foreign manufacturing operations that has emerged in the late 1960s." It had been enabled, these writers emphasized, as part of a broader redesign of corporate production and supply: "In developing Asia, more than a quarter of sales of U.S. affiliates went to the United States in 1977, up from less than 10 percent in 1966."[5] Overall, by 1978, the United States accounted for more than half of developing countries' manufactured exports to the rich countries. As Judith Stein put it, "The large American market became the safety valve for the export industries of U.S. allies, who quickly became economic competitors." The "historic role" of the American economy was to constitute "the market of first and last resort for the rest of the world."[6] The outsized importance of the U.S. market as a source of world economic demand came about not as a reflex of narrow economic relationships but also owing to political and strategic calculations. Within the context of the Cold War, the United States deployed its unmatched national market as a carrot, using economic policy to draw other nations into its orbit of influence and to pull them away from the socialist sphere.

Capitalist globalization received a giant boost from—and was itself powerfully reinflected by—the collapse of Soviet socialism and the decision by China's party-state to reinsert China into what now became a truly planetary capitalism. In 1997, TNC production systems accounted for a gross product of $8 trillion, or around one quarter of global GDP; the United Nations Commission on Trade and Development (UNCTAD) underlined in 2000 that "international production now spans—in different degrees—virtually all countries, sectors, industries and economic activities."[7] Between 1980 and 2008, all told, companies from the advanced capitalist countries increased their outward stock of foreign direct investment far ahead of the inflation rate, from $503 billion to $13.623 trillion.[8] Dozens of investment and free-trade agreements, as Hart-Landsberg underlines,[9] were indispensable as political enablers of this movement.

If FDI now could be directed virtually anywhere and everywhere, however, then the sources of that FDI also began to recompose and diversify. Earlier in the postwar period, the buildup of transnational capital had progressed from the United States to Britain, Germany, Japan, the Netherlands, France, Italy, and other developed countries. During the 1990s and early in the twenty-first century, however, smaller but significant quantities of FDI began to pour forth as well from the Republic of Korea, Taiwan, Hong Kong, India, Singapore, Brazil, Mexico, and, notably, China. (Outward FDI from China increased from $20 billion annually in 2007 to $84 billion annually in 2012, moving China to third place behind the United States and Japan.[10]) The United States remained by far the largest source of outbound FDI, but the United States was, increasingly, only first among equals. "The global crisis," declared UNCTAD in 2010, had "not halted the growing internationalization of production"[11] (though mergers and acquisitions and trade slowed,[12] and the volume of FDI fell[13]), but its pattern continued to alter. In 2012, for the first time ever, developing countries absorbed more FDI than developed countries, even as what UNCTAD dubbed "emerging investor countries" also generated a greater share of global FDI outflows than ever before—nearly one-third.[14] The five BRICS[15] countries alone had accounted for just $7 billion in FDI outflows in 2000, but this figure rose to $145 billion in 2012, giving them 10 percent of the world total.[16]

Capitalist globalization forged innumerable new links in commodity chains and worked correspondingly radical changes in production and trade. "Today," wrote the director general of the World Trade Organization in 2011, "the concept of country of origin is obsolete. . . . No car or commercial jet could now be built with inputs from just one country."[17] For large companies, intermediate components might be produced in-house or contracted out and moved offshore. Top-tier contractors might be co-located with a transnational company's own assembly plants, but tier-two and tier-three contractors entered extended commodity chains obliquely. This fractionalization of production altered the very meaning of "trade." No longer centered on exchanges between autonomous producers based in different countries, trade denoted the flows of raw materials, components, intermediate products, and finished commodities among subsidiary corporate units and their contractors and distributors. By 2012 transnational companies coordinated a staggering four-fifths of world trade through their affiliates, contractual partners, and independent suppliers.[18] At the apex of this system, these companies—perhaps one thousand possessed truly far-reaching significance—wrought profound changes to the commodity chains they dominated.

"The revolutionary aspect of international production," wrote two perceptive analysts forty years ago, "is that widely dispersed productive facilities can, thanks to such innovations as containerized shipping and satellite communications, be integrated into what is, conceptually, a global factory."[19] What they accurately called "advances in the science of centralization" made feasible the coordination at the headquarters level of the multinational corporation—for, they perceived, "the science of centralization is based largely on the sophisticated control of communications."[20] "The permissive technological environment," Bluestone and Harrison added in 1982, "allows huge corporations to operate hundreds of smaller, geographically dispersed plants in place of a small number of politically vulnerable, large local complexes," effectively reversing what had long been taken to be the natural order of things: "the relationship between the centralization of control over production and the concentration of productive activity in large, centrally located facilities."[21] "Corporations," in Hart-Landsberg's assessment, "began dividing the production process into ever finer segments, both vertical and horizontal, and locating the separate stages in two or more countries, creating cross-border production networks."[22]

In themselves, efforts by capital to coordinate and control dispersed work processes were not new. The London-based officers of the Hudson's Bay Company were experimenting with remote management of their agents and employees located in remote northern Canada by 1680.[23] Nor have information networks supplied the sole basis for industry's continual efforts to rearrange its operations. Railroads and electrical grids were also pivotal during the late nineteenth century; and gas turbines, diesel engines, and container shipping play vital roles today.[24] The dispersion and rearrangement of contemporary coordinated production, however, depended in essential ways on capacious, versatile digital connectivity. Dramatically heightened cooperation, sometimes—not always—in real time, could be instituted within and among labor processes that were chopped up and relocated to multiple sites. This reorganization might span from engineering research to final assembly, and from back-office functions to customer service. Often, it externalized "low-value" functions to contractors, who "merely" had to guarantee delivery of so many units at such-and-such a date and time. In general, more types of work could be relocated to more places, as corporate strategy might dictate. Alongside workplace automation, in turn, digital networks conferred newfound locational flexibility. Harley Shaiken captured an essential dimension of this transformation in 1984: "Computer technology is the vehicle to unify the separate elements of the entire production system . . . from the designer to the assembly line throughout the various layers of management, and geographically from Detroit to Sao Paolo."[25] Cross-border commodity chains entered an era of seemingly perpetual innovation and upheaval as networks rendered more elastic the sequencing, location, and interrelationship of different steps in the process of production.

Executives and managers were keenly interested in this evolution and tracked it through the business press.[26] Specializations in "supply-chain management" proliferated, and lists of corporate leaders in the emerging field of logistics were published: Apple's elaborate network of suppliers was "regularly cited as one of the most sophisticated and effective" in 2010.[27] True breakthroughs could be counted; again, however, they offered no guarantees of profitability—or even of security. In some ways, indeed, their reliance on far-reaching networks rendered big companies more susceptible to natural disasters, political risks, and other contingencies. During the 1990s, a journalist reported, "whole industries embraced just-in-time supply chains and lean manufacturing techniques." In 2003, as a result, when the U.S. Homeland Security Department imposed regulations requiring shippers to inform border officials between four and twenty-four hours ahead that their freight would be entering the United States—depending on whether it would arrive by truck, air, or rail—the major arteries for "just-in-time" supplies became destabilized. "Is just-in-time becoming just too difficult?" the reporter asked?[28] Similarly, Ford, Honda, and PC makers such as Dell were among more than one thousand manufacturers whose delicately balanced logistics were hit by a triple disaster in 2011: the Japanese earthquake and tsunami, followed by the worst Thai flooding in half a century.[29] Other kinds of disruptions also impinged. Following revelations that its Chinese contract manufacturer had been using lead-based paint, Mattel was compelled to recall nearly one million toys in 2007.[30] Apple, cited for its "best practices" year upon year, reeled when it was exposed for relying on contractors who subjected legions of young workers to fierce exploitation. Within the general field of logistics a new specialization was quickly established: "supply chain risk management."

The ICT industry itself helped pioneer the trend to parcelized production systems, intracorporate trade, and exports back to the wealthiest markets. "A capital spending surge heavily concentrated in information technology," related Morgan Stanley economist Stephen Roach, "is one with a bias toward imports. At present, foreign-produced high-tech capital goods account for almost 25% of the U.S. market," he noted in 1988.[31] By 2001 this effect had increased: "A component may cross a foreign border several times as it moves up the assembly chain into a finished computer, network router or cellphone. More than 60% of the value of new computer purchases in the U.S. is imported," stated *Wall Street Journal* correspondent Greg Ip.[32] This carried economic importance because, as Ip observed, the United States was spending more on semiconductors and computer accessories made abroad than on crude oil.

Networks in turn acquired ever-greater strategic importance throughout the decades that saw this renewed surge of capitalist globalization. The Business Roundtable, a trade group that lobbies on behalf of the largest U.S. companies, underlined that this linkage was already tight in 1985: "Instead of each plant producing a whole line of products, one plant produces one product, or even one basic component, while other plants assemble components into specialized products. This means of manufacturing also depends upon the unhampered flow of information among the company's various branches. Similarly, the ability to coproduce in other countries depends upon access to common data bases . . . because a product cannot be manufactured from two different sets of specifications."[33]

The sourcing of thousands of intermediate product inputs across many plants in multiple countries, the scheduling and tracking of complex and dispersed production processes, the distribution and marketing of final products: all of these needed to be brought into unison. Ever-expanding network functionality and liberalized terms of network use were essential correlates, because "every step is accompanied by a body of information required to do the work."[34] The network side of restructured commodity chains presented complexities in its own right, however—and again these were not solely technical.

"Government policies about how networks are organized will massively influence which possibilities for sustained, competitive economic growth are captured and which are missed. Those policies will result in differently configured telecommunications networks with distinct potentials for use and industrial development," explained two analysts in 1987.[35] Beginning in the 1970s and 1980s, large corporations strived to liberalize the terms of their access to network systems and specialized equipment, and to repel governmental restrictions on the services and the data flowing across their proprietary networks. They did so, moreover, across the length and breadth of their transnationally distributed operations[36]—that is, by the 1990s, anywhere and everywhere. Even before the World Wide Web was rolled out, the internet was becoming a battering ram—or, perhaps, a Trojan Horse—for transnational capital's project of extraterritorial network liberalization.[37]

As liberalization proceeded, the floodgates of capital investment opened. Spending on ICTs ultimately called forth worldwide expenditures, reckoned in the tens of trillions of dollars, and consumed perhaps 6 to 7 percent of the world's total GDP.[38] Corporate, or enterprise, network spending represented the lion's share of network-related expenditures overall.[39] (Consumer spending on ICTs comprised less than one-third [29 percent] of the total market—business and government accounted for 71 percent.[40]) Manufacturers, in particular, became a major sector of overall ICT demand; U.S. manufacturers of durable and nondurable goods spent no less than $30 billion on ICT equipment and software in the crisis year of 2009, making them the third largest source of business demand for network systems and applications.

The auto industry vividly illuminates how digital technology was repeatedly absorbed by manufacturing and enables us to connect capitalist globalization to a planetary recomposition of the wage-earning working class.

Digital Auto

It is a little-known fact that, early in the 1980s, Detroit counted as one of the top ten U.S. cities with respect to overall computer installations by dollar investment. The world's largest automaker, General Motors claimed 1984 revenues of $84 billion and employed nearly 750,000 workers—two-thirds of them in the United States. The auto giant also possessed more than thirty thousand suppliers, making it a cornerstone of U.S. manufacturing in general. Its GMAC subsidiary, which had loaned money to automobile buyers since 1918, boasted 314 branches (253 in the United States). Facing militancy from its factory workforce and escalating market pressure from Japanese rivals, during the 1970s GM began to embark upon a huge, long-lasting program to bring ICTs into every aspect of automobile production. GM's initiative needs to be set within a wider offensive on U.S. working-class living standards and social power, being conducted not only by manufacturers led by GM, but also by a financial system determined, after Paul Volcker took the helm at the Federal Reserve Bank, to induce austerity in order to wring out inflation, and a Reagan administration waging frontal attacks on social programs and collective-bargaining rights.

As a contemporary recognized, "Managing the G.M. information flow is like managing the information flow of a small country."[41] GM used 250,000 telephones to conduct its operations; employees at its various dispersed units made eight million long-distance calls each month. One 1984 estimate of the automaker's total costs for internal corporate data processing, communications, and office automation came in at $2 billion (another writer put it at $6 billion).[42] GM was undertaking what may have been "the largest shift in technological, human and capital resources in American history."[43]

The auto giant acquired a leading computer services supplier, Electronic Data Systems (EDS), at a price of $2.5 billion in 1984. As a "systems integrator," EDS's new remit was to unify and rationalize GM's fragmented, functionally disparate data processing and communications systems. EDS was asked to engineer online connections to support orders, shipping, finance, inventory, and materials management across GM's sprawling complex. The "islands of automation" that it had already built were to be bridged. GM engineers were developing the so-called Manufacturing Automation Protocol to permit previously isolated machines on factory floors to exchange information with each other and with GM's central computing facilities, which reputedly included several hundred mainframes.[44] The automaker's proprietary Electronic Data Interchange system would link its many suppliers to its own design, manufacturing, and distribution systems.[45] GM became the first manufacturing company to install its own supercomputer (there were then around one hundred super-computers worldwide) for use in three-dimensional modeling, aerodynamic testing, and simulation. The automaker took equity stakes in Isuzu, Suzuki, Fanuc, Toyota, Diffracto, Teknowledge, Philip Crosby, and Daewoo to help it produce robots, artificial intelligence and machine vision systems, manage-ment consulting services, and software.[46] Finally, in 1985 GM acquired Hughes Aircraft ($5.2 billion), a major satellite manufacturer. Its goal was to use Hughes to interconnect its sprawling transnational operations: more than two hundred major facilities scattered across three dozen countries, and no less than fifty thousand additional sites, covering dealers, suppliers, and financial offices.[47] All this signified a veritable orgy of spending on computerization and factory robots—billions just between 1979 and 1984, and a stupefying $90 billion al-together by 2008.[48]

The actual results of GM's surging network investments, which altered and extended automotive labor processes and swelled the flows of data between GM's far-flung units and its partner companies, were painfully contradictory. GM's ambitious and seemingly coherent strategy for unifying its mammoth information systems was ultimately shredded: the automaker disposed of EDS in 1996 and, for all the trumpeting about systems integration, in 2009, by one account, GM still "needed weeks, not days," to assemble its corporate balance sheet. "Executives had to e-mail around the world and then stitch together a patchwork of reports" out of many disparate systems scattered across different countries.[49] Despite these and other shortcomings, however, GM's networking project—akin to its peers in other big manufacturing companies—did con-tribute to a decisive widening of the process of capitalist globalization. During the late twentieth century, networks helped enable industrialization to burst through its prior territorial constraints and to draw upon new pools of wage labor across the world.

The wage relation constitutes the essential continuing basis for capitalist development. In the same historical heartbeat during which extraterritorial networks were being urgently modernized and extended, the collapse of So-viet socialism, the embrace of capitalism by China, and the failure of the Third World political project[50] were impelling hundreds of millions of workers into direct and indirect relations with capital. *The Economist*, a leading proponent of neoliberal policy, recognized that China's "extraordinary mobilization of la-bour is the biggest economic event of the past half-century."[51] The International Labour Office estimated that between 1980 and 2007 the overall global labor force grew from 1.9 billion to 3.1 billion—a rise of 63 percent.[52] This hugely en-larged and rapidly recomposing wage-earning class constitutes a fundamental hallmark of the contemporary world. Its mobilization by transnational capital underpins the contemporary reorganization of global manufacturing and the colossal increase in manufacturing output.

Manufacturers such as GM deployed networks in order to coordinate the high-tech production systems that they were innovating and extending transnationally to export-processing zones being established in poor countries, as Harley Shaiken documented in the case of Mexico's border-hugging maquiladora plants in 1990.[53] While research and development, design, marketing, and perhaps final assembly were performed by transnational manufacturers, characteristically, far-flung chains of contractor- and outsourcer-run plants became charged with producing components and ultimately with final assembly. This rapidly changing production system, with its reliance on embedded networks, engendered far-reaching and often painful ramifications—both for capital and, above all, for labor.

Tony Smith explains that "information technologies have enabled enterprises . . . to coordinate production and distribution activities more intimately," enabling an "asymmetry of economic power within core/ring networks which allows core firms to control production and the flow of information, and to shift economic burdens onto ring firms, thereby leading to the super-exploitation of workers in those ring firms."[54] On one side, as we have seen, this "asymmetry" enabled unprecedented levels of automation coupled with self-service—albeit with no guarantee that profits would rebound. Overcapacity, rather, was becoming a chronic threat to profitability, so that GM's profits veered up and down during the final decades of the twentieth century, while its share of North American auto sales dropped.[55] On the other side, as David Harvey states, networked production was linked to a "revival of sweatshop and family labor systems, putting-out systems, subcontracting systems and the like"; and Harvey detects as a result of this multiformity a "competition between different labor systems [which] becomes a weapon to be used by capital against labor" in struggles over surplus generation and distribution.[56] Kim Moody likewise underlines that corporations combined information technology "with archaic forms of work organization such as contracting-out, casualization, old-fashioned speed-up, and the lengthening of working time."[57] There occurred no worldwide leveling of economic differences; to the contrary, inequality increased virtually everywhere.

The coming-into-existence of a hugely enlarged wage-earning working class contributed to the mounting pressure on labor—notably including manufacturing labor—throughout the wealthy countries. Real wages in the United States dropped by 10 percent between 1978 and 1983 and, beginning in 1979, the value of U.S. labor power fell for the remainder of the century.[58] Working-class

America had to contend not only with spiraling income and wealth inequality but also with the economic deprivation that this betokened.[59] Low-wage, contingent, and part-time employment boomed, so that Italian autonomists discerned a "precariat" even within lead-edge industries and developed market economies.[60] David Harvey pinpoints how this result was doubly destabilizing: capital's pursuit of what he calls "wage repression" succeeded beyond any expectation, and lower wages meant that capital now also faced chronically weakened consumer demand throughout the world's wealthiest market.[61] This contradictory stress built up over decades, while the auto industry seesawed.

On the ground in the United States, the redesigned automotive production system engendered devastating results. In 2008 GM was building autos in thirty-four countries, but now it confined itself to assembly and directly employed a workforce of 243,000—one-third of the number it had employed merely a quarter-century earlier—of whom fewer than ninety-one thousand labored within the United States.[62] U.S. autoworkers all told still numbered over one million, but most worked for independent parts suppliers, and some for subsidiaries of foreign car companies—as Toyota, Nissan, Honda, and Hyundai built up their own operations in the United States.[63]

Parts suppliers and assembly plants established in the United States by foreign auto companies between 1980 and 2009 were anchored, not coincidentally, in a belt of "right to work" states, particularly Indiana and Tennessee.[64] But the problem lay not only with these interlopers. Gregg Shotwell, a radical autoworker and writer, underlined at century's end that GM's 1999 spinoff of its entire parts division, called Delphi Automotive Systems, came as a culmination of the company's longer-term embrace of lean production, subcontracting, modular assembly, and outsourcing to nonunion independent parts suppliers—and as a response to the autoworkers' protests that these had provoked. The workers' earlier hard-won gains thus underwent a grinding reversal. A declining fraction of U.S. autoworkers resided in the union town of Detroit and were represented by the once-powerful United Auto Workers union. As membership in the UAW plummeted, the weakened and overly bureaucratic union continually offered concessions, further sapping the autoworkers' bargaining power. The auto companies responded by intensifying their demands for givebacks in wages and benefits, job security, pensions, and work rules.[65] In the 1990s, GM executives had bet on high-profit gas-guzzlers—SUVs—and GM's spiking profits seemed momentarily to vindicate this strategy. After the turn of the new century, however, the problem of overcapacity in auto manufacturing became global—and chronic.[66] Production[67] and sales boomed in China, and Chinese carmakers exported record volumes to developing countries. But while global unit sales

reached an all-time high—seventy-five million in 2011—the higher-cost producers in North America, Japan, and especially Western Europe were pummeled.[68]
Double-digit sales declines had become characteristic, as steep increases in the
price of gasoline put an end to GM's SUV strategy. Even before the onset of the
depression in 2008, to keep its production lines going GM had become "addicted
to incentives," including cash-back offers and discounts.[69]

The onset of the slump showcased how political priorities impinged on au-
tomaking. GM executives came to Washington, hats in hand. Steven Rattner, a
private equity executive who was chosen to manage the ensuing federal bailout
of GM (and Chrysler), trumpeted that "the auto rescue remains one of the few
actions taken by the administration that . . . can be pronounced an unambiguous
success. Detroit should count itself lucky."[70] His verdict was both self-serving
and unwarranted. GM's "controlled bankruptcy," in which the company received federal commitments totaling nearly $50 billion,[71] enabled GM under
government operation to shutter twenty factories, cut tens of thousands of
jobs, eliminate decades of work rules, generalize nonunion standards and work
practices, curtail workers' right to strike, walk away from "legacy costs" such
as employee health care, and pare the company's UAW workforce to around
fifty thousand.[72] (Ford Motor, which did not enter bankruptcy, used the same
opportunity to close plants and renegotiate contracts with its workers.)

Only ingrained class privilege could account for calling this a success. And
indeed, as Neil Barofsky later noted, the federal officials who were at the same
time showering trillions of dollars on banks did adhere to a "consistent double
standard."[73] Autoworkers—but not bankers—seemingly could be dispensed
with. Peremptorily rejecting what he called "an extreme provision of the UAW
contract under which laid-off workers received 95 percent of their normal pay,"[74]
Rattner's team adhered to what he hailed as "a firm capitalist perspective." In
Rattner's willful delusion, employees and retirees "ought to share the pain."[75]
Unionized autoworkers had possessed outsized importance in setting U.S. living standards historically so that, when the government rained body blows on
them—as Shotwell concluded—the result was nothing less than "the degrada-
tion of the working class."[76]

While the average age of cars on roads in the United States was at a record
high—11.4 years—within two years of its bankruptcy GM was celebrating a
sales recovery in the United States. Operating several of its North American
assembly plants (the number of which had been reduced from twenty-three
in 2006 to seventeen) on a profitable, round-the-clock, three-shift basis, GM
looked to increase its 18 percent market share.[77]

GM's downsizing furnished an object lesson in more than one respect. In
the United States as a whole, consumption by wage-earners remained weak,

while corporate investment in network systems and services surged—and productivity-enhancing automation along with it; after the crisis hit, the U.S. economy produced as much as it had before the downturn, but with seven million fewer jobs. The decade to 2011 indeed was unique over the course of eighty previous years, in that employment declined while productivity rose.[78] (While employment spending increased by a marginal 2 percent in 2011, business spending on equipment and software increased by 26 percent.[79]) At the fringes, the renewed cycles of automation (above all when they began to bite into "knowledge work" associated with middle-class occupations) prompted economist Paul Krugman to express sympathy for the English Luddites, who had resisted capital's technological incursions into the woolen industry around the turn of the nineteenth century.[80] The *Financial Times* cited "job-destroying technology";[81] MIT economists Erik Brynjolfsson and Andrew McAfee conceded that computer-based automation of skilled labor indeed was acting to drive net job displacement.[82] In 2014 Google's chairman, Eric Schmidt, affirmed before the World Economic Forum at Davos that jobs that had earlier seemed beyond the reach of automation now were endangered.[83]

Corporate profits in 2010 accounted for the highest proportion of U.S. national income ever recorded—and captured still a greater share during early 2011. GM's North American profits, likewise, rose strongly in 2013.[84] Workers, reciprocally, saw the share of national income devoted to wages and salaries dip to its lowest level; even if employee wages and benefits were added together, the 2010 total was the lowest since 1965, and slipping.[85]

By contrast, in Europe, as the *Financial Times* noted, "efforts . . . to tackle excess capacity have been less decisive,"[86] such that capacity utilization at European car plants remained too low to support profitable production. In 2012, the existing Europe-based industry was capable of manufacturing fully ten million additional cars each year beyond those that could be consumed there—and conditions worsened during 2013.[87] The European auto market was in dire straits, as price wars accompanied slumping sales. Some manufacturers fared better, some worse; but by summer's end in 2013, European car sales had slumped to their lowest level since 1990.[88] The crisis in the Eurozone collapsed demand for cars and, as the *Financial Times* had consistently understood, "laid bare the chronic excess capacity problems of an industry that, unlike America's, did not downsize after the 2008 banking crisis because of political and union hostility to closing plants."[89] The CEO of Fiat, Sergio Marchionne, might rail that decisive action was needed and that consolidation had become unavoidable[90]; and Europe's auto executives might seek to rouse European states to broker plant closures. However, resistance from the EU's 11.3 million autoworkers—5.3 percent of employed workers overall—

signified, amid conditions of mass unemployment, that capacity cutbacks still remained "politically charged."[91]

Across the Atlantic, the politics of manufacturing production continued to tell a different story. In the aftermath of the state-guided pummeling administered to union autoworkers, right-wing capitalists mounted a concerted drive for legislation that transformed Michigan, the historical center of U.S. industrial collective bargaining, into a right-to-work state.[92] In such a context, we must view additional cycles of network-enabled reorganization as parts of a larger program of reactionary modernization.

"A modern car," by one account, had become "a computer on wheels," typically encompassing around one hundred electronic systems (when an earthquake knocked out a specialized Japanese computer-chip factory in 2011, it struck "a severe and lasting blow to the global auto industry").[93] U.S. auto executives, seeking to differentiate their vehicles by linking into more encompassing digitization trends, hired hundreds of software developers.[94]Meanwhile, the problem of "global gridlock," as Ford CEO Bill Ford artfully suggested, should lead to widespread establishment of "intelligent transport systems."[95] Supported by city, state, and federal largesse, new and existing companies, such as Waze (acquired by Google midway through 2013), Uber Technologies, and Apple, were applying sensors, mobile phones, and data analytics to transportation systems.[96] The idea was to send out internet-connected vehicles using wireless technology to traverse roads thick with sensors that, theoretically, would allow cars to sidestep growing congestion. In addition to in-car navigation, digital autos would be packed with ever more extensive electronics, from Wi-Fi hotspots to voice-activated information systems, presumably so that travelers could amuse themselves as traffic ground to a standstill.[97] Hacking cars, the *Financial Times* reported, "is fast becoming a serious threat."[98] In 2013, self-propelled "autonomous" vehicles—driverless cars—had been authorized in three U.S. states.[99]

This project linked with still more encompassing infrastructural changes, including not only digitally metered roads and power grids but also machine-to-machine communications—"M2M" or, as it sometimes was called, an "internet of things." The cost of the modules needed for M2M—which included a sensor, a SIM card, and wireless electronics for sending and receiving data over mobile networks—dropped below ten dollars per unit in 2012, qualitatively enlarging the range of prospective application. Garbage bins could be designed to "request" visits from trash companies; refrigerators could call out for a fresh milk carton; automobiles could communicate a need for oil or a replacement part—or inform insurance companies that a given driver was exceeding the local speed limit.[100] M2M enthusiasts fantasized about a trillion-dollar market, and high-tech manufacturers began to herald what General Electric called an "industrial Internet."[101] The diminishing cost of sensors (Cisco estimated that there would be fifty billion operating by 2020) and a buildup of corporate data analytics (GE planned for one thousand data scientists at its recently opened Silicon Valley facility by the end of 2013) signified a rapid transition toward gigantic, multifarious, always-on data flows between communicating machines, from jet turbines and other industrial equipment to refrigerators, washing machines, and TVs.[102] All-data-all-the-time became the mantra, as people generated data at every turn through the day—at work, on the street, and at home.[103]

A new platform for would-be market participants was being opened: Who would supply the specialized software and services to power this emerging, industrial internet? A modernized and upgraded network infrastructure was the needed predicate for broadening the movement of capital into a raft of commodity-development projects, as we will see in part III—in education, cultural heritage, government services, medicine, and biotechnology. To assist them, digital equipment vendors, systems integrators, cloud service suppliers, and data analytics companies thronged in from all points of the compass. A planned venture between Microsoft and Toyota, for example, aimed to use the software company's cloud service software to integrate information transfers between a customer's home or mobile device and his or her electric car. This would allow a driver to turn on the heat or check the auto's battery power remotely, and to decide to charge an electric car during off-peak times when electricity cost less. Toyota's CEO offered what he obviously intended as an appealing suggestion, that people would be enabled to "dialogue" with their vehicles each morning— throughout no less fewer than 170 cloud-accessible countries.[104]

General Motors, seemingly unconcernedly, crowed over its "new" networking strategy, which recalled the one that it had pursued during the 1980s and eschewed during the 1990s. Chairman and CEO Dan Akerson announced in 2013, "Today, every single link of the automotive value chain is wired and connected, and that means from the design to the showroom floor." "That's why," he said, "for any company—not just an automotive manufacturer—to be successful in the 21st century, you have to have a core competency in IT. You have to own it and you have to control it and when you don't, you're at the whim of other companies, their priorities, and, if they have financial problems, their difficulties."[105] The occasion for Akerson's remarks was the opening of a new GM data center, one of four new facilities through which the company heralded operational improvements as it again brought more of its IT workforce in-house.[106]

For all this, there was scant promise of redress for Americans' ravaged living standards. Wage repression had become so pervasive that the Obama administration could praise itself merely for having preserved some thousands of less-well-paid manufacturing jobs in its auto industry "bailout."[107] High-paid, secure union jobs with benefits and pensions, however, had been made an endangered species, while paid jobs of any kind remained all too hard to find. The proportion of U.S. workers represented by unions dropped to its lowest point since early in the twentieth century. In the United States, the median wage had sagged by late 2012 to 8 percent below what it was in 2000, adjusted for inflation;[108] and real per capita disposable income shrank by 0.4 percent at an annualized pace for five years—its worst record since these data began to be collected (in 1964).[109] Within just a few years of GM's bailout and return to profitability, Detroit—for decades a proud symbol of U.S. working-class power—filed for bankruptcy.[110] The federal government sat by in stony silence.

Greatly accelerated by the Federal Reserve Bank's austerity program of 1979–82, network-enabled reorganization of the production system and of the labor process contributed to chronic wage repression. This in turn placed a secular drag on consumer demand, which acted as one of several factors in propelling the growth of debt-based finance.

CHAPTER 3

Networked Financialization

Financialization denoted another formative aspect of the rise of digital capital-ism in response to the crisis of the 1970s. Information-processing equipment and software were assimilated into a financial system that operated both as an instrument of class power domestically and a pivot of capitalist expansion and imperial control internationally. Network-enabled financialization, however, again possessed contradictory momentum: it was a bearer of crisis rather than of stable accumulation.

Financialization evolved out of multiple impulses. One spur came as millions of workers who experienced wage repression were brought to depend on debt for immediate consumption as well as for housing and automobiles, education, and medical care. Another came from the fact that finance bulked ever larger in the strategies of transnational manufacturers, retail chains, agribusinesses, and service suppliers, whose investments and operating expenditures required multiple currencies, were subject to varying tax jurisdictions, and threw off prof-its that needed to be managed. Foreign direct investment altered the pattern of global consumption, savings, and trade, contributing to financial imbalances between and among nations. These imbalances destabilized the fixed-exchange rate regime that had endured since World War II—adding complexity, that only increased after the early 1970s, when fixed exchange rates were abandoned by the Nixon administration. The "immense managerial capacities"[1] that had enabled the United States to become the financial impresario for a burgeoning global capitalism now became fraught with uncertainty. Interest rates, exchange rates, shifting current account surpluses, and sovereign debt all became hot potatoes; liquid capital ("hot money"), in the meantime, poured across borders in search of instantaneous returns. The onset of financialization thus bespoke deep-seated trends rather than merely bankers' avarice.[2]

As Cees Hamelink underscored in 1983, it also bespoke a growing convergence with new information technology.[3] Financialization was animated by and reliant on burgeoning network systems: in 2008 financial services companies constituted the United States' second-largest sectoral source of demand for ICTs[4]—$46.7 billion, or 18.4 percent of all annual spending by nonfarm U.S. businesses on information and communications technology equipment and software.[5] The purpose of the discussion that follows is to clarify this complex link and to show that networked financialization introduced its own stressors into capitalism's crisis tendencies.

Throughout the first two postwar decades, the U.S. financial system reached the pinnacle of its stability during the twentieth century. New Deal reforms had rescued and strengthened the system by fragmenting it: issuance of stocks and bonds by investment banks, the provision of insurance, commercial banking to gather in savings and make loans, real estate transactions, and the trading of stocks and bonds by brokers had all been structurally separated. Working closely with Wall Street bankers and, through them, with the banking system overall, were the U.S. Treasury Department and the Federal Reserve Bank. These institutions interlocked with international agencies. One anchor was a system of fixed exchange rates, originally set by forty-four nations for the International Monetary Fund established at Bretton Woods in 1944. Another was the General Agreement on Tariffs and Trade, which since 1947 had mandated policies stressing freedom of investment. A third was the International Bank for Reconstruction and Development, otherwise known as the World Bank, which coordinated finance for strategic and/or profitable projects in less developed countries. Finally, the U.S. Treasury and the Federal Reserve forged close relations with the central banks and private financial systems of U.S. trading partners including, above all, the City of London. Domestically, as they profited from what has been called a "golden age" of prosperity, big U.S. banks also worked closely with the individual states. The result was that, for an extended period, the United States could act as the coordinator, guarantor, and chief beneficiary of a dynamic global capitalism.[6]

Ramifying stresses and strains began to appear during the mid-1960s.[7] The paradoxical consequence of the U.S-led reconstruction of Western Europe and Japanese capitalism as bulwarks against the U.S.S.R. and China had been to revive intercapitalist competition. This, as we already saw, placed pressure on corporate profit strategies and accentuated U.S. capital's need for additional investment outlets and market opportunities. Escalating U.S. foreign direct investment—above all, to Western Europe—was an overarching response. Transnationalizing companies stashed substantial money assets in foreign countries, to fit accounting and tax strategies or to oblige local laws on foreign investment. A huge pool of what became known as "Eurodollars" developed, engendering challenges for central banks and corporate treasurers.

U.S. strategic initiatives likewise contributed to international financial imbalances. The U.S. policy of "containment" of Soviet and Chinese socialism was underwritten by a lengthening archipelago of foreign military bases. Stationing tens of thousands of troops in other countries drained dollars out of the United States; and when containment escalated into full-scale war making, the outflow grew heavier. In 1971, as the war against Vietnam raged, net U.S. military expenditures abroad exceeded the U.S. balance-of-payments deficit.[8]

A closely related U.S. policy again now began to tear at the structure of international finance. Beginning with the Marshall Plan instituted during the late 1940s, the United States had committed itself (albeit unevenly) to deploying its unmatched domestic market as a political mechanism—a source of economic demand—to support capitalist reconstruction throughout Western Europe and East Asia. As U.S. businesses and consumers increased their purchases of products manufactured elsewhere, the U.S. current account deficit underwent a chronic escalation, flooding its trading partners with "stateless dollars."

Under the combined weight of these stressors, greatly intensified by Vietnam War spending and by oil-price hikes by the Organization of Petroleum Exporting Countries beginning in 1971, the financial order cracked. The Nixon administration took the dollar off the gold standard and initiated floating exchange rates. This measure relieved pressure, but at the price of propelling instability in uncharted directions. Inflation spiked, and big investors began to demand a solution that would prioritize the safeguarding of their financial assets. When Paul Volcker, appointed to chair the Federal Reserve Bank by Jimmy Carter, accommodated them by raising interest rates above 19 percent, the effect of this deliberate "shock" was to plunge the United States into an austerity program that saw unemployment rise into double digits.[9]

This austerity program, and the rebalancing of class forces on which it was predicated,[10] translated into stagnating real wages; and this in turn stimulated household demand for credit. Special-purpose credit cards had been issued by hotels, oil companies, and retailers during the first half of the twentieth century. However, during the 1950s and 1960s banks began to experiment with cards as a general means of payment. Bank of America and Interbank played formative roles, each sending a blizzard of unsolicited credit cards to households in order to establish its own nationwide (and, increasingly, international) credit system.

By 1978, credit cards were issued by eleven thousand banks and reached tens of millions of Americans.[11] Credit cards still were only beginning to filter into widespread use, accounting for a small portion (6 percent) of consumer spending as late as 1984; but, as Cortada relates, by 2000 "it was not uncommon for a household to charge 20 percent of their purchases to credit cards."[12] In 2011, half of consumer payments in the United States were made with cards of different sorts.[13] Fees extracted for credit card use were substantial, and "databases with customer information on purchasing habits began to inform bankers and retailers on marketing issues."[14] Other financial products were devised to target the household market, including home equity loans and innovations based on mortgages.[15]

High U.S. interest rates also crashed into the international financial system, as the huge loans thrust on less-developed countries became intolerable burdens. The U.S. banks, the IMF, and the World Bank were immune, however, to the human suffering caused by the debt crisis that their investor-friendly policies induced. In sometimes-strained concert with these countries' own ruling elites, during the 1980s they used the crisis to advance "structural adjustment"—radical policy changes aimed at strengthening freedom of investment and enabling massive privatization of state assets—throughout poor-world countries.[16] Outflows of hundreds of billions of dollars to the wealthy First World from those Third World inhabitants least able to afford these transfers were another consequence.

Volatility, leverage, and risk, however, all increased. Big corporations clamored for stability-enhancing financial instruments so that they might purchase hedges against exchange-rate fluctuations and other unanticipated events. On the supply side of the financial system, unprecedentedly large bank holding companies, joined by great pools of speculative capital, responded with a cascade of product innovations. Workaday loans, mortgages, and share offerings were supplemented and overshadowed by lucrative, fee-based services: cash management, foreign exchange, hedges, commercial paper, CDs, repurchase agreements, trading in corporate and government stocks, bonds, and securities.[17] Newly constructed, largely unregulated financial institutions threw growing weight: they included "shadow" institutions including hedge funds, private equity funds, pension funds, and venture capital funds. To match their flexibility and freedom of maneuver, big banks created "special investment vehicles," which they were not legally compelled to list on their ledgers.

Aggressive executives had long since begun to chafe against the restrictions that set financial industry structure and governed financial practices. New Deal reformers had placed limits on bank mergers as well as on interest rates, and they had drawn a bright legal line to separate deposit-taking commercial banks from securities-issuing investment banks. First National City Bank's Walter

Wriston launched rule-bending negotiable certificates of deposit in the United States in 1961 and went on to issue CDs denominated in Eurodollars.[18] Many others followed in his tracks.

To develop versatile and far-reaching payment mechanisms, to raise and deploy capital across jurisdictions, to offer new instruments of credit and debt, to accelerate the velocity of capital's circulation—and, of course, above all to add to their own profits—financial institutions needed to overcome entrenched political obstacles. Between the 1970s and the 1990s politicians authorized new financial intermediaries and relaxed or ignored rules limiting existing institutions, enabling them to enter or reenter markets that had been undeveloped or foreclosed. Piecemeal legal reforms smoothed the way for nationwide electronic funds transfers, ATM networks, cross-state banking, and gigantic bank holding companies empowered to underwrite corporate securities, sell mortgages, and engage at every level of the financial system.[19] Of notable importance in this context were the routinization of arbitrage; of spinning off product innovations as quickly as teams of bank mathematicians could dream them up; of own-account trading; and of charging hefty fees on every transaction for every class of customer. None of this signified that the mechanism for payments, lending, and credit had lost its structural importance. However, these essential functions became submerged in waves of speculative trading on behalf of big investors, preeminent among which were financial institutions themselves. Financial-sector profits increased their share of total corporate profits from 15 percent in 1980 to 27 percent in 2006.[20] However, leverage—the quantity of borrowed funds on which banks drew—likewise increased and, although it was often artfully camouflaged, so did risk.

Networks, and the software-driven products and practices that permeated them, became neither more nor less than the infrastructure of this globe-encircling high-tech financial system.

In 1966, the financial sector as a whole—including finance, insurance, and real estate—possessed an estimated 17 percent share of the nation's computer installations, less than half the total then in use in the manufacturing sector.[21] Computer systems had been introduced initially to process ever-growing volumes of checks and to coordinate and control savings and lending.[22] Their sphere of application now grew dramatically.

Of the nation's 13,600 commercial banks in 1968, approximately one thousand already operated computers on their premises, while another two thousand turned to off-site computer services provided by outside banks and independent service bureaus. Some big banks, credit card companies, and independent suppliers were beginning to sell specialized financial computer services to other banks and to corporate customers. Automation of varied financial functions was ongoing, both within and among banks and within segments of the payments mechanism that underpinned commercial transactions. The American Bankers Association, however, envisioned a more comprehensive upgrade of the circuits of finance capital.

This modernization, declared the ABA in 1968, would require "more and more extensive and more and more effective communications—between bank branches and their head office, between affiliated banks and their holding company, between banks and their correspondents, between banks and the Federal Reserve System and other Government agencies, and between banks and their depositors, borrowers, and other customers." Across its length and breadth, it rested on "constant improvements and developments in the related communications facilities and services."[23] At the apex of the emerging electronic finance were the U.S. Federal Reserve Wire System Clearing House Interbank Payments Systems (CHIPS, formed in 1970); the Society for Worldwide Interbank Financial Telecommunications (SWIFT, formed in 1973); and the big credit card networks. By the end of the 1970s, tens of billions of dollars traversed these systems each day.[24]

The ABA reiterated in a separate proceeding in 1970 that as data networks became the operational basis of finance, services "specially designed and tailored to meet the needs of the banking industry and its customers" could become a strategic priority.[25] This fixation was especially intense among the largest banks, which spent disproportionately on networking technology and which held a dominant role internationally. By 1980, Chase Manhattan Bank was using networks to coordinate financial services in more than one hundred countries. Its corporate cash-management services, for example, permitted account information to be retrieved in almost any country—or currency—in Western Europe. This allowed financial officers to consult the latest information, and then to transfer funds instantaneously via Chase's network to "ensure full utilization of money," as Chase boasted. "Telecommunications," reported a Chase executive, "has entered a period of explosive growth," enabling the bank to cater to the demands of its transnational corporate customers.[26]

Among large U.S. commercial and investment banks, Chase was not unique. Manufacturers Hanover possessed an internal, packet-switched network and, by 1981, had interconnected it with GTE Telenet to afford connections, including email, to corporate users in more than thirty countries.[27] Bank of America, active in fifty states and ninety-four countries, set out a five-year plan (to begin in 1985) that projected expenditures of $5 billion across the range of information technology systems and applications.[28] Morgan Stanley raised its data processing budget fivefold between 1979 and 1984, among other things, to develop an automated trade analysis and processing system intended for its internal use.[29]

Citicorp, the undoubted industry leader and then the most important transnational financial services company, by 1980 had built up twenty-three hundred branches in ninety-four countries. Using terminals located on customer-premises and connecting them via satellites and other transmission media, Citicorp linked thousands of business clients for financial information and transaction management. Citicorp spent heavily to research and roll out special hardware and software "to provide customers with new tools and, equally important, to differentiate our own services from those of other service providers."[30] "The ability to ensure access" to a unified computer communications network, "on all levels, and at all times, is absolutely essential to any organization that wishes to function as an international financial intermediary," asserted Citicorp.[31]

Trading of corporate stocks and bonds surged across increasingly capacious and far-flung computer networks. The volume of transactions on the New York Stock Exchange, the nation's largest, increased from 525 million shares in 1950 to 2.94 billion shares in 1970; volume swelled to nearly 40 billion shares by 1990, and to 367 billion by 2004.[32] The percentage of Americans who owned stocks increased in tandem with what turned into a generations-long attack on existing retirement programs, in favor of private pensions and 401(k) accounts. (By 2012, an eye-popping 483,000 individual retirement account plans covered 72 million participants, according to the U.S. Labor Department.[33]) The velocity of transactions accelerated too, as the Securities and Exchange Commission sanctioned electronic trading so that securities prices could be monitored and actual trades executed nationwide.[34] The National Association of Securities Dealers Automated Quotation System (NASDAQ), established in 1971, was a spur to this digital reintegration.[35] NASDAQ cooperated with the New York Stock Exchange to establish a jointly owned subsidiary—the Securities Industry Automation Corporation, or SIAC—in 1972. With clearance and settlement responsibilities, SIAC managed a network serving 290 member firms, which employed 1.5 million miles of carrier circuits supplied by five terrestrial and three satellite carriers. Looking forward from 1977, SIAC anticipated a bright future for innovation of networked financial services.[36]

Networks converged on consumer banking in part as a result of a Scot inventor, John Shepherd-Barron—who thought up the idea of the automated teller machine while taking a bath in 1965; the first ATM was put into service by Barclays Bank north of London two years later. (A fellow countryman, James Goodfellow, is credited with the development of the encrypted plastic card and computerized PIN technology.) In the United States, ATMs in service increased from 7,700 in 1978[37] to an estimated 409,000 in 2012.[38] Internationally, the Visa/Plus ATM network possessed 645,000 ATMs scattered throughout 120 countries; the world as a whole boasted nearly two million of these job-destroying machines.[39] Meanwhile, electronic transactions were reducing the need for paper currency, which began to decline in both the United States and the United Kingdom—where cash transactions diminished from 73 percent of the total in 1999 to 59 percent in 2009.[40] More than one-third of New York City taxi fares in 2010 were paid with some kind of card.[41]

The frontiers for electronic payments were pushed back as online banking attained mainstream status.[42] Used by forty-four million U.S. households in 2011, online banking not only generated lucrative fees but also locked in customers, owing to the cumbersomeness of shifting multiple online bill payments to a different institution.[43] Further extensions of electronic payments were actively developed. Even as the digital depression ensued, credit card companies joined up with tech companies like Google and eBay to rig up payment mechanisms around mobile appliances.[44]

Throughout the 1980s, banks upped their budgets for telecommunications, computer equipment, and software by an average of 19 percent every year.[45] Databases and tools for analyzing and executing investment management, debt management, financial planning, and foreign exchange drew in corporate clients via onsite terminals.[46] Fiat was not unique in deploying computerized cash-management systems in the hope that this would allow it to "keep a tight rein on its 421 companies in 55 countries" via centralized control of the $54 billion in cash which flowed through its operations in 1983.[47] "There is no easy way to describe to you the magnitude of the money transactions that banks transmit around the world every day," asserted Robert B. White of Citibank: "A large part" of world exports "was financed through trade credits arranged by banks, and all of it triggered some kind of international financial transaction which depended on the world's communication media."[48]

During the decades that followed, this nexus became further distended. By 2006, J.P. Morgan boasted an information technology staff of twenty thousand and a $7 billion annual IT budget; recent investments had focused "on building sophisticated trading platforms for institutional investors and hedge fund clients," and "[a] clutch of quants with PhDs have been hired to create algorithmic models that speed up trading."[49] When the crisis hit, 2008, Citigroup employed twenty-five thousand software developers and annually spent an estimated $4.9 billion on ICT, *exclusive* of operating expenses.[50] More than two-thirds of Citi's 260,000 employees worked outside the United States at this point (2010)[51]—enabling the holding company to tap into the gigantic overseas cash balances held by U.S. companies (perhaps $500 billion as of 2011).[52] The volume of trading in currencies leapt 21 percent in the three years to mid-2011—so that foreign exchange trades averaged $4 trillion each day.[53] Because the U.S. financial complex integrated the Treasury Department and the Federal Reserve with the leading international banks, crucially, the dollar remained the world's chief reserve currency; and that core industrial commodities—above all, petroleum—continued to be priced in dollars, enabled U.S. monetary policy to project powerfully beyond national borders.[54]

This titanic buildup of networked finance had pushed debt onto every social institution and packaged it in a staggering variety of instruments.[55] Between 1978 and 2007, the quantity of debt held by U.S. financial institutions grew twelvefold: from $3 trillion to $36 trillion.[56] Long-ingrained habits of thrift and of saving eroded, as U.S. policy encouraged indebtedness as politically expedient and privately profitable. The debt, however, was a powder keg—which, as Panitch and Gindin emphasize, detonated successive episodes of crisis. System managers were able to channel the Third World debt crisis of the 1980s, and they went on to contain the flash stock-market crash of 1987, the savings-and-loan meltdown of the late 1980s, the Asian financial crisis of 1997, the collapse of Long Term Capital Management later that year, and the popping of the internet bubble during 1999–2000.[57] Crisis management was normalized as a substitute for any plan to rebuild the financial system on more stable foundations.

U.S. mortgage indebtedness doubled just between 2001 and 2007, rising nearly as much over this short interval as it had over the country's entire prior history; and trillions of dollars were wagered "on the belief that housing prices would always rise and that borrowers would seldom default on mortgages, even as their debt grew."[58] This turned out to be the most vulnerable point in a system that, by 2007, had left U.S. households, businesses, and governments (local, state, and federal) carrying debt of around 350 percent of U.S. gross domestic product.[59] Big banks and shadow banks compounded the danger by perpetrating calculated illegalities. Some ventured their own account bets against their customers; others manipulated the LIBOR (London Interbank Offered Rate) used to set interest charges for trillions of dollars of financial contracts, from derivatives to mortgages.[60] Others allegedly worked to rig foreign exchange markets.[61] Ratings agencies, no longer independent of the big banks, colluded with their paymasters by assigning blue-chip status to flagrantly dubious securities.[62] When, during the mild recession of 2007, some mortgage holders could no longer make payments, the entire over-leveraged and increasingly fraudulent system crashed.

With the pervasive interlinkage of global finance, the network-enabled tools and products had been used to repackage and spread risk across the world. When disruption began in an obscure corner of the U.S. market for mortgage-backed securities, in turn, networks conveyed its death-ray pulse outward automatically and instantaneously.[63] The "chains of potential contagion," as Hugo Radice put it, "reached to the furthest corners of global finance."[64] Leverage—debt—was the fuel for this fire, and debt was, quite literally, everywhere. And this time, the crisis threatened imminent collapse for the entire global financial system. For what was the actual status of the debt piled high in financial intermediaries of every sort? No one could say. As the all-important credit mechanism froze, therefore, the crisis spilled over even beyond finance. Workaday corporate operations drew on overnight loans secured by financial assets to the tune of many billions of dollars every day; but banks knew that many of the assets that underwrote these transactions were actually worthless, and, having no rational reason to believe that their rivals' assets were more secure, all refused to lend.[65] Though many details of the ensuing crisis remain secret or obscure, managers were barely able to contain the conflagration from engulfing the world.

Central banks led by the U.S. Federal Reserve reacted by flooding the financial system with liquidity. If they had not done so, in the opinion of economist Martin Wolf, "we would surely have suffered a second Great Depression."[66] Estimates differ, but there is no doubt that these interventions were colossal. A report by *Bloomberg Markets* magazine, based on documents journalists obtained under the Freedom of Information Act, showed that the Fed secretly pumped $1.2 trillion into the banking system in a single day—December 5, 2008—and that, as of March 2009, the U.S. central bank had committed $7.7 trillion to preserving the status quo.[67] A later estimate, provided by an inside witness to the government's management of the financial crisis, found that, overall, the U.S. Government's commitments were still larger.[68] Other subsequent disclosures revealed that the Federal Reserve's bailout included as much as $580 billion in liquidity aid to fourteen other central banks, from Sweden to South Korea.[69] Throughout the years following the recovery said to have commenced in June 2009, through its program of "quantitative easing" the Fed injected an additional $2 trillion into the U.S. financial system.

Though the crisis thus was contained, grave damage had been done. Millions of U.S. borrowers continued to owe more on their mortgages than their properties were worth; trillions of dollars in household wealth had vaporized and, even though there had already been millions of foreclosures, many mortgage holders still continued to face home seizures.[70] The housing market improved during 2013, but not to the point of guaranteeing stability; indeed, the spike in housing prices during 2013 may have reflected not a return to health but, rather, the tactics of hedge funds bidding up housing prices in order—they hoped—to make a speculative killing. The Federal Reserve Bank's gigantic programs of quantitative easing likewise stoked renewed stock-market speculation and huge flows of "hot money" into higher-interest investments worldwide. Margin borrowing by investors exploded, and municipal debt grew, each a worrisome sign of strain despite, or because of, the re-inflation of bank profits.[71] Only a full-fledged recovery based on investment and jobs would restore the political economy to health, and a real recovery was nowhere to be seen as this book was completed.[72]

Three Follow-On Trends

First, the toxic mixture of high-tech finance and lack of accountability was permitted to persist. Robert B. Reich relates how Wall Street did everything in its considerable power to prevent meaningful reform: "As soon as it was possible, moneyed interests declared the recession over, saying that the system had worked, and then lobbied intensively against major change—leaving the underlying problem unaddressed."[73] "There will be no return to 'normal,'" he concludes, "because the old normal got us into our present predicament and can't possibly get us out."[74]

The top echelons of the Treasury Department continued to be spiked with graduates of Goldman Sachs and other Wall Street firms. As much owing to shared class interest as to the banks' intense lobbying pressure, many of the same risky practices, institutional structures, and dangerous incentives that brought on the financial crisis remained untouched.[75] The man charged with overseeing the government's rescue program declared that it "had been designed by Wall Street, for Wall Street . . . an unprecedented trillion dollar playground for fraud and self-dealing."[76] In turn, "a status quo that was dangerously broken"[77] was preserved. Authorities undertook some reforms,[78] but under the banner "Too Big To Fail," huge units of finance capital still evaded effective regulatory oversight.[79] A measure aiming to curtail the manifestly corrupt practice of proprietary trading by banks, labeled the Volcker Rule, was stuffed full of exemptions and postponed[80] even after J.P. Morgan reported (in May 2012) that trading on its own account by a London-based employee had produced a $5 billion loss.[81] The encompassing reform legislation known as Dodd-Frank was sabotaged, as bank lobbyists drafted and legislators introduced bills to undo serious changes.[82] Money market funds, asset-backed securities, and the repo market—collectively constituting a multitrillion-dollar "shadow banking" complex—remained unregulated and thus constituted what Gillian Tett called "the Achilles heel of America's financial system."[83] Americans might be paying down household debt,[84] but if their credit card statements looked better, their college student loans looked worse. College debt was pegged at $1 trillion by 2013—and was subjected to the same sorts of manipulation as debt-financed mortgages had been.[85] No sooner had the U.S. Treasury Department and the Federal Reserve confirmed by their actions that, indeed, the systemically important institutions were too big to fail, compensation at the top twenty-five Wall Street firms—$135 billion in 2010—broke records.[86]

A second trend signified that the crisis was unlikely to end without a profoundly conflicted restructuring of the world political economy. Since the Second World War, the United States has constituted the power-structure that rules global finance, not only through its largest banks, the Federal Reserve Bank, and the Treasury Department, but, as mentioned, also the International Monetary Fund, the World Bank, and allied international organizations. Throughout the 1990s and beyond 2000, however, challenges to this system grew. The IMF and the World Bank faced demands for a greater say—for additional voting weight and decision-making power—by Brazil, Russia, India, China, and South Africa.[87] These countries, collectively named the BRICS by an investment banker, turned a financier's fantasy into a political reality when they organized themselves into a political grouping in 2008—just as the crisis hit.

The China Development Bank went on to agree, in 2012, to make loans denominated in Renmimbi with India, Brazil, Russia, and South Africa; the outgoing president of the World Bank (who moved on to a senior advisory post at Goldman Sachs), Robert Zoellick, hoped that a "BRICS bank" might be established within the U.S.-centric World Bank system.[88] Substantive, sometimes serious, disagreements surfaced: the long-venerated U.S. policy of freedom of investment came under attack by nations whose economies had suffered from what Brazil's President Dilma Rousseff called a "tsunami" of hot money created by the ultra-loose monetary policies of the United States and the European Union.[89] The dollar's unique status as the world's reserve currency came into question: Could zombie banks and a grossly indebted government continue to stabilize global capitalism? The strains on this system were evident after a June 2013 announcement that the U.S. Federal Reserve Bank planned to halt its $2 trillion-plus quantitative easing program. The result underlined how vulnerable the global economy remained to U.S. monetary policy, as the announcement provoked a deep decline in commodities prices and a dangerous outflow of "hot money" from countries, including Indonesia, India, South Africa, and Brazil.[90] The Fed, by no means oblivious, unexpectedly announced that it would not withdraw its $85 billion-a-month injection after all.[91] Crisis management continued to be the order of the day, yet the deeper ongoing restructuring of global capitalism interacted with it, sometimes in unpredictable ways. As we will see in part III, this conflicted evolution likewise bore down on networked communications and information.

The third trend signaled that the crisis continued to ramify. Debt had not been diminished: actually, throughout the United States and Western Europe it had been enormously enlarged. But through the legerdemain of the capitalist state, during the first years of the digital depression it was offloaded, in many wealthy countries, from financial corporations onto governments.[92] Proclaiming that there was no alternative, capital and its class allies then pointed to "sovereign debt crises"—Greece remained in the headlines throughout much of the writing of this book, but austerity programs were instituted throughout Western Europe and, soon afterward, in the United States—and targeted the standard of living of working people. This political attack was intense. In the United States, a creditor-friendly class struggle, disguised as a shared austerity, hit residential mortgage holders, pensions, medical care, education, and social programs. Though, in 2013, the credo underlying austerity was discredited as a matter of economic theory, a critic (Paul Krugman) correctly underlined that, in practice, austerity policies remained entrenched.[93] As this book was completed, billionaire investors were bankrolling a calculated frontal attack on the U.S. government's debt limit in hopes of gutting social spending and social security programs.[94]

Networked financialization was patently not part of the solution, and, as the digital depression persisted, it continued to spin unaccountably out of control even as bank network investments spiked again.[95] Citigroup announced an agreement to incorporate access to IBM's supercomputer, Watson, "to rethink and redesign the various ways in which our customers and clients interact with money."[96] J.P. Morgan's total annual expenditures on technology climbed to $8.5 billion in 2011;[97] that same year, it was estimated that hedge funds would spend an additional $2.09 billion on information technology.[98] Finance, in turn, continued to exercise power over network development.

Hibernia's announcement in fall 2010 of its plan to construct a new transatlantic submarine cable offers an illustration. The transatlantic cable market had been heavily overbuilt between 1998 and 2001 as seven new cables were laid at the peak of the internet bubble; the severe price competition and actual bankruptcies that followed led to spectacular price drops by surviving network operators: bandwidth prices in 2010 remained "among the lowest in the world." Hibernia's was the first cable to be built for a decade in this seemingly inauspicious market. What was its rationale? The group anticipated that by using a more direct physical path, its "Project Express" cable would cut five milliseconds off what is called "return-path latency"—the time required by a message to transit back and forth, in this case between New York and London. Once completed, it heralded the fastest available path across the Atlantic.

For ordinary users such a marginal gain made no difference. For one group, however, it promised an insuperable advantage. "Financial institutions engaged in high-velocity trading are speed demons," explained an analyst: "They claim that shaving off just a few milliseconds of connectivity between two trading locations can earn them tens of millions of dollars a year—so they're willing to pay extra for the fastest path."[99]

By 2011 high-frequency trading by hedge funds, exchanges, and megabanks made up as much as 70 percent of U.S. equity trading and about one-third of Europe's.[100] For those able to afford it, playing the market no longer revolved around more or less shrewd estimates of specific companies' earning potential but around exploiting innovations in the network infrastructure. Goldman Sachs, Barclays, Credit Suisse, and Morgan Stanley had instituted trading systems built around algorithms for capturing profits by tracing microsecond stock price movements. "They scan the different exchanges, trying to anticipate which direction individual stocks are likely to move in the next fraction of a second based on current market conditions and statistical analysis of past performance."[101] Then they issued buy and sell orders of their own. These unregulated electronic venues depended most fundamentally on high-speed networks;[102] as one analyst observed, "location is critical; the servers are placed as close as possible to those of the exchange."[103] Hibernia planned to reroute the plumbing for the space of flows in search of advantage for a tiny group of preferred customers.[104] (The company halted construction, however, when it ran afoul of U.S. security strictures concerning one of its contractors—the Chinese equipment supplier Huawei.) Similar ultrafast links were being constructed elsewhere, for example, between New York and the great commodity exchanges in Chicago, and, again to cut latency between Tokyo and London, along submarine routes that traversed the Arctic.[105]

Trading algorithms began to be based not only on stock quotes and earnings statements but also on data posted by social network users and chat rooms as it coursed through private networks and exchange venues.[106] A so-called "flash crash" occurred on May 6, 2010, when computer-driven trading unaccountably caused the Dow Jones Industrial Average to swing wildly: within a couple of hours, U.S. markets lost and then recaptured $1 trillion of value.[107] What exactly had happened remained a mystery in 2013. But these networked product innovations carried a prospect of wider dysfunction, as software failures were cited as factors in Facebook's and other companies' botched initial public offerings. U.S. regulators, however, did not implement reforms,[108] so that another far-reaching malfunction hit the share prices of 148 companies, when Knight Capital—which accounted for 11 percent of all U.S. stock trading in 2012—rushed into the market with a new and untested high-frequency system. "Years into what's been described as a 'high-frequency arms race' among financials," wrote one analyst, "these companies are reaching the limits of available technology and pushing what they have to greater extremes."[109] The result, in the measured words of journalist Floyd Norris, was that "the risks may have increased."[110] The music of networked finance continued to play.

CHAPTER 4

Networked Militarization

A third great vector of reorganization originated in government spending for the United States' unmatched military and intelligence programs. Digital capitalism was cast as a permanent, pervasively militarized social formation.

This was not because spending on weaponry was a recent development. Between the fireballs that devastated Japan at the end of World War II and President Truman's decision to send U.S. military forces into Korea, the nation's political economy had been rebuilt as an armamentarium within which ICTs acquired ever-growing importance. Two fuels streamed together to feed this process. The first was a political countermovement by capital and its allies to find means of boosting government spending without carrying forward the domestic welfare state reforms of the New Deal: these reforms had empowered organized labor and had cut into corporate power. The second was a mobilization by transnationally oriented business, political, and military elites to actualize a global *Pax Americana*.

Why did U.S. leaders work to prepare the political economy for permanent war? The immediate strategic priority after World War II was to combat socialism, although this was often euphemistically called "containment." The Soviet Union comprised the primary initial target, but the U.S. strategy quickly widened to include Europe, China, and the Korean peninsula and soon acquired worldwide scope.

Even if they had not been thoroughly devastated like Japan and Germany, the war had weakened major European states economically and had altered their political and ideological dynamics. They were no longer capable of preventing scores of countries throughout Asia, Africa, and Latin America—a collectivity that soon began to be called the "Third World"—from embracing political projects of national self-determination. Revolutionary nationalists had been working in many countries for decades to achieve this result. In a foretaste of events to come, the United States had frequently used military force to repulse turn-of-the-twentieth-century emancipation campaigns when they broke out in nearby Central America, the Caribbean, or in the Philippines. During the postwar period, however, the challenge faced by the United States became much greater.

Some Third World countries (notably, India and Brazil) initiated import substitution and related economic policies aimed at more self-reliant growth. Others (notably, China in 1949) actually withdrew from the capitalist world market. In this historical context, the Cold War became a contest over nothing less than the dispensation of the world's peoples, states, and resources.

To place its strategic net over Western Europe, home to the largest and most important capitalist classes outside the United States itself, the United States helped partition Germany, anchored troops there, and erected the North Atlantic Treaty Organization. In Japan and the Republic of Korea and Taiwan, camping out on the eastern flanks of the Soviet Union and China, the United States garrisoned tens of thousands of additional soldiers. Throughout many countries in Asia, Africa, and Latin America, U.S. authorities repeatedly provided support for autocrats and genuine dictators, and unseated popular, sometimes democratically elected leaders. From Iran to Guatemala, from Chile to Indonesia, and from the Congo to Vietnam, the United States relied on military interventions, covert and/or overt, on a small or large scale, directly and/or by proxy. U.S. government propaganda campaigns directed against the American people presented these interventions as the defense of democracy. Corporate media complicity helped ensure that, whether led by Democrats or Republicans, the war party prevailed in the battle for domestic public opinion. Success was not foreordained, and it certainly was not taken for granted. Throughout every presidency from Truman to Reagan and beyond, the United States battled to capture and, often, to reorganize the frontiers of the world political economy to serve capital's short- and/or long-term designs.

An encompassing institutional circuitry for this purpose was established. The Defense Department (DoD) was set up to unify the previously separate military services. The National Security Council was created as a super-executive department to foreground analysis, planning, and decision making for strategic issues. The Central Intelligence Agency and the National Security

Agency (NSA) were established, both to conduct covert operations and to develop top-secret surveillance programs employing both human and innovative technical means. The military establishment was turned into a standing force, hugely overrunning its earlier, more limited and ad hoc channels. This Executive Branch formation very quickly became by far the most powerful element of the state.[1] Despite fractiousness between different agencies, the president and the military-intelligence establishment shared basic assumptions about the world and the United States' new place within it.

Under the aegis of little-known or entirely secret organizations—the Interdepartment Radio Advisory Committee, the National Communications System, the National Security Agency—what had been civilian functions, including electromagnetic spectrum allocation for government users and management of the government's own communication, were brought within Executive Branch control. In tandem with this refashioning of the state, corporate America also reoriented. From the 1940s onward, high-tech military innovation and weapons design moved to the forefront. Companies developing every conceivable kind of communications and information hardware and software were showered with military contracts. A cloak of "national security" was draped around many of the high-profit boxes within these war-related commodity chains.

War supply became an enormous, multifaceted, and immensely lucrative industry—with information and communications at its core. This process built on existing precedents. At the peak of U.S. involvement in World War I, as AT&T CEO Walter Gifford relayed in a speech to the Army Industrial College, "over 90 percent of the activity of the research and development departments of the Bell System was on war work."[2] In the aftermath of World War II, however, the military hooked into the nation's science infrastructure on a continuing basis, focusing it on weapons systems that could incorporate advanced communications and on upgraded networks to support the traditional military functions of command, control, and intelligence. This military research effort accounted for perhaps three-quarters of all major computer projects throughout the critical early phase of the transition to digital technologies; all of IBM's early computers were funded by the military, in whole or in part.[3]

Spun out by this militarized projection were microelectronics, digital computing, foundational software programs, and innovative networking approaches stemming out of the Distant Early Warning line and IBM's Semi-Automated Ground Environment. During the 1960s, as the U.S. war in Vietnam was escalated by President Johnson and Defense Secretary Robert McNamara, militarized visions of networks began to cohere around the Vietnam War's innovation of the "electronic battlefield";[4] these fantasies grew successively more grandiose even as military war games as well as actual campaigns episodically took the world to the brink.[5] It was Reagan's Star Wars, or Strategic Defense Initiative,[6] that catapulted weapons spending into the internet era. Multibillion dollar funding continues today in planning and programs for cyberwar, whose crackpot realism (in C. Wright Mills's term[7]) has been institutionalized within military operations and strategy.

A network-intensive military did not unfold, however, as a straight-line projection, cut free of any relation with environing historical trends, conflicts, and contingencies. By the late 1960s, as we have seen, stress factors were mounting. Vietnam War spending was contributing to a gathering fiscal crisis. Intensifying intercapitalist rivalries had been engendered by the U.S. successes in rebuilding Germany and Japan, and U.S. capital faced difficulties across a lengthening list of industries. The Third World political project was reaching its apogee: the Vietnamese continued to hold the United States at bay, albeit at terrible cost, supplying a global object lesson to other movements of national liberation. During the second half of the 1960s, the U.S. domestic scene also was transformed, by a strengthening antiwar campaign, militant civil rights struggles and—early in the 1970s—a "rank-and-file rebellion"[8] that coupled a drive for wage and benefit gains with aspirations to democratize the shop-floor and to induce dramatic changes in domestic and foreign policy.

Policymakers responded with radical measures to try to restore profitable capital accumulation. First, they began to attack directly the limited social welfare programs that had been established by the New Deal and only recently expanded by President Johnson's "Great Society." Second, as part of the larger strategy of targeting information and communications as a prospective new pole of market growth, they boosted network-related investments by military agencies. Albeit with cyclical ups and downs, these two trends have been sustained ever since. Even with the defeat of the Third World's bid for national self-determination during the 1980s and the collapse of existing socialism between 1989 and 1992, U.S. military spending momentarily declined, yet no basic change was wrought in the nation's basic direction: no "peace dividend" (as it was briefly called in the aftermath of the Soviet Union's collapse) materialized; and neither the permanent war economy nor the national security state at its helm was disestablished.

Continuing structural changes, however, characterized the military networking project throughout the run-up to the digital depression (I leave analysis of contemporary trends for part III). First, the policy decision to liberalize telecommunications markets destabilized existing arrangements for joint military-corporate coordination of network infrastructures; new mechanisms needed to be established that went considerably beyond a few major carriers, including, above all, AT&T. Second, as capital investment and government subsidy continued to flow into information systems, weapons-making commodity chains were reoriented around networked armaments. Third, although the theater of U.S. military operations remained global, the strategic orientation of U.S. forces shifted, as old adversaries gave way to new ones. Last but hardly least, processes of ideological construction continued to be closed to meaningful discussion of the basics of U.S. foreign policy: wars continued to be presented deceitfully to the American people as emergency defensive measures serving human rights. These four axes of development require some elaboration.

Historically, the U.S. telecommunications infrastructure posed an issue for the military, in that planning and mobilization required coordination with private carriers (rather than, as in Britain, France, and other countries, a state telecommunications operator) among which AT&T had always been dominant. A workable accommodation had long since been reached. The issue acquired fresh salience, however, as a result of Executive Branch decisions to liberalize access to and use of network systems and applications.[9]

Throughout the 1970s, the U.S. DoD had consistently opposed decisions taken by the Federal Communications Commission (FCC) to open U.S. telecommunications markets to competition. Nevertheless, having gathered initial support from some of the top decision makers in the Nixon administration, this accumulation-driven policy of liberalization succeeded and brought with it a host of new ICT suppliers and network operators. These companies, in turn, frequently contracted with military agencies to produce dazzling new weapons, intelligence, and command-and-control systems. Yet this same process of liberalization invalidated the effectiveness of the intimate relationship that DoD had contrived with AT&T—the vertically integrated company that acted as the de facto network manager of the nation's telecommunications infrastructure. A revealing limit on military power over policy appeared when, despite its best efforts, DoD did not manage to avert the 1982 breakup of AT&T following a Justice Department prosecution. The breakup exemplified Vijay Prashad's finding that at this time "the U.S. government authorized a major assault on its own economy, to reshape it"[10] in order to grant to accumulation a new and improved footing. The radicalism of this action stunned many onlookers: not only were the profit strategies of the capitalist class overall being placed ahead of those of the world's largest unit of capital, but the military coordination mechanism for network operators would also need to be redesigned.

The 1982 divestiture "poses a special problem for the Department of Defense," exclaimed Lieutenant General Lawrence in 1983—because the military "has relied for decades on AT&T's integrated management and unified network." President of the National Defense University, Lawrence spelled out the vexing issue: the sudden "lack of end-to-end control by a single organization jeopardizes effectiveness."[11] The fragmentation of the national network infrastructure as a result of the authorization of competing carriers and open markets for network equipment, Colonel Bolling observed, made it necessary to establish alternative means by which "to reintegrate the separated components into an instantaneously responsive, reliable whole."[12] But how?

The Reagan administration engaged this issue even as it broke up AT&T (1982) by creating a National Security Telecommunications Advisory Committee (NSTAC) to advise the president on telecommunication issues relating to emergency preparedness. NSTAC comprised a shifting matrix of executives and represented the nation's principal telecommunications, computing, and information processing companies. "Establishment of the NSTAC," explained a military analyst in 1983, "gave the industrial captains" of an enlarged sector "a share of the responsibility for preserving capabilities."[13] Crisis management within a progressively liberalized market environment institutionalized closer ties between military agencies and corporate infrastructure operators. It likewise galvanized continuing changes in government organization.

Military dominance in overseeing nationwide network security had been formalized in the National Communications System established by President Kennedy. This system was broadened by President Reagan in 1984 and then relocated in 2003 to the Information Analysis and Infrastructure Protection Directorate of the new Department of Homeland Security (DHS). Coordination and oversight were clarified and strengthened during the 1990s, when President Clinton issued Executive Order 13010 and Presidential Decision Directive 63, mandating policy for "Critical Infrastructure Protection." Under President George W. Bush, the Homeland Security Act of 2002 and related federal policy presented the DHS "as the focal point for coordinating activities to protect the computer systems that support our nation's critical infrastructures."[14] The mission of DHS was to help institute "an effective relationship between the public and private sectors."[15] Behind this continuing organizational flux, the state's repressive apparatus was being recoupled to the corporate economy, and computer network defense and offense were more closely linked.[16]

The effect of the post–9/11 mobilization was to expedite and enlarge this trend to top-down coordination within the seemingly disparate, decentralized context of what was becoming an internet-based network infrastructure. In 2005, the Business Roundtable—a group of 160 CEOs representing the top echelons of corporate America—called on government to "fortify the Internet and the infrastructure that supports Internet health."[17] The vulnerability of U.S. companies was a function not only of terrorists but also of other threats, from outages to antagonistic states, hackers, and disgruntled employees. In February 2006, the DHS, joined by seven other cabinet-level departments alongside Intel, Microsoft, Symantec, VeriSign, and other companies, as well as representatives of the governments of the United Kingdom, Australia, New Zealand, and Canada, staged the first "full-scale cyber security exercise"—"Cyber Storm"—to test response mechanisms to a simulated cyberattack. The military aspect of this and related measures was, as usual, presented as defensive in nature; also as usual, this depiction was misleading.

During the Reagan military buildup, an analyst influenced by the thinking of economist John Kenneth Galbraith called the U.S. DoD "an immense planning system that is larger than any other single economic entity in the noncommunist world."[18] DoD's effectiveness as a planning agency is debatable; but the demise of the socialist world notably did not curtail its economic function: to shore up profits, output, and employment—in that order. After 9/11, the scale of U.S. military expenditure became hugely enlarged; as Roxborough observed, on the threshold of the digital depression, "Each of America's four military services is more powerful than the armed forces of any other country."[19]

U.S. military doctrine began to foreground what the administration of George W. Bush called "force transformation." This strategy formalized reliance on weapons and intelligence capabilities that relied ever more heavily on network systems and applications. To preside over this process, an assistant Secretary of Defense for Networks and Information Integration worked, on the corporate side, with a Network Centric Operations Industry Consortium. Responsibility for U.S. military networks was elevated into a leading unit of the Defense Department, the Strategic Command, or STRATCOM—which, in a significant expression of the continuing U.S. weaponization of space, was merged in 2002 with the Space Command. STRATCOM possessed several overriding missions: global strike, missile defense integration, information operations, and global command, control, communications, computers, intelligence, surveillance, and reconnaissance. In March 2007 General James E. Cartwright, director of STRATCOM, testified forthrightly about these missions before Congress:

> Cyberspace has emerged as a war-fighting domain not unlike land, sea, and air. . . . The National Strategy to Secure Cyberspace describes cyberspace as the nervous system of our country and as such, essential to our economy and national security. It describes a role for all federal departments and agencies, state and local government, private companies and organizations, and individual Americans in improving cyber-security. . . . Fundamental to this approach is the integration of cyberspace capabilities across the full range of military operations. . . . Strategic Command is charged with planning and

directing cyber defense within DoD and conducting cyber attack in support of assigned missions. . . . History teaches us that a purely defensive posture poses significant risks; the "Maginot Line" model of terminal defense will ultimately fail without a more aggressive offshore strategy. . . . If we apply the principles of warfare to the cyber domain, as we do to sea, air, and land, we realize the defense of the nation is better served by capabilities enabling us to take the fight to our adversaries, when necessary to deter actions detrimental to our interests.[20]

In 2010, the Cyber Command was established within the Strategic Command in a further centralization and upgrade of military operations for computer networks. In part III, I will return to the functions of this new battlespace. For now, it is sufficient to underline that an offensive network arsenal was an explicit preoccupation virtually all the way through this history. Occasional acknowledgments that the United States was pursuing offensive network capabilities came through publicly. A *New York Times* account, for example, noted that "both China and Russia have offensive information warfare programs" and conceded—seemingly as an afterthought—that "The United States is also said to have begun a cyberwarfare effort."[21] A 2007 scholarly study was more specific, though the effort it described was purportedly still modest in scope: "The military vision is that by the application of millions of dollars and hundreds of people, viruses, suitable as weapons in military conflicts, can be developed."[22] A hint that such programs might be far reaching was revealed when the BBC publicized a declassified, heavily redacted 2003 Defense Department document—a so-called "Information Operations Roadmap"—which, it related, showed that "The U.S. military seeks the capability to knock out every telephone, every networked computer, every radar system on the planet."[23] By 2014 it had become public knowledge that the U.S. possessed a full-fledged cyberwarfare program: when President Obama nominated Vice Admiral Michael S. Rogers to become both director of the National Security Agency and head of the U.S. Cyber Command, it was reported that Rogers had been helping to develop computer network attacks since the 1980s.[24]

The United States maintains hundreds of major military bases in dozens of countries: the theater of U.S. military operations has long been global. However, U.S. force projection began to undergo a strategic reorientation around the turn of the twenty-first century. With the collapse of the Soviet Union and the rise of threats associated with Middle East oil, China, and still-nuclear-armed Russia, bases were relocated from Western Europe to Eastern Europe, the Middle East, Central Asia, and—under President Obama—the Pacific. The Bush administration had forecast that "this new basing strategy will provide the United States with rapid access to areas where we are likely to be engaged, but where a large permanent presence is not needed."[25] Discerning a rising challenge from China, the Obama administration lavished special strategic attention on East and Southeast Asia.[26]

The substantial purpose of U.S. global force projection likewise altered. For decades, this had been to combat socialist states and to repulse movements for national self-determination. While much of U.S. strategists' attention now turned to "asymmetric" threats mounted by nonstate actors, an equally critical U.S. goal was to deflect, contain, or subdue real and would-be rival capitalist states. Once more, I return to this theme in part III. For now it is important to add that the continued U.S. capacity for force projection anywhere around the globe was supported by further change around networks.

To unify its dispersed operations, the United States rebuilt global communications systems for command, control, communications, and intelligence. In addition to STRATCOM, these were managed and coordinated by the different services—Army, Navy, and Air Force; by intelligence agencies; and by the Defense Information Systems Agency (DISA). DISA, created in 1991 as the Cold War ended, was the successor to the Defense Communications Agency (established 1960); DISA had seven thousand to eight thousand employees— a number whose comparative size may be glimpsed by remembering that the employees of the Federal Communications Commission totaled only 1,850.[27] Within DISA were layers of sub-agencies. The mission of the Strategic Planning Office housed in its Defense Spectrum Organization, for example, was "to maximize global spectrum access for US forces both now and for the future."[28] The U.S. military long has been the single largest spectrum user on the planet, and DoD acknowledged that its ability to operate large weapons systems and satellites "depends on international agreements with other countries that allow DoD to use certain frequencies within other countries' borders." Moreover, military spectrum usage "has grown exponentially since Desert Storm in 1991"; and "since September 11th, DoD's spectrum needs have further increased."[29] Presumably, the Strategic Planning Office worked with European allies via the little-known North Atlantic Treaty Organization Frequency Authority, which helps organize spectrum access in foreign theaters.

The related Global Information Grid (GIG) was slated to be a twenty-year building project, on which investment commenced in 1999. Organizationally, it encompassed DISA, STRATCOM, and other DoD offices, as well as the military and intelligence services. The goals associated with the GIG were breathtaking: It was "intended to integrate virtually all of DoD's information systems, services, and applications into one seamless, reliable and secure network" and thereby "to facilitate DoD's effort to transform to a more network-based, or 'net-centric,' way of fighting wars and achieving information superiority over adversaries." Many weapons systems and sensors under contract were "critically dependent" on this long-unrealized infrastructure.[30]

To succeed, the GIG not only would have to overcome organizational rivalries but also bind together unproven communications technologies, presenting both technical and operational uncertainties: extremely high-frequency communications satellites, software-defined radios, an enhanced ground-based optical network using upgraded routers and switches, and improved cryptography. In 2004, the U.S. Government Accountability Office underscored that constructing the GIG posed "enormous challenges and risks"; two years later, the agency produced an even more critical assessment. However, the GIG's spectacular price tag—which rose from a 2004 estimate of $21 billion (through fiscal 2010) to a 2006 estimate of $34 billion (through 2011)—ensured that whether or not it accomplished its military objectives, it would kick-start ICT innovations based on internet technology. The Defense Department boasted in 2006 that just one component of the GIG, its Navy Marine Corps intranet, constituted "the largest corporate intranet in the world," serving 550 locations and hundreds of thousands of users.[31] The experience gained through building and managing this multibillion-dollar project afforded Electronic Data Systems, its prime contractor, lessons it could apply in non-tax-subsidized customer contexts. Accumulation thus continued to be tightly coupled to repression.

Vast though these initiatives were, they did not exhaust the role of information and communications for the extraterritorial U.S. military. Satellite based, the Global Positioning System was integrated into U.S. weapons systems and electronic warfare strategies. An additional fleet of perhaps as many as one hundred specialized satellites, anchored by downlink listening posts in Europe, Japan, Australia, Cyprus, Ascension, and the United States, delivered streams of data drawn from every corner of the globe; over the previous forty years, the United States had spent an eye-popping $200 billion on spy satellites. The Armed Forces Network, run by the American Forces Radio and Television Service out of Alexandria, Virginia, maintained nine television channels and broadcast to all overseas military installations—located in 177 countries—as well as to Navy ships. Such was the dependence of the U.S. force structure on satellites that any hint of threat to these assets—such as one posed when China "painted" a satellite with an electromagnetic beam in 2007[32]—triggered a rapid escalation of U.S. space militarization. All told, by 2011 the U.S. government spent an estimated $80 billion a year on ICTs—probably half or more of which stemmed from military and intelligence functions—making the U.S. government the world's largest ICT consumer and carrying what was indisputably a profound "ripple effect in the private sector."[33]

Although its modernized networks were monumentally impressive and its killing power overwhelming, the U.S. military still remained, paradoxically, far from omnipotent. Major wars in Iraq and Afghanistan produced, at best, highly ambiguous outcomes. This made it all the more vital to shape a supportive public opinion—not only abroad but, perhaps especially, at home. War propaganda continued to be deployed in order to sustain policies hurtful not only to their immediate targets but also to the interests of the great majority of the U.S. population.

To their credit, mainstream academic journals accorded at least some attention to the mechanics of ideological construction for war making. Most of the research of documenting and rebutting propaganda was performed by radical scholars led by the tireless and prolific Edward Herman.[34] Perhaps deservedly, critical analysts granted the press pride of place; yet not only the corporate press, but also television drama, Hollywood film, and games were recruited for active duty as promoters of militarism. Indeed, in the post–9/11 United States, as David Altheide recounts, "fear as entertainment informs the production of popular culture and news, generates profits, and enables political decision makers to control audiences through propaganda."[35]

This repressive ideological work was not simply a function of manipulative representational strategies but also of carefully structured institutional relationships—such as those put into place by the clumsily named Communications Assistance for Law Enforcement Act of 1994 (CALEA). CALEA, as interpreted by the Federal Communications Commission, ensured that surveillance capabilities could be built directly into all new U.S. network infrastructures, including the internet. Monitoring of international communications had occurred since World War II, and warrantless eavesdropping on domestic U.S. electronic communications by the NSA also had been documented—though only after the *New York Times*'s management sat on the story for a year, deferring to President George W. Bush and releasing this news only after his victory in the 2004 election.[36] The sweep and invasiveness of U.S. surveillance programs came into public prominence with the revelations made in 2013 by Edward Snowden, who had worked for a leading NSA contractor. I discuss these sensational exposures further in part 3.

The essential, enduring feature of the state's campaigns to orchestrate public opinion was that the United States possessed a right to intervene where its leaders might choose, anywhere and anytime. This imperial feature has been amply documented down through the decades. More than thirty years ago, the great U.S. historian William Appleman Williams[37] wrote, "The State used its extensive control of information, and its ability to make major decisions in the name of security, to create an ideology ever more defined in content as well as rhetoric as an imperial way of life." Off limits for discussion throughout recent decades have been the actual reasons for deploying U.S. military power to reshape other economies and cultures.

Thus a militarized digital capitalism carried forward the longstanding structural reliance by capital on government spending, extending and reorienting it. In accord with plans made by a tightknit group of neoconservatives powering the administration of President George W. Bush, and continuing forward under the supposedly more dovish President Obama, the U.S. military budget grew by 67 percent in real terms over the decade that followed September 11, 2001, so that its annual spending was equivalent to the collective spending of the next twenty largest military powers.[38] Outlays on weapons systems increased at an even faster rate, more than doubling between 2001 and 2010, from $62.6 billion to $135.8 billion; over this single decade the United States used $1 trillion to make arms purchases.[39]

The build-up of such a military colossus, however, did not neutralize crisis tendencies. Ten years on, the *New York Times* put the cumulative costs of the U.S. responses to the 9/11 attacks at $3.3 trillion.[40] A "conservative" calculation by Joseph Stiglitz and Linda Bilmes in 2008 set the costs of U.S. wars on Iraq and Afghanistan alone at $3 trillion to $5 trillion, and in subsequent years the authors revised this figure upward.[41] Did this constitute military overreach? Could the unbalanced and politically unsettled finances of the United States support this load?

Signs of strain were apparent in 2013. Retiring Defense Secretary Robert Gates hinted bluntly in a speech to NATO allies that, henceforth, they would have to shoulder more of the financial burdens of war making.[42] French President Hollande was reported to be "frustrated" that the United States had not done more "to help with the war in Mali."[43] After a decade of increases, U.S. military spending dropped in 2011 by around 1.2 percent,[44] and domestic political infighting over how, and how far, to reduce federal spending amid a depression produced additional cutbacks in 2013.[45] Admittedly caught up in partisan posturing, the impact on U.S. global military strategy was nevertheless real.[46] Other strictures placed on U.S. foreign policy were, perhaps, knock-on ramifications: the United States did not contemplate, reportedly, what David E. Sanger called "an Arab Spring Marshall Plan"[47]—that is, an effort to buy its way to a desired outcome—after a popular revolt toppled the Mubarak dictatorship in Egypt. U.S. military contractors responded to the inclemency by seeking to diversify, by increasing their weapons sales to developing countries, and even by closing plants.[48]

The true price exacted by military overreach was in some respects immeasurable, as it included civilian populations antagonized by drone strikes and, in the United States, declining living standards and menaced democratic liberties. In order to keep military budgets sacrosanct, attacks on domestic social programs long had been "justified" on economic grounds. This tension was now stretched to the breaking point, as attempts grew to resolve the conflict between guns and butter on the backs of working people.

An insurrectionary world, in which protests cropped up everywhere from Brazil to Turkey and from South Africa to the United States, and in which serious efforts to replace U.S.-capital friendly regimes with popular democracies were being made throughout much of South America, signified that although U.S. military spending was already far, far too great, it might never be enough. Far from acting as a pacifying force for digital capitalism, militarization contributed powerfully to the crisis.

■ ■ ■

Massive and compounding investments in digital networks therefore became a marked feature across the length and breadth of the political economy. Throughout production, finance, and military spending, ICT investment was a prominent aspect of responses to the 1970s downturn. The result was not only to alter corporate and military practices and to enlarge the realm of capitalist social relations—but also to enable capitalism's crisis tendencies to pyramid. Eventually, we now know, the bright line of the ICT investment led on to a precipice as the financial collapse of 2008 transformed into a digital depression.

What, then, about the industry of communications and information processing itself? Through these same years, communications and information processing became the largest sectoral source of demand for ICTs. What did this fourth axis of change around digital networks signify? Did it seem likely to revive the growth prospects of the wider political economy? Let us turn to examine this dynamic field to complete our survey of the deep structural changes that characterized the run-up to, and the progress of, the digital depression.

PART II

The Recomposition of Communications

CHAPTER 5

The Historical Run-Up

Wide-ranging changes in production, finance, and military spending drew impetus from capital's response to the crisis of the 1970s; across this span, corporate profit strategies were renovated around networks' ever-increasing capacity for connectivity and dispersed collaboration. "This was not the first time that overproduction and competition engendered efforts by elites to rejuvenate the market system," I wrote in 1999, "but the pivotal role accorded to information and communications as a solution was unprecedented."[1] A fourth vector of structural transformation may be glimpsed at the epicenter of an emerging digital capitalism: the communications industry.

Violent technical and institutional changes convulsed the communications industry such that commodity chains that had seemed stable buckled and recomposed. The result was not uniform growth, furthermore, but ragged unevenness: expansionary dynamism alongside devastation. Even amid this maelstrom, however, long-entrenched institutional priorities continued to operate and, indeed, to predominate. The existing system was ripped apart and rebuilt—so that it could enlarge and intensify what it had traditionally achieved. To apprehend this complex movement again requires that we begin by revisiting recent historical trends.

■   ■   ■

By the 1970s the United States possessed the world's most elaborate consumer communications industry. Its institutional mission was well-defined:

Communications formed a cornerstone of the market-building processes that, beginning in the late nineteenth century, reoriented U.S. consumption toward production of nationally branded commodities by giant corporations. Two distinct profit strategies underlay successive cycles of media development, from national magazines and telephone service to musical recordings, radio, and television: providing services funded out of advertising sales to businesses and, alternatively, through direct sales or rentals to consumers. The commercial success of these distinct routes to profit also rested on longstanding government largesse, from monopoly copyrights and patents to rights of way and electro-magnetic spectrum grants. Less tangible, but likewise essential, was quite a different input: the uncompensated human activity—in fact, the labor[2]—needed to read books and newspapers, listen to radio and recordings, make telephone calls, and watch films and television shows.

Often a springboard into new territories of profit, in Gary Fields's term,[3] the communications industry's special role in responding to the crisis of the 1970s was to support and enable the wider "fix" through which capital sought to renew the accumulation process. Popular habits of communication underwent spasmodic changes, in keeping with a period marked by metamorphic policy reversals, technological breakthroughs, investment surges, and transnationalization and business diversification. The companies that had ruled discrete fields—from television to telephone service and from musical recording to news—destabilized, but profit-seeking recolonized an enlarged terrain of communications system development.

This process was neither self-starting nor automatic. Market building in communications was a complex, historical process, playing out not over a month or a year but across decades. Beginning during the late 1960s, the transformation of communications was predicated on a radical and sustained revamp of state policy. Nowhere more than in communications and information, as I underlined in part I, was the process singled out by Vijay Prashad more in evidence—whereby "the U.S. government authorized a major assault on its own economy, to reshape it, to follow the axiom of the German sociologist Werner Sombart, so that 'from destruction a new spirit of creation arises.'"[4]

The U.S. government turned communications into a massive and many-sided construction site whose chief architect was capital. Elsewhere I have detailed how a complex process of accelerated commodification came to grip communications, information, and culture.[5] Simply put, the state granted to capital a sweeping warrant to enlarge the sphere of commercial, profit-maximizing endeavor, even at the cost of uprooting existing practice and breaking up entrenched commodity chains. Capital became authorized to encroach upon nonproprietary or common practices of provision, built and operated using public funds, while the state validated these incursions by strengthening capital's private property rights in information and culture. David Harvey calls this category of political-economic transformation—which possesses a long-standing historical importance—"accumulation by dispossession."[6] Network infrastructures were overhauled to enable a great widening and deepening of connectivity, not only as a reflex of technological breakthroughs but, again, through policy changes that chewed through this infrastructure's institutional foundations.

At the outset and into the late 1970s it seemed that a pair of long-established, giant U.S. businesses would spearhead whatever changes might be required to modernize networks. AT&T and IBM possessed near-monopolies in the specialized industries at the center of the vortex: telecommunications and corporate computing. Would they not simply leverage their longstanding power to take over markets for computer communications as they emerged? Many thought they would[7]—including Brazil, France, and Japan. A top-level French report provided support for policymakers as they tried to repel these two U.S. titans' incursions in "telematics,"[8] or computer communications.

Quite apart from this prospective movement around AT&T and IBM, however, other large companies also were rushing into computer communications markets, both as suppliers and as major network users. Among the former were Exxon, General Electric, General Motors, Citicorp, and Sears, each of which bought into networking systems and services.[9] Motives were disparate: Citicorp packaged financial services and advanced network access into lucrative bundles. Sears partnered with IBM and CBS in an early commercial videotex venture. Exxon got into sales of office equipment. General Motors, as we saw, purchased EDS and started marketing computer services. GE took over military electronics contractor and broadcast network owner RCA. That none of these ventures fully succeeded was less crucial than, as we will see, that on the corporate user side communications markets continued to widen and diversify.

Fresh product and service markets, as they formed, also shifted the ground. I have covered the industrial aspect of this change in other works; here I foreground its consumer dimensions. Lucrative businesses took shape around sales and rentals of new media—videotapes, CDs, and DVDs—and around the playback systems needed to use them. Commodity chains extended as the labor employed to assemble these devices was mobilized by capital, not only in the United States but also in Japan, Mexico, South Korea, and Taiwan.[10] Other entrants appeared at the distribution or retail end of existing media businesses, altering the terms of trade. Book publishers, for example, met pressure as they faced off against chain booksellers led by Barnes and Noble, as well as Wal-Mart, which marketed a growing share of their product. The music industry enjoyed the same kind of love-hate relation with concentrating sales channels via Tower Records and Wal-Mart, while Ticketmaster emerged as a force in the concert business. Hollywood film and TV program package companies found fresh avenues to the consumer via Blockbuster in video rentals and, again, Wal-Mart for DVDs. Specialized big-box electronics stores such as Best Buy and Circuit City—and, yet again, Wal-Mart—took a commanding role in retailing electronics hardware. Video games erupted onto the scene, served by specialized players and both arcade and packaged software products. Cable and satellite television systems began to supplant free-to-air terrestrial broadcasters in the distribution of programming; and program suppliers built new market "windows" both for ad-supported and premium television networks in news, drama, and sports, as local systems became linked by satellite, to sell monthly access to bundles of both existing and new networks. On behalf of big advertisers, cable networks joined consumer magazines and direct mail as leading agents of audience segmentation and targeting.

Communications market leaders did not sit passively as these changes hurtled through their businesses. Throughout the 1980s and 1990s, they embarked on massive conglomeration[11] and transnationalization.[12] With active government support, long-discrete media, from book publishing and film making to television, were united (or at least assembled) into sprawling multimedia corporations. Likewise flouting prior policies, government agencies permitted several non-U.S. companies to swallow substantial U.S. properties in this politically delicate business: Fox and Sony and Seagram and Matsushita and Bertelsmann. Others, notably Atari and Nintendo and Sony, carved out positions in the swelling market for video game consoles and games.[13] The U.S. market and the companies that ruled it reciprocally established a fulcrum for stepped-up transnationalization of the communications industry.[14]

Within each market segment top communications companies, like their peers in other industries, busied themselves with raising barriers to entry by would-be rivals. Nevertheless, as we now know, their continual mergers and other competition-reducing maneuvers did not coalesce in a smooth movement toward oligopoly: the leading units of capital in communications instead were destabilized in the cauldron of digitization. What happened? What accounts for this extraordinary change of state?

Three cumulating factors were responsible. A first push against the existing firmament stemmed from political and regulatory policy changes beginning around 1970: computer communications networks were freed to develop at a distance from the existing centers of market power, while adjacent zones of rapid commodification were authorized. A second propelling force carried forward, as growing pools of investment channeled into disproportionately profitable network systems and media and information services.[15] A third source of destabilization appeared as the complex system we know as the World Wide Web unexpectedly constituted an increasingly general platform for restructuring communications commodity chains.

In sharp contrast to the conventional wisdom, as I have underlined elsewhere,[16] the U.S. government intervened to restrict the domains over which the nation's monopoly network operator and its dominant computer vendor respectively reigned. Placed on the defensive as a result of this policy were both AT&T and IBM. Facing antitrust pressure, the long-transnational IBM was compelled to accommodate previously negligible independent suppliers of software. (A decade later, the computer giant fatefully compounded its misfortune by contracting out to independent suppliers not only the operating system software but also the microelectronic circuits needed for a quick rollout of what became the market-leading line of personal computers.) On the other side, AT&T, which had been focused on the domestic U.S. market since the 1920s, was forced to cede room to high-tech interlopers by insistent market-opening actions taken by the Executive Branch and by its immediate regulator, the Federal Communications Commission. A protracted Justice Department antitrust suit actually broke up the company in 1982.

Under the watchwords of "deregulation" and "liberalization," government decision makers opened multifarious opportunities for investment in information-processing equipment and software. Federal regulators and antitrust officials cleared the way for a high-tech networking industry to grow. Public service strictures that had shaped the nation's core network—accountability and non-discrimination—were relaxed or observed in the breach. The accumulation function now instead was assigned growing priority. Thronging into the market were specialized suppliers of local-area computer networks, satellites, microwave equipment, voice messaging systems, and related instrumentation.[17] An increasing proportion of this network gear was produced by computer companies, rather than by AT&T's captive unit Western Electric or other telecommunications suppliers; and this equipment was purchased not only by monopsonistic telecom operators but also by noncarrier businesses to build their own "enterprise" networks. These changes moved quickly from the edges to the center of the U.S. domestic market; from there, corporations and state agencies projected them outward to the world.

Dynamic emerging industries bored into the existing firmament of communications. Throughout the final quarter of the twentieth century the personal computer became a pivot of market reorganization and cultural habit. Desktop machines were gradually altered to add processing power and storage capacity, to permit portable use, and to assimilate at least some kinds of media content—notably, games. Microsoft and Intel seized a disproportionate share of the profits in this segment, though IBM and several PC-compatible manufacturers (as well as the much smaller Apple) dominated sales of the final product. Prepackaged software from Microsoft—DOS and Word—still left significant applications open to outside software companies such as Lotus.[18] The PC established what Zittrain rhapsodized was a "generative" platform for product development: a relatively open and inclusive means for profit-making endeavors.[19] Local-area networks sprang up throughout corporate America to make more efficient use of desktop computers.[20]

As capital investment in networking advanced between the later 1970s and the early 1990s, multifarious projects concentrated an increasingly formidable industry in data communications. However, both nationally and internationally, and in local and wide-area network environments, disparate and typically rival technical approaches proliferated. Beginning in 1976, an influential standard called X.25 was promulgated by European and other government ministries of communications, with the idea that specialized data networks should be developed nationally under central state auspices, and internationally via cooperation by states within the International Telecommunication Union (ITU). The United States, boasting by far the largest national market for computer networking, adopted a quite different course. Some U.S. companies embraced the state-centric standard X.25 in their own networks; some rolled out proprietary systems (IBM's was the most important, but there were several); and some corporate and university military contractors based their networks on the initial internet standards developed during the mid-1970s (TCP/IP). "Managers of large computer installations," observes Janet Abbate, "tended to want protocols that would put control of network performance in their own hands" rather than in the hands of the government ministries looking to limit the scope of such proprietary data networks.[21] They found support from the U.S. government. The United States lobbied intensively at the 1988 World Administrative Telegraph and Telephone Conference convened by the ITU and, as Richard Hill explains, the ITU "was greatly influenced by the increasingly strong trend towards privatization, liberalization and convergence of services."[22] For the first time, as the U.S. delegation to the conference preferred, "private operators were explicitly allowed to use leased lines to provide services, including data services."[23] The United States then added momentum behind the internet standard when it opened state-supported internet backbone facilities to commercial use and then fully privatized them during the early 1990s.

Corporate users thronged to implement "open" internet standards within and among their subsidiary units as they accelerated their attempts to mesh what had been disparate networks.[24] (For years thereafter, though, as James Cortada explains, many companies also continued to operate data communications networks apart from the internet.[25])

On the supply side, through a fifteen-year merger movement, a pair of large network operators—Verizon and a recreated AT&T—added internet backbone and retail services to their offerings; Sprint, Century Link, T-Mobile, and smaller carriers operated in their shadow. That same process enabled AT&T and Verizon to extend, enlarge, and modernize their transnational networks. On the demand side, they served transnational corporate network users based in banking and manufacturing, retailing, energy, and agribusiness. These users built out more or less extensive data centers and network links, and contracted with the large commercial carriers to integrate their proprietary systems with the carriers' more encompassing infrastructures.

Meanwhile, in adjacent markets, related vectors of commodification destabilized existing arrangements and again led on to giantism. In the United States, regulators' change of heart—to favor new modes of television via paid subscription through both cable and then satellite systems—intruded on existing television commodity chains. Free-to-air television remained a protected market, but, like their rivals Comcast and DirecTV, owners of broadcast stations and networks diversified so that television service suppliers could capture not only advertising sales but also subscriber fees. Worldwide, by 2012, more than 800 million subscribers paid for television;[26] in the United States, something like 85 percent of television subscribers did so.[27] Likewise in the consumer market, America Online, CompuServe, and Prodigy offered non-interconnecting dialup services for online access to email and to proprietary content for which they had contracted with outside vendors. Computer network development was framed, correspondingly, by two influential metaphors: the "information superhighway," most famously associated with Al Gore from around 1990; and a "five-hundred-channel world," a term used by cable TV baron John Malone in 1992.[28] The two metaphors, rooted in private mobility and commercial television, rooted the emerging services in an engineered finitude, though superhighways and five-hundred-channel systems still promised tantalizing market growth. Few at the time understood that the "walled gardens" run by commercial services like AOL were simply too small to accommodate the grandiose ambitions of emerging internet companies. Even as internet services began to proliferate around them, cable television and commercial online companies believed that they possessed an unmatched purchase.

Industry leaders' self-confidence was ingrained yet understandable. New technology, they believed, would be introduced only to the extent that it complemented their preferred profit strategies, as indeed had been demonstrated in different ways before—around television, color television, compact discs, and videocassettes. Their multimedia conglomerates, they thought, would assimilate profitably whichever technological options they decided on and would discard or marginalize others. Spurred by a fear that it might otherwise be sidelined from participating in a grandly lucrative market, Time-Warner adhered to this logic as late as 2000 and thereby committed what soon proved to be one of the costliest errors in world business history: it allowed itself to be taken over by the highflying AOL, a company whose valuation had been hugely boosted by speculative investment and whose proprietary approach to networking was even then being superannuated.[29] But something beyond hubris was also involved: the citadels of the communications industry were not well positioned to foresee how the internet would tear across the mediascape.

What we call "the internet" did not storm the world fully fledged. Considerable momentum had already built up around internal corporate networks using the internet protocol throughout the decade prior to the release of the Web, and specialized networking equipment vendors such as 3Com and Sun enjoyed rapid growth.[30] Within a compressed interval, during the late 1980s and 1990s, a series of further developments radically enlarged the interoperable internet: building up under the auspices of the National Science Foundation—and then privatizing—a rapidly growing internet backbone based disproportionately in the United States; abandoning the noncommercial use policy that had enabled the early growth of this internationally interoperable system; inventing the World Wide Web and distributing it as freely available software; institutionalizing the coordination and management of critical internet resources—addresses and network identifiers—not only for the U.S. market but also extraterritorially; and publicly releasing the Mosaic web browser: these were among the vital innovations. Not one of these occurred as an immediate reflex of capital's self-development; all hinged on nonmarket actors including, most fundamentally, the U.S. government. Even midway through the 1990s, the commercial import of these roiling changes was not easy to specify. But a tremendous cycle of investment and commodification pyramided on them.

Additional research on some of these milestones in internet development, and others, is needed. Matthew Crain[31] clarifies the origins of the buildup of Web-based advertiser services in the aftermath of the launch of Netscape's browser. This was itself a complex phenomenon. It was financed by venture capitalists, hedge funds, and investment banks; abetted by closely coordinated bursts of promotion, publicity, and rah-rah journalism; and aided by an emphatically supportive U.S. Executive Branch. Thereby established were conditions sufficient to support another surge of incoming capital, rushing into the enlarging communications market to establish first-mover advantages with which to popularize digital services. As the internet and related new media became a site of investment and market experiment, existing commodity chains began to be rerouted—sometimes wrenchingly. The popping of the internet bubble in 1999–2000 punctuated this movement but did not curtail it. The extraordinary result, shaped by government policy changes for corporate-commercial network development, and reliant on huge pools of capital looking for outlets, was to radically destabilize the communications industry while allowing it to be reconstructed on an enlarged foundation.

The rationality of this process of recomposition should not be overstated. It was tempestuous, contingent, sometimes cannibalistic. Filtering through the day-to-day churn of revisionary projects, however, was capital's sustained effort to appropriate higher profits. Market relations were freed to subsume other forms of provision, as the for-profit communications system was rebuilt around emergent technological potentials and new and refashioned commodities. Connectivity-enabled products and services shifted from scarcity to surplus across an unprecedented and continually widening range. Web services and applications were able to hopscotch across a growing installed base of desktop personal computers, to and from what, before this, had been separate, specialized networks operated by large organizations: universities, government agencies, and corporations. This unexpected bridging introduced potent and (for existing commercial media) intrusive network effects. Existing nodes of market power were disrupted and had to be recreated in different form.

Legal scholar Tim Wu depicts a recurrent phenomenon, whereby monopoly reasserts its prerogatives: challenges to existing communications lead on to the establishment of a new "master switch."[32] In this and similar portrayals, strategies built on first-mover advantages, network effects, significant patents, control over distribution channels, vertical integration, and, not least, state support, allow a handful of market leaders to consolidate. Research by political scientist Matthew Hindman adds fuel to this argument by way of a distinction between barriers to entry and barriers to participation.[33] On the internet, the former are set very low; it is a cheap and simple matter to set up a Web site, and millions have done so. But the ability to organize the experience of the Web itself is a different matter. Month by month, barriers to effective market participation have been raised higher. Microsoft's multifaceted attempt to keep up with Google, industry analysts estimate, costs it upward of $5 billion a year.[34] Apple's competitive move into digital mapping—a single application—reputedly costs it between $500 million and $1 billion annually.[35]

Only a handful of companies are able to play in this league. A masterful account of the Web as monopoly capital-in-the-making, by my colleague Robert McChesney, pivots on the preclusive and antidemocratic power of five companies.[36] Permeating Amazon, Google, Apple, Microsoft, and Facebook, however, are the pressures, the drives, the incentives, the limits, and the conforming tendencies of an environing political economy. I emphasize these, rather than monopoly in itself, as I track below the workings of extended, internet-based communications commodity chains.

Previous analysts have employed a well-known engineering reference model for data communications as a "heuristic,"[37] and I adopt this usage in the chapters that follow in order to trace the multiple commodity chains that constitute today's internet: equipment that is needed to operate and access the system, and which is sold to network operators and to business and residential customers; services that are often "given" to users in order to generate audience tracking data about the behavior and flow of users from Web site to Web site—which they use to sell advertising; and applications and content that are sold or rented to users via direct charges and subscriptions.

CHAPTER 6

Web Communications Commodity Chains

I commence my appraisal of Web-oriented communications commodity chains with networks and access devices: an expansive, malleable infrastructure. Layered into this infrastructure are services and applications powered by other intermediaries, vendors of everything from operating systems, browsers, search engines, and social networks to program content.[1] Recomposition continued at a frenzied pace across this great range throughout the digital depression, signifying capital's scramble to open and to occupy high-profit boxes.

Networks

Behind the retail end of contemporary communications—the side that we experience as consumers—lies a sprawling telecommunications infrastructure. Kindles allow us to download books and other texts through Amazon's behind-the-scenes arrangements for "sponsored connectivity" with carriers; smartphones transport us to Facebook and Sina Weibo via what are, for most of us, invisible wires, cables, and radio frequencies. Virtual spaces are, in fact, bolted to the material world through spatially organized infrastructures: "the networks of the Internet," writes Andrew Blum, "are as fixed in real, physical places as any railroad or telephone system."[2]

My entry point for engaging these infrastructures is familiar: that both the extent of these networks and their information-carrying capacity—their data transfer rate or effective transmission speed[3]—have experienced qualitative growth.

Toward the end of the twentieth century, repeated surges in network transmission speed prompted effusions about a "telecosm"[4] marked by "infinite bandwidth." Even as it grew, however, network information—carrying capacity actually continued to be distributed and priced differentially—by region, by service, and by type of customer. Capacious networks were built to carry all kinds of messages—voice and video as well as email and other applications—as packets of data, and data carriage grew explosively.[5] As network modernization acquired sweeping scope, at every scale the balance between expansion and constraint, surplus and dearth, spasmodically altered.

In 1960, more than four-fifths of the world's 142 million wired telephones were located in the United States and Western Europe. Half a century later (at the end of 2013), more than a billion landlines were distributed more widely around the world, and subscriptions to an increasingly all-purpose service—fixed broadband—had climbed to 688 million. This expansion was surpassed, however, by the even more spectacular rollout, from virtually none a quarter-century earlier, of more than 6.8 billion mobile cellular connections—including 2.1 billion mobile broadband subscriptions[6] (with a large number of multiple subscriptions among wealthier users). Growth was nothing short of phenomenal; and these extensions of access not only co-existed with but also created new communicative inequalities. In parts of Africa in 2010 barely half of the population could even be reached by a wireless signal;[7] in 2013, 45 percent of Brazilians including 80 percent in the lowest income class, had never accessed the internet.[8] Meanwhile, the number of broadband subscribers passed the half-billion mark worldwide in July 2010, with Asia accounting for 41 percent of all lines, Europe for 30 percent, and North America for 26 percent.[9] Overall, developing countries increased their share of the world's Internet users from 44 percent in 2006 to 62 percent in 2011. Billions of people gained new means of electronic connection; no fewer than three-quarters of the world's mobile phones were in the hands of people outside the wealthy Organization for Economic Cooperation and Development (OECD) countries.[10] However, the overall pattern reproduced unevenness and inequality. While North America and Western Europe migrated to cutting-edge mobile internet services standardized around third- and fourth-generation wireless broadband technologies (3G and LTE), the number of African subscribers to the earlier second-generation wireless standard continued to climb.[11] Africa's international bandwidth demand was projected to grow at a compounded annual rate of 51 percent between 2012 and 2019—outpacing all other regions—but signifying that, at the end date, Africa's fifty-four countries still would generate less demand than Canada taken alone.[12]

My second point is that this spatial, social, and technical enlargement of network access came about as a result of repeated cycles of increased capital spending. During the transition decade spanning between 1992 and 2001, the telecommunications industry accounted for one-third of all new investment in the United States.[13] One study of capital spending by the world's telecommunications carriers projected an increase of 5.8 percent for 2011 over 2010—to $311 billion.[14] According to the FCC, during the first two years of the digital depression—2008 and 2009—"the wireless sector accounted for more than 30 percent of all telecom investment, a quarter of all information/communication industry investment, and two percent total investment in the U.S. economy." U.S. wireless operators invested some $25 billion in 2011.[15] In 2013 China's (and the world's) largest wireless operator—China Mobile—alone planned to invest $30.5 billion.[16]

The story is thus not only one of successful technical improvement but also of unlocking access to pools of investment capital. As I will explain later, this in turn was predicated on a radical reworking of institutional policy.

Throughout much of the world, this investment came mainly from abroad. Foreign direct investment, Verizon observed, "has been the driver of telecommunications sector growth in liberalizing economies"; at the height of the internet bubble, between 1999 and 2001, the telecommunications field drew no less than $331 billion worth of investment in developing countries—more than any other sector.[17] In 2012, a growing share—to about 32 percent—of global IT spending totaling $3.86 trillion was projected to come from "emerging markets."[18] This surge was correlated with demand by corporate and especially by transnational capital. Some of it was generated by the companies that were now headquartered in less-developed countries (principally China), which accounted for around one-fifth of the world's largest corporations. A greater share of global network investment, however, originated within the developed market economies to speed network modernization there.

My third point is that this metamorphosis, whatever uplifting qualities we may ascribe to it, never broke free of the contradictory drives of the capitalist political economy. This problematic feature became manifest in varied ways.

Network modernization originated in a fiercely fought overhaul of the structure and policy of telecommunications. This reorientation occurred through episodes of change induced in the United States—which then pressed itself on the world as a model for neoliberal reforms.[19] Market liberalization commenced on a systematic basis around 1967–1970, marking the formation of a bipartisan commitment by the (Democrat) Johnson and (Republican) Nixon presidential administrations. Domestic liberalization culminated in the breakup of AT&T in 1984 as the result of a consent decree signed with the Justice Department, and in a new Telecommunications Act in 1996. These changes destroyed much of the basis for protected monopolies in each market segment, though with considerable aid to incumbents.[20] In a nutshell, as we saw in chapter 1, political decisions gave priority to a diversely rooted and dynamically expansionary networking industry over the particularistic interest of the AT&T Corporation. The world's single largest unit of capital, this vertically and horizontally integrated behemoth was splintered into fragments within a wider networking industry, so that a "monopoly" broad enough to include much of the capitalist class could replace it.[21]

The outward projection of the impulse to network market liberalization likewise required wrenching changes and engendered attractive investment opportunities. Western Europe and Japan adopted the U.S. policy pattern, but they exercised considerable autonomy in doing so. Throughout many less-developed countries, however, liberalization was induced—even imposed—as a byproduct of global economic policy. Some of this transpired in the context of ravaging debt crises throughout the 1980s and 1990s, under the aegis of IMF-, World Bank-, and U.S. Treasury–mandated "structural adjustment."[22] "Part of the impetus for neoliberal reform in telecommunications and other infrastructural industries," concedes economist Roger G. Noll, "had nothing to do with their performance," but instead with the possibility of using privatization and related changes to further "the larger neoliberal reform agenda."[23] However, the stepped-up network investment that resulted not only extended access dramatically but, as we will see, also established some significant capitalist carriers within less-developed countries.

Market liberalization was a precondition for rendering more porous the boundaries between domestic and foreign connectivity. Major operators built up "points of presence" within a country and interconnected them through directly owned cross-border networks. Tata Communications, headquartered in India, laid cables between Egypt and the Gulf Region and major Indian cities to complete its wholly owned, round-the-world fiber-optic cable network.[24] Level 3 Communications' takeover of Global Crossing in 2011 offers another illustration. The combined company's fiber optic networks on three continents were linked by submarine systems and provided end-to-end service to more than seven hundred cities located in seventy countries. Its customers included a diversified group of organizational users: big business, or "enterprise," users, including at least 40 percent of the Fortune 500; government departments; and hundreds of carriers, mobile operators, and internet service providers (ISPs). One of its largest shareholders was Singapore Technologies Telemedia, exemplifying Asia-based capital's appetite to participate in transnational systems and applications.[25] Bursts of submarine cable building during the 1990s and again after 2000 led to qualitative growth of capacity—sometimes overcapacity[26]—even while some parts of the world were still underserved.

The process of attaching profit imperatives to connectivity upended existing social priorities and public service principles as older and insufficient systems gave way, new sites of commodification formed and stimulated market growth, and the boom-and-bust dynamic of the wider economy was transported directly into telecommunications.

Early connections to the internet had been arranged without much regard for profitability; universities and nonprofit community systems had played an out-sized role in this specialized community of military-project-focused computer scientists. As the Web-oriented internet became popular, service provision was rerouted around profit seeking; just in the United States, literally thousands of companies sprang up to offer onramps for households and businesses. As well, internet backbone facilities, for collecting and transferring huge quanti-ties of data, were either purchased from existing specialized companies, such as UUNet, or built directly by big network operators. One network operator in particular played a formative role: WorldCom, which ultimately flamed out in a blaze of fraudulent finance. By integrating forward into internet service and backward into backbone networks, throughout the 1990s and early in the next decade the largest network operators staved off threats to their core business of connectivity and elbowed their way toward the center of the new network architecture.

Internet service provision for the consumer market passed quickly into the hands of the largest providers; in most localities, consumers faced a mere duopoly—one cable-based and one telecom-based service. Thirteen ISPs con-trolled an estimated 86 percent of all U.S. wireline broadband subscriptions by 2011—and all thirteen had integrated forward from either cable television or telecommunications.[27] Backbone services were even more concentrated. This same pattern held across much of the world. In India, the single largest provider of telecommunications services—the government company BNSL— had amassed a 58 percent share of the nation's broadband subscribers.[28] And in China, by 2010, two network operators together served about one-fifth of the world's 492 million broadband subscribers as well as the preponderance of those located in China;[29] seven backbone ISPs, among which three commercial ISPs were primary, catered to the national market.[30]

Major carriers, from AT&T and Deutsche Telekom to China Telecom, like-wise integrated forward into mobile services—although here they faced compe-tition from different kinds of stand-alone mobile operators, and they also were compelled to negotiate sometimes-large subsidy payments with device makers. Apple's iPhone commanded a premium; when the number of AT&T postpaid subscribers adopting iPhones dropped in the second quarter of 2012, AT&T's subsidy payments to Apple declined and its profits actually rose.[31] This was one sign among several that the carriers' far-reaching diversification was not a mere reflex, as some writers held, of their corporate power.[32] Beginning with the transition from dialup modems to wire- or cable-based broadband access, and continuing on through mobile systems and Wi-Fi hotspots, big wireline and cable operators successfully absorbed successive networking technologies as a matter of competitive survival. Market shares may have been large and their profits high, yet the operators' freedom of action still remained constrained.

Environing changes in technology and policy meant that these giant carriers were now only far and away the most important—but not the sole—enablers of connectivity. A substantial share of equipment for transporting data over the internet was sold directly to business customers. Large corporations of every kind built and/or managed so-called "enterprise networks" of their own, frequently transnational in scope; the largest of these demand-side systems were big enough to rival the national networks of small countries. The extent—the scale—of enterprise networking rose sharply. Cisco, the largest supplier of the equipment used in such networks, boasted that globally it enjoyed "relationships with 52,000 partner companies."[33]

As network infrastructures were rebuilt around internet technology, their provisioning ripped away from a century-old manufacturing base. The suppliers of internet "plumbing" were not the historically dominant companies, such as the United States' venerable Western Electric (now part of the French company Alcatel-Lucent[34]), but instead were newcomers like Cisco and Huawei—a Chinese company that, by 2012, employed 140,000 workers and boasted customers in 140 countries.[35] They were joined by server manufacturers such as Dell and H-P; makers of storage media such as EMC; and long-established suppliers that succeeded in mobile infrastructure markets—above all, the Swedish giant Ericsson.[36] The commodity chains into which these companies intervened were also rerouted, notably via third-party contractors, to China; Cisco outsourced no less than 95 percent of its manufacturing operations in this way.[37]

An apparently neutral technical feature of the emerging system's network engineering attested the changes that characterized the transition to the internet. Operators, whether gigantic telecom companies or demand-side enterprise networks, were, for the purposes of internet engineering and operation, classed as "autonomous systems," and the autonomous system numbers they were assigned by the agencies that coordinate critical internet resources formed the basis of the routing tables that sent traffic across the internet. The number of networks whose interoperation constituted the internet had grown by two orders of magnitude. Where the world's wireline telephone networks had numbered in the hundreds, by 2007 the number of autonomous systems had reached tens of thousands.[38] Autonomous-system operators often negotiated private contracts with one another to coordinate their interconnection, pricing, and routing arrangements: proprietary dealings rather than published tariffs therefore governed data transfers across networks.[39] By no means were all internet service providers equally placed. Wholesalers—so-called backbone or tier 1 networks—numbered only a handful; in the United States they were operated by the likes of AT&T, Verizon, Sprint, and Level 3. These system operators built, and rebuilt, their networks to accommodate exponentially increasing data traffic generated by cities, corporations, and countries, and by an emerging architecture in which data centers and smartphones took pride of place.[40] Who paid whom and how much were, however, matters decided behind an opaque screen. There was little basis for assuming that internet pricing was free of discriminatory practices and, as we will see, good reason to think that it might be becoming less even-handed than telephone service pricing during the preceding era of regulated telecommunications.

The erosion of social responsibility around networks went beyond rate setting and market discrimination. It also hit the living standards of a large cohort of unionized workers. Telecommunications workers represented by unions declined from 55 percent of the U.S. total in 1983 to 27 percent in 1997.[41] All told, U.S. telecom carriers (telecom, cable, and satellite companies) shed nearly four hundred thousand workers over the decade to 2011. Once heavily unionized carriers sometimes also cut free of collective-bargaining agreements: in 2011, only around 30 percent of Verizon's two hundred thousand employees were union members.[42] Putting capital into mobile systems provided opportunities for some wireline carriers to escape these expensive legal commitments. The Communications Workers of America, which early in the postwar period had battled successfully to achieve a national contract for workers across the length and breadth of the Bell System, found itself whipsawed by multiple employers after AT&T underwent divestiture and enterprise networks proliferated. "The CWA has held on to its core constituency and beaten back most major concessions," summed up one analyst in 2007, "but it exists in a rising sea of nonunion outfits in an industry that has become highly competitive and aggressive toward its workforce."[43] In 2011, Verizon provoked the nation's largest strike in four years by demanding that its workers grant it concessions: cuts in benefits, embracing authorized sick days, and contributions to health insurance and pensions.[44] It was not only unionized autoworkers, therefore, who were subjected to wage repression.

Telecommunications liberalization also induced a growing potential for market turmoil. For decades, telecom had been a stable, albeit often underdeveloped, industry. With market liberalization followed by internet commercialization, however, investment piled on investment, and this led on to a crash around 2001—and to the ruin of a considerable number of operators.[45] Transforming networks from an exceptional, heavily regulated zone into just another profit-seeking industry rendered them susceptible to the same dynamic that continually gripped the wider political economy. By 2012 another surge in submarine cable construction was underway, despite "tremendous untapped potential capacity on many existing submarine cables."[46]

The digital depression exacted a varying price on this industry. Network operators faced selective price competition and, as the crisis persisted amid increasingly saturated consumer markets, growth rates—for voice services and, in some countries, overall—turned negative.[47] Across the wealthy-country members of the OECD, carrier revenues dropped by 5 percent between 2008 and 2009.[48] Yet a significant number of network operators continued to enjoy robust profits. Contributing were oligopoly status, bundled service marketing, long-duration contracts, and, as the OECD explained, "the fact that communication services are increasingly perceived as nondiscretionary spending items," so that "households seeking to reduce expenditure seem to be economizing in other areas, at least as a first measure."[49]

Their fortunes depended on how the digital depression was inflecting local experience. Especially in ravaged southern Europe, stagnation and unemployment meant that consumers *did* curtail telecom spending during early 2011, and revenue generated by mobile services and average revenue per user fell.[50] (European regulators responded with efforts to stimulate demand by cutting mobile data roaming fees—a lucrative revenue source for the carriers.[51]) In some of the afflicted countries—Ireland, Greece, Spain—network operators hit the reefs. Even as the proportion of smartphone subscribers throughout the country also grew,[52] Eircom underwent the largest corporate bankruptcy in Irish history.[53] After being compelled to sell a 10 percent stake in its state-owned carrier OTE to Deutsche Telekom (DT) of Germany to contribute to the country's overall debt reduction, OTE saw a 5 percent revenue decline in 2012 first-quarter revenues year on year; its fixed telephone lines in service dropped by nearly 12 percent, and fixed retail broadband lines by 2.3 percent. OTE demanded that its employees acquiesce to wage cuts in return for keeping their jobs.[54] By 2012, DT's stake had risen to 40 percent.[55] Spain's Telefonica announced that, to protect its shareholder dividend, it would cut its workforce by 20 percent—but two years later the carrier still faced subscriber losses.[56] In France, an intense price war among four operators prompted market leader France Telecom, still 27 percent state owned, to undertake disposals and to consider joint ventures and even mergers.[57] Even in the United States, where the top two carriers remained profitable, the slump accentuated a decline in wireline revenues as one-third of U.S. households cut the cord.[58]

A fourth overarching trend was that, as network services and applications developed, scrambles to occupy what were seen as newly strategic, high-profit boxes became recurrent, inducing dizzying changes in communications commodity chains.

An important adjunct of capitalist globalization, international telephone traffic had enjoyed a compounded annual growth rate of around 13 percent for twenty years, to reach an estimated 413 billion minutes in 2010. By the late 1990s, however, it could be foreseen that an effective internet application for voice telephony would soon take off.[59] International voice traffic slowed appreciably in 2008, owing both to the economic slump and to Skype, a voice-over-internet protocol (VoIP) provider that had been founded in 2003 and was acquired by Microsoft in 2011. Between 2008 and 2010, usage of Skype almost tripled—to 190 billion minutes; it claimed 170 million monthly users by 2011.[60] International traffic routed by Skype added more than twice the volume generated by all the world's phone companies combined so that, in merely five years, Skype became the world's largest supplier of cross-border voice communications.[61] Although it upended a huge industry, Skype's own revenues remained paltry when compared to those collected by the conventional cross-border telephone industry ($860 million compared with $83 billion in 2010).[62] Paying subscribers made up only a small fraction of Skype's user base (8.1 million in 2009).[63] Other alternative communications applications also became popular: by 2014, WhatsApp, Facebook Messenger, Viber, Line, Tango, Google Hangouts, and Samsung's ChatOn each had been installed more than 100 million times from Google's Play online app store alone.[64]

The lesson of Skype was well understood: "Much of the value in communication now sits above basic connectivity." Services such as instant messaging, voice and video calling, and Web conferencing were "delivered to consumers by companies like Google, Apple, and Cisco—not the carriers."[65] In the United States, capital invested in these carriers earned single-digit returns, while "companies that depend on their networks, from Netflix to Apple, make returns many times higher."[66] Their networks still played an essential role, however, so network operators were determined to rebalance this ratio—the more so because, as the digital depression reached a nadir in 2009,[67] their infrastructures continued to require costly upgrades to support ever-growing cascades of data.[68] However, several factors conspired to interfere with network operators' ambitions to take over or at least enter strategic, high-profit boxes in Web commodity chains. The carriers contended with a legacy of intermittently restrictive regulation,[69] chronic pressure on average revenue per user, and intense competition from both smartphone suppliers and—as we just saw—destabilizing Web applications.

How would this new cycle of modernization be paid for? How would it shift the terms of trade? The cost to operators of transporting a single text message or voice call was trivial; the cost for a bundle of connectivity sufficient to support a billion search queries a month was not. Who would pay the freight for the streams of internet content surging to and from the enormous server farms that Google, Amazon, Apple, Facebook, and Microsoft were scrambling to build? It was estimated that this cloud-based traffic would amount to nearly two-thirds of total internet traffic by 2016, up from one-third in 2011, as the number of users, the number of devices and sensors, the number of downloaded apps, and the quantity of streamed content concurrently experienced tremendous growth.[70]

Network operators sought to make the most of their position, by bundling their services; diversifying into new boxes in recomposing internet commodity chains ("vertical markets"); and pushing to restructure their terms of trade with network-reliant service suppliers. As a result, conflicts escalated and some of the action shifted to political venues as differently situated competitors battled to enlarge, or preserve, their turf. I will briefly review some of these initiatives.

Many carriers offered consumers bundled packages for voice, television, and internet access, referred to as a "triple play." If they added mobile service, analysts spoke of a "quadruple play." The television market was, we will see, a coveted prize. Before cutting back on this build-out, Verizon lavished $23 billion on a project to connect U.S. homes and businesses in large metropolitan areas directly via fiber optic cables to 3-D TV, ultra-high-definition TV, HD video conferencing, and multiplayer games. Verizon's expansion into video continued into 2014, as its fiber-based video service had collected 5.3 million subscribers, while it also marketed an online TV streaming service and planned to broadcast video over its cellular network.[71] Telecom operator-provided internet protocol television (IPTV) services reached 67 million subscribers worldwide by 2012,[72] giving them an estimated 8 percent share of the world's 812 million pay-TV subscribers. The top three carrier-based TV services (by subscribers), whether via IPTV or through a different mode, were, interestingly, AmericaMovil, China Telecom, and RostelCom;[73] France Telecom, Deutsche Telekom, and Verizon occupied a second tier. Television commodity chains remained dynamic, particularly in Asia, as was signposted by the popularity of online video services, including not only YouTube and Netflix but also China's PPTC, which possessed 105 million active monthly users in 2011.[74]

Their traditional strength in catering to business users conferred an advantage on telecommunications companies like Verizon or AT&T over cable system operators like Comcast, which had been more closely tied to the residential market.[75] Big European and U.S. cable operators reciprocated, however, by entering business services markets and rolling out their own triple-play strategies; by 2011, cable operators worldwide had gained more than one hundred million broadband subscribers and more than sixty-five million voice subscribers.[76] As the cable and telecom companies vied with one another, the United States' largest cable company, Comcast, also became its largest consumer internet service provider. Comcast, significantly, directed resources not only into its network infrastructure (a $45 billion purchase of Time Warner Cable was pending as this book went to press) but also into acquiring media content through a multibillion-dollar takeover of NBC Universal from General Electric—on which the Federal Communications Commission signed off in 2011.[77] Cable and telecom companies jockeyed for control of the market for television service as OTT services destabilized their terms of trade.[78]

Comcast's move into content was one among many in a race by network operators to develop so-called "vertical markets" just adjacent to their existing businesses, from television to machine-to-machine communications, and from finance to healthcare, utility services to e-commerce.[79] Japan's NTT DoCoMo, a global leader in pursuing vertical markets, hoped to generate a fifth of its revenues from them, meaning around 10 billion Euros, by 2015.[80] The carriers' drive into applications was most impressive in East Asia, where some seemed on the way to transforming into applications service providers for everything from ringtones to mobile financial services.

Operators also stepped up their attempts to make internet intermediaries like Google, Facebook, Apple, Amazon, and Netflix pay them for flooding their networks with data.[81] They appealed to regulators, asserting that only by being permitted to charge differentially would they be able to raise the investment funds they needed to continue modernizing their broadband networks.[82] They also offered a carrot: network operators could prioritize and channel traffic flows not only to attain operating efficiencies beneficial to themselves but also to offer internet intermediaries the option—for a price—of preferred delivery.

Such "quality of service" initiatives brought the carriers up against a long-standing tenet of regulatory policy. Nondiscrimination in the carriage of data packets over the internet—sometimes labeled "network neutrality"—had achieved full legislative enactment in only two countries by 2012 (Chile and the Netherlands[83]), but the practice of carrying other entities' data streams without favoritism had been enshrined throughout much of Europe and North America.[84]

U.S. network operators had by and large kept their systems open on comparable terms to multiple internet service providers and had not privileged their own subsidiaries or specific customers. However, as network operators bulked up and integrated forward into content and applications, they also appealed to regulators and the courts for authorization to discriminate in their handling of the data transmitted across their networks.

One result was a years-long series of legal proceedings brought by cable companies and telecom carriers. Seemingly indifferent to lessons learned as far back as the nineteenth-century railroad era, U.S. regulators had not only refused to reclassify internet service so as to subject it to common carrier regulation, but they had also drawn a potentially destabilizing legal distinction between wireline and cable networks, on one side, and mobile networks on the other. Mobile systems were given a freer hand to implement discriminatory practices and to privilege their own commercial interests.[85] Court decisions affirmed that because the FCC did not classify internet service as "telecommunications," the common-carrier precept of nondiscrimination did not apply to the carriers transport of internet data. Verizon Wireless's lawsuit against the FCC charged that the agency's half-hearted attempt to codify network neutrality rules violated free-speech protections—that Verizon Wireless should be permitted to transport its own affiliated video service on more preferable terms than, say, that of Netflix.[86] In January 2014, Verizon won this lawsuit.[87] The court held that the FCC actually possessed regulatory jurisdiction over a wider range of internet intermediaries than it had previously chosen to oversee:[88] the issue thus lay not with the scope of the agency's authority, but in how the FCC chose to deploy it—or not. Absent specific, assertive FCC intervention, attempts to negotiate the terms of trade by carriers and internet companies such as Netflix and Google were likely to overshadow the unaddressed need for democratic and accountable internet communication.[89]

In China's policymaking, according to Henry L. Hu, some of "the values of net neutrality are never considered" because the seven backbone ISPs and many local ISPs fall within a far-reaching but complicated (and incomplete) system of official censorship.[90] However, the terms of trade for assimilating internet connectivity in China still were beset by comparable unresolved battles among state-owned network operators, over-the-top service providers, and rival state agencies.[91]

Throughout Western Europe the debate over the terms for data carriage presented yet another face. The top five Web content providers in that region were all U.S. companies. Network operators like Deutsche Telekom, France Telecom, and Telefonica thus could attack nondiscrimination as an unfair subsidy whose effects were to grant a free ride to Google, Facebook, and their kin and thereby also to lock Europe into a further cycle of dependence on U.S. information, media, and cultural services.[92] By 2013, this dynamic impinged on French—and European Parliament—efforts to mandate the creation of an "Act Two" for the cultural exception policies that had protected French music and filmmaking and that now needed to be adapted for digital media.[93]

Physical infrastructures and basic connectivity remained crucial, therefore, but the terms of trade for data carriage—the practical basis of what had been called "convergence" during the 1980s and 1990s—remained in flux. Andrew Odlyzko suggested that the basic issue was "how much control service providers should have over the bits that society relies on so much."[94] Political interventions were certain to continue, as disparate intermediaries sought market advantage by involving state agencies. The issues also acquired additional dimensions as surging growth in mobile network traffic refocused debate around smartphones and tablets.[95]

Apple's extraordinary success with its iPhone massively disrupted commodity chains linked to the infrastructure of mobile services provision. Indeed, the iPhone shifted the online political economy overall. The explosive take-up of smartphones and tablets made data, rather than voice, the mainstay of mobile services.[96] Wireless infrastructures morphed toward a third and then a fourth generation.[97] Disparate technical standards were backed by different manufacturers and network operators,[98] and each migration from one standard to its successor(s) magnified the potential for industry restructuring. International market conflicts compounded this potential. The Chinese state's efforts to develop a homegrown technical standard were renewed around China Mobile and Huawei, and Bharti Airtel, India's largest carrier by number of users, and Japan's Softbank, which planned to employ standards compatible with China Mobile's.[99]

An important factor here was a need for more efficient use of the electromagnetic spectrum. The volcanic upsurge in data sent to and from mobile devices placed fierce pressure on spectrum availability; some U.S. scholars argued that frequency sharing and common use, notably via unlicensed spectrum services, would prove essential in this transition to mobile broadband.[100] Certainly the inefficiencies that had resulted from exclusive licensing practices—chronic waste, as many frequency bands remained unused or underused[101]—were cited as an argument for a fundamental reworking of allocation policy. In the absence of such an overhaul, Eli Noam argues, spectrum shortages were likely to pose increasing constraints going forward.[102]

"Globally," the then-FCC chair asserted in 2011, "Cisco has projected a nearly 60-fold increase in demand for spectrum between 2009 and 2015."[103] "Spectrum is at the top of the agenda right now for regulators," another analyst suggested in 2011—and it became even more urgent for policymakers during 2012 and

2013.[104] How could spectrum sufficient to support high-profit mobile broadband market building be provided?

One response might be to introduce free nationwide Wi-Fi.[105] Such a strategy might be actualized were powerful market actors to succeed in demanding changes to the existing system on the grounds that it blocked an overarching accumulation project, the way the old AT&T monopoly has done. Only recently, however, a movement in quite a different direction had become entrenched. A position that had occupied only marginal intellectual space in the 1950s,[106] favoring the establishment of property rights in spectrum, had latterly ascended to legitimacy. Spectrum auctions had supplanted prior forms of public-service assignment beginning, in the United States, in 1994; they extended to much of the world throughout the following decade. Auctions, of course, privileged those able to mobilize large sums of capital by conferring on them an exclusionary (though still a limited) right to exploit the spectrum. The FCC's 2008 auction produced $19 billion worth of purchases by U.S. wireless carriers.[107] The fight to gain access to coveted spectrum in this case made temporary allies of mobile carriers, internet intermediaries like Google and Microsoft, and consumer electronics companies, against incumbent television broadcasters and so-called "public safety" (mostly police and law-enforcement) claimants.[108] After the rampaging success of the iPhone, however, the big internet intermediaries contended with the carriers over unlicensed spectrum as a possible means of altering the terms of trade between them. Meanwhile, the Middle-Class Tax Relief and Job Creation Act of 2012 authorized the FCC to hold additional spectrum auctions.[109]

Trends in mobile usage created ever-growing spectrum hunger. Voice calls were not unprofitable; nor was texting, before it began to be eclipsed by smartphone chat clients like WeChat and iMessenger (SMS service had grown by leaps and bounds; U.S. wireless phone users sent 173 trillion text messages between June 2009 and 2010).[110] But as smartphones multiplied, it was obvious that data traffic was the great growth node. Text, email, streaming video, music, and other data services surpassed the volume of voice mobile phone calls in 2009;[111] initially, the top 1 percent of mobile users worldwide consumed no less than 50 percent of wireless data throughput by 2012, via their smartphones, tablets, and laptops.[112] Engineering improvements and the growing density of cell-towers (there were around 260,000 just in the United States by 2012),[113] were not sufficient. AT&T saw an astounding surge in mobile data traversing its network: a 5,000 percent increase from 2007 to 2009.[114]

U.S. carriers responded by locking up spectrum assets in the most favorable frequency bands, establishing what they hoped would serve as another barrier

to entry. Between 2010 and 2013, AT&T negotiated a series of spectrum purchases and bid to take over T-Mobile,[115] which would have increased its spectrum holdings by 60 percent, notably in the urban areas where iPhone customers were concentrated. However, this deal was turned back by U.S. authorities;
ironically, AT&T had to cede some of its own spectrum to T-Mobile to back
out of the deal.[116] Verizon Wireless, for its part, agreed to a joint-marketing arrangement with major cable television groups through which it acquired $3.6
billion worth of spectrum and went on to purchase spectrum in fifty-three U.S.
counties from a subsidiary of U.S. Cellular.[117] The third-largest U.S. mobile network, Sprint, gained full control of Clearwire (a wholesaler of wireless broadband service) in order to boost its spectrum assets, even as Sprint itself was
acquired by Japan's SoftBank.[118] The two largest U.S. mobile carriers exploited
their unrivaled spectrum assets both to consolidate their market positions and
to impose data plans with monthly usage caps on customers.[119]

Network operators also rushed to exploit a different spectrum band, by
assimilating a complementary wireless technology. Unlicensed spectrum had
been authorized by the U.S. FCC during the mid-1980s and began to be integrated into Wi-Fi networks during the mid-1990s; by 2011 there were hundreds
of thousands of free and pay Wi-Fi hotspots scattered throughout public build-
ings, hotels, malls, cafes, restaurants, and other locations spread across 144
countries.[120] Wi-Fi was also used for sponsored connectivity services. Even
before the iPhone, telecom and cable operators also were moving into Wi-Fi:
by 2007, some existing U.S., Western European, and Japanese mobile carriers
had joined the list of top commercial hotspot operators.[121] AT&T became a
large operator after its $275 million acquisition of hotspot provider Wayport
in 2008.[122] Between 2010 and 2013 China Mobile organized what it said was the
world's largest carrier-managed Wi-Fi network, with six million access points;[123]
across the East China Sea, Japan's mobile carrier KDDI planned to increase its
Wi-Fi hotspots tenfold, to one hundred thousand. In the United States, five of
the largest cable TV system operators were developing a joint network with
fifty thousand hotspots.[124] These were not merely attempts to coopt prospective competition; the carriers offloaded onto Wi-Fi an increasing share of the
burden placed on their mobile networks by customers' take-up of smartphones
and, especially, of tablets.[125]

Mobile services cut deeply into the business that had been built up over a
century for traditional local and long-distance telephony; but, as the experience of Wi-Fi demonstrates, this did not prevent the wireline carriers from
becoming leaders in wireless provision as well. Mobile carriers based in the
developed market economies proved unable, however, to capture high-growth

wireless subscriber markets throughout Asia, Africa, and Latin America.[126] This constituted another critical trend: that network operators headquartered in the wealthy countries appropriated a declining fraction of the world's growing subscriber base.

A predisposing factor was that the global migration into wireless was gathering speed just as the internet bubble popped in 1999–2000. This granted opportunities to network operators headquartered in some of the less-developed countries at an especially propitious moment. A further strain for North American and, especially, European operators came from the heavy investments they made both for mergers and acquisitions and for spectrum. By 2012, 4G spectrum auctions had cost operators 3.8 billion Euros in France, 3.9 billion Euros in Italy, 4.4 billion Euros in Germany, and 1.6 billion Euros in Spain.[127] European telecom companies collectively carried debt estimated at 272 billion Euros in 2012; from 2000 to 2012 they had already written off assets worth around 134 billion Euros.[128] By this time, of course, the digital depression had struck. One business consultancy projected in 2011 that three-quarters of telecommunications companies were at some risk, "due to high levels of debt taken on to expand technological infrastructures and to fund acquisitions."[129] This debt might become a crushing liability if, as a result of the economic slump, revenues flattened and operating margins became squeezed.[130] Incumbent operators in hard-hit Europe sought relief through disposals of "non-core" assets; Spain's Telefonica, laboring under a debt of 57 billion Euros, sold nearly half of its 10 percent ownership stake in China Unicom at what analysts deemed a discount.[131] Debt continued to weigh on Europe's network operators in mid-2014.[132]

An engraved disparity thus began to erode. Two of the top ten telecommunications companies, by market capitalization—China Mobile, and America Movil, Carlos Slim's Latin American wireless group—were based in China and Mexico, respectively, in 2008. This seesaw continued to tilt. China Mobile's 611 million domestic subscribers, midway through 2011, increased in number to over 700 million by 2013; by then, China Mobile sported by far the greatest market capitalization of any carrier.[133] By 2010, America Movil possessed 217 million subscribers in eighteen countries, and the company was using its network of 290,000 kilometers of fiber to leverage itself into internet and pay-TV services.[134] With its $10 billion capital investment budget, America Movil expected also to add 100 million new subscribers to its already massive customer base by 2014;[135] in 2012 it began to extend its transnational operations by acquiring stakes in two lagging European carriers.[136] Hutchison Whampoa, based in Hong Kong, likewise owned significant network properties in Europe (even bidding for Eircom after Ireland's phone company went bankrupt).[137] An Egyptian telecoms billionaire, Naguib Sawiris, again looked to take stakes in "underperforming" European network operators.[138]

Network services in consequence acquired a changed geographic profile. As the number of mobile phones climbed above 6 billion worldwide, new subscriber growth continued throughout Nigeria, Egypt, South Africa, India, and China.[139] MTN, based in South Africa, was by 2008 the largest mobile operator in Africa, supplying service to 53 million customers in seventeen African countries as well as a few others in the Middle East; but three years later it had nearly tripled its subscriber base, to over 150 million.[140] Bharti Airtel, India's largest mobile company, was the world's fifth largest telecom operator by 2011, with more than 220 million customers in nineteen countries.[141] With its launch in Rwanda in 2012, Bharti too operated seventeen networks in Africa.[142] Based in Britain, Vodafone operated networks in many less-developed countries and even acquired small ownership stakes in Chinese operators. But this was exceptional. Most large network operators headquartered in Europe and the United States either had dropped out of or had not bought into the higher-growth regions. Crisis dynamics, combined with economic nationalism, varying technical standards, and the business acumen shown by upstart rivals, had limited their options. When it promised $130 billion to buy out Vodafone's 45 percent stake in its U.S. wireless unit, Verizon placed a big bet, instead, on its home market.[143]

Patterns of network use by individuals were also, interestingly, migrating from south to north. It was not just that high-end data applications aimed at those for whom price was not an object were matched by skyrocketing low-end usage of voice and texting. Prepaid service models, popularized throughout less-developed countries, likewise diffused through the heartland of digital capitalism: three of every five new U.S. wireless subscribers adopted prepaid service in 2010, amounting to one-quarter of the overall subscriber base by 2011.[144] In Brazil, by comparison, 82 percent of mobile users—191 million out of a total of 242 million at the end of 2011—used the prepaid model.[145] By 2012, some smartphone service providers were also adopting prepaid plans. Not only in Mumbai, but also in Los Angeles and London, prepaid service plans gravitated from low-income to middling strata, whose members brand-name carriers had previously locked in with two-year contracts. The change in usage expressed something beyond a marketing reset.

Control over network connectivity remained only one competitive factor, however, because other links in Web communications commodity chains in their turn also possessed strategic importance. Network devices figured especially in this overarching process of market recomposition. Steve Jobs had been mindful of this possibility during the final years of his reign as Apple's CEO, even prior to his release of the iPhone in 2007, when he had schemed to use unlicensed Wi-Fi to elude dependence on the existing carriers.[146] Instead, when the iPhone hit the market, Apple bargained to ensure that the terms of trade with its wireless network partners were heavily weighted in its favor.[147] I turn now to examine devices more directly.

Devices

Network modernization programs developed in syncopation with access devices. Smartphones and tablets had particularly momentous impacts on the recomposition of Web commodity chains. In their quest to occupy high-profit boxes, large internet intermediaries identified a strategic need to sell their own mobile equipment or to ally with mobile equipment makers in some other way.

Devices proliferated: TV sets and DVRs, PCs, game consoles, set-top boxes, MP3 players, smartphones, tablets, e-book readers, GPS units, wearables. Imbued with broadband internet connectivity, many devices, or "platforms," added "functionality." Market participants sought advantage by stuffing each piece of hardware with their own or their allies' operating systems, browsers, and services, and by tying them to proprietary datacenters for storage in "the cloud." By 2013, four market leaders were each providing the constituent elements needed for a more-or-less tightly integrated "ecosystem."[148] Beneath this cohesiveness lay tumultuous changes.

Manufacturers shipped an estimated 210 million TV sets worldwide in 2009, with annual set sales growth falling to 2.5 percent. Sales rebounded smartly in 2010, to 247 million units,[149] as consumers enthusiastically replaced their tube sets with flat-panel screens. But this sales growth was accomplished only by lowering prices.[150] Something beyond the much-cited learning curve was responsible: TV sets, including the large-sized liquid crystal display (LCD) and light-emitting diode (LED) flatscreen models that set a new benchmark, were in oversupply, while more people were watching television on computers and mobile devices.

Cutbacks in consumer spending during the digital depression had been accompanied by growing competition between suppliers. Price cuts predictably followed, and, though they moderated, they persisted into 2013 as set sales slumped again.[151] Further innovations—3-D, UltraHD, and internet-connected sets, the latter capturing about one-fifth of global TV shipments by 2010[152]— did not turn the manufacturers' fortunes around. Japanese companies that had taken over control of TV manufacturing back in the analog era gave up ground to Korean and Taiwanese rivals with the ascent of digital flatscreens. While LG and Samsung TV sales held up in 2012,[153] Sony's legendary set-making unit by then had suffered losses for eight successive years. Beset by the industry's chronic overcapacity, Sony closed four of its eight TV factories, eliminated ten thousand jobs, sold its New York headquarters, and outsourced production to lower-cost suppliers; for all this, Sony returned to profit in 2013 only because the Japanese government's financial policies weakened the yen.[154] Hitachi, Sharp, Toshiba, and Panasonic also announced losses, made job cuts, and reduced manufacturing capacity.[155] In China, where the television market was booming, price remained a bedrock factor. Sony and Panasonic had cut some set prices by one-third because they were being outsold six-to-one by a domestic company, Skyworth Digital Holdings. Low-end products and small sets from Skyworth, Hisense Electric, and TCL were the fastest-growing market segments, even as China became the world's largest domestic market for flat-panel TVs.[156] Chinese companies were also playing at the high end of the market, as Baidu, Alibaba, and Xiaomi all planned to launch "smart TVs."[157] Speculation continued as to when Apple might add a TV set to its paradigm-setting "ecosystem."[158]

Smart TVs were a bright spot. Sales of sets able to deliver Web content and applications had benefited from the arrival of Microsoft's Kinect controller, which had sold 16 million units by 2012, and from the popularity of online TV and film-streaming services led by Netflix. Big, high-definition units equipped with Web browsers, Wi-Fi, and an apps store created new frontiers of competition and sometimes-opaque market dynamics.[159]

Initially a specialized platform, game consoles sold strongly as market leaders integrated touch and gesture into game play, endowed their fantasy worlds with ever-greater verisimilitude, and transported the gaming experience online. Development costs skyrocketed, punishing smaller companies; designing a game for a console cost between $50,000 and $400,000 early in the 1990s—but rose to $20 million and involved around one hundred developers by 2010.[160] Large publishers, including Ubisoft and Electronic Arts, competed with deep-pocketed conglomerates such as Warner Brothers and Activision Blizzard to recoup these heavy, upfront expenditures with global blockbusters. Sometimes they succeeded. In its first day of release in the United States, Canada, and Britain, Activision Blizzard's "Call of Duty: Modern Warfare 3" sold 6.5 million copies—setting a new industry record and earning $400 million.[161]

Makers of game consoles faced their own boom-and-bust cycle with each enhanced generation of devices. Nintendo's low-priced, motion-sensing Wii, introduced in November 2006, went into a sales slump after competitors brought out effective imitators—notably, the Kinect controller, with which

Microsoft augmented its Xbox 360.[162] Nintendo responded with a 3-D model, but this proved insufficient to halt declining console sales in 2012.[163] Microsoft announced a spate of deals with media conglomerates to permit subscribing gamers to watch an enlarged range of TV programs via Xbox Live.[164] The motion-sensing Wii retained an overall lead in the market for home videogame systems, as of mid-2011, with eighty-six million units sold; but Xbox and PS3 had each shipped more than fifty million units. Xbox continued to gain, with a worldwide installed base of sixty-six million by 2012, and Microsoft strategized about making the console its pivot in the living room.[165]

Seven years passed before Microsoft and Sony each introduced new consoles.[166] Market conditions altered in the interim.[167] Gamers' turn to tablets and smartphones hit console-makers' profits, even while online sales and subscriptions boomed. The number of active online gaming accounts grew from around twenty-two million to ninety-three million between 2007 and 2010, and continued to increase.[168] One survey of users of Sony's PlayStation 3 showed that gaming online and offline together consumed barely half of users' time: DVDs and Blu-rays, video on demand, and downloaded movies and TV shows consumed 40 percent of it, and music and social networking on the Web accounted for an additional 10 percent.[169] After Microsoft's Kinect controller sold eight million units in its first sixty days after release (price: $150), it initiated a program to extend its uses, collaborating with some two hundred companies based in twenty-five industries, from health care and education to automobiles and advertising.[170] Microsoft's Xbox One and Sony's PlayStation 4 continued this process of reshaping consoles into features-rich media platforms. The strategy reaped blockbuster profits: during the 2013 Christmas season, each company sold a million units in North America within twenty-four hours of product debut.[171]

Another specialized device finally found fanfare and rapidly widening use. After thirty years in development and repeated commercial failure, a tipping point was reached for e-book readers when prices for the units plummeted, and hundreds of thousands of electronic titles became available. In China, two major suppliers—Hanvon and Shanda—controlled nearly four-fifths of a market totaling an estimated six hundred million e-books in 2011; other companies, like Dangdang, sought market entry.[172] In the United States, Amazon got the jump, and well-reviewed models from Sony and from Barnes & Noble, despite backing from Microsoft, never overtook it. E-book readers began to sell strongly after the digital depression hit; there were ten million in use in the United States halfway through 2011.[173] That Christmas (2011), e-book readers were a hot item, so that nearly 20 percent of the U.S. adult population possessed one by January 2012.[174] The popularity of the reader was, again, linked to the availability of digital e-books themselves; and, during 2010 and 2011,

U.S. e-book sales overtook sales of audio books and then began to gain on print editions.[175]

Growing e-book sales were not sufficient, however, to prevent overall book sales from dropping by 2.5 percent during the first part of 2011.[176] Pressures on publishers' traditional business model, which had mounted with the rise of the giant brick-and-mortar retailers, continued to build as Amazon seized pricing power over e-books—and their publishers.[177] Several publishers responded by cooperating with Apple, which had its own incentives for introducing an "agency model" that was intended to allow publishers to regain pricing power while granting to Apple's iPad traction against Amazon's Kindle.[178] Charging collusion, however, in April 2012 the U.S. Department of Justice filed a lawsuit against five publishers and Apple. A year later, all of the publishers had settled; Apple—even after a federal judge ruled that it had conspired to raise prices for e-books[179]—continued to fight the charges in court.[180] But by now tablets were on offer from a throng of suppliers, and the data they produced about reading habits and practices became a coveted commodity in their own right.[181]

The transition to multimedia tablets required improvements in connectivity; unlike e-books, movies and videos and games—even color magazines—required substantial bandwidth for easy access. Amazon (and Barnes & Noble) sponsored Wi-Fi so as to reduce consumers' costs while cutting out of the service the 3G and 4G wireless carriers and their expensive data plans.[182]

The first widely adopted multifunctional platform in the transition to Web-enabled services had been the desktop personal computer. With the embrace of laptops during the years after 2000, however, the PC's centrality came into question. Worldwide PC shipments including laptops grew to around 350 million units in 2010,[183] but over the next two years, worldwide PC shipments began to trail.[184] By the end of 2013, worldwide PC shipments had slumped for seven successive quarters.[185] The leading manufacturers as of 2013 were Lenovo, Hewlett-Packard, Dell, and then Acer. The Chinese-owned Lenovo had acquired IBM's PC business in 2005 and, after an initial slide, had reestablished itself within the topmost ranks of PC manufacturers on the strength of its home market: its sales in China grew by 21 percent from 2009 to 2010, coming to account for nearly half of Lenovo's total revenue. China's booming PC market, however, was exceptional.[186] As the depression hit and Lenovo overtook H-P through a joint venture with NEC and acquisitions in Brazil and Germany, Dell slashed its revenue forecast and moved to reorganize, while H-P nearly withdrew from the business. These companies' razor-thin margins came under renewed pressure as a result of an incursion by a new product category, the tablet computer.[187]

Apple was the chief early beneficiary of consumers' embrace of high-end mobile devices. With the death of Apple CEO Steve Jobs, the success of the iPad became a widely cited element in his legacy and of his company's startling rebirth. After twenty-five years in business, at the turn of the new century, Apple had been stumbling toward irrelevance, even in the desktop computer market, its traditional pocket of strength: in 2001 Apple claimed $5.4 billion in revenues and took a $25 million loss. That same year, however, the company began a roaring comeback, and even the onset of the digital depression seven years later did not slow its success. In 2010, Apple garnered sales of $65 billion and net income of $14 billion;[188] by fiscal year 2013, these numbers had increased to an extraordinary $171 billion and $37 billion, respectively.[189] Jobs hitched Apple's fortunes to a trio of sensationally successful mobile devices, beginning with the iPod (October 2001), and continuing with the iPhone (2007) and the iPad (2010). By the tenth anniversary of its first sale in November 2011, Apple had sold more than three hundred million iPods and held a 78 percent share of what was now a declining U.S. market for MP3 players.[190] Smartphones, led by its own iPhone, subsumed the iPod's functions and cannibalized its sales. IPhone revenues skyrocketed, as sales shot from 47 million in 2010 to 136 million in 2012 and continued their climb in 2013: iPhones suddenly accounted for about half of the company's overall revenue.[191] Worldwide smartphone sales exceeded those of PCs for the first time in 2011, and by a commanding majority: 472 million versus 353 million.[192] During 2013, sales of internet-connected smartphones also overtook those of more basic "feature phone" handsets.[193] Even as it became the world's largest PC maker facing a slumping market beset by overcapacity, Lenovo sold more smartphones and tablets than computers.[194] Apple, however, began to yield ground in this pivotal market to Samsung, which, in the third quarter of 2013, enjoyed a 35 percent share of the global smartphone market—as against Apple's 13.4 percent share (admittedly much more profitable, however).[195] Far behind these two, in third place, was the Chinese equipment vendor Huawei.

The iPad became another phenomenon (fifteen million of the high-priced devices were sold in 2010, seventy-one million in 2013) and vied with Apple's revived line of Macs to be the company's second-biggest revenue generator after iPhones.[196] By the end of 2011, counting iPads as PCs, Apple had become the world's top PC maker.[197] Spending on tablets ballooned as shipment growth continuing to accelerate through 2013.[198]

Other consumer electronics manufacturers had been caught out. With iPads initially claiming 60 to 70 percent of the global tablet market, and Apple struggling to meet demand,[199] rival models began to pour from other suppliers—notably, Samsung and Amazon, whose multimedia Kindle Fire offered a low-priced model with less functionality. Such was the tablet's market-moving success that Google and Microsoft broke with their software-centric strategies to introduce tablets of their own during 2012: Nexus 7 and Surface, respectively.[200]

Apple scooped profits away from big network operators with its devices, but all this transpired against a depressed background. Apple's launch of its iPad 2 in 2011 instantly created a billion-dollar secondhand market for first generation iPads. It was a mark of persistent crisis that this market—like those for used CDs and DVDs before it—became institutionalized, in this case not by local shops but by major retailers including eBay, Radio Shack, and Best Buy.[201] The market for new tablets and smartphones began to expand to lower-income countries such as China and India—markets that Apple cultivated zealously as vital to its growth.[202]

Apple's volcanic success with mobile devices shifted the digital world's tectonic plates. It also expressed a strategy that Paul Krugman called "profits without production."[203] The company outsourced everything, from components to final assembly, to suppliers based mostly in East Asia. The iPhone commodity chain brought parts from nine nations and at least 156 companies to an assembly process performed in Shenzhen, China, by legions of low-paid, stressed-out, young workers.[204] Its largest contractor was the Taiwanese company Hon Hai—the world's tenth-largest employer, pumping out an estimated 40 percent of the world's consumer electronics devices—which operated behemoth factory complexes in China (Hon Hai was extending, however, both to Brazil and, through a purchase from Sony, to Mexico and Slovakia).[205] So as not to be whipsawed by Hon Hai, Apple directed a growing fraction of its manufacturing to a second Taiwanese company, Pegatron.[206] At the U.S. end of its operations, Apple directly employed around forty-three thousand people—a mere fraction of the estimated seven hundred thousand people who toiled for its overseas outsourcers.[207] These U.S. employees labored at software development and industrial design, product differentiating features on which Apple relied in order to charge what the market would bear.

Beginning around 2004, Apple had begun to use its stylish devices as a crowbar to pry open communications commodity chains. As it successively inserted its iPods, iPhones, and iPads, it also "tethered" them (Jonathan Zittrain's term[208]) to iTunes, its proprietary service for selling recorded music and, soon, other audiovisual commodities. This in turn compelled its competitors to mimic it, in attempts to establish digital territories for which they "set the rules and control or limit connections to other parts of the Internet."[209] Operating systems, media stores, and popular applications became key to this thrust-and-parry contest. Apple's leading rival—Google—which had contracted for its Nexus tablets and phones with Asus and LG, responded by purchasing its own device maker, Motorola Mobility.[210] Microsoft confirmed the trend when it acquired Nokia's languishing handset maker in 2013.[211] Competitive strength in the mobile market pivoted around a supplier's ability to embed software and services in physical devices; this ability was not only a function of vertical integration but also of a supplier's patent position. Motorola Mobility's allure for Google stemmed chiefly from its trove of seventeen thousand patents, and Google retained most of these patents when it sold Motorola to Lenovo just two years later.[212]

Patent power may be purchased from an external source, as in this case, or through in-house corporate research-and-development programs. Google spent nearly $5 billion on R&D during 2011 and perhaps $7.5 billion in 2013—although only a fraction of this on mobile technology.[213] Its competitor, Microsoft, possessing twenty-six thousand U.S. and international patents, with another thirty-six thousand pending, spent even more: $9 billion in 2011.[214] Samsung declared in 2011 that it would spend $9.3 billion on R&D during the coming year.[215] Apple reported a 2011 R&D outlay of $2.4 billion;[216] Amazon[217] and Facebook spent smaller sums. Depending on legal interpretations, wrote Google's chief legal officer David Drummond in 2011, a contemporary smartphone might be susceptible to 250,000 different patent claims.[218]

Patent warfare in the market for mobile devices was a predictable consequence, as suppliers tried to encircle or to defend against rivals.[219] Google not only bought Motorola Mobility but also purchased one thousand patents from IBM and came to the aid of HTC in a patent fight with Apple. Apple, for its part, cooperated with Microsoft in dismembering bankrupt Canadian telecom equipment maker Nortel through a $4.5 billion purchase of its patents; and Apple deployed its patents against other companies who might be both rivals and suppliers for its smartphones and tablets. As mobile platforms emerged as a market fulcrum, this patent "arms race"—Apple and Samsung alone were embroiled in more than fifty cases in ten countries—became a formative feature.[220] By the same token, Google and Samsung remained, at best, wary allies. Google sold off its manufacturing unit and reached a global patent-licensing agreement with the Korean company, whose Galaxy smartphones used a customized variant of Google's Android operating system;[221] however, seeking to reduce its dependence on Android, Samsung relied on its own operating system to launch a smart wristwatch in 2014.[222]

During the digital depression, the geographic contours of mobile connectivity and, with this, the prospective reach of the mobile platform, burst through prior limits. Stimulating this expansion were both manufacturers' lower-cost, unbranded models (also running mostly on Google's Android software), and the carriers' rollouts of prepaid service plans. Quarterly shipments of mobile phones dipped during 2009, but by mid-2010 they had recovered somewhat, as more than three hundred million units were shipped each quarter. Price pressure, however, threatened vendors' profit margins.[223] Unbranded handsets hit the combined market share of the five largest suppliers, which declined from 83 percent in 2009 to 67 percent in 2010;[224] and by 2013 four-fifths of handsets shipped ran on Android.[225] Caught within a polarizing dynamic were the two early market leaders. Nokia found itself hammered at the high end by Apple and Samsung and at the low end by suppliers of these unbranded models—to which, in 2012, it responded with a line of $45 devices.[226] (The next year, Nokia sold its mobile handset unit to Microsoft.) Likewise reeling from its competition against Apple and Samsung, as well as against lower-priced Android models, in 2013 Blackberry tried to salvage itself by announcing a billion-dollar loss and firing 40 percent of its staff (forty-five hundred employees).[227] Put differently, "Made in USA" smartphone operating systems (iOS, Android, and Windows Phone) rose from a 5 percent market share of the global total in 2005 to an 88 percent share in 2012. A *Financial Times* columnist headlined this sea change in geo-economic terms: "Europe holds a losing hand in the high-stakes mobile game."[228]

A saturated market also carried other consequences. Even successful smartphone vendors faced declining prices. While sales of high-end models by Apple and Samsung remained strong, notably in China[229]—now the world's largest market for them—additional growth would need to come increasingly "from attracting poorer customers anywhere from Detroit to Mumbai."[230] To reach these customers, manufacturers based in China began to offer—and, sometimes, to export—low-priced smartphones. Lenovo, Huawei, Yulong, and Xiaomi occupied significant shares of China's market, and some vendors, including Huawei, Lenovo, and smaller companies like Meizu, began to develop their own app stores.[231] In 2012, it was forecast, three hundred million low-end smartphones would be sold, and the fractional share of global production made up of smartphones priced at under $200 grew strongly in 2012 and 2013.[232] If, as forecast, smartphones experienced continued rapid market expansion, then this would come about largely through growth in poorer countries—one reason Apple's agreement to sell its iPhones to customers of China Mobile, by far the largest mobile carrier there or anywhere else, was strategically important.[233]

As wireless equipment became embedded in daily life—one in four American drivers reported using their phones to Web surf in 2013[234]—mobile devices became the pivot for a widening industrial transformation. Smartphones and tablets opened vistas onto market building across a potential customer base numbering in the billions. Disparate companies, rooted in everything from recorded music to finance, scrambled to reconfigure their commodity chains around the instruments and to extend beyond their existing niches. This certainly figured in

Amazon's decision to contract with the Taiwan-based HTC for a possible new line of smartphones, sales of which "could help Amazon foster greater consumer loyalty as people increasingly shop via phone and tablets."[235]

Mobile payments for hand-held shopping and the related field of location-based advertising totaled $86 billion in 2011 worldwide and were made by 140 million users;[236] linked to a mobile payments system of some kind, as Richard Waters observed, "a smartphone becomes the perfect tool for translating inchoate desire into instant gratification."[237] In the United States, operators, including Verizon and AT&T, pitted themselves against rivals based in what had been disparate industries. Again, by combining in alliances as volatile as they were opaque, Google, Apple, Facebook, bank groups, and credit card companies Visa and MasterCard, as well as eBay's PayPal, all attempted to establish mobile-payments platforms.[238] The competition was extraterritorial. From Japan to Nigeria and from Russia to Mexico, these and other units of capital vied for position.[239] Stealing a march on rivals, "Google Wallet" opened for business in the U.S.—though initially only for those who happened to possess a Samsung 4G phone (equipped with a near-field communications chip) running over Sprint's U.S. network, *and* a Citibank MasterCard or a prepaid card issued by Google itself.[240] It was a wedge: the U.S. market for anytime, anywhere shopping, while it continued to lag behind its counterparts in Europe and East Asia, was opening for business.[241] Apple was readying its own payments system early in 2014.

The question of which market actors would preempt the high-profit boxes in this commodity chain was not going to be answered merely by this already wide-ranging group.[242] To actualize point-and-purchase habits was also a job for retailers. Midway through 2010, many U.S. retailers had not yet optimized their sites to allow this; indeed, a mere 12 percent of the top five hundred U.S. online retailers had sites compatible with mobile browsers.[243] Location-based advertising known as "geofencing," based on satellite positioning technology, directed promotions at customers wandering toward chain outlets for Starbucks and Best Buy.[244] Two other aspirants—Google and Apple—were chagrined, following exposures of their respective covertly intrusive data-collection schemes.[245]

Apple's announcement, at its 2012 developer conference, that it would shed its dependence on Google's entrenched mapping application by trying to create its own, testified that mobile maps had become "simply too important to be left to a rival"[246] (though Apple's mapping application proved a gaffe). The heightening importance of location also underlay Google's acquisition of the mapping and navigation company Waze in 2013.[247] Online intermediaries were vying to insert digital mapping within mobile-centric commodity chains for no fewer than three sets of boxes: local commerce, location-based advertising, and mobile payments. Microsoft's Windows did so through a tie-up with Nokia, whose mobile handset subsidiary Microsoft purchased in 2013; Google, through its own Android and mapping units; and Apple, through its iOS and a contract with the Dutch digital mapping company TomTom.[248]

How societies would cope with the intrusion of mobile devices into settings little prepared to accept them—freeways and city streets, churches, hospitals, and classrooms—remained unsettled, sometimes dangerously so. Sales of a couple of billion mobile phones each year also inflicted punishing environmental damage, as Richard Maxwell and Toby Miller explain in revelatory research.[249] Not only did these products heighten pressure on straitened energy supplies, but they also resulted in torrents of e-waste, as throwaway units leached chemical contaminants into the earth as well as into the bodies of those who worked to dispose of them.

Far more important from the point of view of capital was who would profit from these recomposing communications commodity chains. Any answer would also have to encompass another set of boxes beyond those occupied by networks and devices: those housing the applications and content that relied on this infrastructure.

Software and Applications

The process of populating the Web with content and providing tools to create, explore, and share it, has been one of immense magnitude and social complexity. Motivations have been multifarious: individuals eager to advance their fortunes and to publish personal creations and collections; cultural heritage organizations initiating "mass digitization" projects of libraries, archives, museums, and governments; nonprofits and grassroots organizations circulating information and communications; and for-profit companies, old and new, advancing commodity exchange and adding digital market windows for their copyrighted content.[250] The ease with which one could post to the Web turned it into a vast mélange—by 2011, it encompassed 312 million websites and, by 2013, Google trawled more than thirty trillion web pages:[251] multiform, polyglot, protean. This was no one-dimensional shift, from "print" to "electronics," but a ragged reorganization of society's communicative forms and information resources. To claim a social identity, it seemed, now required a capacity for regular speech acts on the Web; established occupations and existing forms of labor altered, or were supplemented or supplanted, to enable speech with digital characteristics.

Organizing access to this territory emerged, during the 1990s, as a precondition for the Web's commercial exploitation. Attempts to establish stable points of access themselves became a primary axis of market development. Because the Web was built around malleably configured software, competitive advantage was often derived from being first to generate network effects: first to establish a platform that "everybody" wants to join, because it seems that "everybody" already has. Market success, however, rested not only on innovation but, as Matthew Crain shows, on access to investment capital and on sustained commercial promotion.[252]

A fundamental strength of the commodity chain construct is that it looks outward, in an attempt to track the relations and structural ties through which production occurs. Internet-reliant commodity chains encompassed several functional elements, including operating system software and browsers, search engines, social networks, and, beyond them, content and applications. Where might market advantage lodge? Suppliers not only vied within each of these niches but also tried to leverage their initial positions in order to project into other, potentially converging boxes and subchains. Upon building a large user base, providers next sought to diversify and enlarge their profit opportunities by using the versatility of software-defined services and applications to integrate additional functions. Preemptive occupation was the goal, and it exhibited both offensive and defensive aspects.

Robert McChesney has drawn our attention to the big companies that staked out primary roles in organizing Web experience: Google, Apple, Amazon, Microsoft, and Facebook.[253] These companies' market orientations were distinct, facing (respectively) toward navigation and content, hardware, electronic commerce, software, and social networking. But their profit strategies often converged, as mobile devices became a market pivot and media content a common necessity.

Apple set the pattern (though borrowing the idea from RIM's Blackberry) by tightly integrating hardware with its proprietary iOS software. This not only granted to Apple opportunities for its industrial design, but it also allowed the company "to attract huge numbers of software developers to the App store—an advantage in both smartphone and tablet PC markets."[254] As apps developers and content producers flocked to Apple's iOS mobile platform,[255] the company elbowed its way into the media industry. Initially with relief, but increasingly with anxiety, existing media companies passed on to Apple a 30 percent cut on content they sold through its seemingly secure distribution channel.[256] Reoriented commodity chains sent much of the overall profit to Apple and its apps developers—not to telecom carriers, not to Apple's own manufacturing contractors, and certainly not to their low-paid employees.

Microsoft adopted a different strategy, again reflecting its existing strength. Beginning during the 1980s, Microsoft had employed its desktop operating systems as a lever with which to dominate the personal computer industry; it went on during the later 1990s to tie Windows to its Internet Explorer browser and thereby clawed its way onto the Web. Until recently, its 80+ percent share of the market for PC operating systems generated predictable and enviable profits. Might Microsoft now find means of developing a comparable advantage with respect to smartphones and tablets? Several mobile operating systems were circulating. The leaders were Apple's iOS and Google's Android. Microsoft therefore found itself playing catch-up as it tried to negotiate the transition. Pressured by Apple's mobile devices and proprietary business model, it allied with (and then acquired) Nokia's phone unit;[257] it expanded the user base for its Windows Phone software; it stepped into the market for tablet computers and, finally, recognizing that the age of the PC was giving way, Microsoft began to produce its own line of tablets.[258] Microsoft's hold over the enterprise market gave it a base denied to its online rivals; however, despite its success with its Internet Explorer browser, its well-reputed search engine, Bing, and its Surface PC/tablet hybrid, Microsoft's huge expenditures had not yet enabled it to set the pace for recomposition around the mobile Web.

Google pursued yet another approach. Google drew throngs of users to its search engine and funneled them incessantly onward to the open Web; its baseline profit strategy relied on selling advertising to reach the Web traffic flowing to and from its site. Google used this to lever itself into a major role across the entire range of internet functionality, developing many well-regarded tools—notably, mobile operating systems. It also tried to outflank Apple by subsidizing the diffusion of its Android operating system, by extending its advertising network, and by purchasing or underwriting a wide range of applications and content. Google's own Web sites offered higher profits than those to which the search company sent users—a trend it thought would persist[259]—perhaps giving Google a motive for listing its own sites high up in its search rankings. Google unveiled Android in 2008—just as the mobile transition was moving into high gear—as a stealth response to the iPhone; and it licensed Android freely to mobile equipment makers such as HTC, Motorola, and Samsung. Caught out by Apple, these and other rivals were motivated to enter the smartphone market and could do so quickly and at reduced cost by adopting a Google-subsidized Android. As smartphones came into widespread use, generating one-fifth of global handset sales in 2010[260] and more than half by 2013, Google's strategy paid off. Taken together, manufacturers of smartphones built around Android captured the majority of the world market; by 2010, global sales of Android models totaled sixty-seven million and outpaced sales of iPhones.[261] With its Galaxy models, Samsung alone overtook Apple in global sales of smartphones during the third quarter of 2011, though its profit margin was only a bit more than half that of Apple's.[262]

And Google? Disingenuously, then-CEO Eric Schmidt had told Ken Auletta in 2008 that mobile devices would probably remain a secondary focus "because to get on those platforms Google would have to pay large fees and cede control to telephone companies."[263] Three years later, though, Google was activating 550,000 Android-equipped smartphones each day around the world.[264] And its Android app store, sporting half a million apps by 2012,[265] was enabling consumers to download apps in the billions. Late in 2013, Apple's iOS reached around 700 million devices, Google's Android around one billion devices;[266] nevertheless, Apple's precocious success in developing its App Store still translated into a commanding share of app-store spending compared to Google Play's—63 percent versus 37 percent in November 2013.[267]

Apple's success in building a proprietary ecosystem, as already mentioned, helped induce Google to purchase its own captive hardware unit by purchasing Motorola's smartphone subsidiary in 2012. Its principal intention was to lock up Motorola's patents and thereby grant itself a defensive hedge; by 2014 Google's stock of legally protected innovations had made it into one of the topmost corporate patent holders.[268] In meshing its software with products made by its own hardware subsidiary, however, Google also raised the prospect that it might build in advances that it withheld from outside manufacturers who used its Android operating system. On this point, an early reaction by the Republic of Korea offers instruction. Within days of Google's bid for Motorola Mobility, Korean government authorities called on Samsung and LG Electronics—the world's second- and third-largest manufacturers of mobile handsets—to join a consortium whose purpose was "to develop a home-grown mobile phone operating system" and thereby to migrate away from Google's Android.[269] Samsung went on to ally with chipmaker Intel, Vodafone, Orange, and NTT Docomo—all leading mobile phone companies—in a still-unproven bid to develop an insurance policy alternative to Android.[270] And when Google beat a retreat by selling its Motorola unit to Lenovo, one motive was to consolidate its relation to Android-reliant device makers—notably, Samsung, which accounted for about 40 percent of Android sales worldwide.[271]

Android circulated quickly beyond the smartphone. In Fall 2011, Amazon and Sony each announced tablets configured around Google's operating system software. Sony intended to optimize its tablet for its PlayStation games, recordings, and films, while affording wireless connections to its other electronic devices, including video players and televisions.[272] China's Lenovo—contending with Apple's popular iPads in its own domestic market—hedged its bets, launching a line of tablets enabled by either Android or Microsoft's Windows.[273]

Often interlocking with operating systems, browsers became yet another theater of competition. On the desktop, Microsoft's browser, Internet Explorer, remained dominant, while Mozilla's open-source Firefox browser was significant and Google's Chrome browser less so. As mobile devices began to outrun PCs, Apple's Safari browser claimed an early lead, with a three-fifths share in 2011,[274] but Google's Android software displaced it very quickly, as it resided on 80 percent of handsets sold just two years later.[275]

In the "cloud," yet another development impinged on the mobile market.[276] The big internet intermediaries each moved to recentralize operations around gigantic "server farms" built to store and distribute content and applications to users.[277] Intel calculated that one additional server was required for every six hundred smartphones and for every 122 tablet computers; H-P and Dell, which supplied many of these servers, were beneficiaries.[278]

Huge data centers became hubs for the more widely recomposing infrastructure. Customers might worry that storing sensitive data and software with an outside vendor was insecure, and waves of hacker attacks and service outages did little to assuage them. However, on cost and operational grounds, cloud services expanded. As we already saw, cloud services were generating a large and growing share of overall internet traffic. Tipping the balance was the rapid buildup of sensor arrays, and of mobile devices whose relative lack of memory and processing power combined with users' growing need to synch up multiple devices and with the internet intermediaries' quest for greater control, to give a prod to centralized provision.

Big U.S. providers of data-center services included the leader, Amazon, and Microsoft, Google, IBM, Verizon, Rackspace, and AT&T.[279] To supplement an existing facility in Newark, New Jersey, Apple planned to erect a billion-dollar, half-million-square-foot data center in North Carolina.[280] Facebook's data center in central Oregon covered the space of five football fields and was to be enlarged; the company also built a comparable facility in North Carolina.[281] Locations—such as Oregon and Washington—favored with cheap and available land and abundant hydro- and wind-powered energy, were prime real estate: Amazon, Google, and Microsoft each also operated data centers in these Northwest states.[282] Data centers were unevenly distributed, both nationally and internationally. The United States possessed far and away the largest number of any single country; wealthy countries overall boasted a disproportionate share of the total. However, IBM's plan to spread forty data centers across thirteen countries and five continents by the end of 2014 spelled out the pattern of proliferation.[283] In part III of this book we will see how the movement to cloud computing impinged on U.S. international internet policy; for now, I will underline that cloud computing was deeply enmeshed with the profit strategies of internet intermediaries.

This transition moved away from the autonomously configured personal computer as the hub of network connectivity and toward data centers to support mobile devices. A billion PCs were in use worldwide by 2008, and, as we have seen, they continued to sell a few hundred million units each year. However, cloud services made it feasible to consider the PC, as Intel's former chief technology officer put it, as just "one more display device."[284] As they moved through each day, consumers also now often migrated from one device to another; means of ensuring the continuity of their experience became a matter of competitive necessity, as Google related in 2013, "with the transition to a dynamic multi-screen environment."[285]

Internet intermediaries again exhibited different strengths and pursued distinct strategies for cloud services, but Apple's iCloud was symptomatic.[286] Apple possessed two formidable assets, in addition to unequaled cash reserves and its storied brand name: an installed base of hundreds of millions of devices running its iOS software, and a nearly equal number of active credit cards on file from around the world.[287] On these foundations, iCloud—which 300 million people used every day by April 2013[288]—became a key part of Apple's aggressive moves into the distribution of media content of all kinds. Already the world's largest film retailer, with over half of all global online movie transactions, Apple sought to press ahead with its rental model.[289]

Apple's maneuvering contributed to a wider flux, as rival internet intermediaries sought to match it in parlaying content and applications to consumers. The resulting recomposition engulfed a third set of actors—the giant multimedia conglomerates that had dominated the political economy of communications and that now continued to help structure its capital logic.

CHAPTER 7

Services and Applications

By the time of the Time-Warner–AOL merger debacle that rang out the old millennium, the likelihood had evaporated that the existing multimedia companies might simply take over the new digital systems and services. Instead, to their surprise, these conglomerates found themselves on the defensive. Muscling in on their turf were not just broadband and mobile internet operators, such as AT&T, Verizon, and Comcast but—less predictably—well-financed outsiders and upstarts: from Netscape and Yahoo! to Google, Apple, Amazon, Microsoft, Facebook, and Netflix.[1]

It was not only media moguls who were caught out. That the entrenched conglomerates might be in jeopardy was incongruent with the thinking of many critical analysts; beginning in 1983 and continuing through six editions (the last published in 2000), Ben Bagdikian had influentially depicted "The Media Monopoly"[2] as a continually consolidating power node. By conventional measures of revenue and profit, however, and more broadly considered in terms of strategic leverage as well, during the first two decades of the twenty-first century, News Corporation, Disney, Viacom, Comcast, and Time-Warner were equaled or surpassed by giant internet intermediaries, led by Google, Amazon, Apple, and Microsoft. However, far from heralding a rollback of the profit mechanism, the process that was underway denoted a massive extension of the commodification of information and communications. Destabilizing the existing terms of trade was the price paid in attempts to realize this outcome.

Google used its navigational services as a lever. It generated torrents of Web traffic and profited from it both as a gatekeeper and, increasingly, as a topical destination through varied content services. Google's YouTube subsidiary accounted for a major share of Web video traffic, possessing a billion active users by 2013.[3] The company also operated Google Places, Google News, Google Finance, and Google Books, while its vertical search services granted it access to specialized markets in travel, shopping, and local commerce (Maps, Product Search, Flight Search).[4] The scale and scope of the resulting rivalries were noteworthy. In just one of the boxes Google had targeted, travel information, a rival—TripAdvisor—operated thirty Web sites in twenty-one languages by 2013.[5]

Apple and Facebook likewise depended on drawing users to their Web sites and, unlike Google, their profit strategies hinged mostly on what users did there. Facebook built in or purchased numerous functions (think Instagram) and content as it also contracted with outside companies, from Zynga to Spotify, to induce users to linger on its site while it sent them advertising. Apple sold users music, films, books, and games via its App Store and let them access it through iCloud. It also introduced an internet radio service for music streaming. Neither company wished to forward traffic to unaffiliated Web sites, and both found it essential to provide media content.

In 2008, the iPhone freshly launched, users downloaded one hundred thousand apps from Apple's App Store; by the end of 2011, iPhone and iPad users were downloading a billion applications each month, and from 2008 to the end of 2013, Apple's App Store had passed on to developers more than $15 billion from its total revenue of $21.4 billion.[6] Early in 2013, Apple was drawing quarterly revenue of $2.4 billion from music, movies, and apps.[7] Apple's online operation had become entrenched over the course of a mere five years. Apple's App Store led the pack, with 650,000 apps,[8] though it faced stiffening competition from Google and from other app stores in China and elsewhere. Major types of applications, the U.S. FCC reported, included not only navigation and social network services, but news and information, games, location-based services, photo sharing, music and video streaming, and voice calling (VoIP). "In addition," the FCC recounted, "thousands of niche applications have been designed for specific uses, hobbies, interests, and industries by various third-party application developers."[9] By the end of 2013, all told, 2.7 billion internet users worldwide had downloaded more than seventy-five billion applications.[10]

Beyond financing by venture capital and the sale of stock, there are three basic sources of support for communications and media of every description: direct payments—either in the form of fees, subscriptions, site licenses, or rental charges; advertising, in its endlessly updated forms; and noncommercial support, either through governmental or philanthropic finance or voluntary donations. Combining these three basic alternatives, in innumerable variations, communications systems are built and rebuilt. At each juncture in the commodity chains that converged on the internet, companies reset strategy and reorganized operations in light of these three possible forms of revenue generation. Linkages between "old" and "new" media, along with the prospects of specific internet services and applications, were closely related to the concurrent evolution of these varied business models.

Negotiated Transition

The media conglomerates had been neither neutralized nor superannuated by "the internet": underway was not a one-off process of replacement but a complex, negotiated transition. As they continued to wield power over the commodities people read, listened to, watched, and played, conglomerates interacted strategically with their new competitors—the big internet intermediaries. Rivalry was considerable, and the internet companies generally held the better hand, but cooperation was growing. The different groups of companies sought to rearrange commodity chains for communications and information and, if needed, to alter the terms of trade, out of conviction that the profitmaking realm might be enlarged or, at least, rebalanced.

At the end of 2011, just one of the top-ten most-visited U.S. internet properties—Wikimedia—was free of dependence on either advertising or direct consumer charges.[11] The internet services needed access to the conglomerates' copyrighted content and brands, while the conglomerates needed to position themselves more profitably than they had within a digital environment.[12] As one analyst noted, "Music, film and television are to Internet players what the piano stool is to the piano: inseparable."[13]

Battles for position continued to flare. Notably, in 2012–13 the big internet companies and their mobilized nonprofit allies amassed political clout that proved sufficient to halt legislation seeking to impose stringent online copyright policing—legislation that was being shrilly advanced by the multimedia conglomerates.[14] Yet an assimilationist trend was also unmistakable[15] as the newcomers struck agreements with existing communications companies.

Media conglomerates had built diverse revenue sources for their different media products via numerous market windows; the internet intermediaries had not. Apple, Google, and Microsoft were sensationally profitable: their operating margins were each in the vicinity of 40 percent in 2012.[16] Though profitable, neither media companies nor network operators approached this level of performance. But the internet companies' profits were tied heavily to circumscribed market segments. Microsoft generated $40 billion each year from PC software sales; Apple derived most of its revenue from devices; Amazon relied principally on e-commerce. Facebook revealed in its prospectus that 85 percent of its revenues came from advertising;[17] Google, 95 percent of whose revenues were generated by advertising, was also dependent on a single form of patronage.[18] If the media conglomerates needed to integrate forward into digital services, then the big internet intermediaries needed to diversify their revenue streams.[19] Industry-specific evaluations allow us to clarify some of the resultant trends.

Five transnational conglomerates had swallowed dozens of U.S. book publishing labels throughout the second half of the twentieth century (and Gargantua continued to grow, as a result of approvals by state authorities for Random House [Bertelsmann] to merge with Penguin [Pearson], creating the world's largest trade-book publisher.)[20] The subsidiaries of these conglomerates dominated U.S. and European trade publishing via sales of hardcover and paperback books generated by a small cohort of reliable, bestselling writers. The book publishers nevertheless had long since begun to lose their footing, when big-box chains acquired a commanding retailing role, not only Barnes & Noble and Borders, but also Wal-Mart. The publishers then faced entry by Amazon.com beginning in 1995. The internet retailer's killingly low prices (it took losses quarter after quarter to build market share) and its tax-free sales advantage pushed already hard-pressed independent bookstores to the wall; Amazon's tactics also hit the chain stores and the conglomerate publishers. Amazon successfully rerouted the commodity chain for books around its innovative electronic retail channel; it remained a hybrid in that arena until it introduced its e-book reader in 2007, however, because it relied on physically transporting printed copies (and CDs) to consumers. Amazon vice president Paul Misener told a congressional panel in 2010 that Amazon spent a billion dollars a year on outbound shipments, at a rate of two million shipments each week: "The USPS," he added "is an integral part of the service we provide our customers. . . . Online shopping actually *increases* the need for physical shipments" routed via the U.S. Postal Service.[21]

The other shoe dropped when e-books finally gained traction. Paced by the phenomenal success of the Stieg Larsson trilogy, Amazon's e-book sales out-distanced its sales of hardcover books in the three months to July 2010.[22] During that year, e-book sales rose to $878 million, accounting for 6.4 percent of the trade-book market.[23] This change was not foreordained, as e-books had already undergone three decades' worth of experiments and false starts. One precipitant was the publishers' prior take-up of digital technologies for producing books; by the early years of the century, commercially published books were already (mostly) digital files.[24] A second trigger came with Google's plunder of millions of volumes tended on behalf of the public by academic libraries and librarians,[25] which accelerated the mass digitization of cultural property. The rejection by a U.S. federal judge of the terms of Google's deal with publishers and authors only arrested the company's digital book-scanning project—15 million had been scanned—but did not curtail it.[26] In 2013, after Google had settled with the publishers, it won a resounding court victory against authors, reopening the way for its encompassing cultural commodification program.[27]

The rise in popularity of cheap, high-quality e-book readers became a third factor. Amazon's successful Kindle was the final link in establishing a proprietary electronic distribution channel to contend with Apple's. Amazon's pricing of commercially popular e-books, which undercut publishers' list prices by more than half, was the final accelerant. This "first-mover" tactic built market share for Amazon, laying waste to the economics of publishing.[28] By 2013 Amazon was selling around one out every four printed books, creating "a level of market domination with little precedent in the book trade."[29]

The terms of trade swung strongly against existing booksellers and publishers. As the e-book format took hold, one of two big U.S. chain bookstores— Borders—found itself entreating publishers to accept IOUs;[30] when publishers refused, Borders went bankrupt and closed hundreds of stores.[31] Barnes & Noble scrambled to reinvent itself "as a seller of book downloads, reading devices, and apps"[32] and partnered with Microsoft to provide its own Nook e-reader. Nevertheless, while independent bookstores had faced twenty years of carnage,[33] now even the largest traditional U.S. bookseller was in retreat, faced with mounting losses in 2013.[34]

Existing publishers looked frantically for an escape route away from the lower-pricing model instituted by Amazon for e-books. As they watched, a long-entrenched format, the mass-market paperback, faded;[35] Amazon, meanwhile, established its own book-publishing unit and by mid-2011 boasted six separate imprints.[36] Self-publishing boomed, as writers in different genres found means of reaching audiences that bypassed the existing publishers. Conglomerate publishers closed warehouses, sought to lease out office space, decreased the size of print runs, and looked to cut back on author advances. Simon & Schuster, Penguin Group USA, and Hachette Book Group created Bookish.com in an attempt to cut free of Amazon in publicizing and selling their books.[37] They also experimented with raising prices for e-books, especially bestsellers by writers such as Stephen King or Michael Connelly.[38] Apple's intended entry into the market for e-books, built around its iPad, recognized publishers' desperation to find some way of returning retail prices to a level above Amazon's standard $9.99. However, in Europe and, separately, in the United States, authorities charged that this Apple-centric coterie had conspired to limit price competition in the market for e-books.[39] The Justice Department sued, charging that Apple and five big publishers had colluded in restraint of trade "to raise the prices of e-books as a defense against Amazon"—and the publishers all settled, though Apple continued to protest its innocence even after a judge found the company guilty in July 2013.[40] Ironically, this left Amazon in possession of the field. Perhaps more important, no basis for restabilizing book publishing had materialized, and price deflation, as Thompson underlines,[41] continued to pummel the industry.

What about the music industry? A handful of transnational conglomerates had purchased the leading record labels during the 1980s and 1990s, so that four companies came to channel three-quarters of global music sales (EMI, Warner Music, Universal, Sony). EMI was then decapitated, its two major parts shared between Universal and Sony, to leave just three global majors. As in book publishing and film, an industry cartel had held pricing power sufficient to build and rebuild the music business around vinyl, then CD albums, each of which contained a dozen or so recordings. Industry strategy had revolved around star artists and blockbuster hit songs; in 1999 a mere eighty-eight recordings out of nearly three thousand releases garnered a quarter of all record sales.[42] But the music industry, with its intimate connection to the subjectivities of youth the world over, became the classic case of a seemingly durable oligopoly being upended by the arrival of online channels over which recordings circulated as digital files.

Unlike books, considered luxuries and purchased by a small fraction of the population, recorded music sold widely. In an online environment this became, ironically, a vulnerability, for the music industry faced a succession of ingeniously engineered services, through which avid listeners could download or stream unlicensed music for free. The industry turned to lawsuits and technology-based countermeasures in attempts to retain control of copyrighted music and, thereby, of its business model.[43] These tactics did not succeed. Sales of record albums commenced upon a long-term decline beginning in 1999.[44] When Steve Jobs launched Apple's iTunes site and linked it to a succession of smashingly successful mobile devices and, eventually, to iCloud, the music majors breathed a collective sigh of relief as digital revenues again began—finally—to grow. When streaming music services caught on and began to pay royalties for the rights to specific recordings, they relaxed further. However, the music majors also had to content themselves with reduced revenues and an altered industry structure.

Apple possessed credit-card data for a few hundred million clients of its iTunes store, and it funneled to these users a large and growing range of proprietary content.[45] And, as mentioned, Apple demanded a 30 percent cut on content sold through its iPhones and iPads[46] (though—under antitrust pressure—Apple relented somewhat, to give magazine, newspaper, music, and video publishers greater freedom also to sell their content directly without iTunes).[47] Apple, however, had forged a new subchain for the sale of music online. In 2011, global digital music revenues approximated $5.2 billion, and iTunes captured nearly 70 percent of this total.[48] The record companies acquiesced, grudgingly, to the formation of what was, for them, a less-profitable capital logic built around online sales of individual songs rather than entire albums.

Their business conditions eased further as the record companies began to harvest substantial royalties from new market entrants. They arranged payments for licensed use of music directly with streaming music services like Spotify and Deezer, and indirectly (via rights organizations like SoundExchange) with internet radio services such as Sirius XM and Pandora, as well as Apple's own internet radio service. [49] Some of these streaming services, however, faced an uncertain financial future because although they had millions of listeners, only a small fraction were paying subscribers—and advertising revenues were not yet making up for the shortfall in their operating costs.[50] Recording companies also greeted hopefully Amazon's release in Fall 2011 of its low-priced multimedia "Kindle Fire" tablet, anticipating that Amazon's attempt to establish itself as a competitor with Apple's iPad would grant them added leverage. Facebook explored a complementary alternative, by instituting features alerting members to the music their friends were listening to and offering them means by which to access it via streaming services from interlocked suppliers like Spotify and MOG.[51] Google Music, rolled out late in 2011, combined its own download store and its social network site, Google+, to allow customers to share the thirteen million songs it had licensed by offering friends free access—once—to any purchased track.[52] Still, unlicensed file sharing persisted as a widespread norm; in one estimate, it amounted to one-fourth of all internet traffic in 2012.[53] The big record companies continued to pressure Google to cease linking to pirate sites for its search listings even after Google volunteered that it would alter its search algorithm so as to reduce the prominence of sites for which it received takedown requests from copyright owners.[54]

By acquiring the major U.S. film studios throughout the 1980s and 1990s, half a dozen transnational conglomerates had taken control of global movie distribution.[55] The Hollywood majors, built around star actors and directors and blockbuster films, not only remained the hub of a large and lucrative global industry but also united with big music, publishing, and game companies. After U.S. authorities obligingly withdrew existing bans on cross-ownership, the film companies likewise quickly integrated with the U.S. television industry.[56] Build-outs of satellite and cable TV distribution services established important new "windows"—aftermarkets—for theatrical films. An even greater stimulus arrived in the shape of the digital video disk (DVD), which, far from constituting a competitive threat, rapidly became the industry's single most important source of revenue. Could internet-based film and video create new market windows?

The Hollywood majors staved off online competition more effectively than their often-affiliated partners in the recording industry: films took much longer than music files to download. But unlicensed file sharing made inroads as broadband access spread. When the digital depression struck, big film companies were contending not only with dwindling DVD sales, nor only with unlicensed file sharing, but also with the outsized success of Netflix. Netflix had built a very popular online distribution channel from what had begun as a hybrid system, comparable to Amazon's, combining online ordering and postal delivery of DVDs. During the digital depression, however, Netflix rolled out an online service to send film and video product to subscribers, and by autumn 2013 it boasted thirty-one million streaming subscribers in the United States and four million more internationally.[57] Other interlopers, including the big internet intermediaries, swung momentum further toward commercial internet distribution. Hollywood—which had long been accustomed to negotiating with theater chains—after the retail function of exhibition was broken off from production and distribution through a 1948 antitrust action—thus might continue to look forward to growth. A trio of major Hollywood conglomerates even established their own successful online service, Hulu (though profitable, Hulu posed strategic difficulties for its owners).[58]

Fee-based media commodities—books, recordings, films—were experiencing price deflation as they moved online. This devaluation, forecast PwC in 2012, would constitute a "drag" on global media revenue growth going forward.[59] As Hollywood studios shrank, their profit margins "ranged from razor thin to nonexistent."[60] Web-based recomposition, however, was unfolding even beyond these fee-based media boxes. Advertising-dependent media were also encompassed and, here, television was the grand prize.[61]

Many converging initiatives overtook television subchains. "Over the top" (OTT) services again emerged as a disruptive force. Market leaders closely resembled those in the film segment. Netflix became a transnational purveyor of television to subscribers; it then began to pay for original content and, following Amazon's practice, to implement an effective system of commercial suggestions ("if you liked X, then maybe you'd like to try Y"). Hulu proved adept at making a profitable online TV business, which owed in part to the exclusive rights it enjoyed to programs supplied to it by its owners: News Corp., Disney, and Comcast; and Hulu also started producing exclusive original content.[62] Google's YouTube also looked to become a power if Google could secure advertising through a revamp of its video service, partnering with media companies and developing original content for themed channels.[63] Vimeo and other providers were also growing.

Though television's share of global advertising expenditures was forecast to peak in 2013, after three decades of growth,[64] its preeminence could not be doubted:[65] more people watched more television, more of the time, and in more ways. Seven media conglomerates continued to control an estimated 95 percent of U.S. television viewing hours, in keeping with their unmatched expenditures for content (in 2012, Time Warner spent $4.6 billion to acquire video programming).[66] As Google and Apple pondered how to invade television markets,[67] Viacom announced a wide-ranging, multiyear deal for Amazon to acquire exclusive rights to stream thousands of hours of well-proven Nickelodeon programming through its Prime service.[68] Comcast announced that it would promote shows on Twitter.[69] Broadcasters and cable networks defended their business interests, but increasingly they also worked with internet intermediaries to transmit their program feeds online, to desktops, smart TVs, notebooks, tablets, and smartphones. Television companies and internet companies increasingly made common cause. It was symptomatic that the speaker who was asked to address Britain's most prestigious TV industry conference in 2011 was Eric Schmidt of Google.

There were still other uncertainties. Would network operators succeed in capturing chunks of the television market by implementing internet protocol TV (IPTV) services? Which aggregators of programming would succeed at over-the-top television services? How would programming shift, generically and as a commodity trafficked in a global market? Would professionally produced television programs continue to coexist with enormous quantities of user-created video, or would the mix change? Who would control the market data that was generated by and about viewers, as these data streamed back through DVRs, tablets, and online services? (By 2008, DVRs had been placed in around fifty million households, four-fifths of them in North America, though the onset of the depression thereafter slowed their adoption.[70])

Perhaps most important was that the chief mode of TV finance also stood to be reconstituted.[71] For decades, commercial TV had been built around providing stable access to audiences, around scheduled programming, for big advertisers. This commodity subchain, however, now faced multiple fractures. Not only were there an abundance of disaggregated, anytime-everywhere online offerings, but a disparate model for selling advertising was also being constructed online. Might internet companies, ad agencies, and advertisers supplant the existing system of "upfront" TV advertising sales with automated ad-buying exchanges, or "programmatic buying"?[72] How would television advertising be restructured, and which companies would claim the lion's share of it?[73]

And so, having glimpsed changes gripping specific media industries, I turn to examine advertising directly. Threading through Web communications was a legion of initiatives on behalf of advertisers; these demonstrate, better than anything else, how the for-profit communications system was pushed and pulled to incarnate more fully than before the principles on which it had long been based. The sponsor system was undergoing an overhaul—its most thoroughgoing modernization, perhaps, since it was instituted more than a century earlier.

CHAPTER 8

The Sponsor System Resurgent

Advertisers abhor a vacuum. Realms of practice from which they are excluded comprise, for consumer products manufacturers and their affiliates in the specialized industries of marketing and advertising, an onerous cultural white space—because such zones obstruct or resist or are merely indifferent to their selling efforts. If such an area of cultural practice becomes popular, drawing large groups coveted by marketers and giving them reason to occupy themselves for extensive periods, then these limits become positively menacing. Advertisers aim, in principle, to reach most-needed audiences, anytime and everywhere; this translates into a demand to turn cultural white space into signage. This tendency owes less to any transcendent will-to-power and more to a need to keep capital circulating; that is, it is grounded in capital's need to realize the sale of commodities already produced in order to resume the cycle by producing and selling once again. A break in this process of commodity circulation—whether local to a specific company or industry, or sweepingly widespread—is a desideratum of crisis.

Advertisers—makers of consumer commodities of every kind, both goods and services—require routine, extensive access to buyers. The digital depression intensified their need by jeopardizing capital's ability to dispose profitably of mountains of accumulating merchandise. Even as the slump instilled in consumer product companies a more acute need to sell, emerging internet services disrupted advertising and selling as they had previously existed and concomitantly heralded the establishment of more effective means with which to reach buyers. Advertising therefore not only sustained but also deepened its role as a primary source of finance for digital services.

Indeed, the claims on human self-activity now heralded by advertising and marketing were almost unimaginable by the standards of just twenty years earlier. Recognizing that, as one veteran analyst put it, "the impulse to buy can start anywhere" and that rapidly changing habits were drawing billions of people online, marketers of course migrated online.[1] How did they transform this almost unbounded expanse of open terrain into signage and channels for e-commerce?

Simply put, they did so by redesigning advertising and selling so as to give these functions a commanding role in the wider recomposition of communications. This makeover was a complex, dynamic, and unfinished process.

To begin with, even apart from the Web, advertising continued its voracious and uneven globalization. The top one hundred global advertisers spent more than three-fifths of their measured-media budgets outside the United States as the digital depression took hold in 2008. Eleven of the forty-four U.S. companies in the Global 100 sent more than half of their ad spending abroad—including Proctor & Gamble, the world's largest advertiser, with just under $10 billion in measured media spending that year.[2] Under the auspices of a small handful of advertising supergroups—which were frenetically purchasing local affiliates in selected poor-world countries[3]—consumer products manufacturers and retailers moved beyond the long-favored wealthy zones of North America, Western Europe, and Japan. China was the preeminent destination for this renewal of the sales effort. The lure was enlarged discretionary spending on the part of both favored social strata and a huge class of dispossessed peasant-workers for commodities produced by foreign TNCs[4] as well as Chinese companies, at least some of which attained "big-brand" recognition.[5] Advertising thus did not grow merely as an external imposition. Extending to China a practice pioneered in Hollywood, "Transformers 3: Dark of the Moon" implemented product placements for four of China's leading national brands: Meters/bonwe (T-shirts), Lenovo (PCs), TCL (flatscreen TVs), and Yili (milk). The strategy looked to build international brand recognition for these Chinese companies while reciprocally raising their domestic profile via association with Hollywood product.[6] Here advertising bridged between domestic and transnational capital. Proctor & Gamble accounted for 27 percent of the Global 100's China measured-media spending; but there was ample room for growth: China harvested just 3.4 percent of total ad spending by the Global 100.[7] Forecasts also suggested continued rapid growth of e-commerce sales in China which, at $193 billion in 2013, were already half the U.S. total in 2013 and likely to surpass U.S. online sales within just three or four years.[8] Russia and India were likewise flagged as zones for advertising increases, while Brazil, it was forecast, might soon surpass the United Kingdom as the world's fifth-largest advertising market.[9] Advertising's internationalization overspilled the BRICs. In Nigeria, for instance, advertising spending quintupled between 2001 and 2010.[10]

This buildout was selective and therefore far from universal. The depression impelled advertisers to target more assiduously. Beyond their most-needed audiences and growth regions, cutbacks could be savage. Ad spending in Spain contracted by more than one-third between 2007 and 2012; in Greece it more than halved.[11] (This was sometimes called "a flight to safety."[12]) Thus, just as it flooded into higher growth regions and media, so did advertising also flee zones of cultural practice that became unprofitable or that advertisers believed had become superannuated.

This had little to do with popularity: as Raymond Williams noted decades ago, the demonstrated existence of large audiences for a particular program or genre or medium was not of itself sufficient to warrant continued financing. Abandonments occurred, either because audiences declined in value to marketers or because their members now could be reached more effectively or cheaply through other means. Even the most sensationally extended cultural service in history—Facebook, with more than one billion users and annual revenues exceeding $6 billion—faced an uncertain future until 2013, because it had not definitively established a stable platform for advertisers.[13] How much advertising could a social network carry before it alienated its users? Was it more effective for advertisers to buy ads from social networks or simply to build out their own sites and to offer users "branded content" of their own? To wit: Coca-Cola had two million followers on Twitter at the end of 2013. "Advertisers," wrote a journalist, "are, essentially, in the midst of an experiment that has been running for only a year or two." Eventually, they will "pause to assess whether it is working."[14] (By 2014, as it celebrated its tenth birthday, Facebook was making strenuous efforts to refocus on mobile advertising and the social network was said to be "taking money from advertisers like sweets from babies."[15])

The turbulence that ensued could be dizzying. On one side, television soap operas and newspapers and magazines in the United States suffered precipitous declines in advertising revenue[16]—as did television broadcasters in austerity-ravaged Europe.[17] Overall, TV's unmatched share of global ad spending was forecast to decrease slightly for the first time in three decades.[18] By the same token, marketers lavished attention on reliable and burgeoning hotspots. Commercial satellite TV services continued their ascent in China and in the Arab

Middle East.[19] The cost of a thirty-second commercial during the NFL Super Bowl in the United States, one of the world's most watched TV events, reached an all-time high of $4 million in 2014.[20] The number of print newspapers published in India increased by 6 percent during the crisis year of 2008–09, and advertising sales grew by 13 percent—though by 2012, things looked less rosy.[21] Back in the United States, pitches to the burgeoning "Hispanic" market lifted the fortunes of Spanish-language television.[22] And, as relatively well-off baby-boomers drifted into retirement, advertisers and marketers who for decades had disdained the elderly now found them a tempting target.[23]

Ad spending overall declined during late 2008 and 2009 before rebounding somewhat during the following years.[24] In 2012, ad agencies forecast a lift,[25] owing to the combined effects of spending for the London summer Olympics, the European football championships, and the U.S. presidential election.[26] In 2013, in aggregate, the business of global advertising generated an expenditure of half a trillion dollars.[27]

It was in light of this uneven and fraught evolution that advertisers accelerated their drive to revamp communications commodity chains. For them, the technological revolution engendered some positively mouth-watering options. The Web—especially the mobile Web—offered a nearly bottomless well of opportunities to advertise and market to consumers and thus it also swung the terms of trade in favor of big advertisers. As well, because the Web had been constructed around advertisers' demands for user data, it both widened and intensified the sales effort. Both of these trends carried far-reaching ramifications for the wider communications system.

Well before the World Wide Web was popularized, advertisers and markets already anticipated that a bright future might unfold around new interactive media.[28] By the time the digital depression struck, moreover, advertisers had already gained nearly fifteen years of experience with internet channels. To be sure, uncertainties remained, and obstacles continued to arise: for example, a 2013 finding revealed that more than half of online display ads across thousands of campaigns weren't seen by anyone as a result of technical problems, user resistance, and fraud.[29] However, billions of dollars were funneling into internet advertising; the internet was by 2010 becoming the second largest advertising medium after television. It did not require rocket science to divine that an "ad-based business model and marketing-driven culture . . . now permeates tech."[30] Facebook spoke to the unfinished nature of this convergence in its 2012 prospectus, explaining, "Advertising on the social web is a significant market opportunity that is still emerging and evolving."[31] In fact, advertising was undergoing a breathtaking revamp around Web connectivity, especially as it extended from the desktop to mobile devices.[32]

Advertisers' programs for rebooting their interactions to generate and capture identifiable information about individuals possess a long pedigree. Direct mail, nine-digit zip codes, audience demographic segmentation, and bar codes were all robustly expanding lines of advertiser practice before the Web's emergence.[33] Programs for linking such data with other data about specifiable individuals also began to acquire more comprehensive institutional foundations around the time of the Netscape IPO in the mid-1990s.[34] Matthew Crain's study of how the sales effort was reconfigured around the Web during the formative years of the 1990s sheds light on this process.[35] New techniques, new online intermediaries, and, perhaps above all, a supportive federal government boosted commercialized surveillance of individuals. Probability sampling of Nielsen families to chart dynamic connections between viewers and program content thus began to give way to a new-model audience commodity: user tracking data, not only for Web services led by Google and Facebook but also for DVRs and cable television system operators, and not only for television but for services accessed via other devices.[36] Federal authorities permitted the Web to be reconfigured around cookies and clicks and the user data that streamed back to digital services and advertisers. Technologies and practices of data generation and data capture kept pace with, and kept track of, users as they moved through a quotidian that, itself, was increasingly hooked to network infrastructures. Continual efforts were made to extend tracking technologies across each and every frontier. The shift to user tracking was connected to advertisers' growing ability to match it against disparate collections of sales, financial, locational, and demographic data. Unique computer signatures ("fingerprinting"), search histories, and location data allowed internet services and advertisers to track individuals as they shifted from screen to screen throughout their day, complementing the data that they gained by placing cookies on PC browsers.[37]

The average visit to a Web page triggered fifty-six instances of data collection by 2012, up sharply over just eighteen months; and these data were fed into computerized auctions known as "real-time bidding exchanges," in which "as soon as a user visits a Web page, the visit is auctioned to the highest bidder."[38] Search ads and display ads were the most rapidly growing categories and, even throughout the digital depression, they exhibited double-digit growth.[39] A breakthrough was made when it became possible for sellers to target ads to specific Web surfers persistently as they moved from site to site—a practice known as retargeting.[40] Advertisers clamored to take up this option. They also insisted that traditional media, which typically did not generate this kind of user data, needed to find means of doing so—needed to become "accountable" to advertisers' just-emerged online norm.

The transition to user data cut against the grain of the system of media finance, where content was paid for (typically indirectly) out of advertising revenue.[41] Why should advertisers underwrite expensive programming when, on the Web, users tended not to aggregate predictably at a known destination, even for an hour—let alone for an evening—as they surfed from site to site? Advertisers preferred to insert commercial messages into individuals' Web travel so that they would reach members of their most-needed audience wherever their itineraries might lead. The ramifications of this shift to user data remained murky; however, they undoubtedly would carry beyond advertising itself.

Google's roaring success as it explored this option generated a cascade of indicators.[42] To find a Web site, some sort of formalized search function is necessary; and even well-established sites depend on search engines to funnel to them a large share of their traffic. Search, in turn, constitutes a gateway—often, *the* gateway—through which advertisers are connected to users: a 2009 study concluded that an estimated 88 percent of users' clicks were on the links that appeared in the top three search results.[43] The bottleneck character of search made it a hotly contested box in Web communications. In the United States, Microsoft's Bing became the exclusive search provider for both Yahoo! and Facebook, but though it came preinstalled on 70+ percent of new computers sold, it remained in Google's shadow. Worldwide, Google again played the lead role in organizing the experience of the Web outside of China, South Korea, Russia, and Japan, where rivals prevailed.

It is true that search processes are increasingly ubiquitous online. Often, search is embedded unobtrusively within other Web services. Apple's mobile search function is not called "search," but "Siri"—its voice-activated virtual "assistant." [44] Facebook Questions, Google's executive chairman related in 2011, showcased "extensive search and information functions"; shopping sites like Amazon, Wal-Mart, and eBay were likewise "essentially search engines that focus on product search and provide customers with an opportunity to buy at the end of their search."[45] Eric Schmidt might also have mentioned image-based search: eBay permitted users to photograph a car and input it to search eBay's inventory of images of cars for sale.[46] All true; and yet Schmidt was also calculatingly portraying Google as a lesser force than it was.

In August 2011, Google handled 79 percent of Web searches in the United States, and 94 percent in Europe; it garnered 80 percent of paid search advertising in the United States and again a higher share (83 percent) abroad.[47] In mobile search and search advertising, Google's dominance was even greater: around 97 to 98 percent of mobile searches and mobile search advertising revenue went to Google in March 2011.[48] With $40 billion in annual revenue that year, and $48 billion the next, Google dominated Web advertising, drawing 31 percent of *total* global digital advertising revenues in 2013.[49] Google's importance for Web advertising, though, extended beyond its own revenues, because its role included not only placing ads next to its own search listings but also on thousands of outside Web sites through its Ad Sense network. Google was winning a commanding share of Web advertising for itself, but it was also purveying advertising across the Web. In this second aspect, Google competed directly with marketing supergroups: WPP, Omnicom, Interpublic, Havas, Dentsu, and Publicis.[50] Google's drive to be the leading online advertising network was based significantly on its $3.1 billion purchase of DoubleClick in 2007 (it outbid Microsoft and Yahoo).[51] Henceforward (if not already before this), advertising was foundational to Google's structure and strategy and once more carried far-reaching ramifications.

Along what lines is Google's PageRank algorithm constructed? How are its rankings generated? Does Google use its gateway power to steer users in anticompetitive ways, for example, by listing prominently its own affiliated sites (which in 2013 provided no less than two-thirds of Google's overall advertising revenue[52])—or by de-emphasizing those of its competitors?

This is, of course, a proprietary secret. Executive Chairman Eric Schmidt, not surprisingly, cast Google's program in benevolent terms. "One of the great intellectual challenges of our time," he declared, referring to Google's search engine, which drew ever-growing investment in research and development. "From the start," he continued, "Google has constantly refined its search algorithm, which now considers over 200 factors in assessing site quality and relevance."[53] This was indeed an impressive effort. In 2010, Google conducted no fewer than 13,311 "precision evaluations to see whether proposed algorithm changes improved the quality of its search results," and these reviews resulted in 516 changes "that were determined to be useful to users."[54] Google's search technology, Schmidt underlined, was "ever-improving" and the results it generated merely attempts to provide in good faith "a scientific *opinion* as to what information users will find most useful."[55] Drawing on an annual R&D expenditure of around $7.5 billion by 2013, its search service underwent a major redesign in that year.

Yet the logic that structures Google's navigational services and that ties its PageRank algorithm not only to its own growing pile of content and destination Web sites but also to its thousands of advertisers remained a mostly unaccountable secret. Google's gate-keeping role in Web search thus also became a sensitive policy issue: did its dominance over search (and its siphoning off of advertising outlays that might otherwise have been funneled to domestic companies, in Europe and elsewhere[56]) signify that it should be regulated as a public utility?[57] By 2011–12 Google faced antitrust inquiries on three continents.[58] The U.S. Federal Trade Commission issued civil investigative demands relating to Google's potentially anticompetitive monopoly in June 2011, while in September that year the U.S. Senate convened hearings on whether Google was biasing its search results. During 2013 and 2014, however, Google settled on highly favorable terms with U.S. and European antitrust authorities in deals that did not overturn the search company's practice of prioritizing sponsored links and its own shopping service above organic search results.[59] Perhaps, the *Financial Times* editorialized, Web search, akin to other kinds of online services such as Facebook's social network and Apple's App Store, constituted a "winner-take-all" market—an anticompetitive monopoly—meriting "public utility-like responsibilities."[60]

Still other important issues arose from the search giant's entanglement in a larger set of commercial relationships. For Google's market power, however substantial it may be, still does not exhaust the political economy of the commodity chain within which search is embedded. Commercial Web sites of all kinds possess strong incentives to influence their ranking in Google's search listings. A whole industry—search engine optimization—has grown up to serve advertisers' demands that their sites be ranked at or near the top of Google's first page of listings. Companies like SEOP, iProspect, Bruce Clay Inc., Increase Visibility Inc., and SEO Inc. play at the top of this market. A sort of guerilla warfare sets Google and lesser search engines on one side and optimization companies on the other. The commodity chain in which they are enmeshed includes not only search companies but also advertisers, optimizers, tracking companies, and outside content providers—each and all of whom, whether they work for or against Google, contribute to modernizing the profit strategies around which search is structured. Arcane areas of knowledge, such as network science and data mining, vaulted into prominence here; in the five years to 2011, IBM—a leader in social network analysis software—was reported to have spent a stupefying $11 billion buying makers of this kind of software.[61]

Introducing greater competition into search might be a good thing, but, of itself, it will not engage, let alone neutralize, this longer chain of commodity relations. Nor, and above all, will it permit this now-essential cultural and informational utility—search—to be divorced from the self-interested pressures placed on it by contending units of capital. A radical program would, necessarily, reorient this search utility's social purpose in order to guarantee its democratic accountability. New forms and practices of representation, beginning with compelling Google to make its search algorithm public, will need to be established to accomplish this.

Instead, however, Google's navigation service continued to be shaped and reshaped in thralldom to a renewed and much-widened sales effort. Google began to work with Omnicom, one of a handful of ad agency supergroups, to build a global system for making purchases of display ads easier. Google would provide analytics to enable Omnicom to target display ads to niche audiences and then to assess their performance. "We've turned the engineering fire hose at Google toward display advertising" said a Google vice president about this redeployment of social resources.[62] Omnicom established similar partnerships with AOL, Yahoo!, and Microsoft. By attaining "constant access" to the databases of these four online companies, Omnicom hoped "to become more consistent and accurate in targeting advertising to demographics such as car buyers or sports fans, which can be defined differently by different media owners."[63] Attempting to repulse Google's intrusion into digital advertising provision, Omnicom's global rivals WPP and Publicis pursued comparable strategies, some of whose ramifications are discussed below.

The effects of these commercial partnerships on online services were profound, just as their precursors had been for prior media. YouTube, Google's TV unit purchased in 2006 for $1.65 billion, was continually redesigned in light of advertisers' expectations.[64] Millions of users evinced fascination over bits of amateur-produced content on YouTube: so how might advertisers parasitize such a service? Proctor and Gamble's chief branding officer testified in 2010 that video clips about its Old Spice men's cologne—both those created by the company and parodies created by consumers—had been viewed 140 million times on YouTube.[65] But because advertising constitutes Google's spinal column, its dedication to the sales effort must be unceasing; so Google continued to hire squadrons of marketers.[66] In 2013, it announced to users of its YouTube, GooglePlay, and other services that their photos, profiles, comments, and rankings might be deployed in constructing advertising endorsements across the two million Web sites served by its display-advertising network, sites that are viewed by an estimated one billion people.[67]

Once more, Google was only a standout success at accomplishing what other commercial online intermediaries also were doing. AOL sought to transform itself from an internet service provider into a company selling advertisements connected to its own digital news and entertainment properties and to unrelated sites.[68] Amazon was deploying its troves of consumer e-commerce data to sell ads, both on its own account and on its network of other sites; forecasts called for it to generate $800 million from advertising in 2013.[69] The world's biggest marketing services company, advertising supergroup WPP, partnered with Twitter to gain direct access to the microblogger platform so that it could integrate Twitter data into its analyses and create data products for its own customers.[70] Twitter in turn revealed in its prospectus that its top five "data partners" accounted for three-quarters of its data-licensing revenue;[71] Twitter likewise announced that it looked to mine user data to help sell advertising on other mobile apps or Web sites.[72] Facebook, concerned that teenagers might be tiring of it, fell over itself generating both data and desirable points of access to consumers for advertisers, for example, loosening its already lax privacy rules for teenagers.[73]

This was a complex transition, replete with disruptions and attendant uncertainties. Perhaps the most important pertained to mobile devices. In 2012, more people in China accessed the Web via mobile phones than via PCs and, from Indonesia to North America, the rest of the world soon followed. This migration triggered "strategic shifts that run much deeper than simply remaking their services for smaller screens."[74]

One, as we saw, was that Google, Microsoft, and Amazon reciprocated Apple's strategy by moving from software and services into hardware. A second was that online companies sought to diversify their revenue streams by building out services that would harvest a varying mix of advertising, e-commerce fees, and direct sales. The urgency of this effort reflected knowledge that, for all the intense effort put into developing them, advertising sales derived from mobile media remained a shadow of those gained from the desktop (in the United States, $1.5 billion as opposed to $32 billion in 2011, though this figure grew substantially by 2013). Put differently, mobile internet use constituted more than 10 percent of media use overall in the United States in 2011 but drew less than 1 percent of total U.S. advertising expenditures.[75] Smartphones and tablets together were creating a bottomless buyer's market for ads, leaving advertisers awash in new media options; the terms of trade swung decisively toward sponsors and away from media—and not only on the Web. It was symptomatic of the altered environment that at Time Inc.—which had long made much of the separation between "church and state," that is, between editorial and business sides of the enterprise—a new CEO began to talk openly about getting the editorial and advertising sales units of the giant publisher to cooperate with one another.[76] There was also a sustained surge of "branded content," or "content marketing," whereby sponsoring companies like IBM, General Motors, Mountain Dew, and Dow Jones directly produced and presented editorial and entertainment programming.[77]

For advertisers and for the Web services that depended on them, however, the status of the identifiable personal information—of the invasive online surveillance which constituted the foundation of their shared endeavor—perhaps posed the biggest uncertainty. Though presidential campaigners might try to ignore it, this problem remained a political hot potato.

Privacy (Not)

A U.S. presidential candidate might well add to his or her election prospects by making privacy abuses and how to remedy them into substantive campaign issues. In 2012, tellingly, neither the Democrat nor the Republican candidate did so.[78] "Tired of waiting for Congress to pass comprehensive privacy legislation," the *New York Times* editorialized in 2013, "state lawmakers are taking matters into their own hands."[79]

Around the Web, tracking and data-mining were endemic: in 2009, thirty-six of the fifty most visited Web sites stated in their "privacy" policies that they allowed third-party tracking, virtually entirely removing from consumers even the limited opportunities for control offered by their own privacy policies.[80] Mobile devices were differently invasive, in that they did not rely on the small bits of software, termed "cookies," which had acted as the foremost instruments of tracking on desktop computers—but not less so.[81] "If you carry a smartphone in your pocket," noted Miguel Helft, "you are probably doing unpaid work for Apple or Google—and helping them eventually aim more advertising directly at you"—as the phones were programmed to act as sensors to gather data about nearby cell towers and Wi-Fi systems.[82] During a six-month period stretching into 2010, Deutsche Telekom recorded and saved the longitude and latitude coordinates for one documented user more than thirty-five thousand times, obtaining nearly three hundred readings each day. In the United States, network operators did not even have to report exactly which data they were collecting[83] (except, we now know, to government security agencies). A multibillion-dollar industry aimed at capturing and analyzing "big data"[84] for marketing purposes grew up alongside social networks, search services, mobile devices, sensor arrays, and data centers.[85]

Worries about privacy increased (not surprisingly) nearly in step with the phenomenon itself. "The large-scale collection, analysis, and storage of personal information is becoming more central to the Internet economy," conceded Assistant Secretary of Commerce for Communications and Information Lawrence Strickling: "Yet these same practices also give rise to growing unease among consumers, who are unsure about how data about their activities and transactions are collected, used, and stored." Survey after survey showed that Americans were as uninformed as they were unhappy and downright alarmed about privacy abuses.[86] The transition to smartphones and a mobile internet, coupled with evermore extensive tracking facilities and data-mining techniques,[87] guaranteed that what Strickling called "the difficulties of understanding personal data flow" would become "even more acute."[88]

The distinction between criminal incursions and workaday commercial practices remained murky. A drumbeat of disclosures pertaining to thefts and transfers of sensitive consumer data was audible. In April 2011, hackers stole names, user IDs, email addresses, passwords, and perhaps credit-card data for seventy-seven million PlayStation online-gaming accounts in sixty countries.[89] Around the same time, customer lists for JPMorgan Chase, Citibank, and Target were stolen from Epsilon, a company they used for email marketing; hackers took personal information from two hundred thousand Citigroup credit-card holders.[90] Through 2013, analogous break-ins and thefts continued to compromise consumers' data online.[91] In the wake of mobile location data scandals embroiling Apple, Microsoft, and Google, on the other hand, the Dutch satellite navigation company TomTom had to apologize for having sold—to the police—driving data collected from its customers.[92] Even after Facebook claimed to have strengthened its privacy controls, meanwhile, many of its most popular applications were shown by a *Wall Street Journal* investigation to be relaying identifying data to dozens of outside advertising and tracking companies.[93] Google faced accusations that it was illegally wiretapping "in the course of its everyday business—gathering data about Internet users and showing them related ads."[94] A well-regarded independent study found an average of twelve trackers present on each of the top one hundred most popular websites, with one site allowing as many as one hundred different trackers during a month's time: "This means that when a user visits that website, potentially 100 entities—nearly all unseen by the user—will learn about the visit." Online tracking extended from Web browsers on desktops to mobile phones and tablets, televisions, set-top boxes, video-game consoles, and an increasing number of automobiles.[95] Where was the line to be drawn between what had become routine corporate monitoring and unsanctioned invasion of privacy? When, in June 2013, Edward Snowden revealed that the sluices through which electronic life now poured were being operated by the major internet intermediaries in cooperation with the U.S. National Security Agency, the question forced its way into global politics—some further ramifications of which I discuss in part III.

Here it is more important to emphasize that "privacy" was not an adequate conceptual container to house the question of contemporary surveillance. It had become, Raymond Wacks explains, "too vague and unwieldy a concept to perform useful analytical work."[96] A watershed in the political economy of personal information was being traversed, as Web-based commodity chains "fundamentally redefined how, where, and by whom data is collected, used, and shared."[97] The issues were not so much individual and personal as political-economic.

U.S. corporations and state authorities sought to create a cosmetic patch to cover their efforts to integrate ever-expanding troves of data into accumulation and control structures, and to assuage users' anxieties over transgressions. Long before the Snowden exposures, the U.S. Commerce Department and the Federal Trade Commission had groped toward a strategy with which to allay popular fears. The Commerce Department would try to differentiate activities and functions that might be called beneficent from others that might be deemed harmful, and try to establish both a usable rhetoric and legal precepts for publicizing this distinction and enabling reputable units of capital to declare their adherence to it. Enforceable codes of conduct called "fair information practice principles" were put forward as a "central feature" of the Commerce Department's proposed "dynamic privacy framework" for consumer data.[98] In 2012 the Obama administration publicized a "blueprint" for a "privacy bill of rights" for consumers online.[99]

Policymakers were concerned to subordinate any strictures to what they sometimes called "innovation"—a euphemism for profitmaking. The Commerce Department's Internet Policy Task Force held that privacy policies needed to be framed so as to "allow innovation to flourish."[100] Somewhat bolder than the Commerce Department, the Federal Trade Commission thus hoped to restrict any privacy framework by designing it "to keep pace with a dynamic marketplace."[101] Microsoft's deputy general counsel declared that "the challenge that industry and government must address together is how to best protect consumers' privacy while enabling businesses to develop a wide range of innovative products and services."[102] Could the circle be squared?

"If users do not trust that their personal information is safe on the Internet," declared a high government official, "they will be reluctant to adopt new services or fully engage in Internet commerce."[103] Within a swirling policy discourse on consumer privacy, leading units of internet capital sought government help in identifying and drawing a bright line between data-gathering activities that might be deemed acceptable, even necessary, and those constituting transgressions that warranted penalties. A provisional rhetoric of "trust" was propagated. This framework, still delicate, was undercut by Snowden's sensational exposures. However, its central concern—to legitimate extant practices so as to consolidate the new forms of online advertising and selling—bears additional scrutiny.

Justice Louis Brandeis had famously originated the U.S. legal definition of privacy in 1890 as "the right to be let alone."[104] Brandeis's conception possessed a softer focus than the sharp political worry that had motivated early American lawmakers to try to prevent incursions by a despotic executive power. Rather than arbitrary searches and state surveillance of post-office letters, which constituted attacks against political liberty,[105] Brandeis's conception engaged emergent techno-commercial challenges to middle-class domestic sensibilities such as cameras. "Privacy" became a means of subjecting prospective intrusions to a disciplining legal negotiation.

The decades that have passed since Brandeis's formulation, as Oscar Gandy was early to understand,[106] and as Kelly A. Gates, and Mark Andrejevic, have further explained,[107] witnessed the construction of a pervasive institutional apparatus of personal information identification and appropriation. Radio frequency identification systems, smart cards, biometrics, sensors, and workaday commercial and government surveillance systems feed into this mechanism, and Web-based services operate as axes of personal information generation and capture. An online apparatus of commercial intelligence—what Gates calls a "culture of surveillance"[108] has become increasingly coextensive with the quotidian.

In consequence, even Brandeis's wandering definition of a right to privacy became onerous. Because, everyday, people generate "a mountain of data, across a myriad of different devices, that reveals valuable information about users' interests," forthrightly explained Microsoft's Erich Andersen, privacy no longer could be "about being 'let alone.'" Overtaken by their own routine practices, for corporate America and U.S. state agencies this conception had become unacceptable: Brandeis's characterization required fundamental revision. On behalf of Microsoft, Andersen offered up that privacy should be "about knowing what data is being collected and what is happening to it, having choices about how it is collected and used, and being confident that it is secure."[109]

This, however, constituted a carefully worded evasion. While big capital and the U.S. state insisted that individuals must relinquish the right to be left alone in any portion of their lives, they remained institutionally unaccountable themselves. People are told to settle for an artfully ambiguous measure of "transparency, control, and security," as Microsoft put it. Who gets to collect data, and which kinds of data, are left largely for corporations and state agencies to decide. Far-reaching political-economic questions are in turn truncated: rather than how—and whether—democratic freedom and accountability can be carried forward under conditions of omnipresent state and corporate surveillance, the question is merely how to define and publicize a policy that may ease these actors' legitimacy concerns. Corporations based in marketing and advertising again hold up self-regulation, long the favored tactic of their industry.[110] They remain firmly opposed, by contrast, to an easy-to-use, comprehensive "do-not-track" feature proposed (atypically) by the Federal Trade Commission because—as FTC Chairman Jon Leibowitz put it—"self-regulation of privacy has not worked adequately . . . for American consumers."[111]

Numerous proposals competed in this discourse; we need not tarry long on them. Wal-Mart emphasized in 2011 that "privacy solutions" should "help promote global interoperability." This was because considerable gaps already existed in national privacy laws, especially between the European Union and the United States—and they threatened to widen.[112] "As industry develops privacy approaches," Wal-Mart stated, "many companies will need to take a global approach into account, and . . . the challenges inherent in differing privacy regimes." Perhaps, Wal-Mart opined, it would prove necessary for the United States to increase the stringency of its (all-but-toothless) domestic policy.[113] Another corporate leader, General Electric, harmonized by urging that "a stronger privacy framework is key to promoting consumer trust." Operating in more than one hundred countries, GE echoed the need to make "recommendations for consistent privacy standards internationally." Emphasizing voluntary codes of conduct, GE also agreed with Wal-Mart that, to build a usable framework, the United States might need to reform some of its own laws and practices.[114] Reed Elsevier, an Anglo-Dutch publisher and information-service company with a huge U.S. presence, adopted a harder stance, opposing do-not-track mechanisms and "opt-out" provisions for consumers and demanding that the Commerce Department should do all within its power "to facilitate cross-border data transfers."[115] The Department "should encourage other countries to follow our lead and adopt more flexible privacy frameworks that mimic the U.S. approach."[116]

Such was the spectrum of corporate thinking. Accepting it as legitimate, the Commerce Department found "that the U.S. consumer data privacy framework will benefit from legislation to establish a clearer set of rules for the road for businesses and consumers, while preserving the innovation and free flow of information that are hallmarks of the Internet."[117] Because it was opaque, unaccountable, and widely objectionable to the population, the status quo had to *appear* to be altered. In 2011, the Obama administration announced its support for legislation to establish "a baseline set of privacy protections" for consumers; discussion continued over what these "fair information practice principles" should be. In the meantime, debate over the essential, structural power disparity—fully transparent citizenry, opaque companies and state agencies—simmered but produced only cosmetic changes.

Edward Snowden's sensational exposures in *The Guardian* newspaper then decisively altered the picture. His documentation, which was picked up in other news media around the world, revealed how U.S. state and corporate agencies were cooperating to transgress human rights systematically, and on a global scale.[118] The frame that U.S. corporate and government leaders had carefully placed around the question of privacy was blown apart, returning discussion to its profound political fundamentals.

In an angry response before the United Nations General Assembly, Brazil's President Dilma Rousseff—who apparently had been a specific target of NSA surveillance—declared, "In the absence of the right to privacy, there can be no true freedom of expression and opinion, and therefore no effective democracy."[119] It is dangerous to speak freely when one is being monitored. However, Rousseff's protest also prompted corollary questions: What did it signify that the United States could comb through the communications of people and, indeed, of peoples, around the world? Might the interconnected democratic rights to freedom of expression and to privacy attach not only to individuals but to entire societies?

There is indeed a tradition of inquiry that holds that freedom of expression is served best (and perhaps only) when it is anchored in society's ability to engage with the full range of ideas that its members express.[120] A right to privacy must be comparably organic. Unless society ensures a general right to be free of surveillance, then democratic liberties stand to be compromised. It is, then, insufficient to apprehend today's internet marketing by way of a concept of privacy that is cast around mere individual violations. We confront not occasional attacks on specific unfortunates but a wholesale takeover of the now-ubiquitous data trails left by human interaction. The threat that is posed to democratic civil liberties today comes not only from an abusive executive power but also from culture-wide corporate exploitation of personal information. It is shockingly insufficient to put forward an opt-out clause (and this only some of the time) as a solution when, if privacy is truly to be safeguarded and accountability restored, it is the entire society that must be able to opt out.

Both the official politics of privacy and the ongoing modernization of advertising online conspired to deflect and forestall such a solution. The white space demonstrably continued to be narrowed and reduced to allow sellers and spies to watch over all our shoulders all the time. Advertising spending was quickly redirected: not two decades after its popularization, the internet ranked as the second-leading U.S. advertising medium, consuming 20 percent of marketers' ad budgets, amounting to $31 billion in 2011—behind only television, with its 38 percent share, and growing fast. Even as digital depression persisted, search and display-ad spending registered double-digit increases.[121] Both advertising to desktops and, especially, to mobile devices increased sharply during 2012 and 2013, as total advertising expenditures grew 3.5 percent in 2012 and an additional 3.9 percent in 2013.[122]

The battle over personal information was not a mere one-off contest but a grinding campaign that pitted big advertisers, network operators, internet intermediaries, and media conglomerates against popular will. Six months of slow-drip exposures by Edward Snowden cumulated in increasingly widespread certainty that a hugely encompassing, extraterritorial online system had been recruited into the U.S. military-intelligence complex. Who could have guessed, for example, that data supplied by players of Angry Birds—a game app from Finnish software company Rovio that had been downloaded globally more than 1.7 billion times by 2014—had been covertly scooped up by the National Security Agency?[123] Pressure mounted in the United States, still the center of the global internet economy, where privacy advocates pushed for a stronger "do-not-track" option even as advertisers "dug their heels in against changes that would greatly limit the amount of information they can collect."[124] Big internet intermediaries looked to create personal identifiers, in lieu of cookies, presumably hoping in this way to deflect the opposition. This struggle will continue to evolve—likely unpredictably—as it already has.

A final question returns us to the contribution of these recomposing communications commodity chains to economic growth.

CHAPTER 9

Growth amid Depression?

Did the metamorphosis of communications around Web commodity chains establish an exception to the contradictory pattern detected in part I? There, we found that network-enabled reorganizations of manufacturing, finance, and war production eventually led on to a further episode of crisis. Did the U.S. information and communications industry exhibit a different directional pattern? This industry's own investment in ICT and software was greater than that of manufacturing, or banking, or indeed of any other sector: $80.5 billion, or 28 percent of the total in 2011.[1] Might these expenditures, further augmented by outlays made in other national markets, signify that a basis was being laid for a new spatio-temporal fix? For market expansion and economic growth? Or, to the contrary, did investment in Web communications commodity chains siphon revenue and profit mostly from old to new media, so that growth overall remained flat?

Official statistics show that in 2007, U.S. information industry revenues totaled $1.08 trillion, while in 2011 (the most recent annual data) they totaled $1.17 trillion.[2] Modest growth occurred—notable amid a depression.[3] A more granular analysis of the recomposition of communications helps to clarify this finding.

Over the course of the digital depression's now seven years (2008–2014), advertising outlays moved down and then up, advertisers shifted expenditures between media, apps substituted for stand-alone services, and peoples' habits—

their uses of media and their media expenditures—altered. Economic hardship for millions of households throughout Western Europe and North America struck at fee-based communications consumption, and the growth of much-vaunted "middle classes" in China, India, Brazil, and elsewhere did not fully compensate. For a couple of billion people, moreover, disproportionately nonwhite and concentrated in the global south, immiseration remained urgent. Accelerated movement into digital, mobile, and social network services therefore must be set against concurrent expansion of the zones of abandonment and reduced expenditure. Additional research is needed to clarify this complex historical patchwork; for a moment I will focus on the U.S. trends.

Fee based services were hit, especially—as in the United States—where the experience of the slump combined with the availability of unlicensed forms of access. The music industry offers an example. Here, concert-tour revenue fell sharply, "as strapped consumers stayed home": the fifty highest-grossing tours in the world took in 12 percent less money—from $3.34 billion in 2009 to $2.93 billion in 2010, with an even deeper drop (15 percent) in North America.[4] The long drought for global recorded music industry revenues abated in 2012, but only barely, as it showed a 0.3 percent increase, the first since 1999.[5] Digital music downloads accounted for seven-tenths of overall digital music revenues, and music-streaming services claimed strong growth—but unlicensed file sharing remained widespread.[6] Comparable drift overtook the film industry: New DVD sales—until recently, Hollywood's largest revenue source—"collapsed," falling 20 percent in the year to early 2011.[7] Total U.S. spending on filmed home entertainment, including DVDs, Blu-ray discs, and—again—digital downloads, dropped by more than $2 billion between 2008 and 2010, from $21 billion to $18.8 billion.[8] Though unlicensed online viewing of movies and TV shows increased,[9] U.S. box-office revenues also lifted, by 12 percent between 2008 and 2012 to $10.8 billion.[10] Books, finally, likewise demonstrated mixed and uneven results. Industry researcher Albert Greco projected that sales of printed consumer book titles would drop from $18 billion in 2008 to $13.9 billion in 2015—by which time, he predicted, e-book sales would total $3.6 billion.[11] These swings to digital distribution did not compensate for plummeting revenues in conventional audiovisual and publishing markets. Would they?

Communications services again exhibited a dual profile. In the United States, the depressed housing market and economic difficulty translated into a drop-off in cable television and landline telephone subscriptions.[12] The total number of U.S. cable television subscribers fell by nearly 750,000 during the third quarter of 2010—the largest decline in thirty years.[13] The industry regained its footing somewhat the next year, and cable operators looked both to business services and broadband subscriptions for growth.[14] But YouTube's short videos and Netflix's willingness to allow subscribers to share their accounts combined to engender partial—and, symptomatically, cheap—product substitutes. Cord cutting became persistent as erstwhile subscribers embraced online streaming services. The largest U.S. cable operator by subscribers—Comcast—shed video subscribers for six-and-a-half years and focused its strategy on losing fewer customers.[15] In regard to a different access device, the Centers for Disease Control reported that one in four U.S. households possessed only a mobile phone in December 2009, and that this shift was related to income: more than one-third of adults classed as living in poverty in that year had no land line. Product substitution occurred here too, as users shifted from old-style "telephone" calls to free or nearly free VOIP services. And within scarcely three years—by the second half of 2012—nearly two-fifths (38.2 percent) of American homes possessed only wireless telephones.[16] While voice telephony was metamorphosing into a software application, vaporizing a huge industry, however, mobile and residential broadband services continued to expand.

Much advertiser-supported content remained stuck in neutral. Easy access to comparable Web content and hard-hit consumers' propensity to bring shopping lists—and to stick to them rather than indulging in impulse buys—contributed to declining sales of consumer magazines, which never recovered from the downturn of 2008–09. *US Weekly, Star, Vanity Fair, Oprah Magazine, Cosmopolitan, Time,* and *People,* for example, suffered significant drops and, with paid subscriptions flat and advertising revenues declining, digital editions again did not compensate for this shortfall.[17]

Newspapers constituted an extreme case: As readers moved to online aggregators and news sites, and as advertisers abandoned the medium, the long-established urban newspaper faced extinction. Variation persisted even here, though, as chain owners of small, local newspapers clung to their niches. Between 2005 and 2011, the margin of earnings before interest, taxes, depreciation, and amortization at the Gannett newspaper division—which owned around eighty newspapers published in smaller communities, as well as the national newspaper *USA Today*—fell from 29.6 percent to a still-hefty 18.3 percent.[18] The news function, however, remained imperiled.[19]

Slumping disposable income affected media consumption practices; so did the availability of cheap digital replacements, some of them illicit. Because communications commodity chains were recomposing around altered business models, the industry overall grew modestly during the digital depression as its foundations continued to be recast.

Undoubtedly, people were spending much more time with communications and media. An official estimate of the average number of hours adult Americans spent attending to communications (exclusive of telecommunications) put the figure at 3,297 hours in 1996[20]—and at 3,545 hours in both 2007 and 2008 (a small decline was projected for 2009).[21] Added throughout these twelve years was an increment of more than six forty-hour weeks of communications-related activity. Home use of internet services, mobile services, and games, and basic cable television viewing spiked. Putting this differently, the profit streaming into top internet companies was predicated on their appropriation of a greatly enlarged quantity of uncompensated (and typically unrecognized) labor.[22] (It helped that throughout nine successive quarters following a "recovery" officially pegged to the second quarter of 2009, U.S. consumer spending on TV sets grew by 83 percent and on PCs by 50 percent,[23] even while spending on tablets and smartphones also surged.) For the first time, during 2012, U.S. information-technology companies outstripped their counterparts from other sectors in their payouts of dividends to investors.[24]

To clarify further the question of growth, we must also situate the U.S. trend within the world that exists beyond its borders. Between 1995 and 2010, across most of the thirty-four-nation Organization for Economic Cooperation and Development (OECD), the proliferation of mobile and broadband internet services made communications equipment and services the fastest-growing household expenditure.[25] Evident, at this scale—and despite the sagging fortunes of conventional media—was an unequivocal measure of real expansion.

To be sure, the figures ebbed and flowed year to year, especially during the digital depression. Before the crisis, according to a trade group, the World Information Technology and Services Association (WITSA, which tallied its statistics differently than did the OECD or the U.S. Census Bureau), consumers worldwide accounted for nearly 29 percent of $2.7 trillion in total global ICT spending. Fired by demand for mobile data services, in WITSA's 2010 forecast both the consumer share and the total were projected to increase by 2013 to almost one-third of a much-enlarged $4.5 trillion market.[26] In any event, global ICT spending actually dropped by 3 percent in 2009—that is, by $108 billion—so that the industry's projected growth trajectory had to be revised downward. The longer-term trend, however, was toward growth. Midway through 2013, annual global ICT expenditures seemed on track to increase by 4.2 percent, "outpacing expectations of flat growth in the world economy."[27] Growth in connected devices ranging from smartphones to door locks, jewelry, and refrigerators[28] was spurring increases in global ICT spending, and the number of devices with unique IP addresses was projected to rise by an order of magnitude by 2020.[29]

The OECD continued to herald "the Internet Economy on the Rise" in a September 2013 report.[30] A 2014 projection pointed to a rise of 3.1 percent in global spending, to $3.8 trillion.[31] While, overall, the communications and information industry demonstrated growth, individual industry segments—from apps stores and cloud services to film- and music-streaming services, and from high-end smart phones to search engines and social networks—showed enviably strong global market results. The Organization for Economic Cooperation and Development reported in September 2013 that "the Internet economy has become a new source of growth, with the potential to boost the whole economy."[32]

■ ■ ■

If web-enabled commodity chains constituted a rare pole of profitable growth, we may ask, then by whom was this growth captured? How was it distributed within the world system?

By 2013, according to a trade group's projection, Asia-Pacific ICT spending would be just 3.5 percentage points below that of the Americas in the worldwide total—31.1 percent, as compared with 34.6 percent of the overall sum.[33] Market growth rates for Asia and Pacific countries also substantially exceeded those of North America and Europe.[34] Nowhere did the information industry show greater dynamism than in China. Early in 2013, China's Ministry of Industry and Information Technology mandated that newly built homes within areas already wired must be installed with a fiber-to-the-home (FTTH) connection as part of a government plan to connect forty million homes to FTTH by 2015.[35] In August, China's State Council set new targets and predicted that additional investments in both fiber and 3G/4G wireless networks would propel growth of internet-based consumption by "at least 30 percent annually."[36] China's domestic film market, already the world's second largest after surpassing Japan's, bid fair to become the largest within five years.[37]

These shifts in the territorial profile of communications markets signified that the historical mutation into digital capitalism remained ongoing and unfinished. They also introduced a sharp edge to the question of which units of capital, based in and supported by which states, would appropriate whatever growth did occur, especially in the most profitable market segments. Which companies, headquartered in which countries, were in the best position to capture profits from the products and services that issued from recomposing communications commodity chains? And what—whose—new products might generate additional growth and profits still to come?

With this, we enter a final phase of inquiry. For, just as the digital depression accentuated change across the network, equipment, applications, and services industries, it also magnified political-economic conflicts. Benno Teschke has called for "a re-politicization of capitalist development, as a contested and re-gionally differentiated institutionalization of social relations, but also a radical geopoliticization of its historical course."[38] Teschke's findings about the initial widening of capitalism in early modern Europe could hardly be more germane to our epoch of digital capitalism amid depression. Efforts to corral network systems and services in order to capture more of whatever profits might be made introduced a new chapter in the geopolitics of information—one marked by intensifying struggles over control of the extraterritorial internet and of the industries that continued to pyramid around it.

PART III

Geopolitics and Social Purpose

CHAPTER 10

A Struggle for Growth

The digital depression gave no sign of abating. In some places and at some moments, authorities were able to contain the crisis—but not yet to resolve it. Far from being regenerated, the circuits of the political economy that carried the malady functioned largely as they had. Even as the slump became prolonged, however, fresh wellsprings of profitmaking accumulation continually emerged around network equipment, services, and applications.

Who—which companies, which states—would cultivate and control these coveted centers of emerging comparative advantage? Internet connectivity had been woven into the global political economy, enabling new commodities, altering state policy, and revamping the ways in which ordinary people worked, played, and communicated. Vital sites of profit making and, perhaps, of renewed growth were at stake. Cyberspace—and the internet above all[1]—therefore became riven, as rival efforts to shape the destiny of the overall political economy detonated conflicts at the pivot of this domain.

Situating this unfolding dynamic in its international context is the essential task of part III. Were the internet to be considered as a continent (an idea suggested by Serge Halimi, director of *Le Monde diplomatique*), then the fierce geopolitics that were reshaping this jurisdiction might be more easily apprehended. For, during the winter of 2013–14, it seemed that the existing institutional mechanism of "global internet governance" might give way. How it might be altered—even replaced—remained undecided. But further conflicts over this question were foreordained, because the internet remained the forward edge of transnational capitalism's accumulation project. We will see in part III that, as this book went to press, the extraterritorial internet's control structure was balanced on a knife's edge.

■ ■ ■

An abiding structural disparity had shaped the internet. Building on its longtime strengths in communications and information processing and drawing support from a mobilized state, U.S. capital had exercised a conditioning force over its deployment. A snapshot from our current decade showed the picture, both domestically and extraterritorially. The supply of corporate routing equipment was led by Cisco, of search engines by Google, of social networking by Facebook and Twitter, of totemic smartphones and other consumer appliances by Apple and again (in alliance with Samsung) Google. Intel dominated semiconductors, though as desktop PCs gave way to mobile devices, Intel lost ground to Ericsson, Huawei, and another U.S. company, QualComm. Oracle led in databases and faced the German company SAP in business software; Microsoft dominated corporate desktop operating systems. Also in services and mainframe computers for the enterprise market, IBM's profit performance was seemingly untouched by the digital depression; midway through 2012, the $100 billion company had met or beat Wall Street's average earnings estimate every quarter since 2005.[2] The United States boasted the world's two largest telecommunications operators by revenue: AT&T and Verizon.[3] Transnational cloud service suppliers were overwhelmingly U.S. companies. Three of the top four computer services and consulting companies were IBM, EDS (acquired by H-P in 2008), and Accenture (the fourth, Cap Gemini, was French). U.S.-based companies were likewise leaders on the unduly neglected demand side: from Wal-Mart to General Electric to Amazon, U.S. corporate innovation of internet-based systems and applications set a global standard.[4] Crucial to all of this was that the internet's address system and the technical functions connected with it were managed predominantly by U.S. state and corporate actors.[5] Thus U.S. companies were early adopters, further along in assimilating internet technology and exercising disproportionate influence over the internet's continuing evolution.

It bears emphasizing that U.S.-based internet systems and services had preemptively occupied not just domestic but many transnational markets. Looking forward from 2010, Apple's iPhone was a breakaway global hit, beating down protectionist barriers in Korea and China; its user-base of 160 million for its iTunes service mushroomed to 575 million by 2013.[6] Skype's free internet phone service claimed 560 million users;[7] Facebook drew 500 million users (and more than twice that number three years later); Microsoft 789 million; Yahoo! 633 million.[8] There existed both pronounced unevenness and, no doubt, problems of reliable measurement; but U.S. suppliers had carved out entrenched leading positions throughout this extraterritorial realm. Facebook was visited by 92 percent of the internet population in Turkey and 87 percent in Indonesia (compared to 67 percent in the United States).[9] A goodly proportion of the world's internet users—some 944 million people—used Google's services somewhere, just during the month of June, and Google's Android operating system was rapidly extending its role.[10] Twitter was growing strongly: midway through 2013, the microblogging service boasted that its 215 million average monthly users spanned "nearly every country," with more than three-quarters of them located outside the United States.[11]

Through preemptive appropriations of internet connectivity and an assertively helpful state, U.S.-based capital had seized an impressive lead across numerous transnational markets for digital equipment, services, software, and applications. U.S. funding for ICTs in 2010, in one estimate $1.2 trillion, exceeded that of China, Japan, the United Kingdom, and Russia combined. The United States accounted for more than half of global ICT research-and-development spending. In consequence, as a strategic report underlined, "The United States captures more than 30 percent of global Internet revenues and more than 40 percent of net income."[12] U.S. corporate, political, and military leaders were determined to leverage this carefully nurtured comparative advantage to its fullest extent.

For world system theory, the historical cycles of capitalist development divulged a recurrent dominative logic in which core capitalist countries repeatedly reproduced their own preclusive power over the periphery. For centuries this process persisted, with only secondary alterations. U.S. global market dominance over digital systems and services thus may be portrayed as a fresh confirmation of this engraved pattern. Was it?

Let us not be hasty to answer, for the signs are mixed. On one hand, the U.S.-based internet giants had entrenched themselves and would be very difficult to dislodge; they also had continually succeeded in penetrating the defenses of many of their competitors—even in their home markets. On the other hand, internet connectivity became a general prerequisite of the capitalist political economy during a singular historical moment, when capitalism itself was taking hold across the planet. This broadening of capitalism produced, or conditioned, many other emergent changes. One was to diversify the composition of transnational capital. Foreign direct investment spread outward, as we saw in part I, first from the United States, then from Western Europe and Japan, then beyond this.[13] Not only did developing countries, led by China, in 2012 absorb more foreign direct investment than developed countries; led by China, Brazil, Russia, India, and South Africa, developing countries also *generated* nearly one-third of global FDI outflows.[14] This occurred partly owing to a second contemporary feature: the persistent digital depression. As the economies of the United States and Western Europe slumped, South-South commodity chains and trade flows burgeoned. Transnational companies headquartered in big cities throughout the world—by 2010 only one-third of the top five hundred global companies were based in the United States—in turn were actively deploying internet connectivity to link to suppliers and customers wherever they might be profitably found.

This shift altered the topology of the global internet. Put simply, while international internet capacity grew by 33 percent in 2013—and this was the *slowest* annual increase recorded during the preceding decade—so the internet was becoming less U.S.-centric: By 2010 and beyond, regional hubs were being built in Singapore, Tokyo, Hong Kong, Turkey, Kenya, and Brazil; intraregional data flows were expanding while reliance on internet connections through the United States declined;[15] and Asia and Europe (which built up its dominance over African connectivity and increased its traffic with Asia) were becoming major hubs of global connectivity.[16] Additional routing options were being brought forward, increasing and diversifying city-to-city connections among one-hundred-odd major backbone carriers worldwide: the London–New York route share of total transatlantic capacity dropped from 46 percent in 2005 to 30 percent in 2011.[17] In part, this reconfiguration reflected U.S. internet intermediaries' own transnationalization: when Amazon opened a data center in Singapore in 2010 "to give customers in Asia, India, and Australia speedier access" to its cloud services—both "Asian customers and Western companies that have many users in the region"[18]—this thickened traffic flows in Southeast Asia. However, in good part, the movement away from a U.S.-centric internet expressed the political economy of what was now a planetary capitalism. An increasingly far-flung and diversely rooted industry supplied internet equipment, services, and applications. Significant suppliers catered to different market segments from bases in Europe and Japan, but also from Korea, Mexico, India, South Africa, China, and elsewhere. Business users of the internet were still more widely dispersed.

A particularly important sign of prospective wider change was that extraterritorial internet connectivity became a site not of consensus and stably administered accumulation but of sustained political contestation. How, on which principles and with what ramifications, had this particular incarnation of the global space of flows been established? In her valuable study of internet history, published in 1999, Janet Abbate concluded, "As the Internet becomes more of an international resource, the continued authority of the United States in administrative matters will, no doubt, be challenged more and more."[19] Jack Goldsmith and Tim Wu had highlighted in 2006 how, as the internet intruded further into domestic economies and cultures worldwide, reciprocal efforts to strengthen national state oversight had in fact increased.[20] In the United States, thinking about this issue consolidated around the notion that state "control" over "access" was undergoing a widespread and dangerous upswing.[21] However, this perspective evaded another profound and pointed political-economic question: Were existing arrangements for "global internet governance" evenhanded, that is, was management of the extraterritorial internet organized so as to make it equally accountable to all members of the global community? Adjacent to these were other questions, often open-ended and again fractious: Who would shape and profit from the emerging connectivity-enabled commodities that were crucial for a renewal of capitalist growth? How and why were states across the world attempting to realign the mechanisms needed to coordinate and further develop the extraterritorial internet? Might these initiatives secure and stabilize the internet for capitalist accumulation? Or might they turn the internet into a combat zone of growing intercapitalist rivalry? (I consider, toward the end, the question of whether the internet may be transformed into a genuinely democratic system "beyond capital.")

Weakened by the crisis, the United States still occupied a unique position with respect to the extraterritorial internet. Though perhaps no one "organizational system" possessed undiluted mastery of global internet governance, as Laura DeNardis suggests,[22] still, operational management, policymaking, and technical standards for the internet were disproportionately structured by agencies bound to U.S. state power; and the forward edge of digital systems and services continued to be defined disproportionately by U.S. internet companies. True, the extraterritorial internet had originated in international collaborations;[23] however, as we will see, with respect to coordination and policy it remained a U.S. redoubt. In particular, the highly centralized internet naming and addressing system was superintended by a U.S.-based entity called ICANN: the Internet Corporation for Assigned Names and Numbers. And ICANN was contractually obligated to the U.S. Executive Branch.

This power disparity created a paradoxical vulnerability. As the digital depression persisted, U.S. policymakers had to scramble, not only to enlarge capital's ability to exploit internet connectivity but also to shore up—to defend—

their own unique prerogatives. Richly revealing conflicts ensued, and these may be scrutinized by reviewing a series of extraordinary initiatives undertaken by U.S. Executive Branch departments. I begin by briefly situating these undertakings in a longer history of extraterritorial communications. Then, after taking up the question of how internet governance was affected by the reverberating impacts of the NSA spying exposures, I return to the transformation of the wider political economy.

■ ■ ■

We may not posit a formulaic preexisting identity between capital and the state. Ever since the American and the French Revolutions, the state has been episodically a theater of struggle, where the universalistic laws and rhetoric of a nominally democratic polity clash with the particularistic interests and demands of capital. The outcome in any given instance is not foreordained, for three reasons: because state managers as well as diverse and sometimes opposed social actors imagine and pursue projects relatively independently; because capital struggles against other social classes; and because capital also struggles against capital. With respect to many issues, capital constitutes neither an integral nor a stationary interest, because capital's general interest in stabilizing the primacy of the accumulation function must contest particular capitals' interests in advancing their own specific profit projects. Outcomes may not be explained, therefore, solely on the ground of theory: understanding hinges on bringing historical specificities to bear.

Networks do not obviate or transcend these conflicts between universal political rights and particularistic social interests. Indeed, networks have often extended and circulated such struggles. Extensive, well-integrated, nationwide telecommunications networks were established mainly in the wealthy countries of Western Europe and North America while, historians have shown, around the same time—the later nineteenth century—great units of capital cooperated with powerful states to build submarine cable networks with which to bind colonies and ex-colonies into preclusive relationships.[24] Telecommunications networks and imperialism became entangled, therefore, at the outset. With decolonization following World War II throughout Asia and Africa, connectivity still remained limited mostly to urban enclaves and transnational circuits, while the management and operation of national networks passed to governments. (To be sure, in consultation with and, often, deference to telecommunications industry interests.) These states, most newly founded, likewise claimed a role within an organization which had previously been a creature of the imperialist countries: the International Telecommunication Union (ITU), whose responsibilities had been broadened to include radio and wireline telephony in addition to telegraphy. After World War II, the ITU was brought into the new United Nations system.

Though the ITU still gave priority to the developed market economies and to the demands of transnational capital, it made policies and issued regulations for networks on a one-nation-one-vote basis. During the 1960s and 1970s, state-centered mobilizations led by Latin American, Asian, and African countries momentarily threatened the established dominative pattern, as pressure was brought to bear behind a "new international information order." This initiative, however, met with unremitting antagonism and, after the elections of President Ronald Reagan and Prime Minister Margaret Thatcher, with an increasingly forceful counterreaction by the United States and Britain. At the same time, the class basis of many states throughout Asia, Africa, and Latin America was hardening as decolonization struggles receded, ruling groups consolidated, and accommodations were made with transnational capital. The possibility opened that the world's information order might be redeveloped, not as an open-ended project driven by the global south's anti-imperialist movements for national self-determination but, instead, as a repressively "neoliberal" movement for transnational capitalist reintegration in which elite social classes cooperated worldwide. Vijay Prashad has given us a cogent history of this historical arc.[25]

By the late 1980s and early 1990s, through a process that is still incompletely understood, an opportunity to rebuild the extraterritorial space of flows became irresistible to U.S. capital and the U.S. Executive Branch.[26] Since the 1970s, U.S.-sponsored liberalization initiatives had chipped away at national public-service principles and multilateral oversight responsibilities for networks; corporate-commercial freedom to redevelop this infrastructure became a topmost policy priority. In reaction to initiatives aimed at a new international information order, the 1980s debt crisis was used to institute privatization programs, and this impulse rapidly widened. Dozens of nations privatized their telecommunications networks. During the 1990s, the U.S. Executive Branch put nails in the coffin of the old order by institutionalizing an extraterritorial internet and then using it as a battering ram against nationally structured controls.[27] Rights rhetoric suffused this endeavor, endowing it with a missionary ethos of uplift, but the resounding triumph of internet connectivity actually was predicated on the projection of state power and a great opening of capital investment into networking to enable further capitalist globalization.

A far-reaching economic program was implicit—and pervasive—in what were presented as democratizing initiatives. President Clinton's agenda for global electronic commerce was to ban from the global internet tariffs, trade barriers, taxes, and content regulation, and thereby to establish a worldwide electronic free-trade zone.[28] Capital was being freed to pursue commodification projects across breathtaking vistas. Encompassed explicitly in the Clinton-era vision were the United States dominated sectors of "computer software, entertainment products (motion pictures, videos, games, sound recordings), information services (databases, online newspapers), technical information, product licenses, financial services, and professional services (business and technical consulting, accounting, architectural design, legal advice, travel services, etc.)."[29] To a remarkable extent, this mobilization of U.S. state power succeeded in its economic designs. In a book published in 1999, I underscored that "no countertrend toward robust multilateral oversight and regulation of the Internet had yet materialized—in a field where each succeeding month saw fresh applications corrosive of existing national media structures and regulatory controls."[30] It is clear in retrospect that this result attested not only U.S. strength during the "unipolar moment" that followed the collapse of the Soviet Union but, also, the newfound receptivity of states whose class bases and economic programs had undergone drastic redefinition—not only Russia, but also Western Europe and East Asia, and much of the global south including, above all, China.

This rebuilt space of flows, however, was erected around an elemental power disparity between the United States and other states, and this imbalance carried an inborn potential for conflict. The digital depression—both the trends that led into it and the hard-to-manage contingencies that the crisis itself generated—magnified this potential. Cyberspace's already conflicted universal jurisdiction then became a site of increasingly serious infighting. The United States sought to portray the challenges as illicit, self-serving interventions undertaken by heavy-handed states and tin-pot dictators; but this was a mischaracterization. Outside the United States, the same challenges often were viewed differently: as an impulse that aimed to redress the unilateral control that had so profoundly structured the extraterritorial internet. Might some portion of this impulse be traced to other states' attempts to privilege units of capital resident within their borders in the face of resurgent intercapitalist rivalries? Of course—though it must not be reduced solely to this impulse. The U.S.-led reconstruction of the space of flows around the internet, so recently a site of unvarnished triumphalism, therefore now generated intensifying counterpressures.

Two kinds of geopolitical challenges threatened U.S. prerogatives over extraterritorial internet connectivity. One involved attempts to reinstitute state authority in the face of perceived usurpations, as national communicative spaces were restructured around a transnational internet. The other targeted the centralized functions of global internet management that were controlled by the United States. Many states, including both antagonists and allies, strived to rebalance this jurisdiction in order to reduce and, if possible, to supplant U.S. dominance. Both challenges expressed heterogeneous interests and values. Neither impulse was simple, and together, as we will see, they triggered a complex and far-reaching U.S. response.

These challenges also produced demonstration effects. On one side, it became more apparent that cyberspace could be reshaped in light of differing goals and priorities. On the other side, transnational capital, intent that its digitized commodity chains should not be destabilized, reacted with mounting anxiety. Any fragmentation of the space of flows—any limits on the interoperability of the internet—comprised a true danger. A multiple fracture into many national or even subnational internets would be deleterious, in an age when transnational capital depended on standardized connectivity worldwide, and when economic expansion was predicated on transnational commodification projects. Potentially competing extraterritorial network jurisdictions also were imaginable; these had predominated, not only during the epoch of high imperialism but also throughout much of the Cold War, when the U.S.-run Intelsat had coexisted with the much more limited InterSputnik, an extraterritorial satellite system operated by the U.S.S.R. A final option also existed: that a globally interoperable internet would be preserved—but reconstituted on an altered, less-U.S.-centric, political-economic basis as a "federated Internet."

In combating these challenges, which commenced even before the digital depression struck, the George W. Bush administration had prosecuted a "damn the torpedoes—full speed ahead" approach. U.S. policymaking for the internet had operated as if the rest of the world was superfluous—which, in a real sense, it was. The extent of the political isolation that attended this course, however, became manifest in 2005, when other countries—among them, startlingly, the European Union—insisted that all governments, rather than only that of the United States, should possess "an equal role and responsibility" for internet policy and for the management of critical internet resources, notably, the system of unique identifiers, without which it could not function.[31] Changes continued to roil this landscape; as Milton Mueller put it in 2010, the privileges over the internet enjoyed by the United States faced "a long-term war of attrition in which those privileges may gradually be whittled away."[32]

As part of its general strategic review, the Obama administration revamped the appearance of U.S. policy without altering its underlying objectives. Initiated even as the presidential transition got underway, and becoming progressively more expansive and multifaceted, was a high-profile Executive Branch mobilization. Its goals were to enact policies by which the United States could continue to commandeer internet connectivity and to channel it as U.S. interests might seem to warrant. But President Bush's bellicose and self-justifying posture was exchanged for one that rang out with rhetoric of respect for democratic process, human rights, and international comity. "Cooperation," "collective responsibility," "transparency," and "multi-stakeholderism" became the watchwords.[33]

No less a figure than President Barack Obama himself proclaimed that the United States would "support civil society actors in achieving reliable, secure, and safe platforms for freedoms of expression and association." "We encourage people all over the world," he said, "to use digital media to express opinions, share information, monitor elections, expose corruption, and organize social and political movements, and denounce those who harass, unfairly arrest, threaten, or commit violent acts against the people who use these technologies." However, Obama took good care to emphasize that these high-minded principles should not operate merely on behalf of individuals: "The same protections must apply to Internet Service Providers and other providers of connectivity, who too often fall victim to legal regimes of intermediary liability that pass the role of censoring legitimate speech down to companies."[34] When the president issued an "international strategy for cyberspace" in 2011, his text again affirmed what, we will see, was a deep-rooted U.S. "expectation that under normal circumstances, data will flow across borders without regard for its national origin or destination."[35]

Obama was signaling U.S. determination to project power over critical internet resources and over the extraterritorial internet. A major purpose was to secure the continued, untrammeled movement of data throughout networked commodity chains. The human rights of individuals were by the same token conflated with the circuits of transnational profitmaking and of state power projection—as, indeed, they had been for generations. In the chapters that follow I examine this project in detail, and I show that it proved to be not only internally conflicted but also unexpectedly vulnerable.

CHAPTER 11

"A New Foreign Policy Imperative"

Several interlocked U.S. Executive Branch initiatives were organized during the digital depression in a loosely coordinated effort to affirm and bolster U.S. policy for the extraterritorial internet. This endeavor claimed a high priority. Cyber issues, declared Secretary of State Hillary Clinton in her announcement of the administration's International Strategy for Cyberspace, constituted nothing less than "a new foreign policy imperative."[1] The Department of State's contribution to this policy program was to project a refurbished rhetoric of human rights centered on what Secretary Clinton in 2010 hailed as "internet freedom."[2]

The stepping-off point for what became a concerted State Department initiative was supplied by Google, whose then-CEO, Eric Schmidt, had been a member of Obama's campaign team. It is not clear whether Google in its turn had already been in contact with the White House, as the search giant arrived at its decision, in January 2010, to close its China-based search service as a result of state censorship and hacker intrusions. It hardly matters. While, according to a highly placed Chinese analyst, the Beijing leadership "suspected . . . that the U.S. government was backing Google in inflaming anti-government sentiment among China's netizens," the U.S. policymaking establishment certainly lost little time in pouncing on Google's partial withdrawal from China.[3] Google's announcement was followed almost at once by an outpouring of fawning publicity.[4] Nicholas D. Kristof set the tone: "Google's decision to stand up to Chinese cyberoppression [is] positively breathtaking." The *New York Times* later editorialized that "Google's decision to stop censoring its search service in China was a principled and brave decision."[5] Secretary of State Clinton's widely publicized "internet freedom" speech came eleven days after Google's announcement.[6]

A right to freedom of expression is fundamental to democratic self-determination, at both the societal and individual levels—and too many have suffered and perished in struggling to actualize this right for it to be compromised or traded on. Rebecca MacKinnon has justly criticized the concept of "internet freedom" for offering a mélange of confused and conflicting meanings: from an open internet architecture, to citizens' use of the internet as an aid to win freedom from political domination, to noninterference by governments in the internet's networks and platforms, to an unhindered ability to connect to the internet.[7] However, what if this confusion of meanings was deliberate? What if official U.S. declarations of support for "internet freedom" invoked an admirable ideal in order to pursue calculatingly manipulative ends?

The United States' deployment of human rights rhetoric as a lever of its foreign policy actually possesses a long history. A recent treatise explains that, as the United States became an imperial power—at the latest, by the end of the nineteenth century—the spread of American constitutional forms and practices often paradoxically became a matter of compulsion instead of popular determination to adopt the U.S. political model: "The United States resorted to force to compel peoples in its colonies, protectorates, and conquered lands to follow its constitutional lead."[8] Within this wider context, the free-flow-of-information doctrine became a durable weapon of U.S. foreign policy beginning early in the twentieth century and emerged as a linchpin of policy during the period of decolonization and cold war that followed World War II.[9]

"Free flow" paints hard-edged economic and strategic interests in an appealing, but misleading, language of universal human rights. Google, a profit-seeking corporation, was transposed in U.S. discourse into a principled freedom-fighter taking action against an authoritarian state. The same rhetoric became more full-throated the next year, when, contrary to U.S. intelligence agency predictions,[10] opposition movements toppled dictators in Tunisia, then Egypt—and used mobile phones, alongside Facebook and Twitter, to help coordinate their protests. Now these digital services garnered a government-sanctioned advertisement as U.S. officials singled them out as supposed stand-ins for the complex and sometimes longstanding social movements that actually undertook these intended democratic revolutions.[11]

Free-flow doctrine had recurrently served U.S. interests, but its importance both altered and grew as transnationally networked commodity chains extended from a limited media-industry base to the political economy at large.

At the same time, the rhetoric was repeatedly modernized so that it could be put to effective service in altering historical circumstances.

Throughout the early postwar decades, free-flow rhetoric had been directed at the newly independent states emerging from decaying European empires and, on the other hand, at the Soviet Union and other Communist states. At this, the high-water mark of U.S. global power and prestige, the Executive Branch deliberately conflated democratic self-determination with the U.S. model of capitalist development. The effort was initially to provide a seeming justification for U.S. news agencies to gain access to what had been closed foreign markets, but now it expanded to encompass media companies' efforts to drench the world in exported American cultural commodities—not only news but also TV programs, musical recordings, and films.[12] Behind these media companies was U.S. foreign direct investment, typically including a phalanx of corporate advertisers waving a narcissistic model of consumer capitalism for which the United States itself functioned as an international magnet. "Coca-Cola's long history," proclaimed its CEO on the occasion of Myanmar's opening to U.S. foreign investment in May 2012, "is richly intertwined with the history of American foreign policy."[13] Coke had made its first entrance into Asia in 1912, moving into the Philippines scarcely more than one decade after the Philippines was taken over by the United States as a spoils of war. Coke had bought into China in 1927 but departed in 1949, when the Chinese Revolution expelled most foreign businesses; when President Carter reestablished full relations with China in 1979, however, Coke "immediately sent 20,000 cases of the soft drink from Hong Kong to the mainland."[14] Today, many refer to this as "soft power."[15]

During the late 1970s and early 1980s, the functions of free-flow rhetoric again had been extended and enlarged. The doctrine continued to be deployed to justify U.S. cultural exports; but now it also came to be applied to what were termed "transborder data flows." As we saw in part I, networked commodity chains were being rapidly forged and extended; their ability to operate was in part a function of streams of business process data. Unduly forgotten are the fierce debates that accompanied—and, for a time, threatened to constrain—corporate deployments of computer communications to convey these cataracts of data with scant accountability to national jurisdictions.[16] Echoes of these debates sometimes sounded later on, for example, in the "data protection" legislation of European and some other states. The controversy over transborder data flows pertained to, at most, a couple of thousand networks, but its resolution—in favor of transnational capital over democratic accountability—made it feasible to accelerate and extend the corporate reorganization of transnational commodity chains.

Additional decades have passed, and the internet bespeaks a further stage in this evolution. The internet is built around numerous "autonomous systems": networks operated by wholesale and retail internet service providers, and corporate and other organizational users. We have seen how transnational companies' dependence on network systems and applications now possesses critical minute-to-minute importance for the conduct of planetary business operations and markets. This, however, denotes not only an end point but also a new frontier of accumulation. As Kitchin and Dodge explain, software is coming to condition everyday life across multiplying contexts, as air travel, consumption, homes, and other spaces are reorganized around "functionalities" controlled by what is typically remotely stored code.[17] The boundaries of this political economy—this digital capitalism—thus continue to be pushed back. Increasingly a target, as mentioned in part II, is a so-called "internet of things," wherein corporate network systems and applications are made to control an enlarged array of functions and objects, and machine-to-machine interactions pervade daily routine. As Kitchin and Dodge detail, software "is imbuing everyday objects, such as domestic appliances, handheld tools, sporting equipment, medical devices, recreational gadgets, and children's toys, with capacities that allow them to do additional and new types of work."[18] Again, however, these are often not stand-alone objects but network-enabled devices reliant on exchanges of data with remote servers.

The free-flow doctrine has in turn reemerged, as a superordinate imperative, aiming to protect not just a specific industry or a fledgling set of business processes but the entirety of the networked commodity chains that operate today's restructured transnational capitalism.

And, perhaps, tomorrow's—if U.S. tech companies' ambitions for cloud computing are realized. Visions of cloud computing are not new; what was called "time sharing" during the 1960s and 1970s was an early version of what is today called cloud computing. More recently, however, moves to store data and applications alike on centralized server farms—data centers—took growing hold. The chairman of the FCC, citing a private consultancy's data in March 2011, stated that cloud computing was already a $68 billion global industry, and growing at an impressive 17 percent annually. "With its ability to enable collaboration in ways no other technology has before," observed FCC Chairman Genachowski, cloud computing is likely to generate "new markets and new businesses" in "health care, education, and energy."[19] At the forefront of this trend, we saw in part 2, were big U.S. internet intermediaries, including Amazon, Microsoft, IBM, Apple, Facebook, and Google (which operated more than thirty data centers by 2011).[20]

The extraterritorial internet's broadening functions for transnational business therefore again heightened the importance of free-flow policy. Innumerable profit projects, actual and prospective, were predicated on the unrestricted cross-border movement of data. iTunes furnishes a familiar example because it serves the consumer market, but "software as a service" forays into the business market were no less portentous.

The technological frontiers of this commodification campaign required not only a stout defense but an assertive offense as well. Genachowski took care to emphasize that "protectionist" policies, notably, "rigid, in-country data center requirements" inhibiting the flow of data across the borders of states, would "undercut the efficiency and cost savings offered by cloud computing."[21] Such restrictions, he and other policymakers held, needed to be rolled back.

As often, developments in the U.S. domestic political economy had positioned big corporations to take this fight forward—in this instance, legally sanctioned ones. Under U.S. law, corporations had long since contrived to gain the legal status of "persons." Since the 1970s, however, corporate "rights" specifically to First Amendment protection had been expanded as a consequence of aggressive campaigns.[22] Indeed in 2010, around when the Google vs. China stand-off hit the news, a Supreme Court ruling in the Citizens United case held that companies possessed a right under the First Amendment to spend unlimited sums of money in candidate elections.[23] Early the next year, AT&T made a bid before the Supreme Court to claim (unsuccessfully, it turned out) that corporations possessed not only rights to freedom of expression but also to personal privacy.[24] This was the domestic climate within which Secretary of State Hillary Clinton seized the initiative, scarcely two weeks after Google's announced withdrawal from China, to iterate a high-profile discourse of "internet freedom."

The issue was not that China—or, indeed, "networked authoritarians" generally—operated technologically sophisticated and all-too-effective systems of censorship.[25] It was that it served U.S. official purposes to blur the distinction between individual persons' human rights and transnational corporations' networked commodity chains. The signature of Clinton's much-publicized speech was her attempt to equate the activities of this private company with democratic self-determination. "We stand for a single internet where all of humanity has equal access to knowledge and ideas," she declared, placing "internet freedom" shamelessly within a historical legacy that included both Franklin Roosevelt's "Four Freedoms" speech of 1941 and Eleanor Roosevelt's initiative on behalf of the Universal Declaration of Human Rights after World War II.[26]

Secretary Clinton went on to specify that individuals worldwide should possess a "freedom to connect—the idea that governments should not prevent people from connecting to the internet, to websites, or to each other."[27] This "freedom to connect" should overarch state policies and national jurisdictions; and it appeared to set U.S. policy unabashedly on the side of democracy and human rights, cut free of strategic interests and corporate profit strategies. This rhetoric lodged deeply in U.S. policy discourse. The next year, the president himself turned to lead the choir, announcing that "assuring the free flow of information" was "essential to American and global economic prosperity ... and the promotion of universal rights."[28]

State Department internet policy had departed from the simpleminded effusions of those who, throughout the 1990s, had sought to endow the internet with an all-but-immanent power to emancipate humanity from its travails. "These technologies are not an unmitigated blessing," Clinton cautioned. "Modern information networks and the technologies they support can be harnessed for good or for ill.... technologies with the potential to open up access to government and promote transparency can also be hijacked by governments to crush dissent and deny human rights."[29] She elaborated by revisiting her talismanic theme: "Some countries have erected electronic barriers that prevent their people from accessing portions of the world's networks. They've expunged words, names, and phrases from search engine results. They have violated the privacy of citizens who engage in non-violent political speech."[30] All true; all a matter for concern; and, again, all fodder for a calculating U.S. policy. That the United States was different—freer, *better*—was an assumption so deeply naturalized as to remain unstated.

Secretary Clinton proposed that "internet freedom" played an essential part not only in winning political freedom but also in engendering economic uplift. The secretary framed the economic promise of networks in terms not of transnational corporate commodity chains, however, but of bootstrapping sub-Saharan women entrepreneurs accessing microcredit loans and Bangledeshi mobile-phone users learning English. Recalling the arrogant ethnocentric arguments advanced half a century before by Cold War adherents of commercial mass media as tools of development (notably, in this instance, those of Daniel Lerner), Secretary Clinton declared that "a connection to global information networks is like an on-ramp to modernity."[31]

The State Department organized a "Global Internet Freedom Task Force" to be a public centerpiece for its campaign. "We are urging U.S. media companies," Secretary Clinton added, "to take a proactive role in challenging foreign governments' demands for censorship and surveillance."[32] This straightforwardly asserted that, whatever had transpired between the Executive Branch and Google with respect to its search service in China, henceforward the Government would expressly coordinate internet policy with forward units of U.S. capital.

Secretary Clinton revisited the same theme in another high-profile speech in 2011. This time, again without hint of embarrassment, she incorporated into the U.S. platform for networks the nation of Egypt, whose people had just managed to overthrow a dictator who had been backed for decades by the United States. Asserting that "millions worldwide" had responded to the Egyptians' demonstrations "in real time"—as if the online communication itself had somehow engendered the fall of the corrupt and authoritarian Mubarak—Clinton went on imperturbably to declare that the U.S. administration counted itself among those who had answered the Egyptians' call: "You are not alone and we are with you."[33] We may assume that the people of Egypt were not, by and large, taken in; and the United States did not find economic resources sufficient for it to purchase the immediate results that it preferred;[34] but "freedom to connect" served a purpose—and an audience—that went much beyond Egypt.

Secretary Clinton underlined that the United States would push back against those who, for whatever reason, rejected the U.S. program for the extraterritorial internet, observing in connection with "states, terrorists, and those who would act as their proxies," that "those who disrupt the free flow of information in our society *or any other* pose a threat to our economy"; the United States "will protect our networks."[35] (In fact, the State Department had already escalated to an action plan for supporting circumvention technologies under President George W. Bush.[36]) Clinton added, "Monitoring and responding to threats to internet freedom has become part of the daily work of our diplomats and development experts. They are working to advance internet freedom on the ground at our embassies and missions around the world. The United States continues to help people in oppressive internet environments get around filters, stay one step ahead of the censors, the hackers, and the thugs who beat them up or imprison them for what they say online."[37] Here, and through related initiatives,[38] the United States moved beyond rhetoric.

Clinton boasted that the State Department had committed tens of millions of dollars "to support a burgeoning group of technologists and activists" in a multifaceted campaign against "internet repression."[39] She did not choose to mention that this campaign explicitly transgressed on national sovereignty— as was exposed by veteran journalists James Glanz and John Markoff, in June 2011. In an initiative reminiscent of some of the covert programs mounted by the Eisenhower administration during the height of the Cold War, Glanz and Markoff found that "the Obama administration is leading a global effort to deploy 'shadow' Internet and mobile phone systems that dissidents can use to undermine repressive governments that seek to silence them by censoring or shutting down telecommunications networks." Beyond circumvention software, which the United States continued to help install in varied contexts, "secretive projects" to innovate and deploy "stealth wireless networks" were underway in Afghanistan, North Korea, and, the journalists hinted, elsewhere. Buried in their article, Glanz and Markoff connected some of the dots: "Mrs. Clinton has made Internet freedom into a signature cause. But the State Department has carefully framed its support as promoting free speech and human rights for their own sake, not as a policy aimed at destabilizing autocratic governments."[40] Even this conclusion was incomplete: it omitted to mention the resurgent economic function of the doctrine of internet freedom.

The rhetorical firepower that the United States devoted to "internet freedom" was far in excess of a mere attempt to align U.S. foreign policy with the strategic interests of any single corporation. The seeming fusion between Google and the U.S. state, however, served overarching strategic interests, and so it continued to claim some of the limelight. President Obama told one of his aides as the Egyptian Revolution unfolded early in 2011: "What I want is for . . . that Google guy to be president." He was referring to Wael Ghonim, a Google marketing executive, who had organized the Facebook group ("We Are All Khaled Said"—after a victim of the Mubarak police) that had helped in coordinating some of Egypt's biggest protests.[41] For its part, Google continually trumpeted its alignment with civil society and human rights, and drew upon and gave financial support to organizations ostensibly committed to human rights. A shadowy network of such organizations was cultivated, staffed by a mix of principled, benighted, and complicit activists and academics. Google Ideas director Jared Cohen was exemplary of the ties established to bind NGOs, foundations, Ivy League universities, government agencies, internet companies, and capital in general.[42] A Stanford graduate and later a co-author with Google CEO Eric Schmidt, Jared Cohen went on to serve on the Policy Planning Staff under Secretary of State Condoleezza Rice in 2006, before transferring to her successor Hillary Clinton. Rice wrote of Cohen that "he would use his position at Policy Planning to begin to integrate social media into our diplomatic toolkit. That would pay off handsomely some years later, when Twitter and Facebook became accelerants of democratic change in the Middle East."[43] Cohen continued to sound the theme that "connectivity benefits everyone."[44] In late 2013, now attempting to repair the damage to its reputation inflicted by the Snowden revelations—of which more below—Google Ideas under Cohen released software that it boasted would promote free expression by enabling citizens under some regimes to evade government censorship and surveillance. (It was symptomatic that this software worked for the Firefox and Google Chrome browsers but not for Microsoft's Internet Explorer.)[45]

Policy continued to link U.S. state and corporate actors in what seemed an effortless unity. This ventriloquism came through on July 4, 2012, when Google's search site invited users to take action to support internet freedom. Susan Molinari, Google's vice president of public policy and government affairs for the Americas, declared on the company's blog, "We've only just begun to see what a free and open Internet can do for people and for the freedom we cherish."

State Department rhetoric resonated widely, including among other U.S. Executive Branch agencies enrolled in the fight—for it was and is a fight—to project power through cyberspace. Their shared primary goal was to keep corporate data flows streaming without restriction as new profit sites were established around an extraterritorial internet managed by the United States.

CHAPTER 12

Taking Care of Business

The Internet at the
U.S. Commerce Department

A displacement of U.S. policy authority had been effected around the internet's emergence. The Federal Communications Commission, an independent federal regulatory agency established during the New Deal, had overseen nongovernmental network system development beginning in 1934. A series of FCC decisions during the 1960s and 1970s was fundamental to the commercial rollout of packet switching services, and indeed to the commercialization of the internet during the 1990s. To accelerate and widen the deployment of computer communications on the terms demanded by corporations and trade associations, however, the FCC had paradoxically relinquished much of its own jurisdiction.[1] When the internet was spun off by U.S. military agencies and began to converge on the core of the U.S. network infrastructure, the FCC's earlier abdication smoothed the way for the Executive Branch to assume a management role.

The Federal Communications Commission, with its New Deal congressional mandate, subsequently revisited the question of whether to regulate internet connectivity as a communications service from a much-weakened position.[2] Meanwhile, however, the National Telecommunications and Information Administration (NTIA)—which had been established by the Nixon administration to operate with far less democratic accountability than the FCC and which had been accorded a mandate for internet oversight by President Bill Clinton's advisor Ira Magaziner—operated as a locus of internet policymaking. Internet enthusiasts favored a thumping rhetoric of democratic transparency in reference to other states and their transgressions; but the United States itself flouted such precepts in its own regulatory mechanism. A government agency vested with considerable power over internet policy was thickly insulated against principles of accountability and popular rule. That internet policymaking came to lodge in the *Commerce* Department, however, rather than some other Executive Department, was also a testimony to the continued ascent of the accumulation function in the wake of the 1970s crisis.

The NTIA was not the sole unit of the Commerce Department to be charged with a role in respect to cyberspace. Commerce established an intradepartmental Internet Policy Task Force during the first year of the incoming Obama administration, declaring that it hoped thereby to "jumpstart our engine of innovation."[3] Staffed by members of several different Commerce Department agencies, the Internet Policy Task Force was accorded a far-ranging mandate and reported directly to the top—the Secretary of Commerce. One of the Task Force's first orders of business was to launch its own inquiry into "the global free flow of information on the Internet."[4]

Economics rather than political freedom was accorded priority, and the Task Force trumpeted a connection with the 2008 "Seoul Declaration on the Future of the Internet Economy." This conferred on its inquiry an appearance of international comity, for the Seoul Declaration, sponsored by the OECD and endorsed by thirty-nine governments and the European Community, had called for governments to "maintain an open environment that supports the free flow of information, research, innovation, entrepreneurship and business transformation."[5] The Commerce Department endorsed this position, and portrayed unrestricted data flows as a component of the economic recovery program from the slump: "The ability to freely and efficiently distribute information on the Internet is at the very core of modern consumer, business, political, and educational activity. Between 1999 and 2007, the United States economy enjoyed an increase of over 500 percent in business-to-consumer online commerce."[6] These benefits, exclaimed the department, had "increased even during the economic downturn" as, during 2008, "sales by the top 100 online retailers grew 14.3 percent" as contrasted to a 0.9 percent decline in total retail sales over that interval.[7]

The inquiry's purpose was "to identify and examine the impact that restrictions on the flow of information over the Internet have on American businesses and global commerce."[8] This was a sweeping warrant. Everything from prohibitions on pornography and on intellectual property infringement to government filters and lack of transparency—from consumer protections to authoritarian impositions—now might be passed through the prism of economic policy.

Nor was it sufficient simply to inventory existing challenges. Of commanding importance was the question of how to craft effective policy for emerging network technology and the commodities it would be used to circulate: How, the department specified, were prospective constraints on the internet likely to impinge on cloud computing?

Commodification strategies based in part on data centers actually supplied a primary entry point for the proceeding:

> The rise of globally accessible cloud computing services—everything from Web-based mail and office productivity suites, to more general purpose computing, storage and communications services available through the cloud—raises a new set of questions regarding local restrictions that countries may impose on services accessible, though not physically located, in their country. Cloud services realize economies of scale and redundancy through flexible location of user data and processing capability. Internet users, in many circumstances, have no knowledge of or control over the precise location of the services they are receiving or the physical location of their data in cloud environments.[9]

An added advantage, though unmentioned here, was that cloud services lent themselves to what we now know were far-ranging U.S. international electronic surveillance programs.

A brief review of the move to cloud computing services helps explain why these were granted prominence in the Commerce Department's free-flow inquiry.

Tradeoffs are practicable, between services and applications stored directly on devices, such as PCs and e-book readers, and those stored instead on an affiliated network. This is not, in itself, a new trend. Telephone directories were for decades outsized paper books kept for ready reference on a kitchen shelf—but telephone systems also employed directory assistance operators to provide callers with telephone numbers on request. Even after the self-service principle gained primacy, so that once-paid work was offloaded onto unpaid subscribers, callers still could choose to consult either a telephone directory or an electronic database accessed via a networked device of some kind. It was only after the digital depression struck that white pages directories finally began to be jettisoned.[10]

Capacious infrastructures and versatile mobile platforms could be combined to alter the architectural balance needed to provide services and applications. Software programs and applications continued to be sold discretely for users to load and download onto their computing devices; but, increasingly, both were being housed on vendors' Web-hosting sites and streamed on request. Broadband internet connections and multifunctional mobile devices accelerated internet intermediaries' schemes for cloud computing, which they pursued in order to recentralize service provision and to gain greater proprietary control.[11] Profit strategies based on cloud computing bid fair to alter internet commodity chains very extensively.

The economic interest that existed in cloud services was already pronounced. The Commerce Department understood that cloud computing was a name affixed to services provided by data centers, the largest of which might house up to one million square feet worth of server-arrays and related equipment.[12] These gigantic server farms fed not only real estate investment trusts such as Digital Realty, DuPont Fabros, and CoreSite; and not only IT suppliers such as Intel, Dell, IBM, EMC, Seagate, and Hewlett-Packard; but also the companies that built their energy-intensive power systems, such as Emerson Electric and Eaton.[13] Revenue garnered by commercial data-center operators in North America was projected to reach $8.1 billion in 2011, up from $5.7 billion in 2009—impressive growth during a deep slump.[14] Cloud service providers also relied on great quantities of hard-drive-based storage, which is why they experienced a momentary setback when Seagate factories in Thailand flooded.[15]

The economic interest in cloud computing, we will see, extended beyond individual users to businesses and governments. Amazon Web Services (AWS) catered to twenty federal agencies in 2010, after the General Services Administration certified it as a prospective supplier to government departments—and Amazon crowed that this market was "one of our fastest growing customer segments."[16] The federal government followed up by extending outsourcing contracts to Google's and Microsoft's cloud services as well.[17] These huge warehouses full of servers also supported activities throughout every business and financial sector. AWS counted Eli Lilly, Pfizer, Adobe Systems, and Netflix among its customers.[18] Microsoft, which advertised its "Windows Azure" software for developing applications to run in Microsoft's data centers, claimed 3M and the Associated Press. [19]

Data centers were constructed not only by real estate investment trusts (for rental to content and service providers) but also directly by internet companies: not only Google, Apple, Microsoft, Amazon, and Facebook, but also Lockheed Martin, Rackspace, Verizon, and IBM. Akamai participated by building a popular "content delivery network" in order to improve the performance of cloud services. Google placed a dozen or so data centers strategically around the United States and the world. ShinJoung Yeo finds that Google's multibillion-dollar investment in building and interconnecting these massive facilities rendered it one of the largest elements in the global internet infrastructure.[20] Amazon was a precocious builder of cloud facilities, and on a huge scale: the number of files stored in Amazon's data centers almost trebled during just one year, 2011, to 762 billion.[21] Some 300 million people were reportedly using Apple's iCloud every day in April 2013, up 20 percent just since January.[22]

The metaphors are strained, but big internet intermediaries were establishing beachheads in the cloud—aiming to construct more encompassing, general-purpose distribution channels and to develop new commodification strategies by applying computer processing power to new tasks. Consumer cloud services were mentioned in part II.[23] However, a consultancy estimated in 2009 that "business processes delivered as cloud services" constituted the largest segment of the overall market.[24] Crucially, moreover, U.S. providers led in purveying cloud services not just domestically but internationally; in fact, they dominated "every market segment."[25] Thirty years ago, I showed how self-organizing efforts by and among a diverse array of big businesses, from retailers to banks and from oil companies to manufacturers, had outflanked AT&T's monopoly over U.S. telecommunications, and induced the Federal Communications Commission to liberalize markets for network equipment and services in episodic steps.[26] The Commerce Department inquiry into free flow on the internet privileged a comparable grouping, as comments streamed in from individual corporations and trade associations. Taken together, these filings demonstrate the breadth of the capitalist interest on whose behalf the Executive Branch mobilized to engage what were identified as critical policy problems.

A key concern was to differentiate the focus of the Commerce Department proceeding from the nonproprietary, unlicensed data flows that continued to plague media content owners. "The Copyright Alliance," representing individual artists, unions, and a diverse array of corporations based in the United States and beyond—from ASCAP and DGA and the Church Music Publishers Association to MPAA, NASCAR, RIAA, and Reed Elsevier—strained to insist that "enforcement of copyright law does not impede the free flow of information but in fact facilitates that flow . . . dramatic innovation occurring in the production and distribution of copyrighted works is tied directly to the maintenance and future assurance of an online marketplace for such works."[27] Truly free culture—works circulating beyond and apart from the commodity form—warranted no place in this proceeding. "It is critical," specified the Copyright Alliance, "that policymakers emphasize that the free flow of information is not equated with a flow of copyrighted works severed from the ownership rights attached to them."[28]

The Global Intellectual Property Center, established by the U.S. Chamber of Commerce to synthesize the interests of its membership in this field, adopted a shriller tone: "Infringing content is not protected speech. Information that flows as an integral part of enterprises that fraudulently hawk counterfeit goods, or that traffic in pirated copyrighted materials, ought to be considered *mis*information, not comparable to other information that flows on the Internet, and sound public policy should not treat them the same."[29] More graceful, but no less ardent, was the comment by the Motion Picture Association of America—which had had plenty of practice, as an exponent of free-flow measures going back to the aftermath of the Second World War: "Enforcing the rule of law online to enforce intellectual property rights must not be confused with restricting the freedom of expression or restricting the flow of information." Anticipating a French policy counterthrust three years later, MPAA likened so-called "cultural exceptions"—efforts to withdraw cultural practices like film and music from trade agreements and commercial mechanisms—to sheer theft. Both inhibited market development around online distribution and, like other policies enacted by countries attempting to monitor and shape the flow of cultural commodities into their national audiovisual space, MPAA insisted, they should be kept to an absolute minimum.[30]

Agreeing with the bizarre, but in this proceeding nearly universal, precept that intellectual property restrictions actually *aid* the free flow of information, the United States Council for International Business's comment demonstrated that this was not a narrowly parochial concern voiced by media companies alone. USCIB members "include top U.S.-based global companies and professional services firms from every sector of our economy, with operations in every region of the globe." It expressed an avowed "user orientation." It sought to elicit U.S. government aid in helping to counter "restrictions on collecting, using or transferring personal information, encryption regulations, restrictions on location or sensor-based information, quotas on digital content, among others." It targeted limits on the use of voice over IP applications—a seemingly compelling argument for a widening attempt to repel state polices aiming to "preclude companies from gaining the economies and efficiencies of global platforms." Rules limiting foreign-direct investment in telecommunications and related ICT sectors needed to be relaxed or removed. Finally, and crucially, service providers must not be compelled to store or process data in-country, "effectively requiring local investment and placing data under local jurisdictions."[31]

TechAmerica likewise generalized these issues to a great swath of capital. TechAmerica represented approximately twelve hundred member companies; it had been formed by a merger of the American Electronics Association, the Cyber Security Industry Alliance, the Information Technology Association of America, and the Government Electronics and Information Technology Association. Declaring that "the U.S. is the undisputed leader in the creation, deployment, and use of information networks," TechAmerica then added a curiously phrased assertion: "the U.S. is on the forefront of thought leadership and public policy development in the areas that touch the Internet and electronic commerce."[32] TechAmerica, however, pointed up a significant tension in U.S. free-flow policy. Calls by the Federal Bureau of Investigation to expand the Communications Assistance for Law Enforcement Act by requiring that all communications services be rendered transparent to and capable of interception by U.S. law enforcement agencies might induce other countries to "see such regulatory authority in the U.S. as a model for their own regime—either just as, or even more onerous for cost and concerning civil liberties." In short, interestingly, TechAmerica urged that policies should be fostered "that enable free flow of information here at home."[33] The obvious target of these comments, and of others (below) was draft U.S. legislation, which would have subjected internet intermediaries to draconian controls; through the years-long struggles that followed, bills continued to be beaten back only to be raised again in fresh guise.[34] In view of subsequent news reports about National Security Agency surveillance of internet traffic, however, such comments offer food for thought about whether a carefully camouflaged debate was already occurring between Executive Branch agencies and internet intermediaries.[35]

TechAmerica expressly singled out a need to safeguard cloud services. "As cloud computing continues to grow, so, too, will the amount of data crossing national borders. If divergent claims to jurisdiction over user content remain, then it becomes quite difficult for providers to manage their legal obligations and their global technology operations while at the same time protect their customers."[36] This issue threatened to extend to the very interoperability of the internet: "In order to preserve the functioning of the Internet in a global fashion," the group underscored, "there is a need for a single authoritative root that includes the resolvability of all top-level domain names."[37] The reference was to the function of assigning each and every Web site an unambiguous and unique identifier. Just such an authoritative address book for the internet was maintained and managed by a U.S. agency called the Internet Assigned Numbers Authority. We will see below that its function constituted not only a vital point of power but also a flashpoint of opposition to power's exercise.

Broadening the compass of the proceeding still further was the Business Software Alliance, whose members included Adobe, Apple, Cisco, Dell, H-P, IBM, Intel, McAfee, Microsoft, Siemens, Sybase, and Symantec. The alliance declared itself "the voice of the world's commercial software industry and its hardware partners . . . working in 80 countries to expand software markets." Stressing that its constituents "represent one of the fastest growing industries in the world," BSA emphasized that the software industry had generated a $37 billion surplus for the U.S. balance of payments in 2009.[38] BSA added its voice to the argument that strong claims to private property in information had been, and remained, essential for the space of flows—"The success of the Internet is built on a foundation of intellectual property rights"—and, in support of this self-serving assertion, quoted an infamous and historically dubious U.S. Supreme Court decision of 1985: "The Framers intended copyright itself to be the engine of free expression."[39]

BSA again expressed a demand to carry forward free-flow precepts to accommodate the ongoing reconfiguration of networking technology: "As the software industry moves increasingly to a cloud computing model, where software and IT functionality is delivered to customers over the Internet, the imperative to reduce barriers to cross-border data flows becomes clear. A key element of the economics of cloud computing is the unrestrained ability to move data and workloads wherever the computing resources to service them are available." BSA elaborated on this strategic point:

> Cloud computing, which represents the next generation of computing, relies on the free flow of information. . . . Government officials increasingly are becoming aware of the barriers to cloud computing presented by the varying international frameworks on data transmission. The United States, European Union and the Asia-Pacific Economic Cooperation each are working separately on various, and often conflicting, privacy and data regulatory frameworks. By harmonizing a framework for cross-border data flows, government could clear the way for the further development of the online marketplace of ideas in the cloud.[40]

By the same token, should it become more difficult for some reason to harmonize such a cross-border framework, the commercial promise of cloud services might be jeopardized.

In its individual submission, Microsoft worked to explicate the issues that it thought should be put foremost by the Commerce Department: "Unprecedented investments in data centers and other computing infrastructure, as well as increasingly ubiquitous broadband networks, have enabled the era of cloud computing in which sophisticated applications and services are provided to consumers and businesses remotely over the Internet. Yet only with the free flow of information and data can these investments bring about their full potential." The software giant specified that the threat stemmed from three distinct kinds of restrictions: censorship "and other direct limitations on content and services within a jurisdiction, limitations on data transfer to other jurisdictions, and broad assertions of jurisdiction over remote data."[41]

In regard to censorship, Microsoft had become a co-founder of the Global Network Initiative and (without mentioning the Secretary of State's use of this term) expressed its support for "internet freedom." The software company warned that it undertook "to identify circumstances where freedom of expression and privacy may be jeopardized" as it entered new markets; "If the country assessment reveals high levels of risk, it may be necessary to limit the services offered in that country or reconsider our plans to invest."[42] Turning to limitations on data transfer, Microsoft suggested that, by inhibiting the export of data, "privacy and data security policies created by governments" were cramping business. The European Union Data Protection Directive seemed to Microsoft less onerous than kindred initiatives: "Some jurisdictions go further than the EU and impose near-complete bans on the export of certain types of data"—for example, the Canadian provinces of Nova Scotia and British Columbia. In other countries, public-sector procurement contracts "frequently mandate that data be stored locally." Summing up this second area of complaint, Microsoft explained that "there is a patchwork quilt of data protection requirements across the globe—resulting in increased economic burdens, greater compliance costs, and reduced incentives to invest for companies that operate globally." As a result, "the provider may be forced to store the data locally in the jurisdiction that imposes the export restriction, thereby eliminating one of the key efficiencies inherent in cloud computing."[43] Again, a prospective threat to maximally profitable cloud services was identified.

"Uncertainty about the extent of governments' reach" in fact posed a third serious type of obstruction to Microsoft's cloud. Some countries asserted that only the country where data was stored possessed legal jurisdiction. Others claimed jurisdiction if a specific service was offered there "or if the user associated with the data resides there." Still others staked a claim to jurisdiction "on the basis that the computing service provider has a place of business in the country." This "unpredictability of jurisdictional reach" harbored the potential of depressing markets for cloud computing "as users concerned about their data being accessed by foreign governments or otherwise governed by foreign laws may hesitate to adopt online services at all." Microsoft added, with studied vagueness, that "potential cloud users overseas also have expressed concerns about having their data stored in the United States, due to a perception that the U.S. government can freely access their information under the Patriot Act."[44] This concern would prove prescient, as the stakes were raised dramatically as a result of exposures of NSA surveillance programs.

Government, declared Microsoft, had a crucial role to play because "the private sector alone cannot resolve the problems created by inconsistent legal frameworks for data," and these problems "will only grow as cloud computing becomes more popular." Intergovernmental collaboration was essential. "A common approach on both sides of the Atlantic to promoting a globally har-monized framework," Microsoft urged, "could also serve as a model for future negotiations in Asia and elsewhere."[45] The reference here was to wide-ranging trade agreements, efforts at which were ongoing between the United States and trading partners across the Atlantic and Pacific Oceans, respectively.[46]

Google, basking in the glow cast by its recent standoff with China, portrayed the Commerce Department's proceeding in smugly self-serving terms: "Pro-tecting and promoting the flow of information and free expression are core Google values."[47] Implementation of efforts to further the free flow and to resist regulations "that hamper and Balkanize the Internet"—which Google cast as inimical to economic growth and job creation—should spur "a multi-pronged governmental strategy." Unfair or disruptive limits on the flow of information services should be catalogued and publicly highlighted. Governments that vio-lated existing trade rules should face "appropriate action." New international trade agreements—bilateral, regional, and multilateral—should be established to aid transparency and to ensure "that Internet intermediaries can function effectively." Because intergovernmental organizations "are slow-moving . . . and increasingly dominated by nations that not only block free expression but also favor companies that are government-controlled or owned by their citi-zens"—as if this were not true for the United States—implementing free-flow policies would require stepped-up coordination "with on-the-ground industry, non-governmental organizations, and academic entities that are best able to act on behalf of global Internet users."[48] Sidestepping the question of whether such organizations actually do operate on behalf of users, Google instead went on to identify its major target.

Attempting to showcase its adherence to high-minded principle, Google agreed that U.S. domestic policies themselves also might merit revision, aver-ring that "the U.S. is the birthplace of the Internet, and it must continue to set an example of responsible regulation that enables individuals and companies to enjoy and build on the many benefits of the free flow of digital information."[49] The company sought to cast opprobrium upon governments that "manipulate the Internet in favor of local firms"—as if, again, this somehow constituted a departure from U.S. practice. More than twenty governments, it complained, "have blocked some or all Google services, or demanded restrictive condi-tions for allowing their access within their borders." In its inventory of these adverse developments, Google drew liberally on the findings of the OpenNet Initiative, a partnership between researchers at leading universities in Canada, the United States, and England.[50] In China, notably, "numerous U.S. Internet services have been kept out or severely restricted, while Chinese versions of the same services have been permitted to operate, despite containing comparable levels of 'offensive content.'" Speaking on behalf of itself and of its rivals, Google quoted an article published in *Foreign Policy* to emphasize that Facebook, Twitter, Flickr, Blogger, and WordPress all were being burdened by this type of state-sanctioned import substitution.[51]

Google frankly positioned its own global commercial ambitions as a preferred policy pivot. As online traffic continued to grow, the world's internet users had become "a massive new consumer base for both Internet services like email and the hard goods and services that are increasingly advertised, marketed, or sold online."[52] Google's efforts to leverage this transnational consumer base placed it squarely among "large U.S. Internet corporations," which, according to a consultant's study, "earn about one-half their revenues outside the U.S." For Google, non-U.S. revenues represented 53 percent of its total in the first quarter of 2010, and "more than half of Google searches come from outside the U.S."[53] (These percentages remained comparable in 2013.[54])

Google portrayed its role as a broker of access to the internet as an expression of a transcendent interest. When governments restricted its functions, it declared, such actions "affect all of the business and individuals that use the site to communicate, trade, and advertise." In fact, it suggested, "the business disruption is particularly pronounced where a government interferes with a so-called Internet intermediary."[55] Such companies, Google itself notable among them, deserved a privileged place in executing free-flow policies because of their importance as enablers of the construction project that is digital capitalism.

Because other governments seemed to be acting to render the extraterritorial foundations of Google's online profit making less secure, the U.S. government should spring into action to negotiate "rules of the road" for the internet. In addition to ensuring a maximum of transparency by governments and abolishing licensing requirements for internet services, these rules should "ensure that services can be provided without local investment and infrastructure." The Korea-U.S. Free Trade Agreement, negotiated in 2007, contained language on cross-border information flows (Article 15.8) which, Google advised, should be rendered binding (rather than conditional), expanded to cover "all electronic information flows," and incorporated into other trade agreements.[56] Google likewise expressly rejected any grant of jurisdiction over rulemaking for the internet to intergovernmental organizations and agencies such as the UN-affiliated International Telecommunication Union—a point to which I will return.[57]

"It may be more cost-effective," chipped in the Entertainment Software Association—representing computer and video game publishers—"to operate a large server farm in one jurisdiction than another, or latency considerations may dictate locating certain processing functions closer to the consumer base." This "diffuse approach to information management," however, "may implicate the laws of multiple jurisdictions simultaneously." Video game publishers confronted disparate standards for "law enforcement access, data retention, data security, censorship, and national security, among other requirements." Giving vivid illustrations of collusive national regimes, ESA stressed that "the uncertainty created by a tangle of competing privacy and security regimes has the potential to hamper the growth of cloud computing services." ESA agreed with Google that redress lay both in implementing free trade agreements, notably, the agreements negotiated between the United States and Korea, Columbia, and Panama, and also in appealing to the precedent-setting commitments already made by members of the World Trade Organization under its General Agreement on Trade in Services—which "may already give cloud-based or Web-based services firms rights to operate abroad and access the Internet—either across borders, or through data centers or other corporate operations on the ground in a host country."[58]

Congruent concerns were aired by the Internet Commerce Coalition, a group of internet service providers, e-commerce companies, and trade associations that targeted "restrictions on collecting, using or transferring personal data, exporting certain products and services, encryption regulations, restrictions on the collection and use of location-based information, and limitations on the use of certain Internet applications, all of which impede global trade and investment."[59]

The Computer and Communications Industry Association voiced the consensus attained by its small and large member companies, companies that collectively employed more than six hundred thousand workers and generated annual revenues exceeding $200 billion. "When we discuss the global free flow of information over the Internet," CCIA emphasized, "there are potentially trillions of dollars of U.S. economic activity at stake." The overarching importance of expanding the free flow of information commodities should prompt the Executive Branch departments to undertake equally far-reaching initiatives. The U.S Trade Representative should bring trade cases based on allegations of information discrimination and internet censorship by trading partners, because "digital goods and services should be a central feature of our trade policy." Both the multilateral framework of the World Trade Organization and bilateral free-trade agreements should be reinvigorated.[60] In the face of transgressions by forty-odd countries—CCIA singled out Iran, China, and Turkey—the State Department should expand its financial support to the Global Network Initiative and similar "censorship technology circumvention projects" in "internet restricting countries."[61]

Hinting that the Commerce Department perhaps was responding to ex parte concerns expressed by U.S. networking companies, CCIA mentioned that "there is an ad hoc group of U.S. hardware, software and services companies that meets in Washington to discuss many of the issues posed in this notice."[62] The advice imparted by this trade group hinted that seemingly distinct stakeholders might be forging a delicate coalition in regard to internet governance issues: "To be effective in this space, any multi-stakeholder organization must have a very broad mission such as 'Global Internet Freedom' and include representation from multinationals in the corporate sector, non-commercial NGOs, and expert academics. The multi-stakeholder organization cannot be dominated by a few nation states, as none should be members. But it's also important that companies or NGOs from the same country or even the same hemisphere not dominate the multi-stakeholder organization."[63] That this proposal actually hoped to extend already-ingrained global power disparities becomes evident, however, when we add that the major existing organizations for internet management were disproportionately staffed by representatives from companies based in the OECD countries and, in particular, from the United States.

Finally, CCIA again picked up the theme offered by TechAmerica, Google, and Microsoft, in framing its conclusion: "We must recognize that Internet freedom starts at home. We must discourage censorship; surveillance; and content blocking, prioritizing, or de-prioritizing whenever possible. If unavoidable, such actions must be time-limited, narrowly tailored, and undertaken in an open and transparent process. Finally, we must eschew attempts to deputize online intermediaries into law enforcement. If the United States cannot maintain a free and open Internet, it is unlikely for [sic] other nations will do so."[64] In view of subsequent exposures concerning U.S. bulk surveillance of different populations of internet users,[65] it is tempting to think that these assertions were coded attempts to revise U.S. government policy before such potentially destabilizing exposures might be made.

Verizon asserted that it had invested "tens of billions of dollars" to supply global IP services covering 159 countries to 98 percent of Fortune 1000 businesses. It then declared that "the U.S. government's international advocacy should continue to promote a single, global, interoperable Internet that is free of government restrictions that interfere with the ability of informed consumers to drive continued development of services and content." Whether consumers actually were "informed" may be seriously questioned. Verizon, however, drove on to reiterate that "myriad different policies and national operating requirements" and "country-specific" complexities of varied kinds "threaten to fragment the global Internet and can slow—and even prevent—the international deployment of important IP services." Examples included voice over internet protocol (VoIP), and open-source development projects, as well as "public, private, and hybrid cloud computing services" such as those Verizon was rolling out from its own data centers. The impetus to fragmentation posed a threat not only to Verizon's profit strategy, therefore, but—as other internet intermediaries had argued—also to those of its transnational enterprise customers, who "demand a uniform set of integrated services from a single supplier."[66]

Verizon stoutly rejected the idea that the internet should be subjected to "the legacy regulatory paradigms of the 20th Century copper telephone industry" and sought to resist efforts by scores of countries to ban or constrain VoIP applications.[67] At the time, these included the United States, where state public utility commissions and the FCC (which still was pursuing its weak-kneed plan for Net Neutrality) were fumbling in the dark.[68] The world's second-largest network operator then added that "consumer protection rules and obligations should not apply to cross-border services rendered by operators with a focus on business customers."[69] Verizon prided itself, it declared, on its formal commitment "to promoting the human rights values embedded in its Commitment and Values and Code of Conduct."[70] What further demonstration of virtue could be needed?

eBay and its PayPal subsidiary operated trading platforms in twenty-three countries and claimed more than 93 million active users globally; including its other specialized marketplaces, such as StubHub for tickets and classified advertising sites, eBay possessed a presence in more than one thousand cities. eBay framed its intervention before the Commerce Department as a broad-based effort to ensure "that consumer and small business empowerment should be a driving principle of the United States government." Consumer sovereignty thus became a battering ram used to drive forward the corporate interests of U.S. internet intermediaries—eBay's, in particular: "eBay strongly believes that every consumer, no matter where they reside, has the fundamental right to purchase any legal product or service at a fair and reasonable price." Already, 25 percent of all of the business on eBay "comes from cross border trade" and "we predict cross border trade will continue to become a greater share of the business." However, some manufacturers were adopting "anti-consumer" strategies "to resist the increased competition that e-commerce has brought to the retail market." Examples were prohibitions on distributors from selling products online, demands that e-merchants also operate brick-and-mortar stores, and predetermined minimum prices for manufacturers' goods. These "unfair and anti-competitive strategies" were likely to continue "without proper government guidance or intervention."[71]

Throughout this proceeding, policies to ensure unrestricted proprietary data flows constituted a sweepingly general demand on the part of transnational capital. Indeed, that an extraterritorial cyberspace had grown to prominence throughout the two prior decades is inexplicable, as we saw, without crediting U.S. transnational capital with an anchoring role. In turn, exactly whom the Department of Commerce represented in its free-flow proceeding merits question. Acknowledging that, in its role as an official agency of the U.S. state, the department accords routine priority to what it deems U.S. corporate interests, it should be added that a policy of unrestricted proprietary data flows applies to, and benefits, *both* U.S.- and non-U.S.-based units of transnational capital. *Both* rely on cross-border data flows and commodity chains. In and through its work in this proceeding, the U.S. Commerce Department sought to spearhead U.S. corporations but, in doing so, secondarily it also represented big capital *beyond* that fraction of it that happened to be headquartered in the United States. To this extent, even though perhaps unintentionally, the U.S. state was supporting a more generalized capitalist interest.

Additional qualifications are needed to clarify this formulation. Multifarious market factors reduce the capacity of competing transnational capitals to find and project a shared interest (and, as we saw in part 2, likewise of different units of U.S. capital[72]). So does the U.S. government's sometimes-glaring favoritism toward U.S. companies. The United States Trade Representative's preference for Apple over Samsung when, citing "policy reasons," it overturned a legal finding by the International Trade Commission for the first time since 1987, provides a noteworthy illustration.[73] Finally, as we will see herewith, the assumptions that infused existing strategies and structures of accumulation were not set in stone, while the coherence of the U.S. state itself also must not be overstated. Additional U.S. proceedings revealed that conflicts in setting a policy trajectory for the internet split through the U.S. power structure.

CHAPTER 13

Beyond a U.S.-centric Internet?

The geopolitics of today's internet are powerfully illuminated in a concurrent Commerce Department undertaking concerning the Domain Name System (DNS) that is used for internet communications. Undertaken and conducted as an extraterritorial projection of U.S. policymaking, this Executive Branch proceeding was extraordinary for transforming into a venue where other countries mounted a concerted diplomatic challenge to U.S. power. The resulting stalemate, furthermore, threatened to give way when, soon afterward, U.S. power over the DNS experienced a disruption as unexpected as it was severe.

The DNS was formalized in the 1980s (and further elaborated in 1994),[1] as the U.S. Defense Department agreed to split the early internet to form a walled-off military system and a more open civilian one. The DNS became the civilian internet's address book: it provides a convenient and human-friendly way of finding the address of a particular computer system. It enables users to access websites by way of domain names expressed in ordinary languages rather than through the numeric network server addresses (IP addresses) that are assigned to each device connected to the internet. (Unique assignments are no longer as prevalent, however, owing to widening reliance on Network Address Translation [NAT] and dynamic IP address assignments.) IP addresses are encoded in the specialized routers whose interoperation actually constitutes internet service. The DNS is both hierarchical, centrally coordinated and managed, and globally distributed. Specific servers maintain data needed to access their local domains and navigational data about how to process requests for information stored elsewhere. As the Department of Commerce explains, "The accuracy, integrity, and availability of the information supplied by the DNS are essential to the operation of most systems, services, or applications that use the Internet."[2]

The United States had, even prior to the formalization of the current management procedures for this system of identifiers, built up a multifaceted and still incompletely mapped control system over the internet. Participation in core technical standards development continued to be sustained by the internet's much-acclaimed voluntarism; but practice departed from ideal principle. The volunteers' work was coordinated by the Internet Engineering Task Force (established in 1979)—some of whose funding continued to come from the U.S. Defense Information Systems Agency—and the volunteers themselves were funded by their employers or sponsors. As late as 2007, eleven out of sixteen of the area directors who guided the IETF's work were American or employed by American-based organizations; most were "senior officials with major corporations or senior researchers at government or academic institutions."[3] This, in an understated assessment, "provides some protection of U.S. interests."[4] In addition, many of the volunteers who worked within the nonprofit U.S. corporation that was set up to house the DNS and to manage related network functions—which supposedly operated at arm's length from the U.S. government—were employees of such agencies as the U.S. National Institute of Standards and Technology, the Department of Commerce, the Department of Homeland Security, and the Department of Defense.[5] All told, in 2007, 71 percent of the IETF's 120 working group chairs were from the United States, while developing country representatives counted for 6 percent of the total; and 78 percent of these key technical experts were employed by private companies such as Cisco Systems: governments supplied 4 percent and NGOs 6 percent of the total.[6]

The mechanism of U.S. internet control over the DNS specifically was formalized after President Clinton directed the U.S. Commerce Department to privatize the DNS in 1997. Legal contracts were drawn up, binding the Department of Commerce to a for-profit corporation called VeriSign, and also to a private, not-for-profit corporation, the Internet Corporation for Assigned Names and Numbers (ICANN, established 1998). ICANN housed the vital Internet Assigned Numbers Authority (IANA), an agency designated since the internet's early days to manage the irreplaceable identifiers that form the "root" of the addressing system.[7] The Commerce Department contracted with ICANN to have it manage the so-called "IANA functions," which include assigning address space and processing requests for delegation of top-level domains. The Commerce Department approves any proposed change to the root zone-file before it is completed, however—at which point VeriSign enters the change on the master root-zone server on which it maintains the authoritative root-zone file and commences to distribute it across the internet through the thirteen registries that operate root-name servers.[8]

Through these contracts, the functions that enabled operation and development of an extraterritorial internet were institutionalized. These functions pertained not only to the allocation of internet numbering resources used all over the world but also to the administration and management of authoritative data for accessing top-level domains and related technical and policy matters.[9] Around these procedures, and the institutions devised to support them, what some political scientists call a global regime for "internet governance"[10] was projected outward from the United States to the world.

ICANN, the coordinating hub of this mechanism, constituted what Milton Mueller calls "a revolutionary departure" from existing state-based arrangements for coordinating international communications.[11] Global in its reach, ICANN provided a "centralized point of control over the Internet"[12] and used private-contract law to bind foreign entities to its management of the domain name system.[13] Regional internet registries were developed and tasked with managing the allocation of addresses procured in blocks from ICANN for Asia-Pacific, Africa, Latin America, and Europe. Generic top-level domains were managed by other entities within the ICANN system; the most important by far, ".com" went to the U.S. company VeriSign. ICANN managed policy for the internet's operation and continued technical development, working with the Internet Engineering Task Force and the Internet Architecture Board— affiliates of another not-for-profit organization, the Internet Society, based in Reston, Virginia.[14] Also not a part of ICANN but working concurrently with it, the World Wide Web Consortium focuses specifically on international standards development for the Web. Several years after it was founded, ICANN— which remained legally in thrall to the U.S. government—began to promulgate a "multi-stakeholder" model of decision making, supposedly incarnating a robustly democratic procedure. I will explicate the multi-stakeholder model shortly.

At its inception in 1998 and ever since, ICANN's other distinguishing feature pertained to its "unilateral construction of a global regime," as Milton Mueller put it: ICANN "was supervised and accountable to a single sovereign . . . the United States."[15] Sometimes subterranean controversies[16] punctuated what Mueller called ICANN's "unilateral globalism,"[17] as other states recognized that the operation, management, and further development of the space of flows were being skewed. The geopolitics of networks[18] had provided repeated object lessons in how great powers had attempted historically to manage the world's information flows so as to support their far-flung economic and strategic interests. Albeit sometimes opaquely, the extraterritorial internet conformed to this pattern.

Country code authorities that had been set up, or delegated quite informally in the early days by the U.S.-based academic, Jon Postel, who singlehandedly performed the IANA functions for scores of entities (often academic) in individual states, attracted the interests of governments, who sought to manage this fast-growing category of top-level domains (more than 250 at the present writing). Political opposition to the U.S. regime of extraterritorial internet control became insistent even as this regime became established. Brazil's government "took the lead in articulating the challenge" at a multilateral forum, the World Summit on the Information Society (WSIS), between 2003 and 2005.[19] As I wrote in *How to Think about Information* just prior to the onset of the digital depression, "Internet governance is destined to become more controversial during the years ahead."[20] We will find that this forecast has been amply confirmed.

WSIS eventuated in some U.S. concessions, but the result was ambiguity rather than a decisive institutional break with existing practice. The United States acquiesced to the establishment of a new organizational actor, the UN-affiliated Internet Governance Forum (IGF), which was propelled by the mobilization at WSIS into the global internet governance regime—and, thus, into ICANN's operating environment. Trying to head off more radical reforms, ICANN nominally elevated the status of its own Government Advisory Committee (GAC), which had been established in 2002. An indeterminate measure of authority over the mechanisms of internet governance was ceded to other states through the creation of both IGF and GAC; how and even whether states might try to use IGF and GAC as fulcrums to induce other changes remained dubious. Still more opacity was created by a different U.S. effort to assuage other nations' fears: through a 2009 alteration in ICANN's contract with the Commerce Department, formal U.S. control over ICANN was diminished.[21] Although these arrangements may have camouflaged the underlying power relations somewhat, U.S. Executive Branch jurisdiction over the critical IANA functions visibly persisted.

The Commerce Department's contracts with IANA to perform the DNS functions, and with VeriSign to enter changes in the master root zone file, required episodic renewal. As the expiration of the term for IANA functions contract neared (in September 2011), a replacement contract would have to be drawn up. This requirement offered an occasion for the Commerce Department to request public comment on apparently technical and administrative, but in fact power-laden, questions about whether and how to modify the existing legal instrument. The result was extraordinary: U.S. policymaking for the extraterritorial internet was opened to polite but nevertheless fierce contention.

To understand this conflict it will be useful to begin with a brief discussion of the "multi-stakeholder" model that had been established to mediate internet governance. This model was not unique to ICANN. The UN's Internet Governance Forum and the European Union's broadcasting policy adhered, for example, to comparable multi-stakeholder tenets. This innovation merits careful evaluation, however. For Rebecca MacKinnon, the multi-stakeholder model provides a welcome alternative to relying on governments on grounds of supporting freedom of expression. "If civil liberties are to be preserved and protected," she writes, "Internet governance cannot be left up to governments alone.... [T]he nation-state system is not the appropriate framework for governing the Internet."[22] Within ICANN, a nonprofit corporation endowed with political functions, states participate alongside private corporations and trade associations, nongovernmental organizations and individuals; but states are accorded a lesser role: the Government Advisory Committee representative to the ICANN board is a mere observer, whereas these other "constituencies" are voting members. Downgrading both states and treaty-based interstate organizations (notably, the International Telecommunication Union), "multistakeholderism" within ICANN is often credited with elevating "civil society" within a globalized democratic process.

Was multi-stakeholderism equivalent to democratic accountability? Hardly. Providing a venue at which different voices are accorded some kind of a hearing, multi-stakeholder organizations grant functional interest groups direct representation in the political system. For this reason, as Mueller emphasizes, they constitute a variant of corporatism. Mueller follows Marina Ottaway in acknowledging that "corporatism is being revived as a solution to new problems of *global governance* and also as a response to the growth in the number and militancy of transnational NGO networks."[23] This formulation is highly pertinent to ICANN, in which "relations ... are far from balanced ... and throwing large corporations into the mix makes the disparities even more obvious."[24] Mueller saliently observes that "the participation of multiple stakeholder groups ... does not determine how power is distributed among these groups or how much weight they are given in decision-making processes."[25] Considered in terms of principles of representation and democratic accountability, multistakeholderism is not only an incomplete solution, it is also a flawed one.[26]

It is telling that a foremost proponent of this approach has been the U.S. government. The Executive Branch has insisted, against considerable pressure, that ICANN's "multi-stakeholder model" should be retained and, indeed, that it should be extended to other institutions. No less a figure than U.S. President Barack Obama declared that "Internet governance efforts must not be limited to governments, but should include all appropriate stakeholders," and that the United States will "seek the private sector's participation in Internet governance as essential to upholding its multi-stakeholder character."[27] The U.S. government continued to push its "private-sector-led, multi-stakeholder model of Internet governance" into 2014.[28] The merit of multi-stakeholderism for the United States was that, behind a screen of solicitousness for democratic rights, it sustained the U.S. project of "unilateral globalism" while reducing opportunities for other states to exert influence over the extraterritorial internet. To be sure, the model made some room for individuals and NGOs to express their views. However, its essential function was to sustain the primacy of one government—that of the United States—in exercising extraterritorial internet governance even as it also concealed this reality.

Other interested power-holders in addition to the Executive Branch lent avid support to multi-stakeholderism. In an article co-authored with Jared Cohen (who moved from the State Department to direct Google's research arm, Google Ideas[29]), Eric Schmidt—then CEO of Google—positively venerated the emerging "virtual space" constituted by the internet. Herein, they declared, "governments, individuals, nongovernmental organizations, and private companies will balance one another's interests."[30] In this vacuous pluralism, which Schmidt and Cohen hailed as the "interconnected estate," "any person with access to the Internet, regardless of living standard or nationality, is given a voice and the power to effect change."[31] Schmidt and Cohen elevated dispossessed peasants to the status of gigantic transnational corporations. Real power, nevertheless, remained where it had been: in a seemingly stable articulation of U.S. capital and the U.S. Executive Branch.

This much-vaunted but insubstantial democratic process operated, in fact, to conceal and safeguard what was actually an aggressive drive to renew and extend a U.S.-led digital capitalism. This objective surfaced explicitly in 2013 in a study for the Council on Foreign Relations, which concluded, "The United States is well positioned to reap the benefits, known and unknown, of the expansion and deepening of this worldwide platform for sharing information and data."[32] The rhetoric of "multi-stakeholder governance" thus was fundamentally deceptive. It promised to empower individuals, NGOs, and civil society, but its actual effect was to forestall other states—individually and collectively, via interstate treaty organizations—from participating as equals with the U.S. government in managing the extraterritorial internet. Meanwhile, U.S. corporate capital continued to saturate internet governance with its demands and objectives.[33]

Corporations, trade associations, NGOs, individuals, and—in a striking departure from the norm—sovereign states each lodged comments in the venue created by the Commerce Department's public inquiry into the IANA functions contract. While transnational companies predictably supported the status quo, however, some states' responses attested a remarkable rejection of the internet's control structure. The campaign to reincarnate pluralist political doctrine around a corporatist, U.S.-led internet regime was to this extent revealed to be unpersuasive.

On one side, the United States Council for International Business (USCIB) insisted that "the technical coordination of Internet resources and preservation of a unified Domain Name System (DNS) is of critical importance to all of our members given the amount of their business that is conducted over it." Representing three hundred U.S.-based transnational companies and providers of professional services, USCIB referenced the existing tripartite arrangement for managing the IANA functions (ICANN, Commerce Department, VeriSign) and allowed that "some stakeholders have concerns about the current model." In contrast, they stated, "We support the current model, and feel that such concerns are best addressed by focusing on specific suggestions to enhance the transparency or the operation of the IANA functions process. This should be done within the existing model and contract framework."[34]

"Stability" and "security" were the watchwords employed repeatedly by corporations with a stake in the existing order: they asserted again and again that this extraterritorial system must not be altered. Cisco, the world's leading supplier of routers and an array of other tools for internet functionality and applications provision, was one such claimant. Cisco identified "five core principles" that, it declared, had been incarnated in the internet's successful institutionalization: stability, trust, transparency, interoperability, and technical competence. Real damage might be perpetrated on internet operations if these precepts were undercut by reorganizing the IANA functions. That simply could not be permitted to occur: the status quo should be preserved. Akin to other corporate interveners, Cisco allowed that institutional "transparency" might be increased—so that the legitimacy of the existing system might be enhanced.[35]

Sharing this concern to ensure the "stability and security" of DNS management, Google's intervention was again unsurprising. Google "strongly believes" that ICANN should "remain the executor of the IANA functions."[36]

The "bottom-up, multi-stakeholder model, which is accountable to all stake-holders and is embodied by ICANN, is both effective and necessary." Google supported one reform: it hoped to augment ICANN's management role over the IANA functions by transferring to it—from VeriSign—specific operational responsibilities in defining and posting authoritative address data. "As it is currently practiced, there is a potential for the updates requested by ICANN to be altered after receipt by VeriSign. If ICANN generates the fully signed root zone and conveys it securely to VeriSign for distribution, the integrity of the process would be increased."[37]

Behind this arcane technical issue lay the politically charged power disparity that drew international concern: ICANN's vaunted attempts at transparency, in deference to its many diverse "stakeholders," contrasted with—even contradicted—VeriSign's direct bond with the Commerce Department to operate the identifiers needed to run the system. Now that a global internet governance regime was being successfully institutionalized, Google implied, it was time for the Commerce Department to grant ICANN the independent authority that it had vowed it would at the time of ICANN's establishment.

Google underlined that it was "strategically important for the NTIA to send a strong signal in support of the private-sector, multi-stakeholder Internet governance model."[38] In addition to this management revision, Google wished to see ICANN's institutional status rendered durable. As matters stood—and this in itself testified to the sensitivity of the earlier process of institutionalization from the perspective of the U.S. Executive Branch—ICANN served at the pleasure of the Department of Commerce, via a one-year base contract with four additional one-year options to renew. This arrangement, Google presciently warned, "creates unnecessary and even potentially harmful instability" and lends itself to "speculation that the IANA functions will be moved to another entity." Not only was this unfortunate for ICANN's internal organizational processes, its effects were "even more visible in domestic and international forums where other parties are motivated to advocate for the transfer of the IANA functions to parties beyond the reach of the present governance structure." That is, the continued provisionality of this management structure lent itself to dissident nations' efforts to alter internet governance. As Google discreetly asserted, "The one-year options unnecessarily highlight to an international audience the U.S. government's unique role in the Internet governance process." A "longer-duration" agreement between ICANN and NTIA would improve things by clarifying the "important"—that is, implicitly, the enduring—"relationship" between the two entities, while "highlight[ing] the U.S. government's continued commitment to the private-sector-led governance model."[39] Google, notably, said nothing about curtailing the Commerce Department's substantive management function itself. That the Commerce Department did not accept Google's proposal only further confirmed the strength and, indeed, the power of the U.S. state interest in ICANN.

Other commenters dissented strongly, in a frontal challenge to U.S. internet management. The very fact that they lodged comments before the U.S. Commerce Department, of course, constituted a symptom of the larger inversion. Still more extraordinary was the presence at this venue of a multilateral treaty organization, the International Telecommunication Union. The ITU is a UN affiliate with a membership including 192 governments (whose apparent primacy within the organization camouflages widespread corporate penetration of its functions). For decades the ITU had been the centerpiece of the institutional regime for international spectrum- and cable-based telecommunications policy; indeed, its jurisdiction had been enlarged throughout the mid-twentieth century. Shut out of internet governance from the outset, by contrast, at the request of some of its members the ITU repeatedly struggled to regain a place in policymaking for this modernized infrastructure. Its efforts were consistently rebuffed. Within, and behind, the ITU, however, were scores of member states dissatisfied with the United States' "unilateral globalism." Now, the ITU placed itself in the incongruous position of pleading for a minor functional role (regarding the domain name ".int") before an agency of one of its member states.[40] Perhaps there is no better illustration of the underlying power dynamics in this proceeding. A UN-accredited international organization, representing the states of the world, took the position of a marginal supplicant. Adding to the injury, the Commerce Department simply ignored the ITU's request—which had been approved by consensus by its member states (including the United States).[41] For some, including principled democrats such as Rebecca MacKinnon, this result was all to the good: "Putting the UN in charge of coordinating the Internet's practical functions would be a setback for freedom of expression."[42]

Perhaps so, but U.S. dominance itself formally disserved democratic ideals on its face. For much of the world, until the United States shed its unilateral control over internet management, both its constitutional protections and its attacks on the UN system continued to ring hollow. Several sovereign states responded by making their opposition to the prevailing arrangements palpable. The government of Kenya proposed a "transition" away from management of the IANA functions by the U.S. Department of Commerce's NTIA. A true "multistakeholder relationship," declared Kenya, would require that, in NTIA's place, there should be a combination of organizations offering strengthened global and governmental representation. These should include not only root-server operators, protocol developers (including the Internet Engineering Task Force), the five regional internet registries, and address functions performed by ICANN, but also the country code top-level domain operators and the Government Advisory Committee. In keeping with the WSIS Tunis Declaration, both principles of global representation and "national policy processes" needed to find application in the IANA functions. Indeed, "more stakeholder oversight" should be institutionalized and expressed "in all UN languages" and over a wider span, "including but not limited to the root zone."[43] Kenya had notably extended the realm of intended reforms by including the IETF in its proposal to reorganize internet governance, recognizing that, before this, the IETF had managed to elude reformers' scrutiny.[44]

The government of India voiced a congruent view through the comment made by its Department of Information Technology. As currently constituted, India charged, "the procedure being followed by ICANN does take into consideration the views of broad spectrum of entities including Governments, Industry, Civil society and other stakeholders." Management of IANA should "be made broad based where the entire ecosystem and the community could take part in its reviewing regarding the transparency, accountability and enhancing its performance." This enlarged group specifically included the regional internet registries and country code top-level domains.[45]

Egypt, perhaps emboldened by its ongoing popular revolution, chipped in through its representative to ICANN's Government Advisory Committee. The aim of Egypt's submission again ingeniously deployed ICANN's commitment to "multistakeholderism" *against* the prevailing institutional arrangements. "Egypt," it declared, "supports that the Internet Corporation for Assigned Names and Numbers (ICANN) continue to perform the IANA functions and believes that the ICANN model, through its bottom-up process and the involvement of all stakeholders, is the right place for discussing improvements of the IANA functions rather than through a contract between ICANN and an individual government." Egypt's submission continued: "That the final approval is being sought from NTIA/DoC negatively affects the responsiveness, predictability, transparency and accountability of the process." As presently organized, indeed, "the IANA is currently more of an isolated black box within ICANN. It is unclear how agreed policies affect or are reflected into the IANA functions. It's unclear how GAC principles are reflected into the IANA delegation and re-delegation process." However, "the IANA functions," they pointed out, "could be enhanced through more transparency and through accountability to the whole community which could be significantly improved by removing (or at least narrowing the scope of) a unilateral contractual oversight." Both ICANN's supporting organizations (for example, the Country Code Name Supporting Organization) and its advisory committees (notably, the GAC) should take a direct managerial role.[46] More democracy—real democracy—could be attained if the United States were compelled to relinquish its dominating role.

More subdued, but no less definite, was the Secretary of Communications for Mexico—a U.S. ally—who commented that "we believe that is necessary to enhance the transparency and accountability in the IANA functions in order to find some mechanism to the evolution of the IANA contract in the final transition to ICANN." ICANN, that is, should become more genuinely representative, and the IANA functions more transparent, "to create better mechanisms and procedures to interact with all the stakeholders."[47]

Rounding out this picture of dissent was a submission from East Asia. Perhaps the most portentous comments addressing the power disparities that suffused the IANA functions were those lodged by the Peoples Republic of China. "Conflicts over the flow of information through cyberspace," one high-profile analyst had written in 2010, "will further complicate the already troubled U.S.-Chinese relationship."[48] Actually, by this time China and the United States had already clashed over global internet governance for some years[49]—and this conflict persisted.

The China Internet Network Information Center (CNNIC), a Beijing-based organization vested with national responsibilities for internet operation in China, again sought to turn the expressed concern for "security and stability" and "multi-stakeholderism" against the purposes expressed both by U.S. corporations and the Commerce Department. IANA, CNNIC spelled out, should function "completely without involving DOC and VeriSign." IANA, that is, should be made "a real independent organization or run by an independent organization, which is supervised by the global Internet communities themselves." In turn, "IANA should strengthen the multi-stakeholder model, and ensure all the root server operators to follow the policies and instructions that are developed by the community."[50] "The best multi-stakeholder model," CNNIC's deputy director general repeated insistently in an accompanying letter, "is to change the DOC-supervising-only model, and make IANA to be a real independent organization or run by an independent organization, which is supervised by the global Internet communities themselves."[51] How this might be accomplished was not specified; but, especially in light of subsequent developments, it is worth underlining the congruence that existed on this point between the Chinese proposal and those entered by India, Mexico, Kenya, and Egypt.

Wang Chen, minister of China's state Internet Information Office, declared before a conference held in Beijing in September 2011 that "while the Internets in various countries link with each other, they belong to different sovereign jurisdictions." Western critics have concentrated overwhelmingly on how states abuse their "sovereign jurisdiction" to engender repression. This indeed is always of concern. However, sovereignty likewise gave states the grounds for demanding that the internet's management should be reorganized internationally. Wang went on to assert that "countries are in urgent need of strengthening international cooperation" over the internet. In an unmistakable rejoinder to U.S. rhetoric, Wang tartly underlined that "the international exchanges and cooperation over the internet should respect the principles of full equality, mutual respect, mutual help and mutual benefit, and should refrain from using 'network freedom' to seek 'network hegemony.'" "Open and participative methods" together with "joint formulation of international rules" were, he held, the preferred option for internet policymaking; he closed by saying that China "would like to play an active role in this process."[52]

Regarding China's resolve with respect to global internet governance, additional Chinese internet organizations filed like-spirited comments.[53] The China Organizational Name Administration Center (CONAC), a nonprofit organization established in 2008, was authorized by the Chinese government to run the registry for ".cn" for Government Affairs and Public Interest agencies. CONAC allowed that it "actively participates in the global Internet community." Suggestively fusing political and market rhetorics, CONAC asserted that "it is imperative for IANA to incorporate muti-stakeholder [sic] model and establish a formalized mechanism to collect IANA functions users' inputs and feedbacks to improve the overall customer experience. Also, more information concerning IANA functions performance and management should be released to enhance transparency and facilitate the multi-stakeholder's supervision on the performance of IANA functions." However, CONAC continued, it was confident that ICANN's existing officers could transform the organization so that "a new pattern of the IANA functions contract can better serve the development of the Internet."[54] Meaningful reforms could be instituted by ICANN's present leaders if only they could be granted permission.

Milton Mueller, who disapproved of a more state-centric model, nevertheless discerned that the approach "which is desired by many governments around the world, is to multi-lateralize the contracting process. The U.S. would share its authority over the IANA function with other governments, either on a one-country, one-vote basis or through some subset or club of privileged governments."[55] Beyond this demand, it is important to note, the extent of the consensus among these states remained both ambiguous and open to political and economic pressure. The extraordinary submissions to the Commerce Department signified, however, that the concerns of other states were not dissipating—that they would not be brushed aside. Did they likewise attest a unity of political purpose beyond opposition to U.S. unilateral globalism?

Virtually the entire poor world—Africa, the Middle East, South Asia, East Asia, and Latin America—was represented in this U.S. proceeding. Can this have been mere coincidence? In any case, it did not signal a rebirth of the Third World political project—whose historical moment had passed during the 1980s—though it carried forward into internet policymaking a still widely shared legacy or, at least, a shared rhetoric, of anti-imperialism. Nor was it an anticapitalist "united front"; these countries were integrated into transnational capitalism, and their leaders were (mostly) committed to it. Vijay Prashad explains that, as it mutated in the cauldron of the 1980s and 1990s, the Third World political project had transformed into a kind of "neoliberalism with Southern characteristics."[56] Initiatives including the South Commission, IBSA (India, Brazil, South Africa) and, latterly joined by China and Russia, the BRICS, constituted a nascent or perhaps only a potential political movement, which took for granted actually existing transnational capitalism but which demanded to gain greater power within it. Political unity remained difficult to attain and even more difficult to sustain. The ambiguity was further heightened by the existence of ongoing social-political struggles within these countries—struggles that continued to interact with their international direction. All this admitted, it was also unmistakable that, however "neoliberalism with Southern characteristics" might evolve, its leaders shared the goal of reducing U.S. unilateral dominance over the extraterritorial internet.

Indications of the gravity accorded to their initiative by U.S. leaders surfaced continually after the close of the proceeding's comment period. In May 2011, Assistant Secretary of Commerce for Communications and Information Lawrence E. Strickling conceded that "one of the greatest challenges facing the Internet in the next five years is its political sustainability, which of course forces us to confront the question of what is the collective role of nation-states with respect to the multi-stakeholder model." Strickling stoutly repeated, "the United States is most assuredly opposed to establishing a governance structure for the Internet that would be managed and controlled by nation-states."[57]

The U.S. preference for multi-stakeholder governance over an interstate jurisdiction was expressed especially forcefully at the Group of Eight summit meeting in Paris in May and early June 2011. This venue was doubly telling: the G8, which traced its lineage back to a 1975 response mounted by France, the United States, and a handful of major trading partners to the global oil crisis was, most revealingly, *not* the G20—whose members included dissenting commenters in the IANA proceeding, notably, China and India, as well as Brazil. And, prior to the formal G8 deliberations, an extraordinary preparatory meeting, dubbed eG8, was organized by the French public relations and advertising firm Publicis;[58] here, around one thousand participants, including internet and media leaders representing eBay, Facebook, News Corporation, Microsoft, Google, and Amazon, rubbed elbows with international leaders. Eric Schmidt attempted to give an object lesson to Nicolas Sarkozy (and Rupert Murdoch) with regard to how much government regulation should be applied to the internet.[59] Despite some squabbles, the G8's official declaration following its meeting in Deauville in 2011 affirmed the U.S. preference: "For the first time at Leaders' level, we agreed, in the presence of some leaders of the Internet economy, on a number of key principles, including freedom, respect for privacy and intellectual property, multi-stakeholder governance, cyber-security, and protection from crime, that underpin a strong and flourishing Internet."[60] In view of subsequent developments, this avowed "respect for privacy" stands out as exceptionally hypocritical.

The G8 declaration reads like the playbook that had been used the previous year by the U.S. Commerce Department's Internet Policy Task Force. Here is the G8:

> The global digital economy has served as a powerful economic driver and engine of growth and innovation. Broadband internet access is an essential infrastructure for participation in today's economy. In order for our countries to benefit fully from the digital economy, we need to seize emerging opportunities, such as cloud computing, social networking and citizen publications, which are driving innovation and enabling growth in our societies. As we adopt more innovative internet-based services, we face challenges in promoting interoperability and convergence among our public policies on issues such as the protection of personal data, net neutrality, transborder data flow, ICT security, and intellectual property.[61]

Scarcely one month later, the OECD followed up with its own "Communiqué on Principles for Internet Policy Making," which built on the Seoul Declaration of three years before, to hammer on a need for "free flow of information," promotion of "cross-border service delivery," and "multi-stakeholder cooperation in policy development."[62]

The U.S. Commerce Department also pressed forward. Its "Further Notice of Inquiry" regarding the IANA functions seemed to flaunt the U.S.'s expansive power over "critical Internet resources."[63] Yet international opposition persisted. China's comments before the Commerce Department became more pointed, and Namibia joined the chorus of dissenters.[64]

The Internet Society of China directly attacked "the status quo of the unilateral control [by] the United States," exclaiming that, "unfortunately," the revised draft proposal issued by the Commerce Department bore no "substantial improvement on most concerned issues from the Internet community." Its comments, significantly, were submitted both in English and, by way of a completely separate document, in Mandarin.[65] Vowing that a way had to be found "so that all countries can equally participate in the management of Internet critical resources," China's powerful Ministry of Industry and Information Technology explicitly invoked WSIS in advocating for multilateral principles of internet governance.[66]

The Internet Society of China was responding to a U.S. Commerce Department announcement of mid-June, 2011, when, after reviewing the eighty-odd comments elicited by its notice of inquiry, the Commerce Department released a Further Notice of Inquiry calling for public comment on a Draft Statement of Work. In its discussion of the comments, NTIA purported to concede that "there is a need to address how all stakeholders, including governments collectively, can operate within the paradigm of a multi-stakeholder environment and be satisfied that their interests are being adequately addressed. Resolving this issue is critical to a strong multi-stakeholder model and to ensure the long-term political sustainability of an Internet that supports the free flow of information, goods, and services. NTIA's continued commitment to openness and transparency and the multi-stakeholder model is evidenced by the manner in which it is proceeding with this procurement."[67] However, NTIA also peremptorily declared that it would brook no changes to its policy of U.S. control over IANA: "Consistent with the 2005 U.S. Principles on the Internet's Domain Name and Addressing System, the United States is committed to maintaining its historic role and will take no action that would adversely impact the effective and efficient operation of the DNS.... [W]ith this FNOI, NTIA reiterates that it is not in discussions with ICANN to transition the IANA functions nor does the agency intend to undertake such discussions."[68] NTIA offered some concessions in its draft statement, for example, in recognizing the legitimacy of country code operators' efforts to develop a policymaking role, and it invited additional comment on these proposed alterations. Conflict over digital capitalism's operational power structure thus gave no hint of receding.

Indeed, it sharpened. The Administrator of NTIA, Assistant Secretary of Commerce for Communications and Information Lawrence E. Strickling, reflected on the passage of events in June 2011. Reaffirming his conviction that "we were at an 'all hands on deck' moment," Strickling elaborated: "Events over the last year have only confirmed the need for action. We have seen more and more instances of restrictions on the free flow of information online, disputes between various standards bodies, and statements by international organizations and some governments to regulate the Internet more directly." These

developments had only strengthened his commitment to the existing mechanisms of multi-stakeholder governance, and so, anticipating that this stance
would continue to face challenges, Strickling asserted:

> We need to find a way to bring governments willingly, if not enthusiastically,
> into the tent of multi-stakeholder policymaking. While some nations persist
> in proposing such measures as giving the International Telecommunication
> Union (ITU) the authority to veto ICANN Board decisions, the United
> States is most assuredly opposed to overturning the proven governance
> model that has built and spread the internet around the world with extraor-
> dinary openness, speed and innovation. Subjecting the leading internet insti-
> tutions such as ICANN, and the IETF, to traditional treaty-based regulation,
> such as the ITU, would certainly lead to the imposition of heavy-handed and
> economically misguided regulation and the loss of flexibility the current sys-
> tem allows today, all of which would jeopardize the growth and innovation
> we have enjoyed these past years. The United States government will work
> with other nations to protect existing global Internet institutions by better
> defining the role of governments as a set of stakeholders. We do not seek to
> supplant these institutions with a United Nations or treaty-based regime.[69]

It is fanciful to understand this discourse as supporting individual human
rights as against the grasping efforts of states. This issue is real—indeed, vital;
but the proceeding's true pivot lay elsewhere. It centered on disagreement over
the skew that existed within the interstate system in relative power to manage
critical internet resources: in the "unilateral globalism" exercised by the United
States. Throughout succeeding months, the conflict over global internet governance continued to simmer.

U.S. transnational business backed the U.S.'s hardening stance. Late in 2011,
the Software and Information Industry Association joined with the National
Foreign Trade Council "to promote the global flow of data across national
boundaries," referencing the OECD's communiqué of 2011—which now served
as a touchstone—indicating a seeming convergence between U.S. policy and
the preferences of transnational capital.[70] There existed, indeed, an additional
imperative because, as presently constituted, "The global trading system does
not spell out a consistent, transparent framework for the treatment of cross-
border flows of digital goods, services or information, leaving businesses and
individuals to deal with a patchwork of national, bilateral and global arrangements." Intervention was needed both to harmonize the existing system and
to smooth the way for "a new generation of networked technologies [that]
enables greater cross-border collaboration over the Internet."[71]

As if to hurl the fact of its control back at its critics, in March 2012 NTIA announced that it was canceling its RFP for the IANA contract "because we received no proposals that met the requirements requested by the global community. The Department intends to reissue the RFP at a future date to be determined so that the requirements of the global internet community can be served."[72] While this move fueled intense speculation as to motive and may have subverted the identity of interest that seemed to have been forged between big capital and the U.S. Commerce Department,[73] the agency's RFP for the IANA functions contract was reissued the next month—and in July 2012 a new contract with ICANN was awarded.[74]

Meanwhile, in June 2012, a proposal had been submitted to the Internet Engineering Task Force by three engineers from China Telecom and China Mobile to establish "autonomous internets."[75] The aim, as Mueller reported, was to provide "a way to alter Internet standards to partition the Internet into autonomously administered national networks, using the domain name system."[76] The engineers singled out the existing DNS's "central control," charging that it was "not suitable to autonomy," and that a "national internet network" "owning" "its independent root DNS server" could not be constructed within the existing DNS. In its technological assumptions and thus also in its projected solution, this proposal may have been faulty—but its importance was arguably more political than technological. It showed that the Chinese aim of rebalancing the U.S.-centric internet still carried forward, albeit nominally within the existing mechanism of global internet governance.[77]

The United States was, in its turn, waging what it undoubtedly hoped would amount to a preemptive campaign. Policymakers took the offensive by asserting throughout 2012 that advocates of multilateral internet control were planning a palace coup, to occur at an upcoming conference of the International Telecommunication Union.[78] Early salvos were fired by Lawrence E. Strickling, assistant secretary of Commerce for Communications and Information, at public presentations between September 2011 and January 2012,[79] and by FCC Commissioner Robert M. McDowell in a much-bruited op-ed for the *Wall Street Journal* on "the U.N. threat to Internet freedom."[80] The theme that the United States must resist government control and continue to manage the internet under existing arrangements then attained expression before Congress. A bipartisan congressional declaration held that Executive Branch agencies "should continue working to implement the position of the United States on Internet governance that clearly articulates the consistent and unequivocal policy of the United States to promote a global Internet free from government control and preserve and advance the successful multistakeholder model that governs the

Internet today."[81] Hearings in the House of Representatives were arranged so that high-level U.S. policymakers at the State Department and the Federal Communications Commission as well as representatives from the Internet Society and Google could proclaim congruent views.[82] A U.S. congressional resolution (H. Con. Res. 127) originating in the House Energy and Commerce Committee on June 20, 2012, was crafted to "express the sense of Congress that the Internet should remain free from international regulation and that the United States should continue its commitment to the current 'multi-stakeholder' model of governance." This resolution, possessing bipartisan sponsorship, specifically "reject[ed] international proposals, expected to be discussed at the December World Conference on International Telecommunications (WCIT) in Dubai, to treat the Internet like an old-fashioned telephone service." For months prior to WCIT-12, people were warned that this was to be an epochal clash between upholders of an open internet and would-be government usurpers, led by authoritarian states like Russia, Iran, and China. The terms of reference were set so rigidly that one European telecom company executive soon afterward called this a campaign of "propaganda warfare."[83]

Again, let me emphasize that freedom of expression is no trifling issue. No matter where we live, there is reason for worry that the internet's relative openness is being usurped, corroded, canalized, parasitized. This, as succeeding developments would underline, does not necessarily imply armies of state censors, or "great firewalls." However, "internet freedom" was—again—a red herring. Calculatingly manipulative, it told us to entrust a fundamental human right to a pair of powerfully self-interested social actors.

During the first half of December, the geopolitics of the internet broke open at the ITU's Dubai conference.[84] In answering the question of whether ITU members should vest the agency with oversight responsibilities for the internet, responsibilities comparable to those it has exercised for decades for other forms of international communication, the United States said "No." The question was rhetorical, however, because no such proposals had been formally presented to the Dubai conference; perhaps this made it less a surprise when the U.S. position won out. The revised ITU treaty document did not grant the agency a formal role in global internet governance. However, a majority of countries voted to attach a resolution "invit[ing] member states to elaborate on their respective position on international Internet-related technical, development and public policy issues within the mandate of the I.T.U. at various I.T.U. fora," and this resolution was approved by "consensus," where, in this case, "consensus" signified the absence of formal opposition.[85] Objecting to "even symbolic global oversight," as a New York Times writer put it,[86] the United States thereupon refused to sign the treaty. So did all European Union countries, Australia, Japan, India, Kenya, Colombia, Canada, Britain—fifty-five nations in total. If the United States won the battle, however, the outcome of the war over global internet governance now became palpably uncertain: more than two-thirds of the attending countries—eighty-nine, all told—endorsed the document. Adding to the sense that a watershed was near, many of the nonsignatories stated that they would conduct further consultations and decide later whether to accede to the treaty.[87]

The deliberations at WCIT-12 were multifaceted and encompassed crosscutting concerns.[88] One was the terms of trade between internet services like Google and the companies that transport their voluminous data streams—network operators and ISPs like Verizon, Deutsche Telekom, or Free. This business fight harbored implications for the more general and important policy issue discussed in part II regarding who should pay for the continual modernizations of network infrastructure on which recurrent augmentations and enhancements of internet service depend. Averted was an edict in favor of content providers paying network operators—the goal of the telecom companies, and already a quietly observed occasional practice—which would have carried prospectively grave consequences for net neutrality policies.

With respect to the paramount issue looming over WCIT-12—who would wield the power to manage the continued integration of the internet into the transnational capitalist political economy—we may be confident that, behind the scenes, U.S. officials intensified their bilateral lobbying in an attempt to bring dissenters back into the fold. India[89] and Kenya notably joined the United States in rejecting the WCIT-12 treaty; equally telling, however, was that Korea and Mexico did not reject it, nor did U.S. allies from the Arab states. The political challenge to U.S. "global unilateralism" was breaking open. A *Wall Street Journal* editorialist called Dubai "America's First Big Digital Defeat."[90]

Though it receded somewhat from public view, in the aftermath the conflict persisted. On one hand, Russia held a high-level international meeting in May 2013, at which ITU Secretary General Dr. Hamadoun Toure joined other participants in exploring the question of whether WCIT-12 in Dubai "should be regarded as . . . a watershed after which a political confrontation on the control over the Internet follows."[91] "What is the price of consensus?"[92] the conferees asked, in an inversion of typical U.S. rhetoric. In this connection, Andrey Kolesnikov, director of Russia's .ru country code, pointedly praised China "which never—and WCIT-2012 is not an exception—loudly announces and promotes its position in the world arena or pushes on the coalition approach, but still demonstrates a breathtaking progress in national IT sector."[93]

The World Information Technology and Services Alliance, a trade group representing a very broad range of member companies, worried that "global companies may face an uncertain regulatory environment based on the division between countries at WCIT-2012"—and reaffirmed its support for "multistakeholder dialogue" over "government control."[94] U.S. officials also regrouped. NTIA's Lawrence Strickling purported to demur in June 2013, when an academic expert pronounced at a Columbia University conference that a "federated model for Internet governance" now stood a real chance of superseding the U.S.-centric extraterritorial system.[95] What concrete content and procedures this "federated model" might entail remained unspecified; and we may wonder what U.S. officials thought privately about this proposal. In any case, a high-level task force report to the U.S. Council on Foreign Relations expressed real worry about the status of global internet governance in June 2013,[96] just before Edward Snowden's exposures of invasive and ubiquitous NSA surveillance of global internet traffic began to crash into global politics—and put paid to U.S. hopes of preempting the issue.

Snowden's intervention carried profound consequences, which went beyond the grave question of bulk surveillance to "destabilize the foundations of international internet governance."[97] This was not because Snowden told the world something new, something of which it had been genuinely ignorant. U.S. surveillance of international communications in general (and programs undertaken by the National Security Agency, which was established in 1952, and by its precursors) dates back to the early twentieth century.[98] Diplomatic cables to and from delegates to the United Nations' founding conference in San Francisco in 1945 were intercepted by U.S. military surveillance round the clock.[99] During the mid-1970s, abuses by U.S. intelligence agencies including, for the first time, some committed under the codename Project Shamrock by the NSA, were investigated by Senator Frank Church. In the 1990s, reports circulated that, through its "Five Eyes" partnership with Britain, Canada, Australia, and New Zealand, the U.S. NSA operated a signals intelligence program to monitor and intercept international satellite communications. The scope of this surveillance and, specifically, whether it was limited to military and diplomatic purposes or also encompassed commercial intelligence of value to United States companies, surfaced during European investigations of this so-called "Echelon" program.[100] Already circulating before Snowden's exposures were also more recent reports that the U.S. National Security Agency sifts wholesale through electronic transmissions transiting satellite and cable networks at its far-flung "listening posts" and its gigantic data center at Bluffdale, Utah.[101] It was also patent, finally, that the U.S. government was deadly earnest in its stepped-up attacks against proponents of freedom of expression: whistleblowers and leakers.[102]

Snowden's exposures nevertheless engendered far-reaching effects, for three interlinked reasons. First, they confirmed for the world to see that the United States was systematically exploiting its unique position with respect to the extraterritorial internet. Prior to 2013, while the U.S.-centric internet was well-recognized, U.S. authorities had camouflaged their internet capabilities. Only in desultory and limited ways had the extent of U.S. power flashed into view. The largest U.S. employer of mathematicians, the National Security Agency, employed thirty-five thousand workers overall and so, with a $10.8 billion annual budget, constituted the largest unit in the U.S. intelligence complex. Now it was revealed that NSA's "strategic mission" expressly included not only diplomatic, military, and antiterrorist objectives, it also was intent on "ensuring U.S. economic advantage and policy strategies." Presumably, this was why, in 2010, the NSA was monitoring both the government and personal emails of the top ten Venezuelan economic officials while also seeking "economic advantage" over Japan and Brazil.[103] Allegations surfaced that U.S. and British intelligence agencies had spied on the European commissioner responsible for sensitive antitrust investigations, including one that involved Google.[104]

A small group of courageous journalists conveyed Snowden's documentation to the world's press, demonstrating that, albeit sometimes apparently surreptitiously, the U.S. state had fused with leading U.S. internet companies to effectuate what U.S. insiders called "a golden age of signals intelligence."[105] Through its heavily reported PRISM program, the NSA had gained access to communications and internet companies' data; however, other "far more secret and far more invasive" programs permitted the NSA to gain direct access to the fiber optic cables and related infrastructure through which all electronic communications passed.[106] Never before had populations both foreign and domestic been subjected to such sweeping invasion of communications: it was reported that the NSA could observe 75 percent of the internet traffic passing across or through the United States.[107] The scope of NSA's mass surveillance programs encompassed email messages, social network posts, Web traffic, credit card transactions, and telephone calls; the NSA was collecting entire email address books from Google, Hotmail, Yahoo!, and Facebook.[108] World of Warcraft, Second Life, and other online games had been infiltrated: supposedly, each evinced a potential to be a "target-rich communication network" used by would-be terrorists. So, too, the NSA had tapped data streaming from leaky smartphone apps, led by Angry Birds.[109] It had accessed supposedly protected servers in unwitting data centers located in Germany, South Africa, Taiwan,

Russia, China, and Singapore.[110] Not only had the NSA reputedly used foreign listening posts located in dozens of embassies, including in Bogota, Caracas, Mexico City, Panama City, and Brasilia, to spy on people and governments.[111] The NSA had spied on elected leaders, installed bugs in the European Union's downtown Washington offices, infiltrated the European Union's internal computer network, and hacked United Nations communications.[112] Julian Assange, evidently, had been correct to claim months before that witting and unwitting cooperation between the government and internet intermediaries had turned the Web into a "surveillance engine."[113]

Second, however, public recoil against U.S. internet surveillance now became a politically destabilizing element, as angry "blowback"—fueled by a drip-feed of further exposures—funneled into the debate at both national and international levels.[114] Bolivian President Evo Morales's plane had been compelled to make an unplanned landing in Austria on its return journey from Moscow to La Paz because of extralegal U.S. intervention—apparently in the belief that Morales might be harboring Edward Snowden aboard.[115] Facing a backlash, some of Europe's elected leaders discerned both a political need—and, increasingly, an opportunity—to launch strategic responses to the NSA's bulk surveillance programs.[116] France used the revelations to push for its "cultural exception" within the negotiations between the European Union and the United States over a transatlantic trade agreement and to expand its own digital spying programs; while some European lawmakers strengthened their resolve to uphold tougher data protection standards as part of any forthcoming trade deal, some also proposed to suspend the SWIFT agreement covering bank data transfers from the European Union to U.S. security agencies.[117] Responding to disclosures that their elected leaders had been spied upon, Mexico, Germany, France, and Spain each summoned their U.S. ambassadors.[118] Germany's privacy commissioners called for a review of whether European internet traffic could be kept within the European Union, and when a European Commission report was released, it declared that internet governance was too U.S.-centric and that the European Union needed to take steps to further its role in internet governance.[119] Brazil and Germany together drafted a United Nations resolution calling for the right to privacy on the internet.[120] India advised government employees not to use Google's Gmail service and apparently warned its diplomatic staff in London to prepare sensitive documents using typewriters rather than PCs.[121] Indian officials likewise charged that multi-stakeholderism was a sham, and they renewed their push to multilateralize IANA in order "to free the internet from U.S. control."[122] South American leaders, including Argentina's President Christina Fernandez Kirchner and Brazil's Dilma Rousseff, protested to Mercosur, the common market of South America, that their national sovereignty had been violated and, thereafter, laid similar charges before the United Nations General Assembly.[123]

The U.S. political leadership in turn was compelled to assume a defensive posture. While Ron Wyden and a few other principled legislators opposed the NSA self-aggrandizing power grab on grounds that it trampled human rights, discomfited—and sometimes complicit—congressional leaders looked for political cover as they sought to bolster the NSA.[124] Hillary Clinton, a front-runner for the 2016 presidential election, stepped forward to offer what she no doubt hoped might pass for thoughtful comment: that it was time to hold a "sensible, adult conversation" about spying—hardly a substitute for real redress.[125] The FBI tried to reframe the issue around a need to defend against threatened cyberattacks on the United States.[126] Even after the U.S. government decided to charge Snowden with having violated the Espionage Act, early polls revealed that more Americans continued to consider him more a "hero" than a "traitor."[127] That sentiment continued to resonate.[128] The *New York Times* editorialized that Snowden should be considered a "whistle-blower" and offered clemency or a plea bargain.[129] The European Parliament invited the refugee to testify (via a video link) in its investigation of U.S. surveillance practices.[130]

While U.S. leaders continued to scramble, during fall 2013, revelations broke that the communications of presidents and prime ministers in Brazil, Mexico, Germany, France (and likely others) had been monitored.[131] President Rousseff insisted before the General Assembly of the United Nations that global internet governance needed to be overhauled.[132] Asian governments joined in demanding explanations after reports surfaced that U.S. and Australian embassies had secretly collected signals intelligence from Beijing to Jakarta and Kuala Lumpur; and that the NSA had also reportedly gathered billions of pieces of information from internet and telephone communications in India, making that country the number-one NSA target among the BRICS countries.[133]

Responses to these exposures spanned beyond rights rhetoric and led directly to consideration of power structures. Brazil—which already produced three-quarters of Latin America's internet capacity—proposed a series of programs to reduce its dependence on the U.S.-centric internet and to strengthen its own internet industry.[134] Among the proposals: increasing its domestic internet bandwidth; building and diversifying its international internet connectivity; supporting domestic content production and setting up its own national email service; and encouraging reliance on domestically produced network equipment.[135] Local data-storage provisions were added to "Marco Civil de Internet" legislation moving forward in Brazil's House of Representatives[136]—and were immediately contested by U.S. internet intermediaries.[137] An alliance of German phone and internet companies proposed that German email service and German Web site access be reorganized on a national basis, so that this particular internet traffic remained within the country's borders and therefore did not pass through U.S. internet exchanges.[138] Worries about U.S. industrial espionage also prompted Germany to push (at least as a momentary tactic) to add data protection strictures to the Transatlantic Trade and Investment Partnership then under negotiation between the European Union and the United States.[139] German Chancellor Angela Merkel embraced proposals to establish European data networks that purportedly would safeguard Web communications from U.S. spy agencies.[140] The European Commission called for "concrete and actionable steps to address the globalization of ICANN and the IANA functions."[141]

Third, therefore, longstanding opposition to U.S. "unilateral globalism" with respect to the extraterritorial internet now finally found a sharp point at which to renew struggle over the IANA functions. Long diverging political-economic interests obtained new ammunition in the international outrage over U.S. spying such that, as Milton Mueller recounted, "U.S. credibility as a neutral steward of the Internet has been severely damaged."[142] At an October meeting in Bali of the Internet Governance Forum, a United Nations affiliate that had been substantially assimilated into the U.S.-centric ICANN system, almost all of the 135-odd workshops and sessions among fifteen hundred representatives drawn from 111 countries proceeded in the shadow of the U.S. spying exposures.[143] The United States' rhetoric of internet freedom lay in tatters, and, its moral authority severely strained, participants pondered the possibility of a "post-Snowden Internet."[144] Still more significantly, the very organizations charged with responsibility for coordinating the internet's technical infrastructure met in Montevideo, Uruguay, and jointly "called for accelerating the globalization of ICANN and IANA functions, towards an environment in which all stakeholders, including all governments, participate on an equal footing."[145] With IANA itself as the sole exception, all of the expert groups involved in the coordination and development of the internet—the regional internet registries, the Internet Architecture Board, the Internet Engineering Task Force, the Internet Society, the World Wide Web Consortium and, not least, ICANN—endorsed this historic break.

After a concurrent report that the NSA had cooperated with its British counterpart agency (Government Communication Headquarters, or GCHQ) to tap into Yahoo! and Google data centers around the world in order to intercept and copy their massive data flows, internet intermediaries began to break ranks with the U.S. government: the *New York Times* explained that the spying scandal had grown to "[threaten] the foundation of their businesses, which rests on consumers and companies trusting them with their digital lives."[146] As headlines began to query, "Where Does Facebook Stop and the NSA Begin?"[147] U.S. internet intermediaries tried to reposition themselves as ardent foes of governmental trespasses; Eric Schmidt used a Hong Kong-based platform to protest, while Google complained formally to the NSA, the White House, and congressional representatives.[148] It was unclear, however, that this public-relations blitz would prove sufficient. Abiding damage to U.S. internet companies' transnational interests threatened—not least to their rapidly growing cloud services and the myriad commercial applications piled atop them.

It was a remarkably fluid moment, wherein the direction of change remained both vital and indefinite—perhaps even a historic turning point. The multipronged U.S. internet policy offensive in support of a transnational digital capitalism had been widely discredited, at home and especially abroad: the U.S. was compelled to regroup.[149] It was not yet evident, however, who else would, or who could, step in to recharge or adapt this existing policy program. Brazil, interestingly, stepped forward to announce that it would host a "Global Multi-stakeholder Meeting on the Future of Internet Governance" in April 2014. Was this a bid for autonomy from the U.S.-centric system—or a feint? Might a coalition of nations and corporations emerge that was sufficient to assemble a formally different, though substantially similar, policy for global internet governance? Where might this leave the United States? Bureaucrats, strategists, and independent analysts pondered whether Brazil's initiative might further some kind of accommodation and help rebuild legitimacy for a version of the status quo—or move beyond it.[150]

In the predominant U.S. discourse, the question of whether different states might fracture the interoperable internet as they imposed greater national jurisdictional controls still continued to be a touchstone; but other questions were now intervening, more far-reaching and portentous ones. Would U.S. corporate and state power over the extraterritorial internet finally be reduced? If so, this would constitute a sea change, the profound ramifications of which would give rise at once to other questions: What would replace U.S. unilateral globalism? Would ICANN's corporatist "multi-stakeholder" model be elevated, to transpose into a full-fledged global regime? Or, far less likely, would a multilateral model of internet governance be instituted? Or, instead, would the previous unstable stalemate find a new lease on life as U.S.-centric internet governance and its erstwhile allies continued to vie against dissatisfied stakeholders such as China and Russia? How would the U.S. leadership respond to the varied reform proposals? What roles would be played in forthcoming initiatives by other power groupings: the European Union, Mercosur, the BRICS, the Shanghai

Cooperation Organization? Only after this book goes to press will we learn whether the U.S.–centric internet may be modified and, if so, how. Surprises, assuredly, remain in store. But the essential questions have to do not with "balkanization," as Eric Schmidt referred to the specter of a fractured internet,[151] but with whose political-economic interests may predominate in any restructuring and, above all, with how—and how far—democratic principles of representation and accountability might be imagined and established.

A neglected aspect of these profound questions brings us back once more to the U.S. state—which was not bound necessarily to act in a single, unitary way. The NSA spying scandal revealed that the seeming fusion of interests between the U.S. Executive Branch and U.S. networking and internet companies was actually far from stable. Not only had the spiraling business threat posed to U.S. internet companies caused them to look for means of appearing to distance themselves politically from the U.S. state, so that they vowed to "harden" their systems and pressed publicly for tighter laws against backdoor surveillance programs by their own government's spy services[152]—indeed, Microsoft even boasted that it would allow foreign users of its systems to store their personal data on servers located outside the United States.[153] And not only had President Obama reciprocated, ignoring U.S. public opinion (which opposed NSA data collection policies) in his attempts to shore up NSA surveillance programs and to shift the blame by declaring, "The challenges to our privacy do not come from government alone."[154] Amid this fractiousness between U.S. internet capital and the U.S. administration, other powerful U.S. state actors also expressed alarm at what they had long perceived as the internet's strategic vulnerabilities. The longstanding U.S. approach to global internet governance in turn faced additional challenges not only from without but also from within.

CHAPTER 14

Accumulation
and Repression

A sustained and often secretive mobilization by the U.S. Executive Branch engendered little-known challenges to the existing internet by elements of the United States military and security establishment. The issues pertained to cyber-conflict, as it came to be called, in which, akin to air power decades before, network-enabled weapons launched a far-reaching reappraisal of strategic imperatives.

The 1990s and the decade that followed witnessed scattered cyberattacks, occasionally quite serious ones.[1] Estonian banking and government Web sites were struck during May 2007 by an assault supposedly perpetrated from within Russia. Israel reputedly used cyberweapons (or, perhaps, a hardware-based Trojan horse?) to knock out Syrian air defenses before swooping in with bombers to destroy a nuclear facility there in 2007.[2] U.S. analysts charged that China-based hackers had repeatedly broken into U.S. military organizations, corporate contractors, and digital services,[3] and that they had insinuated "logic bombs" into U.S. networks for possible later use.[4] "Cyber attacks from China," stated one, "have resulted in the loss of extraordinary amounts of private sector proprietary data, in addition to sensitive military information such as the engineering data for the new F-35 fighter aircraft."[5] More than $300 billion worth of F-35s had been ordered by the U.S. Air Force, Navy, and Marines—nearly twenty-five hundred airplanes:[6] had this huge expenditure, and the dominance it promised, been compromised? Where, moreover, was the dividing line in this new battlespace between espionage and acts of war?

Social as well as technical factors made it difficult to verify what was happening. Companies and Executive Branch departments were reluctant to admit publicly that outsiders had hacked into their networks; as well, military officials and contractor companies managed the scant publicity accorded cyberweapons in light of visions of the national interest that were frequently as misdirected as they were self-interested. Furthermore, because sophisticated attackers might succeed in covering their traces, companies and state agencies might be ignorant that their networks had been compromised, or of the identities or even the national base of the perpetrators. Whatever the extent of the transgressions, a near-perfect terrain had been established for the kind of hyperbole and fear mongering that, especially after 9/11, sowed anxiety and confusion throughout the U.S. population.

A sketchy record of U.S. cyber-conflict policy would make room for a few relatively well-known landmarks. The Gulf War of 1991 was packaged by one insider as a watershed in the emergence of infocentric warfare, though whether this was actually true was questionable.[7] Be this as it may, the 1990s saw intensive, and secret, preparation of weapons, and of offensive as well as defensive capabilities. U.S. military agencies actively probed the potentialities of network-enabled operations, training specialized personnel for info- or net-centric war. The "signature event" of "the takeoff period" in U.S. cyber-conflict planning, which one authority dated to 1998, was that year's Presidential Decision Directive 63; it was followed by a succession of additional organizational changes during what this same writer called the era of "militarization" which, he held, commenced in 2003 with the classified National Strategy for a Secure Cyberspace.[8] A National Security Presidential Directive issued in July 2002—NSPD 16—reportedly ordered the government to develop guidance for determining when and how the U.S. would launch cyberattacks against enemy networks. A 2003 "DOD Information Operations Roadmap" recommended that the United States issue a declaration of policy for offensive operations; and a 2006 *National Military Strategy for Cyberspace Operations* had gone on record with the claim that "as a war-fighting domain . . . cyberspace favors the offense."[9] The offensive mission was continually expanded, reorganized, and refined but, vitally, the National Security Agency remained one of its anchors throughout this process of "weaponizing the internet."[10] Strategic deterrence was likewise being reshaped to make room for the tools of cyber-conflict as new understandings emerged and technologies altered in the face of "the unauthorized penetration by, on behalf of, or in support of, a government into another nation's computer or network, or any other activity affecting a computer system, in which the purpose is to add, alter, or falsify data, or cause the disruption of or damage to a computer, or network device, or the objects a computer system controls."[11]

A classified Comprehensive National Cybersecurity Initiative was adopted in January 2008 under National Security Presidential Directive 54 and Homeland Security Presidential Directive 23; Congress allotted the initiative a five-year budget of $17 billion.[12] The incoming Obama Administration released a *Cyberspace Policy Review* in 2009, the analysis of which warned, "The Nation is at a crossroads," and called for "a national dialogue on cybersecurity."[13] The National Research Council had already convened an expert Committee on Offensive Information Warfare in 2006, and it released its report in 2009. The committee's finding—that "enduring unilateral dominance in cyberspace is neither realistic nor achievable by the United States"[14]—was not only ignored, it was soon outpaced by events.

One salutary finding had been that "secrecy has impeded widespread understanding and debate about the nature and implications of U.S. cyberattack"; no less commendable was a committee recommendation congruent with that of the *Cyberspace Policy Review*: that the U.S. government should conduct "a broad, unclassified national debate and discussion about cyberattack policy."[15] However, despite a stream of ensuing military and intelligence analyses, newspaper reports, think-tank studies, and congressional hearings, the United States was crossing a watershed without any of the debate over fundamental assumptions that stands as an absolute prerequisite of democratic accountability—and no graver issue confronts any polity than the decision to undertake conflicts that may constitute, or lead on to, war.

On one hand, U.S. military dependence on networks was becoming ever-more comprehensive; on the other, a fast-growing, profit-making institutional complex had coalesced, to develop, manage, and coordinate connectivity-enabled weaponry.

As we have seen, just as they also had penetrated deeply into finance, production, and communications, networks had been made intrinsic elements within the modernized machinery of war. This went beyond endowing Abrams tanks and Bradley fighting vehicles with digital gun sights and communications capabilities.[16] Networks had comprehensively diffused across the war-making function. Deputy Secretary of Defense William Lynn summed up the military's assimilation of connectivity in 2010: "Information technology enables almost everything the U.S. military does: logistical support and global command and control of forces, real-time provision of intelligence, and remote operations. Every one of these functions depends heavily on the military's global communications backbone, which consists of 15,000 networks and seven million computing devices across hundreds of installations in dozens of countries. More than 90,000 people work full time to maintain it."[17] By 2013, the Defense Department was operating six hundred thousand mobile devices from multiple vendors.[18] DoD's IT budget ($36 billion in 2011) approached half of the federal government's overall spending on information technology ($80 billion), and outlays made by the intelligence agencies apparently were not included in this estimate.[19] Fresh infusions were presented as an urgent national necessity, a matter of "protecting" the nation's now-indispensable cyber infrastructure—like the above-mentioned $1.2 billion data center being built near Salt Lake City by the Army Corps of Engineers for the National Security Agency, to balance the load placed by its global spying operation on the NSA's Fort Meade, Maryland, facility.[20]

To supply the needed weaponry, a further front opened in the arms race. The largest U.S. military contractors, including Northrop Grumman, General Dynamics, Lockheed Martin, Boeing, and Raytheon, all obtained major "cyber contracts" with U.S. military and intelligence agencies; Northrop Grumman, which in 2011 identified "cyber" as one of its four growth markets, estimated that overall federal spending on offensive and defensive cyber operations had reached $10 billion annually and was headed upward.[21] Legislation sought to create room explicitly for corporate vendors, called "cybersecurity suppliers," in a bill introduced (but not passed) in 2011.[22] A trade association, the Internet Security Alliance, offered an institutional nexus for military contractors[23]— which in turn "invested heavily" to establish what the *Financial Times* called "a cyber-industrial complex"; mergers and acquisitions in the sector heated up, and overall information technology employment in the greater Washington, D.C., area reached 280,000—more than in Silicon Valley or New York City.[24] Implementing a plan drafted by his predecessor, President Obama established an operational military Cyber Command, and hundreds of companies mushroomed around its headquarters near the mammoth National Security Agency facility at Fort Meade, Maryland. More than a dozen other nations, including France and the United Kingdom, followed suit by setting up their own cyber command units.[25]

That U.S. strategy incorporated offensive cyberattacks belatedly became a matter of public record: U.S. militarization of cyberspace far outran the attenuated public discussion that did ensue. The *New York Times* had used an artful headline—"Halted '03 Iraq Plan Illustrates U.S. Fear of Cyberwar Risk"—to imply that a concern for human welfare had informed the U.S. decision not to execute a cyberattack against the Iraqi financial system in preparation for its invasion. In fact, the *Times* revealed in the body of the account, the U.S. decision had been taken largely on grounds of "collateral damage": principally, that it might have triggered "worldwide financial havoc, spreading across the Middle East to Europe and perhaps to the United States."[26] Of course, we know now that it did not require cyberwar to crater the U.S. financial system. In October 2011, however—well after the fact—the *Times* revealed that the Obama Administration had "intensely debated" whether to commence its military strikes against Libya the previous March with a "cyberoffensive to disrupt and even disable the Qaddafi government's air-defense system." Again the plan had been rejected, and again the decision bespoke not concern for its human consequences but operational uncertainties: some military officers had argued against this offensive, reported the *Times*, by "questioning whether the attack could be mounted on such short notice."[27] However, the *Washington Post* later reported on a classified intelligence budget, leaked by Edward Snowden, to show that U.S. spy agencies had mounted no fewer than 231 offensive cyber operations in the same year—2011[28]—that this particular option was forsaken in the case of Libya.

A treatise by U.S. General Martin Dempsey stated matter-of-factly that "disrupting the enemy will require the full inclusion of space and cyberspace operations into the traditional air-land-sea battle space ... [They have] critical importance for the projection of military force."[29] A high-ranking NATO official added, "Clearly in the future all conflicts are going to involve people trying to disrupt the information technology systems, which are not only necessary for communication, but also for the operation of highly sophisticated weapons systems."[30] Three years after the need for a "broad national debate" was underlined, a *Financial Times* editorial called merely for the U.S. and U.K. governments to "be more open about their capabilities."[31]

Crucial decisions were being taken without any real effort at accountability. Most spectacularly, after months of speculation about who had perpetrated a military-grade computer virus—dubbed "Stuxnet"—and how it might have appeared on the open internet in 2010, it was confirmed in 2012 that it had been created by the United States and Israel. The two nations' military intelligence services had worked concordantly, beginning during the George W. Bush administration and continuing uninterruptedly through the Obama presidency, to develop the virus—originally code-named "Olympic Games"—in a successful campaign to sabotage Iranian nuclear facilities at Natanz. "From his first months in office," David E. Sanger reported in a *New York Times* front-page retrospective, "President Obama secretly ordered increasingly sophisticated attacks on the computer systems that run Iran's main nuclear enrichment facilities."[32] The "Olympic Games" deployment constituted "the most dramatic field test in history of a new weapon in America's arsenal,"[33] signaling that the world's most network-dependent nation was determined to take the lead—just as it had sixty-five years before, at Hiroshima and Nagasaki—in this new battlespace. Nor did the Obama administration then discontinue its deployment of cyberweapons—both against Iran and, it was hinted, other states.[34] Reports circulated that another virus, called "Flame," had been sent to corrupt the computers used by high-ranking Iranian leaders.[35] And, as already mentioned, the United States was also pursuing scores of other offensive cyber operations, notably against China, Russia, and North Korea, as well as Iran.[36]

As a result of constricted, belated, and heavily managed publicity, we do not yet completely understand the process that led to the presidential decisions to "secretly launch the country into a new era of cyber combat."[37] David E. Sanger suggests that pressures from Israel played a part in the launch of "Olympic Games" at Iran.[38] Be this as it may, other precipitants rendered cyberattacks a more widespread option. First, the attractiveness of cyberweapons stemmed in part from the fact that they seemed to enable war on the cheap. Cyberattacks of the kind mounted against Natanz, though more elaborate, expensive, and time-consuming than in popular depiction, need not necessitate also putting "boots on the ground" to mount "kinetic" campaigns (as the military calls these)—with an accompanying imperative for expensive logistics and resupply (around $2 billion each week in the case of the U.S. campaign in Afghanistan). This makes cyber conflict appropriate for—even emblematic of—the digital-depression-induced "age of austerity," in which even the U.S. military faced (modest) cutbacks.[39]

Second, cyberweapons, together with drone aircraft, offered means of making war with only the barest involvement by citizens, or even by their legislative representatives; the new weapons, writes David E. Sanger, "dramatically expanded the president's ability" to conduct "clandestine conflict," deeming it practical "to wage nonstop, low-level conflict, something just short of war, every day of the year."[40] U.S. cyberwarriors might hope to deploy these new-model weapons without suffering U.S. casualties, no matter what "collateral damage" they produced on others—and thus without arousing strong domestic protest, a standing concern in an era of permanent war.

A third factor was dispositive, as it underlay the other two: that U.S. global military supremacy remained an overriding—indeed, an unshakeable—official commitment. For going on three-quarters of a century, the U.S. mission had been to project force on behalf of transnational capital's long-range and, often, its immediate interests; this mission now came to encompass the deployment of offensive cyber operations. It was, simply, unacceptable to U.S. leaders that any rival should dominate this battlespace—not primarily owing to hubris, but rather to an abiding U.S. commitment to exploiting "the prerogative of offensive defence"[41] in policing the world.

This, however—to return to the finding of the Committee on Offensive Cyber Weapons—was easier said than done. In the *Dr. Strangelove*-ian world of U.S. military decision making, a good offense may be made superordinate even when deterrence raises intractable problems. Cyberattacks may make strategic use of computing resources located in third countries, owing to the interoperability of the networks that mesh to form the extraterritorial internet. This fact not only threatens to draw nonbelligerents into the conflict, it also introduces a critical element of indeterminacy into hair-trigger calculations in responding to whomever may have launched a cyberattack. A major cyberattack against the United States, observes Richard A. Clarke, "is likely to originate in the U.S., so we will *not* be able to see it coming and block it": cyberwarriors, presumably from the United States as well as other countries, were infiltrating civilian networks, implanting "logic bombs" in electric power grids, and "seeding infrastructure for destruction."[42]

Ramifications arising out of the United States' need to defend against cyberattacks were therefore profound. Analysts agreed that until and unless the fundamental problem of defensive security could be solved, the deployment of offensive cyberweapons would remain strategically uncertain[43]—though this, as we have seen, did not prevent the United States from deploying them. In part, this was because U.S. cyberattacks imparted a strong motive to other countries for ramping up their own cyberweapons programs.[44] More important, it was because of the asymmetry that characterized this domain: for all its power in conventional and nuclear armaments, the United States—the originating host for digital capitalism—remained singularly vulnerable to cyberattack.

Though, owing to its ubiquitous network-dependence, the United States probably had the most to gain from a treaty that would demilitarize cyberspace, that option was not pursued. Eschewing a political solution, the United States instead opted for technical and organizational patches. While his administration ramped up the applications of internet connectivity, President Bill Clinton substituted for an antimilitarization program a sustained federal effort to upgrade "critical infrastructure protection" around networks embedded in communications, energy, transportation, and financial commodity chains. This imperative persisted through subsequent administrations. "When the subject of cyber comes up," writes David E. Sanger, "Obama and his advisers almost always turn the conversation to cyber *defense*—how to harden and protect America's power grid, its banking system, and the rest of its critical infrastructure."[45] The U.S. drive to deepen and extend digital capitalism itself thus accentuated a condition of chronic strategic *insecurity*.

Because the state had invested prolonged effort in expanding capital's freedom to develop and apply network connectivity; because a huge array of internet systems and services had come to support commodity chains of every description, penetrating deep into the political economy, including into the heart of the military establishment; because this network of networks had been deliberately built out and configured extraterritorially; because, as President Obama's *Cyberspace Policy Review* underlined, "the digital infrastructure's architecture was driven more by considerations of interoperability and efficiency than of security";[46] and of course because all this had transpired in a world riven by dominative power relations and deep-seated inequalities, the U.S. government's ability to safeguard society from destructive cyber-actions was anything but assured. "A growing array of state and non-state actors," declared the *Review*, "are compromising, stealing, changing, or destroying information and could cause critical disruptions to U.S. systems."[47] A series of government reports and news stories provided a torrent of diagnostics, but the essential and, as the U.S. began to deploy cyberweapons, the urgent, point was that the federal government needed to do much more to erect safeguards over the nation's own networks.[48]

Programmatic efforts continued around "critical infrastructures,"[49] while a widened protective screen was sought—as the U.S. political economy became ever more network reliant and as awareness focused on how the internet's vulnerability reflected its initial design (which had not included security measures typical of other public networks).[50] The need to extend defenses instigated the Internet Policy Task Force in 2010–12 to review security in areas adjacent to already-identified critical infrastructures, throughout a so-called "Internet and Information Innovation Sector."[51] This did not comprise the sole such extension. The Defense Department began to coordinate cyberdefense with the Department of Homeland Security.[52] A U.S. cybersecurity framework also began to be extended transnationally. Having organized close relations with its counterparts in Canada, Australia, and the United Kingdom, the United States also brought an agenda of cyberdefense before NATO.[53] Early in 2012 NATO's twenty-eight member countries signed an ambitious cyberdefense contract "to secure its network across 50 sites";[54] during 2012, all NATO networks, both civilian and military, were to be brought under the NATO Cyber Incident Response Center. Of course, there was a world beyond NATO, and the new U.S. cybercommand turned its attention next to Japan, South Korea, and New Zealand.[55] Any fallout on these arrangements from the Snowden exposures remained uncertain in mid-2014.

A "broad national debate" over how networks had been integrated into the political economy was desperately needed. During the presidential campaign of 2012, however, any trace of such a debate was submerged. In its stead, the distended apparatus of managed publicity produced a surrogate discourse, pivoting not around "Why?" but rather, merely, "How?" Democrats disagreed with Republicans about meaningful details, such as whether tier 1 ISPs instead of a government agency should be vested with the power to perform deep-packet inspection, or whether information sharing between military agencies and corporations would be a sufficient safeguard. But the discourse's basic character expressed a bipartisan aspiration to securing a connectivity-enabled transnational capitalism. Proclamations of U.S. vulnerability in this context perversely became a pretext for prospectively wrenching changes to the internet. Longtime White House National Security aide Richard A. Clarke understood the issue in just these terms, as he asked whether "hardening" U.S. domestic network infrastructures might allow the United States to go "on the offensive, using our new cyber warriors to achieve military dominance of cyberspace for the United States of America?"[56] Clarke was a proponent of international arms-control measures to limit the impact of cyberwar on civilian populations. But he was uncompromising that any such agreements should "[allow] the U.S. to continue to do what it is good at, cyber war against military targets, including going first."[57] Still being exercised, unmistakably, was "the prerogative of offensive defence."[58]

The prospect of a cyberattack on the United States itself was real enough. When approached from the target side, moreover, the prospect of cyber-conflict was terrifying. As network infrastructures became hardwired into social and political life, society as a whole was made vulnerable. Banks, schools, stoplights, supermarkets, hospitals, even households: the operations of each and every network-enabled organization and function stood to be compromised—possibly with lethal effects. A clear-eyed analysis of combat must take it as axiomatic that—in Oettinger's[59] artfully understated formulation in 1980—"The line between the civilian and the military seems to have grown thin." Yet it did not bear much acknowledgment that cyberweapons portended attacks on noncombatants and daily life.[60] One authority observed that, although apparently "no one has yet been killed" by a cyber-conflict, "it is likely that cyber conflicts will become more destructive" as nations "put more physical infrastructure online, such as the Smart Grid."[61]

Attempts at ensuring greater security could follow one of two paths. Network dependence could continue to be reorganized through technological, legal, and organizational means, on the understanding that digital capitalism had progressed beyond any possibility of actually pulling the plug. This was the option preferred by Richard A. Clarke, who held simply, "It is impossible to reduce our dependence on networked systems at this point."[62] Alternatively, a global campaign could be undertaken to forge a comprehensive treaty banning cyber weapons. To stand any chance of success, admittedly, this option would necessitate a far more sweeping U.S. policy reversal to redress the dominative relationships that helped make U.S. policy an object of attacks in the first place. A beginning might be for the U.S. to withdraw its troops from its several hundred foreign military bases and to abrogate the "structure of forces" agreements that enabled them. For U.S. policymakers in general, however, such a response was all but unimaginable.

A multilateral dialogue, based on fully shared information, constituted an obvious first prerequisite for meaningful engagement with the issue of security across cyberspace's extraterritorial jurisdiction.[63] However, political-economic relationships, sorely aggravated by the digital depression, conspired to marginalize even this minimal prospect. At the national level, these same factors, alongside a huge military industry and a pervasively corrupted process of campaign finance, likewise weighted the scales against an officially sanctioned "broad national discussion." What, then, substituted for the process of democratically accountable decision making?

The Obama administration mounted concerted attempts to reorganize the functionality of the internet in both institutional and technical terms. Often proceeding within secretive and technologically opaque contexts, these endeavors were congruent with entrenched practice and with Armand Mattelart's astute characterization of the current trajectory: "The heads of the world-system network resort to strong-armed management of inequalities instead of declaring war on the mechanisms that reproduce them and reconstructing damaged systems of solidarity."[64] Federal initiatives to "secure" the nation's networks were replete with fearsome implications.

The problem was simple to state but highly complex in its ramifications: Securing military networks and corporate commodity chains against attack was practically impossible, in like measure that these systems interoperated with the existing internet. So far-reaching did this threat appear, that erstwhile White House security advisor Clarke declared in 2010 that "at present the U.S. would be better off if cyber warfare never existed, given our asymmetrical vulnerabilities to such warfare."[65] The efforts that followed to reduce internet vulnerabilities, however, exacted a steep—indeed, for democrats, an inadmissible—price. A repressive authoritarian potential was intrinsic within the strengthening impulse to "cybersecurity."

Beginning well before 9/11, hackers and state-sponsored cyberattacks had already become occasions for instituting preemptive measures. I have already mentioned programs to protect cyber infrastructure. Apparently commencing in March 1998 and seemingly originating in Russia, sustained intrusions into hundreds of computers at the Pentagon, NASA, and private universities and research laboratories likewise prompted the U.S. Defense Department to order that even its unclassified communications would thereafter be routed "through eight large electronic gateways that will be easier to monitor"—anticipating the more encompassing Trusted Internet Communication directive covering the entire federal government a decade later.[66] In the wake of 9/11 such initiatives strengthened. The Patriot Act and a great number of additional measures established a seemingly permanent "state of exception," in which the government arrogated to itself the right to take any measures it might deem necessary against threats, real or imagined. To choose only one example, which surfaced a year before Snowden's exposures commenced: cellphone carriers reported that, in 2011, U.S. law enforcement agencies of every kind had made a total of 1.3 million demands (many encompassing multiple individuals) that they divulge subscriber information, what the *New York Times* called a "startling" figure, testifying to "an explosion in cellphone surveillance" involving the turnover of subscriber records thousands of times *each day*.[67] As a consequence of Snowden's whistle-blowing, we now know that these transgressions merely scratched the surface: the National Security Agency, which was charged with offensive as well as defensive functions, was plowing through billions of emails, telephone calls, texts, chat messages, blogs, and other electronic communications, not only domestically[68] but internationally.[69]

Overarching surveillance seemed rational—indeed, urgent—when the commodity chains that fed U.S. military procurement were themselves transnationalized. In 2008, President Bush had signed Presidential Decision Directive 54, a secret outline for defending the United States against cyber-conflict, one of whose provisions concerned "Supply Chain Security."[70] Computer chips manufactured by U.S. companies in the Pentagon's "Trusted Foundry" program accounted for a mere 2 percent of the $3.5 billion in annual military purchases of integrated circuits. Because (so the assumption went) globally sourced computer hardware could be tampered with more easily than chips produced on U.S. soil, it might be a Trojan horse.[71] Obama carried forward this objective but recognized that it raised a more general problem: "Globalization of the commercial information and communications technology marketplace provides increased opportunities for those intent on harming the United States by penetrating the supply chain to gain unauthorized access to data, alter data, or interrupt communications. Risks stemming from both the domestic and globalized supply chain must be managed in a strategic and comprehensive way over the entire lifecycle of products, systems and services."[72] Faced with such a threat, of course, U.S. companies could wave the flag in order to outmaneuver foreign competitors in bids for U.S. government contracts. Threat management, however, also encompassed other dimensions.

A far-reaching plan for internet security issued from the White House in March 2010, much of it said to have been carried over from the classified program developed by the Bush administration.[73] "Firewalls" and "intrusion protection systems" that inspected every packet seeking entry began to be introduced throughout government networks. Legislation was brought forward to expedite the movement of deep-packet inspection technology into the networks of major ISPs. A technology known as Secure DNS, or DNSSEC, began to be pressed into service to ensure that internet users could communicate "with high confidence that the identity of the person or organization that they are communicating with is not being spoofed or forged."[74] Kindred measures were pursued, pertaining to everything from the Internet Protocol's architecture and the Border Gateway Protocol that was needed to route packets, to technical standards for the Web, to hardware vulnerabilities.[75] Might these often-arcane technical measures be sufficient to eliminate the security loopholes?[76] A revealing part of the problem was that efforts to universalize or, at least, to generalize strong encryption were repeatedly rebuffed by leading units of capital.

A Commerce Department Internet Policy Task Force proceeding on cybersecurity sought to elicit reports on the current situation and to systematize an official remedy for it. Corporations spanning many segments of communications commodity chains participated. AT&T, Cisco, Google, IBM, Microsoft, PayPal, and VeriSign filed comments. So did major trade associations, whose members encompassed many diverse units of capital: the Business Software Alliance, the Cellular Telecommunications Industry Association, the Information Technology Industry Council, the Internet Security Alliance, the Messaging Anti-Abuse Working Group, the Online Trust Alliance, and TechAmerica.[77] A status report on this proceeding was published as a "Green Paper" by the Commerce Department, one month after the president issued his administration's overall "International Strategy for Cyberspace" in May 2011.[78] Three features of the Green Paper command attention.

First, a tripartite approach to "security" was instituted. Military networks fell under the aegis of the Defense Department, the National Security Agency, and their corporate contractors. Other government networks, and so-called "critical infrastructures" used for energy, transport, banking, and communications across the wider society, were under the purview of the Department of Homeland Security, working with the CIO Council, whose members were the chief information officers of twenty-eight federal departments and agencies. The Commerce Department (especially NIST), finally, would coordinate security for a more far-flung "Internet and Information Innovation Sector," which encompassed commercial information services and content providers, transactional services, storage and hosting services, and "user support" providers such as application, browser, social network, and search services.[79] Taken together, and coordinating with the co-headed U.S. Cyber Command and NSA,[80] these three Executive Branch agencies were developing "a public/ private collaboration that spans multiple government agencies, more than 30 security tool vendors, and a host of end-user organizations."[81] Because, again, the internet constituted an interoperable network of networks belonging to corporations and government agencies, only sweeping coordination between state and capital—dubbed a "public-private partnership" to generate "trust"— could anchor "security best practices."[82] In specific relation to the internet, the "public-private partnership" had originated earlier as a hallmark of the Clinton administration's "framework for global electronic commerce."[83] Did the Obama administration's adaptation amount to what it had previously called "an organized and unified response"[84]—a structural fusion of interests? Or was it to be a mere amalgamation, subject to flaring conflict and instability?

A momentary answer to this question was suggested through a second feature of the same Commerce Department proceeding. Rather than resisting government-mandated internet security on principle, corporate commenters instead tended to agree to it if it were treated as an externality—a cost to be absorbed by taxpayers. This was not the only possible solution: security could instead be mandated as a cost to be borne by corporations. Companies indeed were allotting substantial sums to secure their network systems internally; beyond the borders of their own proprietary networks, however, why should they assume the burden of addressing disparate and costly security issues? (This behavior established a partial parallel with financial practices that had helped to trigger the digital depression: credit default swaps and other such instruments had reduced individual corporate risk but radically increased systemic risk.) The government should step in to do so. A program was indeed devised to diagnose security risks inhering in what is called the Border Gateway Protocol, which helps enable the interoperability of the internet. Intensive analysis was undertaken by the Internet Engineering Task Force—a voluntary organization which, recall, was supposedly a neutral representative of the global community—in concert with both the U.S. Department of Homeland Security and the National Institute of Standards and Technology, a unit of the U.S. Commerce Department.[85]

The reach and coherence of this response, however, were not assured, because corporate commenters were united in their conviction that the government should not introduce additional regulatory measures. "Security" mandates could be suggested, even modeled—just not enforced. The units of capital that operated 85 percent of the nation's critical infrastructure[86] stoutly opposed federal actions to compel them to "harden" their network systems and services. This went beyond rejecting the expense that such regulations would require—and had nothing to do with the defense of civil liberties that bulked so large in reference to other countries' censoriousness. No, corporate opposition to regulation stemmed from an assumption that had been pervasive from the moment the internet began to be commercialized during the 1980s and 1990s: that capital should enjoy freedom over and above common needs, in this sphere as in others, with any necessary measures being paid for by the government.[87] To impose such regulation over the internet—the supreme vehicle of contemporary efforts to regenerate capitalism—flouted this longstanding article of faith.

The outcome was thus to establish a protracted and contradictory standoff rather than a coherent policy. Beginning in 2009, the Obama Administration had worked to pass legislation that would grant the Department of Homeland Security power to enforce minimum cybersecurity standards over critical infrastructures that, a *New York Times* reporter explained, "if damaged, would lead to mass casualties or economic loss."[88] The continued absence of mandatory regulation drew fierce critics, both military and civilian, who charged that incentives and voluntarism would not suffice to safeguard the American people.[89] During 2011, however, two additional attempts at cybersecurity legislation became casualties of popular opposition.[90] During 2012,[91] the central state remained divided about coercive impositions. While President Obama editorialized in favor of "comprehensive cybersecurity legislation" to address "an urgent national-security challenge,"[92] a significant number of liberals and Republicans (and the U.S. Chamber of Commerce and other business lobbyists) opposed expanding the enforcement role of the Department of Homeland Security.[93] Resurrected, draconian legislation was rebuffed again in 2013, only to reappear once again.[94] The Commerce Department, whose reason for being sprang from its proximity to U.S. business interests, itself continued to throw its support to "a multi-stakeholder approach" and "voluntary codes of conduct."[95]

The extraterritorial ramifications of the problem constituted a third key aspect of the Green Paper—and again a source of dissension. "The fact that cybersecurity is not defined by national borders and that the United States cannot afford to ignore global considerations," declared the Green Paper, "was a large topic of comment . . . and plays a major part in how the Department of Commerce views its role in cybersecurity." One proposal was that the United States establish an Ambassador for cybersecurity at the State Department and, soon thereafter, the State Department did in fact establish a Coordinator for Cyber Issues.[96] This constituted what the President had singled out as a necessary diplomatic dimension of international policy for cyberspace.[97] The Messaging Anti-Abuse Working Group requested that the Commerce Department establish "its own specialized, technical 'boots on the ground' abroad, staffed by career employees with specialized cyber knowledge and expertise."[98] Education, technical assistance, international standards promotion, and other forms of support should be concentrated in "nations facing the most acute challenges."[99] The president himself expressly called for such initiatives under the rubric of "development."[100] Those with some knowledge of the history of imperialism might discern analogies to the educational initiatives carried out by missionaries and, after World War II, to earlier "development" programs that in some cases looked like what historian Bradley Simpson called "economists with guns."[101]

Sandwiched between "diplomacy" and "development" within the president's clarion call was a third keyword: "defense." Obama declared that "a globally distributed network requires globally distributed early warning capabilities" and "enhanced computer network defense."[102] Through "ongoing operational and policy relationships," "collaborations in the technical and military defense areas," the United States would deploy its unmatched global military presence to advance cybersecurity extraterritorially. One set of initiatives would be multilateral; it would be pursued in concert with the international institutions forged in concert with U.S. dominance: the Organization of American States, the Association of Southeast Asian Nations, the Organization for Cooperation and Security in Europe, the African Union, the OECD, the Group of Eight, the North Atlantic Treaty Organization, the European Union, and the Asia-Pacific Economic Cooperation Organization.[103] Related exercises were organized around the so-called Meridian Process, which pursued information sharing on behalf of closer international cooperation around "Critical Infrastructure Information Protection" (CIIP). The 2011 Meridian Conference, whose theme was "CIIP and International Dependencies," was hosted by Qatar (the previous three annual events had been hosted by Taiwan, the United States, and Singapore); preparations were made by a program committee made up of representatives from Qatar, Germany, Hungary, Japan, Netherlands, Singapore, Taiwan, United Kingdom, Argentina, and the United States.[104] Also encompassed would be bilateral undertakings,[105] presumably connected to the "structure of force" agreements that set out terms for the hundreds of U.S. military bases located in dozens of other countries. Across this range, governmental work "in consultation with industry" would "enhance the security of the globalized supply chains on which free and open trade depend."[106] This was also the framework to which NSA spying initiatives were fitted. Only unbroken, global, omnidirectional electronic intelligence might suffice to provide warnings of threats that might originate and be expressed anywhere within the distributed, interoperable network.

Would even these ambitious measures be enough? A xenophobia-tinged notion arose, stressing that the internet might need to be rebuilt so as to incorporate technological fixes for what was portrayed as its "faulty initial design" around protocols that had emphasized interoperability built around trust and anonymity. One such plan, called Project Phoenix, that would include biometric identification and encryption of all keystrokes, drew praise from the head of security at PayPal. Google's vice president, Vinton Cerf, who had helped devise the original internet protocols, affected an interest "in the clean-slate ideas."[107]

Whether such a radical restructuring might be undertaken, let alone whether it might succeed, remained open questions. Throughout 2010–14, however, an institutionally strengthened U.S. cyber-industrial complex made repeated efforts to expand in this direction. Invasive and encompassing online surveillance programs granted what the ACLU called "virtually unchecked power to conduct dragnet collection of Americans' international emails and telephone calls without a warrant or suspicion of any kind."[108] Richard A. Clarke gestured enviously at the fact that, unlike the United States, "the Chinese government has both the power and the means to disconnect China's slice of the Internet from the rest of the world, which it may very well do in the event of a conflict with the United States."[109] The *Financial Times* reported that an executive at a Boeing subsidiary had asked, in the same vein, "If China can block any packet from entering the country and we can't, how can we win?"[110] Not China or Iran, but a professor at the U.S. Naval War College simply posited that henceforth an internet policed by intelligence agencies "will be reshaped to fit country borders."[111] Clarke himself recommended that, in addition to greater governmental centralization of the security function, the United States should pursue more secure network designs. Specifically, the United States should develop what he called a "Military Internet Protocol," replete with monitoring features, and should build out specialized networks with "no real-time connection" with the internet and use protocols, applications, and operating systems that were incompatible with it. "Those devoted to one big everybody-goes-everywhere, interconnected web won't like it," Clarke insisted, "but change must come."[112] Ian Bremmer forecast that transnational companies might need to learn to coordinate their operations across "a set of interlinked intranets closely monitored by various governments."[113] We must not underrate their ability to do so.

Though U.S. authorities stridently objected to such measures when other countries proposed them, efforts to reconstruct the internet around territorially bounded networks imbued with connectivity restrictions found influential adherents in the United States itself. Were the extraterritorial internet to be sectioned and splintered, however, then cross-border data flows (around which transnationally parcelized commodity chains had been constructed) and the rapid migration to cloud computing (services delivered via centralized data centers) and even, perhaps, the ideology of "free flow of information" would be subordinated to preparation for cyber-conflict.

U.S. officials paradoxically pursued both initiatives. Proposals that would fracture the internet to "harden" U.S. networks persisted alongside others that aimed at bulwarking global network interoperability. President Obama himself expressly rejected "a fragmented internet," but he glossed over the tensions that existed between the free-flow policy and international military, diplomatic, and development cybersecurity initiatives.[114] A high-level task force report to the Council on Foreign Relations affirmed in 2013 that "*a global Internet increasingly fragmented into national Internets is not in the interest of the United States*" and concluded that "by building a cyber alliance, making the free flow of information a part of all future trade agreements, and articulating an inclusive and robust vision of Internet governance, Washington can limit the effects of a fragmenting Internet." It also concluded, however, that "the trends do not look good."[115]

This uncertainty escalated dramatically in the wake of the Snowden exposures. A Washington, D.C.–based research outfit convened a meeting for business representatives to discuss with a former U.S. State Department coordinator for International Communications and Information Policy "The Impact of PRISM on Digital Trade Policy" and warned that the United States' "widespread, clandestine surveillance of digital communications . . . will likely have an impact on the ability of the U.S. government and tech sector to fight back against anti-competitive policies, such as server localization, that impede the global free flow of information while potentially legitimizing countries who wish to engage in such practices."[116] Shortly after this, the same group suggested that an effect of the spying revelations might be to cut tens of billions of dollars from the revenues of U.S. cloud services providers.[117] The third quarter of 2013 showed that new orders gained by U.S.-based Cisco Systems indeed had dropped 25 percent in Brazil and 30 percent in Russia, as the transnational supplier of internet equipment contended with "the furor over disclosures that the NSA had used the strong position of US technology companies to extend its surveillance"[118] and, it should have been added, U.S. offensive capabilities in cyberspace.

The debate at a U.S. academic conference in June 2013 around the idea that a "federated internet" might provide U.S. leaders with a relatively acceptable alternative to the existing U.S.-centric extraterritorial system may be placed in this context.[119] The concrete content of this proposal for a "federated internet" was not comprehensively specified, and its probability of actualization remained unknown. Perhaps, however—even if ultimately under some other name—it signaled a drive to fashion a differently advantaged U.S. policy synthesis. U.S. military planners continued to insist on a makeover of the internet to accommodate an "offensive defence"; while U.S. economic diplomacy continued to stress the interoperable internet as the pivot of unrestricted foreign investment, mutable cross-border commodity chains, and transnational corporate information flows. Might a means be contrived by which to reconcile these diverging U.S. policy requirements for both state repression and capital accumulation?

This was but the first of several profound open questions. Clashing U.S. policy imperatives of course also interacted with goals and programs set by other social and political actors, not only nationally but internationally. Just where the struggle to control and channel the extraterritorial internet might lead, in turn, became suffused with unprecedented contingency. This work concludes with a sketch of some of the larger forces that propelled digital capitalism into what was evidently a fraught future.

CHAPTER 15

From Geopolitics to Social and Political Struggle

The historical movement of the political economy is shaped both within and beyond a top-down, state-oriented geopolitics. The dispositive and dynamic factor is the political balance of social forces both within particular societies and globally.

"Can the capitalist class reproduce its power in the face of the raft of economic, social, political and geopolitical and environmental difficulties?" asks David Harvey. He believes that it may, but that this will come about, if it does come about, only as an outcome of social and political struggle. In order for capital's class project to succeed, Harvey explains, there will "have to be wrenching and painful shifts in the geographical and sectoral locus of capitalist class power. The capitalist class cannot, if history is any guide, maintain its power without changing its character and moving accumulation on to a different trajectory and into new spaces (such as east Asia)."[1] This reorganization was rendered contingent, not only by the titanic scale on which it was unfolding, but also because of generative conflicts among its participants.

Foregrounding digital sites of accumulation gave rise, we have seen, to an increasingly fractious geopolitics of information. Attempts by numerous states to multilateralize control of the U.S.-centric extraterritorial internet need to be referred both to structural alterations to the interstate system, and to competing efforts to regenerate the political economy in ways that might capture an outsized share of overall profits for specific units of capital and particular fractions of the capitalist class.

The onset of the digital depression brought changes to the interstate system, expressive of altering political-economic relations. The so-called Washington Consensus, which had codified U.S. power to set rules for the global political economy, was discarded. As the panic hit, it looked briefly as if the G20—which included five Asian nations in addition to Japan—might replace the smaller Atlantic-oriented G7 as an economic policymaking body.[2] Even after this impulse receded, Christine Lagarde, in ascending to the top executive role at the IMF, found it necessary to court Brazil, India, and China for support. China soon after became the third-largest member country by quota share within a restructured IMF; Brazil, India, and Russia were also elevated.[3] Other multilateral organizations and policymaking institutions likewise opened—selectively, often conflictually—to what were now called "Big Emerging Market" countries, led by China. On the other hand, the U.S.-EU–led drive to institute the so-called Doha Round of the World Trade Organization ended in failure, owing mostly to the opposition by the global south.[4] Disagreements over economic policies compounded. "Ironically, some of the countries that are responsible for the deepest crisis since the Great Depression, and have yet to solve their own problems, are eager to prescribe codes of conduct to the rest of the world," was the tart comment by Brazil's finance minister, Guido Mantega, in 2012.[5] The U.S. National Intelligence Council had projected that, going forward, "the United States' relative strength . . . will decline and U.S. leverage will become more constrained."[6] U.S. power was under challenge—but, crucially, it had not been supplanted: "Power structures," a journalist wrote in 2012, "still largely reflect the old state of the world."[7] If the U.S. was weakening, then no other power yet stood ready to replace it as a global hegemon: a rule-maker and -enforcer for capital. The United States predictably pressed its advantage. It attempted to revise the 1996 Information Technology Agreement under the auspices of the World Trade Organization.[8] It tried to negotiate transatlantic and transpacific trade agreements, which circumvented the global regime of the World Trade Organization and other multilateral institutions. All three of these initiatives, however, were under pressure at the time of this writing.[9]

Many commentators believed that China aspired to take over as a global power. But the U.S. economy remained more than three times as large as China's, while Chinese capital's impressive efforts to transnationalize perforce occurred within a global economy that was simultaneously awash in surplus capacity and overseen by entrenched transnational enterprises.[10] Even had the country decided to bid for global supremacy, moreover—not a small matter in its own right[11]—neither China's military nor its financial institutions were yet equal to the task of exercising interstate dominance. China's surplus, moreover, had been invested in supporting the United States as one of its two largest export markets (the European Union was the other) rather than in restructuring its own profoundly unbalanced political economy with its exceptional dependence on investment and exports. Such a change in priorities would not be easily accomplished, though there were signs that the Xi Jinping administration might move in this direction.[12] Chinese efforts to find and hold diplomatic, political, and ideological ground, finally, were conducted within a resistant international context.

All this admitted, China constituted one of two unsurpassed poles of growth for the capitalist political economy in general. The other growth pole was not territorial but sectoral: the information and communications industry.[13] How did these two poles interact—and combine? What, in particular, was the status of China's own information industry? I focus on this question in order to clarify some of digital capitalism's urgent pressure points.

China's industrialization, a correlative of the transnational reorganization of commodity chains throughout the late twentieth century, was itself—as Yu Hong shows—simultaneously a process of informationization.[14] Although China's party-controlled state welcomed unprecedented quantities of foreign direct investment into many industries, it was also impressively successful in setting terms of entry into the national market for the strategic communications and information sector.[15]

Between April and June of the crisis year 2010, the best record in PC shipments among top manufacturers was posted by Lenovo, for which its home market in China accounted for half of its sales and all of its profits. "Retreating from the west looks wise," commented the *Financial Times*;[16] and throughout the succeeding years, Lenovo's strong record continued to be based disproportionately on domestic sales.[17] Google and News Corporation, in contrast, each had to beat at least a partial retreat from China's national market.[18] Facebook remained a bystander, pondering a bid to enter China.[19] Not Amazon, but Alibaba, dominated China's e-commerce. Leading Western financial news Web sites, including those of Bloomberg, Thomson Reuters, the *New York Times*, and the *Wall Street Journal*, found themselves stymied in China.[20] As the U.S. internet intermediaries looked on, units of capital formed and took leading roles as purveyors of equipment and services across a wide swath: CCTV and Shanghai Media Group, Alibaba, Tencent, Sina, Baidu, China Mobile and China Telecom, Huawei and ZTE and Xiaomi (which crowed that its low-cost Red Rice smartphone sold out its first batch of one hundred thousand units in ninety seconds),[21] Xinhua, Sohu, Youku, and RenRen.

This by no means signified autarky. Chinese internet and communications companies often listed on the U.S. NASDAQ stock market; some found means of incorporating in the Cayman Islands or the Virgin Islands. Many exhibited opaque ownership structures, in which—as ShinJoung Yeo shows—institutional investors bulked large, including many U.S. private equity and hedge funds as well as various sovereign wealth funds.[22] Alibaba, an e-commerce giant with a prospective valuation that vied with that of Facebook, was nearly 35 percent owned by SoftBank of Japan;[23] SoftBank, likewise, owned a chunk of RenRen's parent, Oak Pacific Interactive. U.S.- and British-based investment funds T. Rowe Price and Oppenheimer were among the more substantial investors in Baidu and Sohu. Tencent operated four wholly owned foreign enterprises. Chinese internet companies thus drew liberally on foreign investment capital, which in turn was hungry for returns drawn from the booming Chinese market.

Nor were these the only means by which foreign capital participated in and profited from China's internet. Transnational internet intermediaries were allowed to establish a direct presence in some domestic industry segments as, for example, Microsoft in operating-system software and Apple in mobile devices.[24] IBM mainframe computers actually possessed a reputed 100 percent market share of China's "tier 1" state owned banks—for which Oracle and SAP were the principal suppliers of business software.[25] As of 2011, nearly half of the software and hardware procured for the Chinese central state's e-government services were foreign products.[26] China was increasingly a pivot of Global Hollywood,[27] as it began to displace the United States as the largest national film market; and Hollywood worried that Chinese audience preferences might drift away from its own "high-budget fantasies in 3-D and large-screen Imax formats" and toward domestic releases.[28]

For all this porousness, the domains of information, communications, and culture also were designated by China's party-state as "pillar industries," meaning that they were awarded a strategic priority within the state's overall economic policy.[29] Already sizable, this vital pole of economic growth drew a multipronged state initiative aiming at additional expansion. "Digitalization of content, and cooperation with the private sector are considered the next steps in the development," according to a report on 2010's Central Economic Work Conference.[30] It was reported in 2013 that China's powerful Ministry of Industry and Information Technology intended to shepherd investment of a spectacular $325 billion to extend and modernize wireline and wireless broadband infrastructure nationwide by 2020.[31] Based on as many as two hundred Chinese companies, and designated a strategic emerging industry in the State Council's 12th Five Year Plan (2011–2015), China's cloud computing platforms, applications, and hosting and storage were surging.[32] China's party-state, one U.S. analysis underscored, was acting strategically in light of its insight "that digital media in general and the internet in particular are critical to the country's economic development."[33]

Like the United States Government, China's party-state cultivated large units of capital in the internet sector. Paralleling U.S. President Obama's hobnobbing with Eric Schmidt, both PRC President Hu Jintao (in 2010) and his successor, Xi Jinping (in 2012), made well-publicized visits to Tencent—a Shenzhen-based company whose QQ social media service boasted 700 million users and whose CEO had amassed a fortune estimated at $6.4 billion.[34] Also like the United States, China's government often intervened to set the terms of access to the national market.[35] Both Microsoft and Apple, for example, were required to make strategic concessions in the design of their products in order to offer their goods in China.[36] State-owned wireless giant China Mobile (with 740 million customers in 2013), whose capital investments in next-generation 4G mobile network equipment greatly exceeded those being committed by Verizon, AT&T, and Vodafone, threw its support to a homegrown technical standard on which Chinese companies held significant patents. The move, commented the *Wall Street Journal*, "instantly gave that standard critical mass," and promised to grant China "greater say in how the global wireless industry works."[37] Not unrelated was an antitrust probe of Qualcomm, the world's largest maker of chips for smartphones, by China's foremost economic planning body and regulator, the National Development and Reform Commission.[38]

Relations and ownership structures linking a specific Chinese company's management to foreign portfolio and direct investors and, on the other hand, to Chinese state authorities, were typically opaque. Though the importance of these analytically distinct interests was ambiguous and fluid so that, therefore, the overall balance-of-power over China's information industry could not be definitively fixed, that the party-state was aiding units of Chinese capital to win important roles in the domestic market was beyond question. China's success in shaping its national information and communications market must be seen as an exceptional historical achievement in its own right.

Despite repeated efforts throughout several decades, including formally instituting "cultural exception" policies for French music and film and, more recently, insisting that "Act Two" of the cultural exception could only reach the stage if digital media services were similarly protected—France never fully managed it. Britain gave up decades ago, after its precocious computer industry died a slow death. Late in 2013, the chairman of the German software company SAP declared that "[If one wanted a strong European IT industry], then one shouldn't have let it die out 20 years ago."[39] (It might be noted that SAP's own CEO, Bill McDermott, was American.[40]) The regenerated capitalism of post-war Western Europe continually engendered mere niches in the ever-mutating fields of communications and information; and continually even these failed (as with the French champion Bull) or were abandoned (as in Nokia's sale of its wireless phone manufacturing unit to Microsoft), or they simply languished (as with Alcatel-Lucent).[41] SAP and Ericsson were the major exceptions. Comparable was the recent record compiled by Japan, despite its prior success in forging an industrial policy to develop a domestic computer industry,[42] and its decades-long lock on electronics hardware; by the 2010s, Sony, Panasonic, and other once-mighty consumer electronics companies were seeking shelter from Apple and Samsung on one side and Huawei and ZTE on the other.

China was not altogether unique. The "decolonization of information" that had inspired the Third World political project went down to defeat during the 1980s as a result of intense pressure from the United States as well as of hardening social-class relations in many poor countries.[43] Yet the import-substitution policies that had been forged by some of the largest Third World states succeeded in creating elements of national information industries, and these became foundations for subsequent projects. Brazil, whose "market reserve" policy throughout the 1970s built up a domestic capacity in "informatics," altered course after 1990 by granting subsidies, tax breaks, and tariff reductions aimed at reconfiguring its market to accommodate investment by foreign (largely U.S.) tech companies. Joining Dell, Sony, H-P, and Lenovo in what became the world's third-largest computer market, Hon Hai today assembles iPhones in Brazil.[44] Even as Brazil implemented economic policies to adapt the national market, however, established Brazilian IT companies partnered with transnational IT suppliers through licensing and distribution arrangements, while state administrators focused effort on internet development. By 2013, Brazil boasted a regionally dominant status over internet infrastructure, and Brazilian companies played growing roles both nationally and extraterritorially.[45] In this light, President Rousseff's willingness to stand up to the surveillance practices of the United States looks to be, in part, a form of economic diplomacy on behalf of Brazil's own high-tech companies.

India's satellite program and computer industry initiatives during the 1970s and 1980s likewise constituted a late expression of the state's attempt to pursue independent national development; after this, as India's leaders radically reoriented toward the global market, Indian IT software and business process outsourcing companies, led by Infosys, TCS, and Wipro, emerged as genuinely transnational suppliers—though it has been argued that, more recently, they have ceded priority to foreign capital.[46] South Korea created impressive niches in digital games and birthed a national champion that won global importance in consumer electronics: Samsung, which teamed with Google to challenge what had initially appeared to be an Apple preserve, advanced mobile devices.[47] Taiwan's information-technology industry, originating in establishment of the

Industrial Technology Research Institute in 1973, boasted microelectronics chipmaker TSMC, a pair of PC makers (Acer, ASUSTEK), and low-margin manufacturers like Quanta, Wistron, Compal, and Hon Hai.[48] A $63 billion industry by revenue in 2012, accounting for more than one-fifth of global semiconductor sales, Taiwan's chipmakers struggled even as they furnished the technology their big customers—notably, Apple and Samsung—used to generate jaw-dropping profits.[49] We stand in real need of comparative research into the internet industries of these countries and others, including Russia, where far-reaching Soviet state planning and science and technology education were followed by Presidential Modernization Programs: "Electronic Russia" (2002–12) and "Go Russia" (2009–), and where national units of capital played outsized roles in the domestic market for internet services.[50]

China, however, offered the most far-reaching, multifaceted, and successful model of state-directed development for ICT industry.[51] In 1949, Mao had announced, China was standing up; and, notwithstanding the "reform" that commenced in 1978—a period that is now longer than the Mao era that preceded it—China continued to stand up, now not as a recognizably socialist pioneer but as a rising capitalist power. The state's role in supervising the buildup of national capital in information and communications, moreover, did not diminish during the "reform" era. By 2010 it had become evident that, apart from the United States itself, no other country beside China possessed a multifaceted and technologically sophisticated information and communications industry, anchored by a large and still rapidly growing domestic market, and overseen by a strong and capable state. Chinese businesses and state agencies stood out, for these reasons, as increasingly vital actors within a globally mutating digital capitalism. (Late in 2013, China announced that it would reorganize the state's national security structure, perhaps bringing it more in line with the U.S. model, in order to grapple more effectively with both domestic and international challenges.[52])

Chinese policies to channel the national market in order to benefit home-based companies were not applied solely to this one vital sector. Disparate other strategic industries—oil and chemicals; aerospace; automotive equipment; power generation and distribution; military equipment; banking; genomics— also pursued comparable programs successfully, though, as Peter Nolan clarifies, far from comprehensively.[53] This said, the effectiveness of Chinese policies in the high-growth field of information and communications constituted, for foreign (and, especially, for U.S.) capital an intermittently onerous constraint.

Restrictions on the Chinese domestic market placed a limit on transnational capital's expansion in an exceptional locus of growth, which in turn made them a fixture of U.S. political venom. U.S. policymakers demanded that China should place itself on the receiving end of this trading relationship. U.S. companies, Hillary Clinton urged in 2011, "want fair opportunities to export to China's growing markets . . . as well as assurances that the $50 billion of American capital invested in China will create a strong foundation for new market and investment opportunities." The U.S. Secretary of State elaborated on this agenda: "China still needs to take important steps toward reform . . . to end unfair discrimination against U.S. and other foreign companies or against their innovative technologies, remove preferences for domestic firms, and end measures that disadvantage or appropriate foreign intellectual property."[54] However, the U.S. goal of acquiring bigger chunks of China's high-growth information and communications market was often stymied.

A reciprocal tendency was also marked. China's success in reserving or contouring its national market granted some maneuvering room to Chinese capital. Yet, if and when they succeeded within their home market—not a foregone conclusion, as the closure of state-backed operating system supplier Red Flag Software demonstrated in 2014[55]—Chinese communications companies then also needed to push out beyond domestic horizons. Their ambition for "going out," for launching themselves into the world market, was not matched by their record of performance, however—though, as mentioned, after 2007 Chinese outward foreign direct investment burgeoned remarkably, so that during 2012 Chinese companies spent more than $57 billion on foreign acquisitions.[56] Chinese capital in communications and information thus remained below par with its U.S., European, and Japanese-based transnational competitors. Only exceptionally did Chinese communications companies boast global status. Network equipment vendor Huawei secured an estimated $30 billion in new contracts during 2009, not only in China but also in Europe and Africa, so that it became the world's largest supplier of mobile infrastructure; ZTE, a second Chinese network equipment manufacturer, likewise became globally significant.[57] I have already mentioned Lenovo, which continued its growth by agreeing to purchase IBM's server business for $2.3 billion and Google's Motorola Mobility for $2.9 billion early in 2014.[58]

Most foreign communications and information ventures, however, were less substantial. Principally to serve transnational companies based in both countries with internet and outsourcing services, China Telecom set up a unit in Brazil.[59] China Telecom's deal to gain interconnection to AT&T's networks in the United States was likewise predicated on providing cross-border services to corporate users.[60] Tencent's WeChat messaging application struck a deal with Google to gain access to users in Asia, South Africa, Spain, and the United States.[61] Dalian Wanda, which harbored grandiose ambitions for Chinese movie making, purchased the U.S. cinema chain AMC Entertainment in 2012.[62] In general, China's communications and information companies were still limited internationally by the formidable pressures and constraints placed upon them by an entrenched U.S.-centric digital capitalism.[63]

These included both political restrictions imposed by governments and barriers to entry instituted by transnational companies straddling virtually every profitable sector. The United States introduced a "cyber-espionage" review process for government ICT purchases, which was specifically aimed at Chinese vendors Huawei and ZTE; U.S. lawmakers also urged U.S. companies and, more brazenly, allied states to shop elsewhere.[64] In a cable released by WikiLeaks, it was reported that Hillary Clinton had asked Australia's prime minister, Kevin Rudd, in March 2009: "How do you deal toughly with your banker?"[65] It was a searching question (though, even with its large purchases, China still accounted for only a fraction of U.S. public debt).[66] Despite trade talks aimed at easing investment rules[67] and some Chinese investments, as of mid-2013 the growth movement of Chinese capital continued to face throttling U.S. restrictions. U.S. authorities denied Chinese foreign direct investments in the U.S. domestic market in industries as diverse as petroleum, pork, and internet routers; but the U.S. government unfailingly deemed the internet industry—a primary growth pole for digital capitalism—"strategic" and, therefore, off-limits to Chinese capital. Huawei repeatedly tested the politically sensitive U.S. market before being compelled to withdraw in 2013.[68]

Political-economic structures constituted global, rather than merely national, obstructions to the expansion of Chinese capital. Just a few of what Nolan terms "system integrator" TNCs dominated global markets in everything from aerospace and semiconductors to soft drinks.[69] Three-quarters of these were headquartered in the wealthy nations. They had spent recent decades building up concentrated power via mergers and acquisitions, research and development, and brand marketing and, as we found in part 1, they now possessed far-reaching cross-border production systems—notably extending into China itself.[70] The big U.S. internet companies made up the most recent exemplars.

Yet the result was not a simple stasis but a volatile force field. U.S. companies had reacted to the first shocks of the digital depression by building up great stashes of liquid capital, with an eye to protecting themselves against further unpredictable risks. As a result, corporate America possessed an estimated $1.9 trillion "sitting idly on balance sheets" by 2011—the largest proportion of total U.S. corporate assets in half a century.[71] The rate of increase slowed thereafter, U.S. companies and their European counterparts[72] together held nearly 2 trillion Euros in cash early in 2012 and the figure mounted through 2013.[73] High-tech companies, disproportionately profitable, claimed the lion's share of this hoard. Just three of them—Apple, Microsoft, and Google—together held cash amounting to around $90 billion in December 2010.[74] These enormous liquid assets continued to multiply beyond any relevant yardstick of risk; by June 2012 Apple alone possessed $117 billion in cash, and by the third quarter of 2013 Apple's stash amounted to $147 billion.[75] The U.S. tech sector overall was sitting on $775 billion.[76] Were these signs of strength—or vulnerability?

Despite another spike in high-tech mergers and acquisitions;[77] despite President Obama's urging early in 2011 that U.S. businesses "get in the game";[78] and despite investors' tolerance of Amazon, whose practice of piling on investment at the expense of its profit was exceptional,[79] executives mostly withheld these great reserves of money capital from flowing back into nonfinancial investment. "There are no signs of a revival of capital spending despite the continuing low cost of capital," stated a journalist late in 2013.[80] As U.S. capital spending continued to languish into 2014, the *Financial Times* agonized about what it called "a prolonged corporate investment strike"[81]—a term associated with the Depression-era presidency of Franklin Delano Roosevelt. The underlying problem was that—as is typical during a depression—companies were not able to identify sufficient profitable opportunities. Instead, they fixated on how much to preserve as hoards, and how much to expend on shareholder dividends and stock buybacks. Battles broke out over this issue. Cisco spent $72 billion on share buyback programs over the decade to 2012, "dwarfing [its] spending on acquisitions."[82] Under pressure from predatory investors, Apple acted in a comparable way.[83] Were internet capital to be permitted to flow more freely into China's information and communications sector, there was no shortage of it to draw upon.

In principle, of course, it was possible to break this logjam. U.S. and Chinese authorities could cooperate to release these huge reserves and help them flow through both national markets and beyond. There were indeed numerous forays of this kind: U.S. hedge funds continued to invest in Chinese internet companies, for example, and Microsoft and Huawei partnered to market low-cost Windows smartphones in Africa.[84] These, however, were small potatoes. Brokered by the two states, might not foreign direct investment, mergers, and other joint ventures and combinations between Chinese and U.S. units of capital be stepped up to accelerate the growth of the information sector?

The force field of transnational capitalism was not constituted as a neutral political-economic space. Would it be U.S. or Chinese capitals that presided over such combinations? Who would buy whom? How much access would be accorded to each respective national market? Which companies would be granted pole position in the race for emergent profitable fields, from "big data" analytics and cloud computing to genomics? How would the ground rules be set for taxation, repatriation of profits, and investment? How would the costs, as well as the gains, from any "great rebalancing" be distributed?[85] How would attempts to solve these issues interact with the altering structure of the greater transnational political economy—which, of course, included scores of additional states, each also facing domestic pressures?

With this question we reach bedrock. For the geopolitics that animated digital capitalism's restructuring was forged not merely out of maneuvers by states and giant corporations but—most elementally—in light of the ever-changing balance of social forces within nations and internationally. Both the general crisis and the mode of growth of digital capitalism signified that the geopolitics of the internet were, and would remain, profoundly fraught.

Internationally, U.S. capital and the U.S. state sought to extend their carefully built advantages with recalcitrant trading partners. They demanded concessions from already-hard-pressed populations throughout lower-growth regions, including the United States and Western Europe—in living standards, in environmental quality, in social provision, and in democratic liberties. Attacks commenced from the moment that U.S. and European capitalism averted financial collapse, as political and corporate leaders put the crisis itself to use, deploying their power over states in order to inflict "austerity" measures. (Francis Fukuyama admonished Tea-Party Republicans for demonizing the federal government, on the grounds that the power of a "strong state" was now needed "for the purposes of national revival."[86]) Authoritarian tendencies were a correlative of measures that struck at wage-earning and "informal"-sector workers, because, as the exactions bit into social experience, popular opposition to capital's class project also escalated.

Some system managers were precocious in recognizing this. Dominique Strauss-Kahn (not equally responsible in all respects) recounted that at a special conference convened by the IMF and the International Labour Organization, "they spoke of the 210 million people currently out of work worldwide—the highest level of official unemployment in history." By 2010 the IMF was warning that, because of this jobs crisis, America and Europe risked "an explosion of social unrest."[87] This forecast began to be borne out as, in Greece, France, England, Spain, Portugal, and Italy, mobilizations began to challenge state policies enacted on behalf of capital. In the United States, demonstrations mounted by the Occupy movement dramatically altered the tenor of political discourse: a concoction that had been made up of the class dogmas and entitlements of the Party of Wall Street was, in a matter of weeks, compelled to make room for considerations of economic inequality and injustices arising out of corporate, especially bank, profit-hunger.[88] As the slump persisted, so did simmering resistance to an unaltered status quo. In Europe, midway through 2011, José Viñals, IMF director of monetary and capital markets, concluded, "We are entering a new phase of the crisis—I would call it the political phase of the crisis."[89] From Athens to Oakland, from Johannesburg to Seoul, and from Lisbon and Madrid to Sao Paolo, popular opposition to prevailing policies signified that the "political phase of the crisis" would not soon end. Austerity drives pursued on behalf of capital energized resistance among people who saw their lives and, for the young, their futures crumbling. In November 2013 Greek workers were staging a twenty-four-hour general strike against austerity—the latest in more than thirty nationwide shutdowns since 2010.[90] That, heading into 2014, protests had not produced political change in the centers of transnational capitalism was no guarantee that they might not yet do so.

This dynamic, however, requires additional specification. Social-political struggles were generated not merely as an adjunct of the economic slump and the austerity policies that accompanied it, or even owing to longstanding forms of inequality and domination—but also as a corollary of more specifically salient trends: this was, after all, a *digital* depression. On one side, recalling a similar pattern set during the 1930s, even as mainstream commentators acquiesced in a "lost decade,"[91] the architects of U.S. economic policy continued to prioritize network-based profit projects. "Digital infrastructure," pronounced Lawrence Summers, then head of the National Economic Council, "will be a key source of competitive advantage in the knowledge economy."[92] On the other side, these insistent efforts to extend the sphere of the profit mechanism in and around digital networks engendered opposition on this same terrain.

The commodification process—the birthing of industries for profitmaking—does not typically arise out of a consensus attained among interested parties. Far from it! Network-based systems and services have been typically destructive, inasmuch as they have been predicated on the plunder of public goods[93]—shared resources of culture, education, government, and biological life. Michael Perelman and David Harvey call this process of preemption, whose history is as old as that of capitalism, "accumulation by dispossession."[94] Nearly every vector of digital capitalism not only extended capital's takeover of what had been (admittedly often inequitably) shared resources, but concurrently engendered countermobilization and protest. The oppositional movements became co-participants in this unfolding history.

Consider the case of education. Computer-assisted instruction may be dated, in a U.S. context, to the origination in 1959 of what became a longstanding program undertaken at the University of Illinois—with heavy involvement by military agencies and corporations and also (reality being under no obligation to be one-dimensional) by principled educators.[95] Network-reliant education initiatives gained adherents internationally. A tele-school movement pioneered by Mexico in 1968 as a temporary expedient before new schools could be built, spread to the point that by 2012, one out of five Mexican children was enrolled in a tele-school.[96] By the mid-1980s, it was feasible to identify a nascent online education business, whose checkered rollout I examined in *Digital Capitalism*.[97] This business accelerated throughout the years leading up to and through the digital depression, from numerous national bases. From China to Chile, from South Korea to South Africa, from the United States to India to Mexico to Brazil, private purveyors of educational goods and services laid claim to what they hoped to make into a multi-trillion-dollar transnational market.

Internet connectivity constituted a taproot for this metamorphosis, in which a public good was transformed into a commodity. In poorer countries, where schooling institutions typically had never come close to being sufficient, proprietary outfits positioned themselves within a wide-open field; "The gaps in public education," intoned a *Wall Street Journal* article, "have created an opportunity for nonpublic institutions."[98] Despite protests by students seeking expanded access to nonprofit education provision,[99] the prospect of widening access to schooling was often handed off to corporate providers.[100] This project faced a different historical context in the developed market economies. Here, government funding for public schools had created a near-universal system—subject, to be sure, to deeply coded class inequalities—and public colleges enrolled a large proportion of postsecondary students. In this context, commodification projects proceeded in tandem with attempts to discredit, defund, and reorient the public system.[101]

Attacks proceeded across the range of the education system, as the digital depression was used as a pretext for establishing additional points at which private corporations might "enter"—actually, reestablish—education. At the preschool level, examples could be found of municipalities shifting taxpayer money away from public institutions and toward proprietary schools—with predictable effects on class size and quality in the former.[102] At the primary school level, some cities—Chicago, the third-largest U.S. school district, was the preeminent case—summarily shut down dozens of public schools over protests by tens of thousands of community members and militant unionized teachers.[103] Meanwhile, for the one-third of U.S. households with annual incomes of less than $30,000 and teens living at home that lacked a broadband internet connection, McDonald's—with twelve thousand Wi-Fi–equipped U.S. locations—became a preferred place to study.[104] Community colleges, which enrolled 44 percent of U.S. college students, including a disproportionate number of poor and minority students, received a declining proportion of federal funds for education.[105] Public universities also saw chronic and deliberate resource cuts. The nation's preeminent public university system, California's, had established a no-tuition policy in its much-vaunted 1960 Master Plan.[106] Fifty years later, the idea of a free college education lay in ruins. In 2013 Cooper Union, one of the last tuition-free colleges in the United States, announced that henceforward it would charge undergraduates to attend.[107] These were attacks on working-class Americans, whose presence in elite schools at any level remained miniscule.[108]

U.S. funding patterns revealed a stark realignment by government toward the side of capital: as public education was starved of basic resources, becoming part of a wider regression that critics aptly called "failure by design,"[109] the volume of federally guaranteed loans to students enrolling at proprietary colleges inflated that side of the enterprise.[110] This incentive proved tempting to suppliers such as the University of Phoenix, and Education Management, a conglomerate 41 percent owned by Goldman Sachs, enrolling around 150,000 students. The majority of proprietary college revenue actually came not from their success in the marketplace but from government. It turned out that several of these colleges were enrolling students with deceptive promises, and that their student loan default rates were double those of students enrolled at public colleges.[111] With exposure of these practices,[112] U.S. new-student enrollments in the for-profit colleges lurched.[113]

However, the probability was slight that public education institutions would be equipped to respond adequately, through sustained large-scale funding increases. Instead, incentivized by business-minded boards of trustees, their own administrators sprang to team up with commercial online course vendors. Start-up ventures like Coursera, edX, and Udacity parasitized universities in a joint scramble to turn a new commodity—the college course—into a blockbuster profit generator.[114] Their massive open online courses, or MOOCs, garnered hugely enthusiastic publicity,[115] and vendors moved to create courses available to students for college credit.[116] Purveyors of "learning management systems" such as Blackboard[117] and Moodle cultivated adjacent market segments.

The proprietary education companies, from the ITT Educational Services and the University of Phoenix to DeVry Institute of Technology, Corinthian Colleges, Kaplan Higher Education, and Pearson Education, also moved strongly into overseas markets. DeVry and Pearson bought into Brazil; Pearson invested in China[118] where, research showed, as many as three-quarters of primary school students obtained some kind of supplementary education from an outside—and often profit-driven—"shadow" provider.[119] Japan and the Republic of Korea likewise boasted many distance learning companies. U.S. purveyors looked enviously at these already well-developed markets. U.S. online provider Udemy, half of whose one million students lived outside the United States, launched its Web site in nine languages (including Chinese), targeting people hoping to earn $10 an hour through its vocational training courses, such as its popular tutorial on how to use Microsoft Excel.[120] Internet companies such as Apple[121] and conglomerate media groups like News Corporation also moved in. News Corp. announced, for example, that its education division would partner with AT&T "to tap into the multibillion-dollar public education market," by selling "digital learning tools" to students from kindergarten through high school. The executive leading this effort, Joel I. Klein, had been New York City's schools chancellor prior to joining the company, where he became one of Murdoch's closest advisors (and helped him to ward off the threat posed by a phone hacking scandal in Britain).[122] All over the world, the online purveyors posed as agents of deliverance by widening "access" and purporting to free it from the elitism and class privilege that had for so long encrusted formal education. To the extent that they succeeded, ironically, their cheapening of the value of skilled labor would grant the reproduction of capitalist social relations an enlarged foundation.

Not all participants in the educational enterprise acquiesced in this progression. A *New York Times* reporter underlined that "among educators, digital learning tools are a contentious issue. Many teachers see them as a way to make classes larger, add an extra burden to the job or cut down on teachers' jobs altogether."[123] University professors were also wary; from San Jose State University to Harvard, many of them greeted impositions of for-credit, for-profit college courses with unhappiness, anxiety, and sometimes anger.[124] Fiscal attacks on public education triggered protests by students from Britain to Chile and from Quebec to Taiwan. The Chilean movement demanding more affordable education brought out thousands of students for demonstrations over the course of a year;[125] Michelle Bachelet, the victor in the 2013 presidential election, "answered recent mass student protests by vowing to increase corporate taxes to partly pay for an education overhaul."[126] In Quebec, which had legislated a 75 percent increase in tuition fees for implementation over five years, student protestors ignited a radical movement that brought down the provincial government in 2012.[127]

The overall process provoked more multifarious opposition, as analogous vectors of commodification laid waste to other public goods. We possess no inventory of these movements across their unaccustomed range and variety.

Aided by an austerity-based resurgence of 1980s-style privatization, with hundreds of billions of dollars worth of state assets sold worldwide during 2010 and 2011,[128] cultural heritage, government services, pharmaceutical, medical, and agricultural biotechnology were alike in the grip of commodification projects. India tied government welfare benefits (as well as bank accounts and cellphone service) to an ID program encompassing what would be the world's largest biometric database, replete with retinal scans and thumbprints.[129] An intended "IT Future of Medicine" project aimed to integrate DNA analysis with disease management, depending on the rapidly declining cost of commercial gene sequencing and using software provided by a growing number of bioinformatics companies, such as Spain's Integromics and Sweden's Qlucore.[130] Scandals broke out over public procurement for IT systems to put Britons' medical records online,[131] over revelations that digital records actually might not cut costs as promised,[132] over systematic transgression of medical ethics as pharmaceutical companies failed to reveal their pervasive commercial sponsorship of research,[133] and over privacy breaches as thousands of patient files were posted online.[134] A globe-spanning battle over genetically modified foods was intermittently reported.[135] Having digitized some 20 million books at academic libraries, Google Books slowed its pace momentarily to fight the legal battles that ensued;[136] carrying forward, however, was a wider process of for-profit content appropriation via mass digitization.[137] The arts and cultural production were symptomatically swept up into a totalizing economic discourse: an official report calculated that, in 2011, "the arts and cultural sector's contributions" to U.S. GDP accounted for an impressive-sounding $504 billion.[138] In this context, policies pursued by U.S. government authorities and decisions taken by U.S. courts often harbored global implications.

Many of these vectors of commodification incited resistance. By the dawn of the twenty-first century, "right to know" mobilizations were occurring in many countries—India's was prominent—and were helping to root a more expansive "Access To Knowledge" (A2K) initiative that encompassed everything from free software to biotechnology.[139]

This wrenching commodification of public goods also must be related, as David Harvey has emphasized, to changes to the built environment. The construction and episodic rebuilding of the material spaces within which social life unfolds have long required great investments. Historically, these have been directed to such things as roads, highways and street grids, bridges, and housing, as well as on port facilities, airports, dams, water, hospitals, sewer and waste disposal systems, and electricity and telecommunications grids. Today, a revamped information infrastructure constitutes another key basis for the recreation of the built environment, to support the distribution of both existing and nascent commodities. We have seen in parts I and II indicators of the scale of investment that now channels into these capacious network infrastructures. But of course this is not merely a physical process or an anodyne matter of "investment." Unevenly across the world, the social relations that are etched into the built environment are being restructured, often violently, to support multiplying commodification projects.

Land seizures are the global predicate for this larger shift[140]—from South Sudan and Democratic Republic of Congo to Indonesia to Argentina to China. The case of China is especially important. As China's huge peasant class journeyed to the southeast coast, its members metamorphosed into a class of real and would-be wage earners. In 2011, more Chinese citizens came to live in cities than in the countryside; a mere thirty years before, fewer than 20 percent of Chinese people had been urbanites. Globally, inhabitants of cities exceeded rural dwellers in 2008,[141] and throughout Latin America, Africa, and South Asia, sprawling, jerry-rigged megacities became sites of frequent conflict over rights and social justice. In China, by contrast, urbanization involved rebuilding from the ground up.

In 2010, China overtook the depressed United States as the world's premier builder—spending more than a trillion dollars that year, as political authorities sought to avert a slump by opening the spigots of finance. Innumerable projects commenced.[142] Property values rose, as did the sales of cement and construction machinery companies. Economists began to discuss whether China's construction boom exhibited the dynamics of a classic speculative bubble.[143] Some forecast a "hard landing."[144] Economic policy ascended in priority, as did its possible political ramifications.

China's urbanization impelled a host of converging initiatives around dozens of mid-sized new cities: "Huge, almost unimaginable infrastructure projects are being put in place not only in the big centres, in Beijing, Shanghai and Hong Kong, but in these secondary cities."[145] A city of 7 million located in central China, Changsha, unveiled plans in 2012 to spend $130 billion on airport and road construction, waste treatment, and other projects.[146] Under the rubric "Smart+Connected Communities," in 2011 the Chinese city of Chongqing was pursuing not only smart energy technology but also e-government programs, and transformed education and health-care information provision.[147] Worldwide construction expenditures were forecast to reach nearly $100 trillion over the course of the decade to follow.[148] Such projections might be wildly inflated, and yet still signify that, as David Harvey has long argued, "urbanization has been a key means for the absorption of capital and labor surpluses" and that, in

particular, "the Chinese urbanization boom is playing a central role in stimulating the revival of global economic growth for a wide range of consumer
goods."[149]

This process, however, again was based on sanctioned land grabs—accumulation by dispossession—which, as they occurred, provoked intense, though
mostly local, social-political resistance.[150] Harvey speculates that, as it continues, China's lopsided urbanization may create further ground for anticapitalist
mobilization.[151] The socialist legacies carried by many Chinese workers and
peasants might factor in here.[152] On the other hand, it is possible that the net
gain will be both sufficiently large and—if China's economic policy is altered—
so redistributed that the dispossessed will tend to acquiesce. The question again
will be settled politically: What sort of social life is being constructed? What
is the balance of social forces between proponents and opponents?

The digital depression will be resolved on terms favorable to capital only by
wrenching away existing structures of provision, characteristically inadequate
and partial though they are, in favor of high-tech, for-profit surrogates. This is
not a recipe for democratic self-determination, let alone for political harmony.
Society is not of one mind that these public goods should be placed in capital's grip. Accumulation by dispossession takes away from those with little in
order to create territories of profit for those with much. If, as Gregg Shotwell
writes, "liberals fight for a cause, radicals fight for their lives" then, as it intrudes
ever further into social experience, accumulation by dispossession is likely to
increase the number of radicals.[153] What forms their radicalism may take, and
what effects it may carry for the greater political economy, constitute profound
open questions.

It is not sufficient that communications and information may help resuscitate
growth. Growth for whom? Growth of what kind? And, as an environmental
agenda grows urgent, how much growth? The prevailing answers to these questions are unacceptable to much of the world's population and unsustainable
for all of it. Resources of hope spring from awareness that no variant of digital
capitalism serves the human condition—and from the concrete activisms that
follow.

Notes

Introduction

1. Richard Walker, "The Golden State Adrift," *New Left Review* 66 (November/December 2010): 5–30.

2. Rick Lyman and Mary Williams Walsh, "Struggling San Jose Plans to Cut Worker Benefits," *New York Times*, September 24, 2013.

3. Neil Irwin, "Fed's Aid in '08 Crisis Stretched Worldwide," *New York Times*, February 24, 2014.

4. Financial Crisis Inquiry Commission, *The Financial Crisis Inquiry Report* (New York: Public Affairs, 2011), 354. The most persuasive account is Leo Panitch and Sam Gindin, *The Making of Global Capitalism* (London: Verso, 2012), 301–30. Carrying forward through late 2012, though with less analytical bite, is Robert Kuttner, *Debtors' Prison: The Politics of Austerity versus Possibility* (New York: Knopf, 2013).

5. Neil Barofsky, *Bailout: An Inside Account of How Washington Abandoned Main Street While Rescuing Wall Street* (New York: Free Press, 2012), 162.

6. Carmen M. Reinhardt and Kenneth S. Rogoff, *This Time Is Different: Eight Centuries of Financial Folly* (Princeton, N.J.: Princeton University Press, 2009).

7. National Bureau of Economic Research, available at http://www.nber.org/cycles/sept2010.html (accessed January 10, 2014).

8. Matt Kennard and Shannon Bond, "Number of Americans in Poverty at Highest in 50 Years," *Financial Times*, September 14, 2011.

9. "Bipolar Bearish," The Lex Column, *Financial Times*, May 13, 2011.

10. John Bellamy Foster and Robert W. McChesney, *The Endless Crisis: How Monopoly-Finance Capital Produces Stagnation and Upheaval from the USA to China* (New York: Monthly Review, 2012).

11. Paul Krugman, "The Big Shrug," *New York Times*, June 10, 2013. Also see Kuttner, *Debtors' Prison*, 36; Paul Krugman, *End This Depression Now* (New York: Norton, 2012).

12. J. Bradford DeLong, "The Second Great Depression," *Foreign Affairs* 92, no. 4 (July/August 2013): 159.

13. Brian Blackstone, "Euro Zone Braces for Stagnation," *Wall Street Journal*, June 21, 2013; Annie Lowrey, "I.M.F. Trims Global Growth Forecast as Emerging Markets Lag," *New York Times*, July 10, 2013; Julia Werdigier, "Jobless Rate Will Continue to Increase in Europe, O.E.C.D. Forecasts," *New York Times*, July 17, 2013; Neil Shah, Ben Casselman, and Jon Hilsenrath, "Tepid Growth Restrains Fed," *Wall Street Journal*, August 1, 2013.

14. Claire Jones, "Deflation Fears Spark Shock ECB Rate Cut," *Financial Times*, November 8, 2013; Robin Harding, "IMF Warns of Growing Threat from Deflation," *Financial Times*, January 16, 2014; Claudia Jones and Chris Giles, "ECB Poised for Battle to Ward Off Deflation," *Financial Times*, January 27, 2014.

15. Ed Crooks, "US Capital Spending Set to Slow to Four-Year Low in Sign of Caution," *Financial Times*, January 24, 2014.

16. Farhad Manjoo, "Beware of Tech Bubble, Maybe," *Wall Street Journal*, December 30, 2013; Nick Bilton, "If It Looks Like a Bubble and Floats Like One . . .," *New York Times*, November 25, 2013; David Streitfeld, "In Silicon Valley, Partying Like It's 1999 Once More," *New York Times*, November 27, 2013.

17. Delphine Strauss, John Paul Rathbone, and Jonathan Wheatley, "Argentine Peso Plunges amid Emerging Markets Sell-Off," *Financial Times*, January 24, 2014.

18. Annie Lowrie, "Household Incomes Remain Flat Despite Improving Economy," *New York Times*, September 17, 2013; Shawn Donnan, "Trade to Remain Sluggish, Says Unctad," *Financial Times*, September 13, 2013; David Jolly, "World Economy Growing Unevenly, O.E.C.D. Says," *New York Times*, September 3, 2013; Satyajit Das, "Post-Crisis Policies Offer Only Chronic Stagnation," *Financial Times*, September 12, 2013; United Nations Conference on Trade and Development, *World Investment Report 2013* (New York: United Nations, 2013); John Authers, "Risk of New Crisis Drives Fed Doubts over Taper," *Financial Times*, September 7–8, 2013; Gillian Tett, "Insane Financial System Lives on Post-Lehman," *Financial Times*, September 13, 2013.

19. Michael A. Bernstein, *The Great Depression: Delayed Recovery and Economic Change in America, 1929–1939* (Princeton, N.J.: Princeton University Press, 1987), 49, 51.

20. Bernstein, *Great Depression*, 88–89. See also Alexander J. Field, *A Great Leap Forward: 1930s Depression and U.S. Economic Growth* (New Haven, Conn.: Yale University Press, 2011).

21. National Commission on the Causes of the Financial and Economic Crisis in the United States, *The Financial Crisis Inquiry Report* (New York: Public Affairs, 2011), xvi, 3, 4.

22. Carmen M. Reinhart and Kenneth S. Rogoff, *This Time Is Different: A Panoramic View of Eight Centuries of Crises*. Princeton: Princeton University Press, 2009.

23. Barofsky, *Bail-Out*; Simon Johnson and James Kwak, *Thirteen Bankers: The Wall Street Takeover and the Next Financial Meltdown* (New York: Pantheon, 2010); Charles H. Ferguson, *Predator Nation: Corporate Criminals, Political Corruption, and the Hijacking of America* (New York: Crown, 2012).

24. Robert B. Reich, *After-Shock: The Next Economy and America's Future* (New York: Vintage, 2011); Joseph E. Stiglitz, *Free Fall: America, Free Markets, and the Sinking of the World Economy* (New York: Norton, 2010).

25. Foster and McChesney, *Endless Crisis*.

26. Doug Henwood, *After the New Economy* (New York: New Press, 2003), 203.

27. Kuttner, *Debtors' Prison*, 43.

28. Dan Schiller, *Theorizing Communication: A History* (New York: Oxford University Press, 1996), 161–72.

29. Raymond Williams, "Literature and Sociology: In Memory of Lucien Goldman," *New Left Review* 67 (May–June 1971): 11.

30. Manuel Castells, "An Introduction to the Information Age," *City* 7 (1997): 6–16.

31. Manuel Castells, *The Rise of the Network Society* (Cambridge: Blackwell, 1996), 1.

32. Dan Schiller, *Digital Capitalism: Networking the Global Market System* (Cambridge, Mass.: MIT Press, 1999).

33. Jones, "Deflation Fears"; Hannah Kuchler, Tim Bradshaw, and Arash Massoudi, "Life Is Tweet for Twitter Founders after Company Valued at $30bn," *Financial Times*, November 8, 2013.

34. Dan Schiller, *How To Think about Information* (Urbana: University of Illinois Press, 2007), 36–57.

35. Fredric Jameson, *Representing Capital: A Reading of Volume One* (London: Verso, 2011), 87.

36. David Harvey, *The Enigma of Capital* (New York: Oxford, 2010), 117.

37. Immanuel Wallerstein, "Protection Networks and Commodity Chains in the Capitalist World-Economy," in *Frontiers of Commodity Chain Research*, ed. Jennifer Bair (Stanford, Calif.: Stanford University Press, 2009), 83. This has been a consistent emphasis: "The transnationality of commodity chains is as descriptively true of the sixteenth-century capitalist world as of the twentieth century." Immanuel Wallerstein, *Historical Capitalism* (London: Verso, 1983), 31.

38. Jennifer Bair, "Global Commodity Chains: Genealogy and Review," in Bair, *Frontiers*, 10–13, 7–9.

39. Steven Topik, Carlos Marichal and Zephyr Frank, "Commodity Chains in Theory and Latin American History," in *From Silver to Cocaine: Latin American Commodity Chains and the Building of the World Economy, 1500–2000*, ed. Steven Topik, Carlos Marichal, and Zephyr Frank (Durham, N.C.: Duke University Press, 2006), 14.

40. Terence K. Hopkins and Immanuel Wallerstein, "Conclusions about Commodity Chains" in *Commodity Chains and Global Capitalism*, ed. Gary Gereffi and Miguel Korzeniewicz (Westport, Conn.: Praeger, 1994), 49.

41. Terence K. Hopkins and Immanuel Wallerstein, "Commodity Chains: Construct and Research," in Gereffi and Korzeniewicz, *Commodity Chains and Global Capitalism*, 17.

42. Hopkins and Wallerstein, "Commodity Chains," 17.

43. Hopkins and Wallerstein, "Conclusions," 50.

44. Hopkins and Wallerstein, "Conclusions," 50.

45. Hopkins and Wallerstein, "Conclusions," 49.

46. As Wallerstein says of the "boxes" of fragmented individual production that populate more extended commodity chains: "They are not a given but a matter of social definition, and in fact of constant social redefinition." Wallerstein, "Introduction," *Review, A Journal of the Fernand Braudel Center* 23, no. 1 (2000): 5.

Chapter 1. Network Connectivity and Labor Systems

1. David Harvey, *Enigma of Capital* (New York: Oxford University Press, 2010).

2. Vijay Prashad, *The Poorer Nations: A Possible History of the Global South* (London: Verso, 2012).

3. Judith Stein, *Pivotal Decade: How the United States Traded Factories for Services in the Seventies* (New Haven, Conn.: Yale University Press, 2010), 102.

4. Kim Moody, *U.S. Labor in Trouble and Transition* (New York: Verso, 2007), 12.

5. Stein, *Pivotal Decade*, 127.

6. Stein, *Pivotal Decade*, 106–7.

7. For more recent overviews see Robert Brenner, *The Boom and the Bubble: The U.S. in the World Economy* (London: Verso, 2002); and Stein, *Pivotal Decade*. Still valuable is Bennett Harrison and Barry Bluestone, *The Deindustrialization of America: Plant Closings, Community Abandonment, and the Dismantling of Basic Industry* (New York: Basic, 1982); and Bennett Harrison and Barry Bluestone, *The Great U-Turn: Corporate Restructuring and the Polarizing of America* (New York: Basic, 1990).

8. Stein, *Pivotal Decade*, 115.

9. Jefferson Cowie, *Stayin' Alive: The 1970s and the Last Days of the Working Class* (New York: New Press, 2010); Aaron Brenner, Robert Brenner, and Cal Winslow, eds., *Rebel Rank and File: Labor Militancy and Revolt from Below during the Long 1970s* (New York: Verso, 2010); Thomas Borstelmann, *The 1970s: A New Global History from Civil Rights to Economic Inequality* (Princeton, N.J.: Princeton University Press, 2012).

10. Prashad, *Poorer Nations*; Dan Schiller, *How to Think about Information* (Urbana: University of Illinois Press, 2007), 37–39.

11. David Harvey, *The New Imperialism* (Oxford: Oxford University Press, 2003), 87–88; Moody, *U.S. Labor in Trouble*, 13.

12. Prashad, *Poorer Nations*, 52.

13. Moody, *U.S. Labor in Trouble*, 11–36.

14. James P. Womack, Daniel T. Jones, and Daniel Roos, *The Machine That Changed the World: The Story of Lean Production* (New York: HarperPerennial, 1991). Often this was actually only a variation on an older tune. David Harvey, *A Companion to Marx's Capital* (London: Verso, 2010).

15. Moody, *U.S. Labor in Trouble*, 28–34.

16. The labor process was identified as a major concern for communication and media studies by Andrew Herman and Vincent Mosco in "Radical Social Theory and the Communications Revolution," in *Communication and Social Structure*, ed. E. G. McAnany, N. Janus, and J. Schnitman (New York: Praeger, 1981), 58–84.

17. Oz Frankel, *States of Inquiry: Social Investigations and Print Culture in Nineteenth-Century Britain and the United States* (Baltimore: Johns Hopkins, 2006), 10, 39–71.

18. Karl Marx, *Capital, Volume I: A Critical Analysis of Capitalist Production* (New York: International, 1967), 360.

19. Marx, *Capital, I*, 368.

20. Marx, *Capital, I*, 368.

21. Marx, *Capital, I*, 310.

22. Marx, *Capital, I*, 420.

23. Marx *Capital, I*, 763. Marx elsewhere makes the following suggestive statement about this process: "The *real lever* of the overall labour process is increasingly not the individual worker. Instead, *labour-power socially combined* and the various competing labour-powers which together form the entire production machine participate in very different ways in the immediate process of making commodities, or, more accurately in this context, creating the product. Some work better with their hands, others with their heads, one as a manager, engineer, technologist, etc., the other as overseer, the third as manual labourer or even drudge. An ever increasing number of types of labour are included in the immediate concept of *productive labour*, and those who perform it are classed as *productive workers*, workers directly exploited by capital and subordinated to its process of production and expansion." From *A Critical Analysis of Capitalist Production* in Marx, *Capital, Volume 1: A Critique of Political Economy*, trans. Ben Fowkes, (Harmondsworth: Penguin, 1992), 1039–40 (original emphasis).

24. Eric Hobsbawm, *Industry and Empire: The Birth of the Industrial Revolution* (New Press, 1999), xi.

25. Harvey, *Companion to Marx's Capital*, 212.

26. E. P. Thompson, "Time, Work-Discipline, and Industrial Capitalism," *Past and Present* 38 (December 1967): 56–97.

27. David S. Landes, *The Unbound Prometheus: Technological Change and Industrial Development in Western Europe from 1750 to the Present* (Cambridge: Cambridge University Press, 1969); Sidney Pollard, *Peaceful Conquest: The Industrialization of Europe 1760–1970* (Oxford University Press, 1982).

28. Glenn Porter, "Foreword," in D. A. Hounshell, *From the American System to Mass Production, 1800–1932* (Baltimore: Johns Hopkins, 1984), xv.

29. Gary Fields, *Territories of Profit: Communications, Capitalist Development, and the Innovative Enterprises of G. F. Swift and Dell Computer* (Stanford, Calif.: Stanford University Press, 2004).

30. Richard B. Du Boff, "The Introduction of Electric Power in American Manufacturing," *Economic History Review* 20, no. 3 (December 1967): 509–10, 513, 514, 518.

31. U.S. Department of Labor, Bureau of Labor Statistics, *Handbook of Labor Statistics, Bulletin 2175*, December 1983 (Washington, D.C.: U.S. GPO), table 71, pp. 165–68.

32. Mark McColloch, *White Collar Workers in Transition: The Boom Years, 1940–1970* (Westport, Conn: Greenwood, 1983), 15.

33. Dale C. Johnson, ed., *Class and Social Development: A New Theory of the Middle Class* (Beverly Hills, Calif.: Sage, 1982), 197.

34. Jorge Reina Schement, "Porat, Bell, and the Information Society Reconsidered: The Growth of Information Work in the Early Twentieth Century," *Information Processing and Management* 26, no. 4 (1990): 449–65.

35. Seymour Melman, "The Rise of Administrative Overhead in the Manufacturing Industries of the United States, 1899–1947," *Oxford Economic Papers*, New Series, 3, no. 1 (February 1951), 67, 90, 91, 92.

36. C. Wright Mills, *White Collar* (New York: Oxford University Press, 1953); McColloch, *White Collar Workers*, 15, 83; Daniel Bell, *The Coming of the Post-Industrial Society* (New York: Basic, 1974); Marc Uri Porat, *The Information Economy: Definition and Measurement*, PhD diss., Stanford University, published by U.S. Department of Commerce, May 1977; Schement, "Porat."

37. Geoffrey D. Austrian, *Herman Hollerith: Forgotten Giant of Information Processing* (New York: Columbia University Press, 1982), 203.

38. Austrian, *Herman Hollerith*, 125.

39. Mills, *White Collar*, 193.

40. Margaret Davies, *Woman's Place Is at the Typewriter* (Philadelphia: Temple University Press, 1982); James W. Cortada, *Before the Computer: IBM, NCR, Burroughs, and Remington Rand and the Industry They Created 1865–1956* (Princeton, N.J.: Princeton University Press, 1993); JoAnne Yates, *Control through Communication: The Rise of System in American Management* (Baltimore: Johns Hopkins University Press, 1989); Vincent E. Giuliano, "The Mechanization of Office Work," *Scientific American* 247, no. 3 (September 1982), 149–64.

41. David Alan Grier, *When Computers Were Human* (Princeton, N.J.: Princeton University Press, 2005).

42. "Office Automation: How Much Is Too Much?" (advertisement), *Wall Street Journal*, August 6, 1985, 11.

43. Harry Braverman, *Labor and Monopoly Capital* (New York: Monthly Review, 1974), 9.

44. Braverman, *Labor and Monopoly Capital*, 37.

45. Ursula Huws, "Crisis as Capitalist Opportunity: New Accumulation through Public Service Commodification," in *The Crisis and the Left: The Socialist Register 2012*, ed. L. Panitch, G. Albo, and V. Chibber (Pontypool, U.K.: Merlin, 2011), 74, 76 (quote).

46. Such linkages were posited as an explicit goal in the information society discourse of Japan at the time. See Nick Dyer-Witheford, *Cyber-Marx: Cycles and Circuits of Struggle in High-Technology Capitalism* (Urbana: University of Illinois Press, 1999), 20; Tessa Morris-Suzuki, *Beyond Computopia: Information, Automation and Democracy in Japan* (London: Kegan Paul, 1988), 8–13.

47. J. C. R. Licklider and Robert W. Taylor, "The Computer as a Communication Device," *Science and Technology* 76 (April 1968): 22 (original emphasis), 27, 28, 30.

48. Licklider and Taylor, "Computer as a Communication Device," 30; on Licklider and time-sharing systems, see Arthur L. Norberg and Judy E. O'Neill, *Transforming Computer*

Technology: Information Processing for the Pentagon, 1962–1986 (Baltimore, Md.: Johns Hopkins, 1996), 68–118; Janet Abbate, *Inventing the Internet* (Cambridge, Mass.: MIT Press, 1999).

49. Abbate, *Inventing the Internet*, 96, 100, 104–6.

50. BBN Communications Corporation, Report No. 4799, "A History of the ARPA-NET: The First Decade," prepared for Defense Advanced Research Agency, April 1981, III-100–102.

51. BBN, "History of the ARPANET," II-2. Norbert and O'Neill, in *Transforming Computer Technology*, state: "ARPANET was a large-scale experiment that was started to solve the problem of resource sharing between computers and among researchers. The goal was to connect computing systems, and through the systems the researchers, so that research could be accumulated and duplication of effort avoided through the sharing of resources and improved communication" (192).

52. BBN, "History of the Arpanet," II-2. "[V]arious computer systems of different ages and degrees of incompatibility always exist concurrently, which means that some digitized data residing in a computer can't easily be shared with other parts of the enterprise. To be sure, much progress has been made since the late 1960s to address this problem; however, one can reasonably assume it will never be fully resolved." James W. Cortada, *Information and the Modern Corporation* (Cambridge, Mass.: MIT Press, 2011), 93.

53. BBN, "History of the Arpanet," II-3. What can best be termed utopian gestures to the wider societal applications of networked tools are also evident in Licklider and Taylor, "Computer as a Communication Device," 39–40.

54. BBN, "History of the Arpanet," II-7, 8.

55. James W. Cortada, *The Digital Hand, Volume 1: How Computers Changed the Work of American Manufacturing, Transportation, and Retail Industries* (New York: Oxford University Press, 2004), 24.

56. James W. Cortada, "New Wine in Old and New Bottles: Patterns and Effects of the Internet on Companies," in *The Internet and American Business*, ed. William Aspray and Paul E. Ceruzzi (Cambridge, Mass.: MIT Press, 2008), 415, 417.

57. Michael E. Porter and Victor E. Millar, "How Information Gives You Competitive Advantage," *Harvard Business Review* 63, no. 4 (July–August 1985): 149–60; "capitalizing" quote from Irving P. Canton, "Learning to Love the Service Economy," *Harvard Business Review* 62, no. 3 (May–June 1984): 89–97.

58. "Business Is Turning Data into a Potent Strategic Weapon," *Business Week*, August 22, 1983, 92–98.

59. F. Warren McFarlan, "Information Technology Changes the Way you Compete," *Harvard Business Review* 62, no. 3 (May–June 1984): 98–103; "Cost-Cutting that Goes to the Bone," *Business Week*, July 12, 1982, 65–66; Gregory L. Parsons, "Information Technology: A New Competitive Weapon," *Sloan Management Review* 25, no. 1 (Fall 1983): 3–13.

60. "TRW Leads a Revolution in Managing Technology," *Business Week*, November 15, 1982, 130.

61. Michael Palm, "Phoning It In: Self-Service, Telecommunications, and New Consumer Labor," PhD diss., New York University, 2010.

62. Lewis M. Branscomb, "Computer Communications in the Eighties—Time to Put It All Together," International Conference on Computer Communications, Atlanta, Georgia, October 27, 1980, 5.

63. Cortada, *Information*, 47.

64. Harley Shaiken, *Work Transformed: Automation and Labor in the Computer Age* (New York: Holt, Rinehart, and Winston, 1984), 218–19.

65. "The Car of the Future Will Have New Skin and Bones," *Business Week*, July 29, 1985, 50; Turner Whitted, "Some Recent Advances in Computer Graphics," *Science* 215, no. 4534 (February 12, 1982): 767–74; C. A. Hudson, "Computers in Manufacturing," *Science* 215, no. 4534 (February 12, 1982): 818–25; and especially, Harley Shaiken, *Work Transformed*, 136–246.

66. Also see Bob Davis, "Computers Speed the Design of More Workaday Products," *Wall Street Journal*, January 18, 1985; and "Computers in Design and Manufacturing," in *New Pathways in Science and Technology*, U.S. National Academy of Science, 214–34 (New York: Vintage, 1985).

67. Hudson, "Computers in Manufacturing," 819.

68. Electronic Data Systems, Inc., *Annual Report 1984*, 10; "Industry's Hot New Find: The Mathematician," *Business Week*, July 4, 1983, 88; Urban C. Lehner and John Marcom, "Auto Automation: To Battle the Japanese, GM Is Pushing Boldly into Computerization—If the Program Succeeds, It May Dramatically Affect Much of Manufacturing; Leaning on Computer Firms." *Wall Street Journal*, July 9, 1984.

69. John Reed, "Integration of Design Tools Speeds Up Car Production," *Financial Times*, September 29, 2010.

70. Ernest Mandel, *Late Capitalism* (London: NLB, 1975), 191.

71. Alvin Toffler, *The Adaptive Corporation* (New York: Gower, 1985); David Noble, *Forces of Production* (New York: Oxford University Press, 1984).

72. For one casual reference, see Brent Scowcroft, "A World in Transformation," *National Interest*, May/June 2012, 8–9.

73. Yochai Benkler, *The Wealth of Networks: How Social Production Transforms Markets and Freedom* (New Haven, Conn.: Yale University Press, 2006).

74. Graham Murdock, "Political Economies as Moral Economies: Commodities, Gifts, and Public Goods," in *The Handbook of Political Economy of Communications*, ed. Janet Wasko, Graham Murdock, and Helena Sousa, 13–40 (Chichester, U.K.: Wiley-Blackwell, 2011).

75. Cortada, *Information*, 11, 12–13.

Chapter 2. Networked Production and Reconstructed Commodity Chains

1. The international share of U.S. corporate profits was around 5 percent during the 1960s, but by 2007 it accounted for perhaps one-quarter of all declared profits. Ed Yardeni, citing U.S. Commerce Department figures in Timothy Appel, "Overseas Profits Provide Shelter for U.S. Firms," *Wall Street Journal*, August 9, 2007. See also David Harvey, *Enigma of Capital* (New York: Oxford University Press, 2010).

2. Mira Wilkins, *The Maturing of Multinational Enterprise* (Cambridge: Harvard University Press, 1974), 411–39.

3. Judith Stein, *Pivotal Decade: How the United States Traded Factories for Services in the Seventies* (New Haven, Conn.: Yale University Press, 2010), 12. Two other incisive analyses of this recent episode are Martin Hart-Landsberg, *Capitalist Globalization: Consequences, Resistance, and Alternatives* (New York: Monthly Review, 2013); and Leo Panitch and Sam Gindin, *The Making of Global Capitalism: The Political Economy of American Empire* (London: Verso, 2012).

4. Jeffrey A. Frieden, *Global Capitalism: Its Fall and Rise in the Twentieth Century* (New York: Norton, 2007), 371.

5. Joseph Grunwald and Kenneth Flamm, *The Global Factory: Foreign Assembly in International Trade* (Washington, D.C.: Brookings Institution, 1985), 3.

6. Stein, *Pivotal Decade*, 174 (LDC exports to U.S.), 8 ("safety valve"), 156 ("first and last resort").

7. United Nations Conference on Trade and Development [UNCTAD], *World Investment Report 2000* (New York: United Nations, 2000), 3.

8. Peter Nolan and Jin Zhang, "Global Competition after the Financial Crisis," *New Left Review* 64 (July/August 2010): 101.

9. Hart-Landsberg, *Capitalist Globalization*, 90–130.

10. UNCTAD, *World Investment Report 2013, Country Fact Sheet: China*, available at at http://unctad.org/sections/dite_dir/docs/wir2013/wir13_fs_cn_en.pdf (accessed January 10, 2014).

11. UNCTAD, *World Investment Report 2010* (New York: United Nations, 2010), xviii.

12. Helen Thomas, "Tax Fears Prompt M&A Rush," *Financial Times*, May 16, 2011.

13. UNCTAD, *World Investment Report 2013* (New York: United Nations, 2013).

14. UNCTAD, *World Investment Report 2013*, vii.

15. Brazil, Russia, India, China, and South Africa.

16. UNCTAD, *World Investment Report 2013*, 2.

17. Pascal Lamy, "'Made in China' Tells Us Little about Global Trade," *Financial Times*, January 25, 2011.

18. UNCTAD, *World Investment Report 2013 Overview*, x, available at http://unctad.org/en/PublicationsLibrary/wir2013overview_en.pdf (accessed January 10, 2014).

19. Richard J. Barnet and Ronald E. Muller, *Global Reach: The Power of the Multinational Corporations* (New York: Simon and Schuster, 1974). 27–28.

20. Barnet and Muller, *Global Reach*, 40, 42.

21. Bennett Harrison and Barry Bluestone, *The Deindustrialization of America: Plant Closings, Community Abandonment, and the Dismantling of Basic Industry* (New York: Basic, 1982), 178. For a more abstract claim by an MIT management analyst about how computer communications "[eliminate] spatial and temporal constraints on organizational design," see Peter G. W. Keen, "Telecommunications and Business Policy: The Coming Impacts of Communication on Management," CISR no. 81, Sloan WP no. 1266–81 (Cambridge, Mass.: MIT Center for Information Systems Research, 1981), 27.

22. Hart-Landsberg, *Capitalist Globalization*, 91.

23. Michael O'Leary, Wanda Orlikowski, and JoAnne Yates, "Distributed Work over the Centuries: Trust and Control in the Hudson's Bay Company, 1670–1826," in *Distributed Work*, ed. Pamela Hinds and Sara Kiesler (Cambridge, Mass.: MIT Press, 2001), 27–54.

24. "Permissive technologies," Bluestone and Harrison called them in *Deindustrialization of America.*

25. Harley Shaiken, *Work Transformed: Automation and Labor in the Computer Age* (New York: Holt, Rinehart, and Winston, 1984), 217.

26. Tim Scannell, "'Fortune' Survey Finds No Loss of Corporate Control in Move to DDP," *Computerworld*, March 23, 1981, 10–11.

27. Paul Taylor, "Supply Chain Is a Strategic Discipline," *Financial Times* Connected Business, January 26, 2011.

28. Daniel Altman, "Uncertain Economy Hinders Highly Precise Supply System," *New York Times*, March 15, 2003.

29. Ben Bland and Robin Kwong, "Sunken Ambitions," *Financial Times*, November 4, 2011.

30. Paul Taylor, "Supply Chain."

31. Stephen S. Roach, "Dark Side of a Capital-Spending Boom," *Wall Street Journal*, June 2, 1988.

32. Greg Ip, "Tech Bust: What Goes Around, Comes Around," *Wall Street Journal*, July 16, 2001.

33. The Business Roundtable, "International Information Flow: A Plan for Action" (New York: Business Roundtable, January 1985), 10–11, quoted in Herbert I. Schiller, "National Sovereignty and the World Business System," paper presented to the International Political Science Association, XIII World Congress, Paris, July 19, 1985, 10–11.

34. James W. Cortada, *Information and the Modern Corporation* (Cambridge, Mass.: MIT Press, 2011), 36.

35. Stephen S. Cohen and John Zysman, *Manufacturing Matters: The Myth of the Postindustrial Economy* (New York: Basic, 1987), 193.

36. Dan Schiller, *Telematics and Government* (Norwood: Ablex, 1982).

37. Dan Schiller, *Digital Capitalism: Networking the Global Market System* (Cambridge: MIT Press, 1999), 37–50.

38. Cortada, *Information*, 80.

39. AT&T, for example, derives about half of its wireline revenues from corporate or enterprise customers. Andrew Parker and Paul Taylor, "Tough Calls Are Queuing Up for AT&T's Chief Executive," *Financial Times*, July 19, 2010.

40. Cortada, *Information*, 80.

41. Ann Knight of Paine, Webber, in Daniel F. Cuff, "General Motors Goes Courting," *New York Times*, May 19, 1984.

42. Electronic Data Systems Corporation, *1984 Annual Report*, 10; "GM Moves into a New Era," *Business Week*, July 16, 1984, 49.

43. Martin Anderson, writing in Technology Review in 1982, quoted in Cortada, *Digital Hand*, vol. 1, 134.

44. Richard Brandt, "Finding the Missing Link in Automation," *Business Week*, June 17, 1985, 39; Sydney Shaw, "Pact Signed for Standards on Computers," *Washington Post*, April 25, 1984; "Communication Barriers in the Factory Are Falling," *Business Week*, May 14, 1984, 148–52; "A Push to Make Computers Talk to Each Other," *Business Week*, May 7, 1984, 37–38; Urban C. Lehner and John Marcom Jr., "To Battle the Japanese, GM Is Pushing Boldly into Computerization," *Wall Street Journal*, July 9, 1984; Marjorie Sorge and Michelle Krebs, "New Automation Setup Due for GM Plants," *Automotive News*, March 18, 1985, 26, 43, 45.

45. James W. Cortada, "New Wine in Old and New Bottles: Patterns and Effects of the Internet on Companies," in *The Internet and American Business*, ed. William Aspray and Paul E. Ceruzzi (Cambridge, Mass.: MIT Press, 2008), 393; on the U.S. auto industry in general, see Cortada, *Digital Hand*, vol. 1, 131–39.

46. *Business Week*, "GM Moves," 48–54, esp. 49; General Motors, "How to Use Computers Intelligently" (advertisement), *Wall Street Journal*, May 4, 1987. For a different example, one rooted in the television manufacturing industry, see Jefferson Cowie, *Capital Moves: RCA's Seventy-Year Quest for Cheap Labor* (Ithaca, N.Y.: Cornell University Press, 1999).

47. Amal Nag and Roy J. Harris Jr., "GM's Winning Offer for Hughes May Set Heavy-Industry Trend," *Wall Street Journal*, June 6, 1985; General Motors, "How to Use Computers Intelligently."

48. A total of $33 billion was spent on "restructuring" between 1979 and 1984. *Business Week*, "GM Moves"; General Motors, "How to Use Computers Intelligently"; Steven Rattner, *Overhaul: An Insider's Account of the Obama Administration's Emergency Rescue of the Auto Industry* (Boston: Houghton Mifflin, 2011), 15.

49. Rattner, *Overhaul*, 185.

50. Vijay Prashad, *The Darker Nations* (New York: New Press, 2007).

51. "What a Waste," *Economist*, May 13, 2013, 14.

52. International Labour Office, *Economically Active Population Estimates and Projections*, 5th ed., rev. 2009, in John Bellamy Foster, Robert W. McChesney, and Jamil Jonna, "The Global Reserve Army of Labor and the New Imperialism," *Monthly Review* 63, no. 6 (November 2011): 21.

53. Harley Shaiken, *Mexico in the Global Economy: High Technology and Work Organization in Export Industries* (La Jolla: Center for U.S.-Mexico Studies [University of California, San Diego], 1990); "Free Exchange: Chains of Gold," *The Economist*, August 4, 2012, 68.

54. Tony Smith, *Technology and Capital in the Age of Lean Production* (Albany: State University of New York Press, 2000), 117.

55. Martin Anderson, writing in *Technology Review* in 1982, quoted in Cortada, *Digital Hand*, vol. 1, 134.

56. David Harvey, *A Companion to Marx's Capital* (London: Verso, 2010), 225–26.

57. Kim Moody, *Workers in a Lean World: Unions in the International Economy* (London: Verso, 1997), 86.

58. David McNally, *Global Slump: The Economics and Politics of Crisis and Resistance* (Oakland: PM Press, 2011), 36; Simon Mohun, "Aggregate Capital Productivity in the U.S. Economy, 1964–2001," *Cambridge Journal of Economics* 33, no. 5 (2009): 1023–46, quoted in McNally, *Global Slump*, 48.

59. Sylvia A. Allegretto, "The State of Working America's Wealth, 2011," Economic Policy Institute Briefing Paper 292, March 23, 2011; Emmanuel Saez, "Striking It Richer: The Evolution of Top Incomes in the United States (updated with 2009 and 2010 Estimates)," available at http://elsa.berkeley.edu/~saez/saez-UStopincomes-2010.pdf (accessed January 10, 2014).

60. Vincent Mosco and Catherine McKercher, *The Laboring of Communication* (Lanham, Md.: Lexington, 2008).

61. Harvey, *Enigma of Capital*, 12. See also Doug Henwood, interview, "Austerity in the Face of Weakness," *The Real News*, August 26, 2010, available at http://therealnews.com/t2/index.php?option=com_content&task=view&id=31&Itemid=74&jumival=5518 (accessed January 10, 2014).

62. Rattner, *Overhaul*, 184, 247.

63. "How Many Auto Workers Are in Your State?" *USA Today*, December 4, 2008, available at at http://usatoday30.usatoday.com/money/autos/2008-12-04-auto-workers-by-state_n.htm (accessed January 10, 2014).

64. Bill Vlasic, Hiroko Tabuchi, and Charles Duhigg, "An American Model for Tech Jobs?" *New York Times*, August 5, 2012 (with maps).

65. Gregg Shotwell, *Autoworkers under the Gun: A Shop-Floor View of the End of the American Dream* (Chicago: Haymarket, 2011), 7–66, quote at 19.

66. For another example, Japanese carmakers Toyota, Honda, and Nissan were moving a higher proportion of their production overseas as they struggled with idle facilities at home. Chester Dawson, "For Toyota, Patriotism and Profits May Not Mix," *Wall Street Journal*, November 29, 2011.

67. China was forecast to surpass Europe as an auto producer in 2013 for the first time. Peter Marsh, Chris Bryant, and Richard Milne, "Milestone for China Car Output," *Financial Times*, January 2, 2013.

68. Keith Bradsher, "Cheap Chinese Cars Make Valuable Gains in Emerging Markets," *New York Times*, July 6, 2012; John Reed, "Car Industry Grows to Record Size Despite Challenging Year," *Financial Times*, December 19, 2011; Li Fangfang, "Auto Industry Roars into Life," ChinaWatch, *China Daily*, November 30, 2011. By 2013, world production was projected to reach 82.4 million cars and light trucks. Peter Marsh, "U.S. and China Look to Drive Car Industry," *Financial Times*, January 2, 2013.

69. Rattner, *Overhaul*, 16.

70. Rattner, *Overhaul*, 13.

71. Neil Barofsky, *Bailout: An Inside Account of How Washington Abandoned Main Street While Rescuing Wall Street* (New York: Free Press, 2012), 177.

72. Stein, *Pivotal Decade*, 299; Shotwell, *Autoworkers*, 175.

73. Barofsky, *Bailout*, 175, 179.

74. Rattner, *Overhaul*, 29, see also 68.

75. Rattner, *Overhaul*, 53, 57.

76. Shotwell, *Autoworkers*, 175; Lee Sustar, Afterword, in Shotwell, *Autoworkers*, 230.

77. Robert Wright, "GM Plants at Full Tilt to Feed U.S. Car Demand," *Financial Times*, October 1, 2013. Chris Woodyard, "Autoworkers Pushed to Limit as Many Plants Max

Out," *USA Today*, May 23, 2012; Bill Vlasic and Jack Ewing, "After a Loss, GM Plans Fast Action in Europe," *New York Times*, August 3, 2012; Jeff Bennett, "GM Offers Free Car-Care to Bolster U.S. Sales," *Wall Street Journal*, June 7, 2013; Bill Vlasic, "Car Sales Climb Sharply in Strong Start to 2013," *New York Times*, February 2, 2013.

78. Paul Krugman, "Sympathy for the Luddites," *New York Times*, June 14, 2013; International Labor Organization, *World of Work Report 2013*, available at http://www.ilo.org/global/research/global-reports/world-of-work/lang—en/index.htm (accessed January 10, 2014).

79. Rattner, *Overhaul*, 53, 57.

80. Paul Krugman, "Sympathy for the Luddites," *New York Times*, June 14, 2013. Decades earlier, a previous Nobel Prize–winning economist had prioritized this issue. Wassily W. Leontieff, "Technological Advance, Economic Growth, and the Distribution of Income," *Population and Development Review* 9 no. 3 (September 1983): 407–8.

81. "The Lex Column," *Financial Times*, August 10, 2010.

82. Erik Brynjolfsson and Andrew McAfee, *Race against the Machine* (Digital Frontier Press, 2011). E-book.

83. John Gapper and Richard Waters, "Google Chief Warns of IT Threat," *Financial Times*, January 24, 2014.

84. Nathan Bomey, "Strong North American Sales Propels GM to $1.2 Billion Profit," *Detroit Free Press*, July 25, 2013. Available at http://www.freep.com/article/20130725/BUSINESS0101/307250080/General-Motors-earnings (accessed January 10, 2014).

85. Floyd Norris, "As Corporate Profits Rise, Workers' Income Declines," *New York Times*, August 6, 2011.

86. Wright, "GM Plants at Full Tilt."

87. Henry Foy, "EU Car Sales Lowest since 1993," *Financial Times*, June 19, 2013.

88. Henry Foy and Chris Bryant, "European Car Sales at Lowest Level since 1990," *Financial Times*, September 18, 2013.

89. John Reed, "Car Industry's Resistance to Change Comes Home to Roost," *Financial Times*, June 7, 2012.

90. Bernard Simon and John Reed, "European Carmakers Must Consolidate, Says Fiat Chief," *Financial Times*, January 12, 2012.

91. Henry Foy and Chris Bryant, "Battered and Bruised Sector Holds Breath over Signs of Growth," *Financial Times*, June 17, 2013; Chris Bryant, "Pressure Rises on Carmakers as Sales in Europe Hit the Skids," *Financial Times*, March 20, 2013.

92. Anthony Riedel, "Know Your Rights: Michigan's Right to Work Law," *Freedom@Work*, July 2, 2013, available at http://www.nrtw.org/en/blog/know-your-rights-michigan-right-work-03212013 (accessed January 10, 2014).

93. Andrew Pollack and Steve Lohr, "The Chip That Powers Cars," *New York Times*, April 28, 2011. Also see "Jonathan Soble, "Tsunami Takes Its Toll on Toyota," *Financial Times*, June 11–12, 2011.

94. Jaclyn Trop, "Tired of Silicon Valley? Try Motor City," *New York Times*, July 1, 2013.

95. Daniel Thomas and John Reed, "Ford Head Warns Rise to 4bn Cars Risks World Gridlock," *Financial Times*, February 27, 2012. Ford added capacity to its North American manufacturing operations during 2013. Mike Ramsey, "Ford to Add 200,000 Vehicles to 2013 North American Output," *Wall Street Journal*, May 22, 2013.

96. Shira Ovide, "Tapping 'Big Data' to Fill Potholes," *Wall Street Journal*, June 12, 2012.

97. Chris Nuttall, "Welcome to the Real Infobahn," interview with Bill Ford, *Financial Times*, October 25, 2011; Thomas and Reed, "Ford Head Warns"; John Reed, "Visions of Mobility in the Megacity," Special Report: The Future of the Car, *Financial Times*, September 13, 2011; John Reed, "Carmakers Weaving on Information Superhighway," *Financial Times*, July 25, 2011.

98. Chris Bryant, "High-Tech Cars under Threat from Hackers on Information Super-highway," *Financial Times*, March 24, 2013.

99. Claire Cain Miller and Matthew L. Wald, "Self-Driving Cars for Testing Are Supported by U.S.," *New York Times*, May 31, 2013.

100. Jane Bird, "'Internet of Things' Breaks through $10 Barrier," *Financial Times*, February 27, 2012.

101. Peter C. Evans and Marco Annunziata, "Industrial Internet: Pushing the Boundaries of Minds and Machines," GE publication, November 26, 2012. Also see John Koten, "A Revolution in the Making," (report: "Manufacturing"), *Wall Street Journal*, June 11, 2013.

102. Richard Waters, "GE Creates a Platform Path for the 'Internet of Things,'" *Financial Times*, June 20, 2013.

103. A perceptive analysis of this emergent development is offered in Mark Andrejevic, "Defining the Sensor Society," *Television and New Media*, forthcoming.

104. April Dembosky and John Reed, "Microsoft and Toyota to Build Car Interface," *Financial Times*, April 7, 2011.

105. Melissa Burden, "GM to Invest $258M in Milford Twp. Data Center," *Detroit News*, May 14, 2013.

106. Alex Luft, "General Motors Announces Fourth Information Technology Center in Chandler, Arizona," *GM Authority*, March 7, 2013.

107. Bill Vlasic, Hiroko Tabuchi, and Charles Duhigg, "An American Model for Tech Jobs?" *New York Times*, August 5, 2012.

108. Robert Reich, "Consumption Drops, Unemployment Rises, and DC Politicians Are Clueless: Here's Why," February 25, 2013, available at www.truth-out.org/news/item/14771 (accessed January 10, 2014).

109. Spencer Jakab, "Income Sinkhole Hurts Consumer Spending," *Wall Street Journal*, March 29, 2013.

110. Monica Davey, "Financial Crisis Just a Symptom of Detroit Woes," *New York Times*, July 9, 2013; Michael A. Fletcher, "Detroit Files Largest Municipal Bankruptcy in U.S. history," *Washington Post*, July 18, 2013, available at: http://www.washingtonpost.com/business/economy/2013/07/18/a8db3f0e-efe6-11e2-bed3-b9b6fe264871_story.html (accessed January 10, 2014).

Chapter 3. Networked Financialization

1. Leo Panitch and Sam Gindin, *The Making of Global Capitalism* (London: Verso, 2012), 79.

2. Panitch and Gindin, *Making of Global Capitalism*; John Bellamy Foster and Fred Magdoff, *The Great Financial Crisis: Causes and Consequences* (New York: Monthly Review, 2009); Geoff Mann, "Colletti's Credit Crunch," *New Left Review* 56 (March/April 2009): 121–24; David Harvey, "Is This *Really* the End of Neoliberalism?" *Counterpunch*, March 13/15, 2009.

3. Cees J. Hamelink, *Finance and Information: A Study of Converging Interests* (Norwood, N.J.: Ablex, 1983).

4. U.S. Census Bureau News, "Census Bureau Reports 11 Percent Increase in U.S. Business Spending on Information and Communication Technology in 2008," May 20, 2010, CB10–71; World Information Technology Services Alliance, "Digital Planet 2008, Executive Summary," 3.

5. U.S. Census Bureau, "Information and Communication Technology Survey," available at www.census.gov/econ/ict (accessed January 10, 2014).

6. Gindin and Panitch, *Making of Global Capitalism*; Leo Panitch and Sam Gindin, "Finance and American Empire," in *American Empire and the Political Economy of Global Finance*, ed. Leo Panitch and Martijn Konings (New York: Palgrave, 2009), 19; Stephen A. Marglin and Juliet B. Schor, eds., *The Golden Age of Capitalism: Reinterpreting the Postwar Experience* (Oxford: Clarendon, 1991).

7. Fred L. Block, *The Origins of International Economic Disorder: A Study of United States International Monetary Policy from World War II to the Present* (Berkeley: University of California Press, 1977).

8. Judith Stein, *Pivotal Decade: How the United States Traded Factories for Services in the Seventies* (New Haven, Conn.: Yale University Press, 2010), 41.

9. Panitch and Gindin, *Making of Global Capitalism*, 168.

10. Panitch and Gindin, *Making of Global Capitalism*, 170–71.

11. Lewis Mandell, *The Credit Card Industry: A History* (Boston: Twayne, 1990), xiv.

12. James W. Cortada, *The Digital Hand, Volume 2: How Computers Changed the Work of American Financial, Telecommunications, Media, and Entertainment Industries* (New York: Oxford University Press, 2006), 33, 61.

13. "Cashed Out," The Lex Column, *Financial Times*, February 11, 2013.

14. Cortada, *Digital Hand*, vol. 2, 63.

15. David Harvey, *Enigma of Capital* (New York: Oxford University Press); Robert B. Reich, *After-Shock: The Next Economy and America's Future* (New York: Vintage, 2011); Charles H. Ferguson, *Predator Nation: Corporate Criminals, Political Corruption, and the Hijacking of America* (New York: Crown, 2012).

16. Vijay Prashad, *The Poorer Nations: Toward a Possible History of the Global South* (London: Verso, 2012).

17. Panitch and Gindin, *Making of Global Capitalism*: 174.

18. Jeff Madrick, *Age of Greed* (New York: Knopf, 2011), 16–19.

19. Cortada, *Digital Hand*, vol. 2, 18.

20. National Commission on the Causes of the Financial and Economic Crisis, *Financal Crisis Inquiry Report, 2011*, xvii. A larger increase in the proportion of profits claimed by financial institutions over this interval is given in Stein, *Pivotal Decade*, 296.

21. Dan Schiller, *Telematics and Government* (Norwood: Ablex, 1982), table 4, p. 24.

22. Cortada, *Digital Hand*, vol. 2, 60–73.

23. Federal Communications Commission, "In the Matter of Regulatory and Policy Problems Presented by the Interdependence of Computer and Communication Services and Facilities," CC Docket No. 16979, American Bankers Association Comment, March 4, 1968, 1, 2, 3, 23, in Dan Schiller, *Telematics and Government*, 28.

24. Cortada, *Digital Hand*, vol. 2, 75.

25. FCC, "In the Matter of Establishment of Policies and Procedures for Consideration of Applications to Provide Specialized Common Carrier Services in the Domestic Public Point-to-Point Microwave Service," CC Docket No. 18920, Comment of American Banking Association October 12, 1970, 1525, in Dan Schiller, *Telematics and Government*, 45.

26. Letter from Kay Riddle, Vice President, Chase Manhattan Bank, to Richardson Preyer, Chairman, Subcommittee on Government Information and Individual Rights, Committee on Government Operations, U.S. House of Representatives, 96th Cong., 2d Sess., Hearings on International Data Flow, March 10, 13, 27, and April 21, 1980, 739–42, in Dan Schiller, *Telematics and Government*, 100–101.

27. Barry D. Wessler, "United States Public Packet Networks: An Update," *Telecommunication Journal* 47, no. 6 (1980), 374; "Electronic Mail Cuts Bank's Phone Dependence," *ComputerWorld*, June 29, 1981, 19, both in Dan Schiller, *Telematics and Government*, 54.

28. "Bank of America Rushes into the Information Age," *Business Week*, April 15, 1985, 110–12.

29. Marilyn A. Harris, "Morgan Stanley's High-Tech Boot Camp," *Business Week*, December 24, 1984, 79–82.

30. Citicorp, *Annual Report 1981*, inside back cover.

31. Citicorp, *Annual Report 1981*, inside front cover.

32. Cortada, *Digital Hand*, vol. 2, 155–56.

33. Gretchen Morgenson, "The Curtain Opens on 401(k) Fees," *New York Times*, June 3, 2012.

34. Cortada, *Digital Hand*, vol. 2, 158.

35. Cortada, *Digital Hand*, vol. 2, 169.

36. Statement of Vincent P. Moore Jr. in U.S. Senate, 95th Cong., Committee on Commerce, Science, and Transportation, Subcommittee on Communications, Hearings on Domestic Telecommunications Common Carrier Policies, 1st Sess., 21, March 22, 1977, Two Parts. Serial No. 95–42 (Washington, D.C.: GPO, 1977), 1048, in Dan Schiller, *Telematics and Government*, 64.

37. Hamelink, *Finance and Information*, 54.

38. Robin Sidel, "ATM's Fall Short on Disability Rule," *Wall Street Journal*, March 8, 2012.

39. Visa credit card letter to cardholder, May 2012; Phil Davison, "Pioneer of ATM technology and Other Bank Innovations," *Financial Times*, May 29–30, 2010.

40. Maija Palmer, "More Flash than Cash," *Financial Times*, March 21, 2012.

41. Binyamin Appelbaum, "As Plastic Reigns, Printing of Money Slows," *New York Times*, July 7, 2011.

42. Palmer, "More Flash than Cash."

43. Nelson D. Schwartz, "Online Banking Keeps Customers on Hook for Fees," *New York Times*, October 16, 2011.

44. Maija Palmer, "Racing to Make the Mobile Wallet Pay," *Financial Times*, December 1, 2011.

45. Joel Kurtzman, *The Death of Money* (Boston: Little, Brown, 1993), 26.

46. Citibank Electronic Banking and Cash Management Division, "Electronic Banking: An Executive's Guide" (New York: n.d. [1981?]).

47. "Clever Cash Management Revs Fiat's Finances," *Business Week*, April 30, 1984, 60.

48. Quoted in John M. Eger, "The Brussels Mandate: An Alliance for the Future of World Communications and Information Policy," address before the Conference on Transnational Data Regulation, Brussels, Belgium, February 9, 1978, 1–2.

49. Mara Der Hovanesian, "JP Morgan: The Bank of Technology," *Business Week*, June 19, 2006, available at http://www.businessweek.com/stories/2006-06-18/jpmorgan-the-bank-of-technology (accessed January 10, 2014).

50. Francesco Guerrera, "Citigroup Ramps Up Tech Cuts," *Financial Times*, May 22, 2009.

51. John Cassidy, "What Good Is Wall Street?" *New Yorker*, November 29, 2010.

52. Helen Thomas and Jeremy Lemer, "US Groups Blame Tax as Cash Held Overseas Tops $500bn," *Financial Times*, July 28, 2011.

53. Jennifer Hughes, "Battle Lines Are Drawn in Changing Landscape," *Financial Times*, October 3, 2011.

54. Panitch and Gindin, *Making of Global Capitalism*.

55. Foster and Magdoff, *Great Financial Crisis*; Martin Wolf, "A Hard Slog in the Foothills of Debt," *Financial Times*, March 14, 2012.

56. National Commission on the Causes of the Financial and Economic Crisis, *Financial Crisis Inquiry Report, 2011*, xvii; Stein, *Pivotal Decade*, 296.

57. Panitch and Gindin, *Making of Global Capitalism*, 247–71.

58. National Commission on the Causes of the Financial and Economic Crisis, *Financial Crisis Inquiry Report, 2011*, 7, 6 (quote).

59. Fred Magdoff and Michael D. Yates, *The ABCs of the Economic Crisis: What Working People Need to Know* (New York: Monthly Review, 2009), 76.

60. David Enrich, "Fresh Charges Readied in Rate-Rigging Case," *Wall Street Journal*, June 18, 2013; Caroline Binham, Phillip Stafford, and Kara Scannell, "'Lord Libor' Trio Put ICAP at Heart of Rate-Rigging Scandal," *Financial Times*, September 26, 2013.

61. Caroline Binham, John Aglionby, and Megan Murphy, "Swiss Probe UBS and Other Banks over Alleged Rigging of Forex Market," *Financial Times*, October 5/6, 2013.

62. Ferguson, *Predator Nation*.

63. International Monetary Fund, "How Linkages Fuel the Fire: The Transmission of Financial Stress from Advanced to Emerging Economies," in *World Economic Outlook, April 2009*, chapter 4.

64. Hugo Radice, "The Next Banking Crisis," *The Bullet* 574 (November 28, 2011), 2.

65. Mark Blyth, *Austerity: The History of a Dangerous Idea* (New York: Oxford University Press, 2013), 23–26.

66. Martin Wolf, "America Owes a Lot to Bernanke," *Financial Times*, June 5, 2013.

67. Bob Ivry, Bradley Keoun, and Phil Kuntz, "Secret Fed Loans Gave Banks $13 Billion Undisclosed to Congress," *Bloomberg Markets*, November 27, 2011, 1–2.

68. Neil Barofsky, *Bailout: An Inside Account of How Washington Abandoned Main Street While Rescuing Wall Street* (New York: Free Press, 2012).

69. Neil Irwin, "Fed's Aid In '08 Crisis Stretched Worldwide," *New York Times*, February 24, 2014.

70. Shahien Nasiripour, "A Million a Year Still Face Foreclosure," *Financial Times*, April 4, 2012. The former Special Inspector General in charge of oversight of the Treasury's Troubled Asset Relief Program calculated that, at their height, federal programs to rescue the financial system "had maxed out at $4.7 trillion." Barofsky, *Bailout*, 162.

71. Floyd Norris, "Shades of 2007 Borrowing," *New York Times*, June 1, 2013; Gretchen Morgenson, "Quantity over Quality in Bank Profits," *New York Times*, June 2, 2013; Floyd Norris, "A Portent of Peril for Muni Boldholders," *New York Times*, June 7, 2013.

72. "To achieve a full recovery and healthy growth of the world economy will be a long and tortuous process," declared Chinese leader Xi Jinping in October 2013. James Pomfret and Randy Fabi, "China's Xi Sees 'Long and Tortuous' World Economic Recovery," *Reuters*, October 7, 2013, available at http://www.reuters.com/article/2013/10/07/us-asia-china-idUSBRE99609L20131007 (accessed January 10, 2014).

73. Reich, *After-Shock*, 8.

74. Reich, *After-Shock*, 75.

75. Simon Johnson and James Kwak, *Thirteen Bankers* (New York: Pantheon, 2010); Brooke Masters, "Alert on 'Shadow Bank' Threat," *Financial Times*, March 15, 2012.

76. Barofsky, *Bailout*, 129, 132.

77. Barofsky, *Bailout*, 149, 160.

78. Brooke Masters, "Banks Are Short $566bn, Says Fitch Study," *Financial Times*, May 17, 2012, available at http://www.ft.com/intl/cms/s/0/d436e1ee-9fec-11e1-94ba-00144feabdc0.html#axzz1v7hZ9MyF (accessed January 10, 2014).

79. "The most pronounced development in banking today is that executives have gotten bolder as their business has gotten worse." Jessie Eisinger, "How the U.S. Shelters and Subsidizes the Banking Industry," *New York Times*, June 30, 2011. For other discussions, see Scott Patterson and Jean Eaglesham, "SEC Probes Rapid Trading," *Wall Street Journal*, March 23, 2012; Edward Wyatt, "S.E.C. Is Avoiding Tough Sanctions for Large Banks," *New York Times*, February 3, 2012; Sheila McNulty, "Speculators Return in Wake of Enron," *Financial Times*, December 2, 2011.

80. James B. Stewart, "Volcker Rule, Once Simple, Now Boggles," *New York Times*, October 22, 2011.

81. Shahien Nasiripour and Tom Braithwaite, "Fed Extends Volcker Rule Deadline," *Financial Times*, April 19, 2012, available at http://www.ft.com/intl/cms/s/0/ffc56a56-8a4d -11e1-93c9-00144feab49a.html#axzz1u7B83aRX (accessed January 10, 2014); William Watts, "U.S. Stock Futures Hit by J.P. Morgan," *Wall Street Journal*, May 11, 2012.

82. Barofsky, *Bailout*, 148; Eric Lipton and Ben Protess, "Banks' Lobbyists Help in Drafting Financial Bills," *New York Times*, May 24, 2013.

83. Gillian Tett, "The Achilles Heel of America's Financial System," *Financial Times*, July 31, 2012; Sebastian Mallaby, "Finance Must Escape the Shadows," *Financial Times*, August 1, 2012.

84. Gillian Tett, "Americans Are Now Ahead in Paying Down Their Debts," *Financial Times*, May 10, 2013.

85. Jessica Silver-Greenberg and Catherine Rampell, "Sallie Mae Will Split as Loans Face Scrutiny," *New York Times*, May 30, 2013.

86. Barofsky, *Bailout*, 217.

87. Alan Beattie, "An Exercise of Influence," *Financial Times*, April 3, 2012; James Fontanella-Khan, "BRICs Call for More Power at IMF," *Financial Times*, March 30, 2012.

88. Henny Sender, "China Offers Other Brics Renmimbi Loans," *Financial Times*, March 8, 2012; James Lamont, "Zoellick Backs Creation of Brics Bank," *Financial Times*, April 2, 2012.

89. Joe Leahy, "Opponents to Free Capital Flows Seek to Sway IMF," *Financial Times*, May 7, 2012.

90. Nathaniel Popper, "Global Sell-Off Shows Fed Reach beyond the U.S.," *New York Times*, June 21, 2013.

91. Patrick Jenkins, "Five Bitter Pills," *Financial Times*, September 13, 2013; Robin Harding, James Politi, and Michael Mackenzie, "Fed Blinks on Tapering of QE3," *Financial Times*, September 19, 2013.

92. Wolf, "Hard Slog."

93. Paul Krugman, "The Big Shrug," *New York Times*, June 10, 2013; Lawrence Summers, "The Buck Does Not Stop with Reinhart and Rogoff," *Financial Times*, May 6, 2013; Robert Kuttner, *Debtors' Prison: The Politics of Austerity versus Possibility* (New York: Knopf, 2013).

94. Sheryl Gay Stolberg and Mike McIntire, "A Federal Budget Crisis Months in the Planning," *New York Times*, October 6, 2013.

95. Paul Taylor, "Bank Tech Expenditure Set to Rise," *Financial Times*, The Connected Business, September 18, 2013, available at http:// http://www.ft.com/cms/s/0/33a6cde2 -13af-11e3-9289-00144feabdco.html#axzz2qfXFvI2L (accessed January 10, 2014).

96. Quoted in Robert Shrimsley, "A Supercomputer for Citigroup," *Financial Times*, March 8, 2012.

97. Francesco Guerrera and Justin Baer, "JPMorgan Cuts Trading Systems," *Financial Times*, February 16, 2011.

98. "Hedge Funds to Spend $2.09 Billion on Information Technology in 2011," *Business Wire*, September 29, 2011, available at http://www.businesswire.com/news/home/ 20110929006008/en#.UtmoR2Tnb9k (accessed January 10, 2014).

99. "Hibernia Pulls Ahead in Trans-Atlantic Speed Race," *TeleGeography*, CommsUpdate, September 30, 2010, quoting TeleGeography Vice President of Research Tim Stronge.

100. Scott Patterson, *Dark Pools: High Speed Traders, A.I. Bandits, and the Threat to the Global Financial System* (New York: Crown Business, 2012), 8.

101. Steve Kroft, "How Speed Traders Are Changing Wall Street," *Sixty Minutes*, CBS, October 10, 2010, available at http://www.cbsnews.com/news/how-speed-traders-are-changing -wall-street-07-10-2010 (accessed January 10, 2014).

102. Patterson, Dark Pools: 9.

103. "Slaves to the algorithm," Lex Column, *Financial Times*, July 13, 2011. Interestingly, in Asia exclusive of Japan, HFT made up a mere 5 percent of equity trading. Jeremy Grant and Telis Demos, "Ultra-fast Traders Braced for Tough Curbs in Europe," *Financial Times*, October 14, 2011.

104. Set up as a unit in Hibernia's so-called Global Financial Network, Project Express was supported by $250 million in financing from a three-year-old joint venture between Chinese network vendor Huawei and Britain's Global Marine Systems—long the largest global operator of cable ships. "Hibernia Atlantic Achieves an Important Milestone for Project Express," *Business Wire*, January 5, 2011, available at http://unified-communications .tmcnet.com/news/2011/01/05/5225567.htm (accessed January 10, 2014).

105. Rich Miller, "More Speed—at $80,000 a Millisecond," *DataCenter Knowledge*, January 24, 2011, available at http://www.datacenterknowledge.com/archives/2011/01/24/ more-speed-at-80000-a-millisecond (accessed January 10, 2014); Sebastian Anthony, "$1.5bn: The Cost of Cutting London–Tokyo Latency by 60 ms," *ExtremeTech*, March 20, 2012, available at http://www.extremetech.com/extreme/122989-1-5-billion-the-cost-of -cutting-london-toyko-latency-by-60ms (accessed January 10, 2014); Andrea Thomer, "Climate Change as a Safe Bet: Beneficiaries and Implications of Trans-Arctic Submarine Cable Projects" (Champaign-Urbana: University of Illinois, unpublished paper, Fall 2013).

106. Maureen O'Hara and David Easley, "The Next Big Crash Could Be Caused by 'Big Data,'" *Financial Times*, May 21, 2013.

107. "Knight Capital," The Lex Column, *Financial Times*, August 5, 2012.

108. Telis Demos, "Traders Still Waiting for Measures to Prevent a Repeat of 2010's 'Flash Crash,'" *Financial Times*, May 7, 2012.

109. Tracy Alloway, "Knight's Woes Shine Light on Succession of Wall St. Glitches," *Financial Times*, August 4/5, 2012.

110. Floyd Norris, "Strong and Fast, But No Time to Think," *New York Times*, August 3, 2012; also see Jessica Silver-Greenberg and Ben Protess, "Trying to Stay Nimble, Knight Capital Stumbles," *New York Times*, August 3, 2012; and Arash Massoudi, "Software Glitch Leaves Brokerage Knight Nursing Loss of $440m," *Financial Times*, August 3, 2012.

Chapter 4. Networked Militarization

1. Gareth Porter, *Perils of Dominance: Imbalance of Power and the Road to War in Vietnam* (Berkeley: University of California Press, 2005).

2. Walter S. Gifford, address before the Army War College, Washington, D.C., in Addresses, Papers and Interviews of Walter S. Gifford, vol. 2, October 13, 1928–December 2, 1937. Compiled by the Information Department of the American Telephone and Telegraph Company, New York, 1937, 203.

3. James W. Cortada, *The Digital Hand, Volume 3: How Computers Changed the Work of American Public Sector Industries* (New York: Oxford University Press, 2008), 54.

4. Michael T. Klare, *War without End* (New York: Vintage, 1972), 165–209.

5. The Cuban missile crisis is the most-well-known episode. However, see Jamie Doward, "How a NATO War Game Took the World to the Brink of Nuclear Disaster," *The Guardian*, November 2, 2013.

6. Vincent Mosco, *The Pay-Per Society* (Toronto: Garamond, 1989), 131–72.

7. C. Wright Mills, *The Sociological Imagination.* (New York: Oxford University Press, 2000).

8. Aaron Brenner, Robert Brenner, and Cal Winslow, eds., *Rebel Rank and File: Labor Militancy and Revolt from Below during the Long 1970s* (New York: Verso, 2010).

9. I devoted considerable attention to this Executive Branch mobilization around telecommunications policy in Dan Schiller, *Telematics and Government* (Norwood: Ablex, 1982).

10. Vijay Prashad, *The Poorer Nations: A Possible History of the Global South* (London: Verso, 2012), 52.

11. R. D. Lawrence, "Preface," in *AT&T Aftermath of Antitrust: Preserving Positive Command and Control*, ed. George H. Bolling (Washington, D.C.: National Defense University Press, 1983), xi.

12. Bolling, *AT&T*, 2.

13. Bolling, *AT&T*, 12

14. U.S. Government Accountability Office, "Critical Infrastructure Protection: Department of Homeland Security Faces Challenges in Fulfilling Cybersecurity Responsibilities," May 26, 2005 (GAO05–434), available at http://www.gao.gov/products/GAO-05-434 (accessed January 10, 2014).

15. P. E. Auerswald, L. M. Branscomb, T. M. La Porte, and M.-K. Erwann, eds., *Seeds of Disaster, Roots of Response: How Private Action Can Reduce Public Vulnerability* (New York: Cambridge University Press, 2006), xv.

16. Jason Healey, *A Fierce Domain: Conflict in Cyberspace, 1986 to 2012* (Vienna, Va.: Cyber Conflict Studies Association and the Atlantic Council, 2013), 36, 65.

17. Business Roundtable, "Essential Steps to Strengthen America's Cyber Terrorism Preparedness," available at http://web.archive.org/web/20080911120233/http://www.businessroundtable.org/pdf/20060622002CyberReconFinal6106.pdf (accessed January 30, 2014).

18. John Tirman, "The Defense Economy Debate," in *The Militarization of High Technology*, ed. John Tirman (Cambridge: Ballinger, 1984), 4.

19. Ian Roxborough, "Weary Titan, Assertive Hegemon: Military Strategy, Globalization, and U.S. Preponderance," in *The Paradox of a Global USA*, ed. B. Mazlish, N. Chanda, and K. Weisbode (Stanford: Stanford University Press, 2007), 123.

20. Available at http://www.gpo.gov/fdsys/pkg/CHRG-110Shrg39441/html/CHRG-110shrg39441.htm (accessed March 4, 2014).

21. Mark Landler and John Markoff, "After Computer Siege in Estonia, War Fears Turn to Cyberspace," *New York Times*, May 29, 2007.

22. Diffie Whitfield and Susan Landau, *Privacy on the Line: The Politics of Wiretapping and Encryption* (Cambridge, Mass.: MIT Press, 2007), 114.

23. A. Brookes, "US Plans to 'Fight the Net' Revealed." *BBC News*, January 27, 2006, available at http://news.bbc.co.uk/2/hi/americas/4655196.stm (accessed January 10, 2014).

24. David E. Sanger and Thom Shanker, "Obama Picks a Cyber Expert to Lead N.S.A.," *New York Times*, January 31, 2014. This chronology is congruent with that given by Healey, *Fierce Domain*.

25. (U.S. Office of Management and Budget 2007), "Department of Defense," The Bush Administration, available at http://www.gpo.gov/fdsys/phg/BUDGET-2008-BUD/pdf/BUDGET-2008-BUD-11.pdf.

26. Peter Baker, "Panetta's Pentagon, without the Blank Check," *New York Times*, October 24, 2011; Elisabeth Bumiller, "U.S. to Sustain Military Power in the Pacific, Panetta Says," *New York Times*, October 24, 2011; Hillary Clinton, "America's Pacific Century," *Foreign Policy* 189 (November 2011): 56–63.

27. L. R. Mayer, "Wired," *CapitalEye*, January 7, 2007.

28. Defense Information Systems Agency, available at http://www.disa.mil/dso/spo.html (accessed January 10, 2014).

29. U.S. Government Accountability Office, *Telecommunications: Comprehensive Review of U.S. Spectrum Management with Broad Stakeholder Involvement Is Needed* (GAO-03-277) (Washington, D.C.: GAO, 2003), 30.

30. U.S. Government Accountability Office, *DOD Management Approach and Processes Not Well-Suited to Support Development of Global Information Grid* (GAO-06-211) (Washington, D.C.: GAO, 2006), 1, 3, 4.

31. U.S. Government Accountability Office, *DOD Management Approach*, 1, 6.

32. William J. Broad and David E. Sanger, "Flexing Muscle, China Destroys Satellite in Test," *New York Times*, January 19, 2007.

33. Sean Collins Walsh, "Federal Push for 'Cloud' Technology Faces Skepticism," *New York Times*, August 22, 2011.

34. For example, Edward S. Herman and Noam Chomsky, *Manufacturing Consent: The Political Economy of the Mass Media* (New York: Pantheon, 2002).

35. David L. Altheide, *Terrorism and the Politics of Fear* (Lanham, Md.: AltaMira, 2006), 2.

36. Jane Mayer, "A Secret Sharer," *New Yorker*, May 23, 2011, 54.

37. William Appleman Williams, *Empire as a Way of Life* (Oxford: Oxford University Press, 1980), 197.

38. David E. Sanger, *Confront and Conceal* (New York: Crown, 2012), 417, 418, citing "Threatening a Sacred Cow," *The Economist*, February 10, 2011.

39. Christopher Drew, "Military Is Said to Make Progress in Modernizing," *New York Times*, October 28, 2011.

40. Including homeland security, wars in Iraq and Afghanistan, and medical costs for American wounded. David E. Sanger, "The Price of Lost Chances," *New York Times*, September 11, 2011; Amanda Cox, "A 9/11 Tally: $3.3 Trillion," *New York Times*, September 11, 2011. Compare with Clifford A. Kiracofe, "Wars Leave Crumbling Infrastructure at Home for US," *Information Clearing House*, April 10, 2012.

41. Joseph E. Stiglitz, "The Price of 9/11," *Project Syndicate*, September 1, 2011; Joseph Stiglitz and Linda Bilmes, "There Will Be No Peace Dividend after Afghanistan," *Financial Times*, January 24, 2013.

42. Steven Erlanger, "Shrinking Europe Military Spending Is Examined," *New York Times*, April 23, 2013.

43. Mark Landler and Peter Baker, "Extending a Hand Abroad, Obama Often Finds a Cold Shoulder," *New York Times*, June 19, 2013.

44. Stockholm International Peace Research Institute, "World Military Spending Levels Out after 13 Years of Increases, Says SIPRI," April 17, 2012, available at http://www.sipri .org/media/pressreleases/2012/17-april-2012-world-military-spending-levels-out-after -13-years-of-increases-says-sipri (accessed January 10, 2014).

45. David E. Sanger and Thom Shanker, "Cuts Give Obama Path to Create Leaner Military," *New York Times*, March 11, 2013; "Squeezing the Pentagon," *The Economist*, July 6, 2013, 26–27.

46. Thom Shanker, "Hagel Gives Dire Assessment of Choices He Expects Cuts to Force on the Pentagon," *New York Times*, August 1, 2013.

47. Sanger, *Confront and Conceal*, 421.

48. Dion Nissenbaum, "Military Contractors Change Tactics," *Wall Street Journal*, January 4, 2013.

Chapter 5. The Historical Run-Up

1. Dan Schiller, *How to Think about Information* (Urbana: University of Illinois Press, 2007), 36.

2. For this insight, Dallas W. Smythe, "Communications: Blindspot of Western Marxism," *Canadian Journal of Political and Social Theory* 1, no. 3 (Fall 1977): 1–27. For discussion, Dan Schiller, *Theorizing Communication: A History* (New York: Oxford University Press, 1996).

3. Gary Fields, *Territories of Profit: Communications, Capitalist Development, and the Innovative Enterprises of G. F. Swift and Dell Computer* (Stanford: Stanford University Press, 2004).

4. Vijay Prashad, *The Poorer Nations* (New York: Verso, 2012), 52.

5. Dan Schiller, *How to Think about Information*, 39–48.

6. David Harvey, *The New Imperialism* (Oxford: Oxford University Press, 2003), 137–82.

7. This outcome was problematized by Daniel Bell, "The Social Framework of the Information Society," chapter 9 in *The Computer Age: A Twenty-Year View*, ed. Michael L. Dertouzos and Joel Moses (Cambridge, Mass.: MIT Press, 1979).

8. Pierre Nora and Alain Minc, *The Computerization of Society* (Cambridge, Mass.: MIT Press, 1980 [1978]).

9. Kevin Robins and Frank Webster, "Information as a Social Relation," *Intermedia* 8, no. 4 (July 1980), 30.

10. Jefferson Cowie, *Capital Moves: RCA's Seventy-Year Quest for Cheap Labor* (Ithaca, N.Y.: Cornell University Press, 1999); Mari Castañeda, "The Development of the U.S. Advanced Digital Television System, 1987–1997: The Property Creation of New Media," PhD diss., University of California, San Diego, 2000.

11. Jack Banks, *Monopoly Television: MTV's Quest to Control the Music* (Boulder, Colo.: Westview, 1996); William M. Kunz, *Culture Conglomerates: Consolidation in the Motion Picture and Television Industries* (Lanham, Md.: Rowman and Littlefield, 2006).

12. Edward Herman and Robert McChesney, *The Global Media* (Aldershot: Edward Elgar, 1997).

13. Steven Kline, Nick Dyer-Witheford, and Greg de Peuter, *Digital Play: The Interaction of Technology, Culture, and Marketing* (Montreal: McGill-Queen's University Press, 2003).

14. Schiller, *How To Think about Information*, 101–44.

15. Bell, "Social Framework," 182.

16. Dan Schiller, *Telematics and Government* (Norwood: Ablex, 1982); Dan Schiller, *Digital Capitalism: Networking the Global Market System* (Cambridge, Mass.: MIT Press, 1999).

17. Ronald A. Cass and John Haring, *International Trade in Telecommunications* (Washington, D.C. / Cambridge, Mass.: AEI Press / MIT Press, 1998), 91–92, 104.

18. Martin Campbell-Kelly, *From Airline Reservations to Sonic the Hedgehog: A History of the Software Industry* (Cambridge, Mass.: MIT Press, 2003).

19. Jonathan Zittrain, *The Future of the Internet and How to Stop It* (New Haven, Conn.: Yale, 2008), 11–18.

20. Urs von Burg, *The Triumph of Ethernet: Technological Communities and the Battle for the LAN Standard* (Stanford, Calif.: Stanford University Press, 2001).

21. Janet Abbate, *Inventing the Internet* (Cambridge, Mass.: MIT Press, 1999), 159, 160.

22. Richard Hill, *The New International Telecommunications Regulations* and the Internet: A Commentary and Legislative History (Zurich: Schulthess, 2013), 7.

23. Hill, *New International Telecommunications*, 8; William J. Drake, "WATTC 88: Restructuring the International Telecommunications Regulations," *Telecommunications Policy* 12, no. 3 (September 1988): 217–33; Peter Cowhey and Jonathan D. Aronson, "The ITU in Transition," *Telecommunications Policy* 15, no. 4 (August 1991): 298–310.

24. Zittrain, *Future of the Internet*, 28.

25. James W. Cortada, *Information and the Modern Corporation* (Cambridge, Mass.: MIT Press, 2011).

26. "IPTV Broadband Penetration Reaches 15 Percent, Growth Prospects are Patchy," *TeleGeography*, CommsUpdate, June 20, 2012.

27. U.S. Government Accountability Office, "Video Marketplace: Competition is Evolving, and Government Reporting Should Be Re-Evaluated" (GAO-13-576), June 2013, available at http://www.gao.gov/products/GAO-13-576 (accessed January 10, 2014).

28. L. J. Davis, *The Billionaire Shell Game* (New York: Doubleday, 1998), 150.

29. Dan Schiller, "Internet Feeding Frenzy," *Le Monde diplomatique*, February 2000, available at http://mondediplo.com/2000/02/02schiller (accessed January 10, 2014); Robert W. McChesney, *Digital Disconnect: How Capitalism Is Turning the Internet against Democracy* (New York: New Press, 2013), 123–24.

30. Between 1983 and 1993, the number of interconnecting computer networks leapt from a mere handful to more than ten thousand. Vinton Cerf, "How the Internet Came to Be," in *The Online User's Encyclopedia*, by Bernard Aboba (Boston: Addison-Wesley, 1993), 5. Also see E. Fleischman, Boeing Computer Services, "A Large Corporate User's View of IPng," Internet Engineering Task Force Network Working Group RFC 1687, August 1994; and Abbate, *Inventing the Internet.*

31. Matthew Crain, "The Revolution Will Be Commercialized: Finance, Public Policy, and the Construction of Internet Advertising," PhD diss., University of Illinois, Urbana-Champaign, 2013; Matthew Crain, "Financial Markets and Online Advertising: Reevaluating the Dotcom Investment Bubble," *Information, Communications and Society* 17, no. 3 (2014): 371–84. Available at http://dx.doi.org/10.1080/1369118X.2013.869615 (accessed January 31, 2014).

32. Tim Wu, *The Master Switch: The Rise and Fall of Information Empires* (New York: Knopf, 2010).

33. Matthew Hindman, *The Myth of Digital Democracy* (Princeton: Princeton University Press, 2008).

34. Steve Lohr, "Can These Guys Make You 'Bing'?" *New York Times*, Sunday Business, July 31, 2011.

35. Quentin Hardy, "Head to Head over Mobile Maps," *New York Times*, June 18, 2012.

36. McChesney, *Digital Disconnect.* For similarly focused (though uncritical) arguments, see John Battelle, "The Internet Big Five By Product Strength," available at http://battelle media.com/archives/2012/01/the-internet-big-five-by-product-strength.php (accessed January 10, 2014); and Farhad Manjoo, "The Great Tech War of 2012," *Fast Company*, October 17, 2011, available at http://www.fastcompany.com/1784824/great-tech-war-2012.

37. Sascha D. Meinrath, James W. Losey, and Victor W. Pickard, "Digital Feudalism: Enclosures and Erasures from Digital Rights Management to the Digital Divide," *CommLaw Conspectus* 19, no. 2 (2011): 431. Alternative conceptions of what is called the "Internet ecosystem" are offered in Internet Advertising Bureau, Hamilton Consultants, Inc., with Dr. John Deighton and Dr. John Quelch, authors, "Economic Value of the Advertising-Supported Internet Ecoystem" (Cambridge, Mass.: Hamilton Consultants), June 10, 2009, exhibits 1–1, 1–2, 1–3, pp. 10–11, 13, 14.

Chapter 6. Web Communications Commodity Chains

1. "Internet intermediaries," declared the Commerce Department, "provide access to, host, transmit or index information created by third parties, or provide Internet-based services to third parties. Internet intermediaries include website hosts, blogging site hosts, social media sites and other services that allow individuals to provide and post information to be

hosted online. The services Internet intermediaries provide are integral to the growth and vitality of the Internet." U.S. Department of Commerce, National Telecommunications and Information Administration, Notice of Inquiry, "Global Free Flow of Information on the Internet," in *Federal Register* 75, no. 188 (September 29, 2010): 60072, available at http://www.gpo.gov/fdsys/pkg/FR-2010-09-29/pdf/2010-24385.pdf (accessed January 10, 2014).

2. Andrew Blum, *Tubes: A Journey to the Center of the Internet* (New York: HarperCollins, 2012), 9. This crucial point was made earlier by Manuel Castells, *The Informational City: Information Technology, Economic Restructuring and the Urban-Regional Process* (Oxford: Basil Blackwell, 1989).

3. As is helpfully specified by Eli Noam, "Let Them Eat Cellphones: Why Mobile Wireless Is No Solution for Broadband," *Journal of Information Policy* 1 (2011): 470.

4. George Gilder, *Telecosm: How Infinite Bandwidth Will Revolutionize Our World* (New York: Free Press, 2000).

5. International Telecommunication Union (ITU), *Trends in Telecommunications Reform 2013: Transnational Aspects of Regulation in a Networked Society* (Geneva: ITU, April 18, 2013), 4.

6. ITU, *Trends in Telecommunications Reform 2013*, 1.

7. ITU, *Monitoring the WSIS Targets, World Telecom/ICT Development Report 2010* (Geneva: ITU, 2010), 14, table 1.2.

8. "45% of Brazilians Have Never Had Internet Access, Reports Finds," *TeleGeography*, CommsUpdate, June 24, 2013.

9. "Forging a True Global Connection—Broadband Passes 500 Million Subscribers," *Broadband Forum*, available at http://www.broadband-forum.org/news/download/pressreleases/2010/500Million.pdf (accessed January 10, 2014).

10. ITU, "The World in 2011 ICT Facts and Figures," available at http://www.itu.int/ITU-D/ict/facts/2011 (accessed January 10, 2014).

11. "The Beginning of the End for 2G," *TeleGeography*, CommsUpdate, February 5, 2014.

12. "Africa's international bandwidth growth to lead the world," *TeleGeography*, Comms Update, October 31, 2013.

13. Judith Stein, *Pivotal Decade: How the United States Traded Factories for Services in the Seventies* (New Haven, Conn.: Yale University Press, 2010), 286.

14. "Global Telecoms CAPEX to Top USD311 Billion in 2011, Report Says," *TeleGeography*, CommsUpdate, November 9, 2011.

15. U.S. FCC, *In the Matter of Implementation of Section 6002(b) of the Omnibus Budget Reconciliation Act of 1993*, Sixteenth Report, WT Docket No. 11–186, March 19, 2013, 20.

16. "China Mobile Launches TD-LTE Tender," *TeleGeography*, CommsUpdate, June 25, 2013.

17. "Comments of Verizon and Verizon Wireless," before the Department of Commerce, Global Free Flow of Information on the Internet, December 6, 2010, 7–8, available at http://www.ntia.doc.gov/files/ntia/comments/100921457-0457-01/attachments/12%2006%2010%20VZ,%20VZW%20comments_Global%20Internet.pdf (accessed January 10, 2014).

18. Mary Lennighan, "Going Global," *Total Telecom*, May 2012, 7.

19. Dan Schiller, *Telematics and Government* (Norwood: Ablex, 1982); Schiller, *Digital Capitalism*.

20. Patricia Aufderheide, *Communication Policy and the Public Interest: The Telecommunications Act of 1996* (New York: Guilford, 1999).

21. I borrow here from Christopher Hill, *From Reformation to Industrial Revolution* (Harmondsworth: Penguin, 1988).

22. On structural adjustment in general, see Biplab Dasgupta, *Structural Adjustment, Global Trade and the New Political Economy of Development* (London: Zed, 1998).

23. Roger G. Noll, "Telecommunications Reform in Developing Countries," in *Economic Policy Reform: The Second Stage*, ed. Anne O. Krueger (Chicago: University of Chicago Press, 2000), 199. See David Harvey, *A Brief History of Neoliberalism (New York: Oxford University Press, 2007)*; and Dan Schiller, *Digital Capitalism: Networking the Global Market System* (Cambridge, Mass.: MIT Press, 1999), on the larger neoliberal agenda and its relation to networks, respectively.

24. "Tata Completes Round-the-World Cable Network Ring," *TeleGeography*, Comms Update, March 22, 2012.

25. "3 Is the Magic Number: Level 3 Merges with Global Crossing in USD3bn Stock-for-Stock Deal," *TeleGeography*, CommsUpdate, April 12, 2011; "Level 3 Completes Global Crossing Acquisition," *TeleGeography*, CommsUpdate, October 5, 2011.

26. Dan Schiller, *How to Think about Information* (Urbana: University of Illinois Press, 2007), 80–100.

27. U.S. FCC, Office of Engineering and Technology and Consumer and Governmental Affairs Bureau, "Measuring Broadband America," August 2, 2011, 3, available at at http://www.fcc.gov/measuring-broadband-america/#read (accessed January 10, 2014)

28. Tushar Tajane, "Top Five Internet Service Providers of India (as of 2010)," *TechZoom. org*, February 24, 2011, available at http://techzoom.org/top-5-internet-service-providers-of-india-as-of-2010 (accessed January 10, 2014).

29. "Broadband Provider Rankings: The Rise and Rise of China," *TeleGeography*, Comms Update, July 28, 2010.

30. Henry L. Hu, "The Political Economy of Governing ISPs in China: Perspectives of Net Neutrality and Vertical Integration," *China Quarterly* 207 (September 2011): 523.

31. Thomas Gryta, "AT&T Gets a Boost from Increased Smartphone Use," *Wall Street Journal*, July 25, 2012.

32. David Carr, "Telecom's Big Players Hold Back the Future," *New York Times*, May 20, 2013.

33. Testimony of Mary Brown, Cisco Systems Inc., before the Subcommittee on Technology and Innovation, Committee on Science, Space, and Technology, U.S. House of Representatives, Hearing on "Avoiding the Spectrum Crunch: Growing the Wireless Economy through Innovation," April 18, 2012, 3.

34. Alcatel's market capitalization in July 2012 was close to one-fifth of the sum Alcatel had paid to acquire Lucent in 2006, and the company continued to face losses and to cut

thousands of jobs. Daniel Thomas, "Alcatel-Lucent to Cut 5,000 Jobs," *Financial Times*, July 27, 2012.

35. "The Company That Spooked the World," *The Economist*, August 4, 2012; Yun Wen's doctoral dissertation on Huawei, ongoing at Simon Fraser University, will contribute to our knowledge of this company.

36. Rex Milne, "Ericsson Suffers as Sales of Older Networks Decline," *Financial Times*, July 19, 2012.

37. "Cisco to Cut Workforce by 15%, Sell Factory," *BusinessWorld*, July 19, 2011; Jeff Gaumgartner, "Foxconn Buys Cisco's Set-Top Factory," *LR Cable News Analysis*, July 18, 2011, available at www.lightreading.com/document.asp?doc_id=210080&site (accessed January 10, 2014).

38. Rick Kuhn, Kotikalapudi Sriram, and Doug Montgomery, "Border Gateway Protocol Security: Recommendations of the National Institute of Standards and Technology," NIST Special Publication 800–54, July 2007, 2–2.

39. Milton L. Mueller, *Networks and States: The Global Politics of Internet Governance* (Cambridge, Mass.: MIT Press, 2010), 226, 239. For a more expansive portrayal of the issues, see Laura DeNardis, *The Global War For Internet Governance* (New Haven, Conn.: Yale University Press, 2014). For a tally of registered autonomous system numbers and names, see ftp://ftp.arin.net/info/asn.txt (accessed March 9, 2014).

40. ITU, *Trends In Telecommunication Reform 2013: Transnational Aspects of Regulation in a Networked Society*, 4, available at http://www.itu.int/pub/D-REG-TTR.14-2013 (accessed January 10, 2014).

41. Jeffrey Keefe and Rosemary Batt, "United States," in *Telecommunications: Restructuring Work and Employment Relations Worldwide*, ed. Harry Katz (Ithaca, N.Y.: Cornell University Press, 1997), 33–43.

42. Anton Troianovski, "Verizon Pursues Tough Line on Labor," *Wall Street Journal*, July 13, 2011.

43. Kim Moody, *U.S. Labor in Trouble and Transition* (London: Verso, 2007), 54.

44. Greg Bensinger and Spencer E. Ante, "Verizon Strike Turns Nasty," *Wall Street Journal*, August 9, 2011; Steven Greenhouse, "Verizon Landline Unit at Heart of Strike," *New York Times*, August 11, 2011.

45. Dan Schiller, "End of the Telecom Revolution," *Le Monde diplomatique*, August 2003, 28–29; Dan Schiller, *How to Think about Information*, 80–100.

46. "Submarine Cable Construction Continues Despite Untapped Potential Capacity," *TeleGeography*, CommsUpdate, April 18, 2012.

47. "Service Provider Revenue Growth Bounces Back in Q3," *TeleGeography*, Comms Update, November 17, 2010; Jenna Wortham, "Data Networks Pose a Threat to Wireless," *New York Times*, May 16, 2011.

48. Organisation for Economic Cooperation and Development (OECD), *Communications Outlook 2011* (Washington: OECD, 2011), 1.

49. OECD, *Communications Outlook 2011*, 1.

50. Andrew Parker, "Telecoms Operators Feel the Pressure," *Financial Times*, June 10, 2011.

51. Kevin J. O'Brien, "In Europe, a Move to Slash Phone Roaming Charges," *New York Times*, July 6, 2011.

52. "Vodafone Ireland Reports 48% of Users Now Own Smartphones," *TeleGeography*, CommsUpdate, February 8, 2013.

53. Robin Wigglesworth and Daniel Thomas, "Hutchison Whampoa Bids Euro2bn for Bankrupt Eircom," *Financial Times*, May 5/6, 2012.

54. Jack Ewing, "In Asset Sale, Greece to Give up 10% Stake in Telecom Company," *New York Times*, June 7, 2011; "OTE's Group EBITDA Up 6.2%, Greek Figure Down 5.5%," *TeleGeography*, CommsUpdate, May 10, 2012.

55. Cornelius Rahn, "Deutsche Telekom's Greek Ambitions End with Cash Crunch," *Bloomberg Business Week*, June 26, 2012, available at http://www.bloomberg.com/news/2012-06-25/deutsche-telekom-s-greek-ambitions-end-with-cash-crunch.html (accessed January 10, 2014).

56. Andrew Parker, "Telefonica to Cut Spanish Workforce by 20% but Vows to Increase Dividends," *Financial Times*, April 15, 2011; "Net Debt Cut but Writedowns and Domestic Woes Hit Telefonica," *TeleGeography*, CommsUpdate, February 28, 2013.

57. Daniel Thomas and James Boxell, "Merger Ruled Out as France Telecom Eyes Other Deals," *Financial Times*, July 26, 2012.

58. Bensinger and Ante, "Verizon Strike Turns Nasty"; Steven Greenhouse, "Verizon Landline Unit"; U.S. FCC, *Implementation of Section 6002(b) of the Omnibus Budget Reconciliation Act of 1993*, WT Docket No. 11–186, adopted March 19, 2013, 25–26.

59. Dan Schiller, *Digital Capitalism*, 26.

60. Richard Waters, Maija Palmer, and Tim Bradshaw," Knocking at the Door of Tech Heaven," *Financial Times*, May 11, 2011.

61. "Microsoft's Acquisition of Skype," *TeleGeography*, CommsUpdate, May 11, 2011; "International Long-Distance Slumps, While Skype Soars," *TeleGeography*, The Feed, January 6, 2011; Joe Nocera, "The Cloud Hanging over Skype," *New York Times*, September 5, 2009; David Gelles and Maija Palmer, "Skype Deal Stumbles over Software Row," *Financial Times*, September 17, 2009.

62. Waters, Palmer, and Bradshaw, "Knocking"; Paul Taylor, "Skype's Changing Traffic Growth," *Financial Times*, May 10, 2011.

63. Maija Palmer, "Valuation Adds to Bubble Fears," *Financial Times*, May 11, 2011; David Gelles, "Skype Begins Move to List on Nasdaq," *Financial Times*, August 10, 2010; "Skype's Share of the Long-Distance Pie on the Increase," *TeleGeography*, CommsUpdate, March 24, 2009.

64. "Skype Traffic Continues to Thrive," *TeleGeography*, CommsUpdate, January 15, 2014.

65. Charles S. Golvin of Forrester Research, quoted in Jenna Wortham, "Data Networks Pose a Threat to Wireless," *New York Times*, May 16, 2011; Daniel Thomas and Tim Bradshaw, "Mobile Groups Face Off with 'Killer Text Apps,'" *Financial Times*, April 29, 2013; Daniel Thomas and Tim Bradshaw, "Rapid Rise of Chat Apps Slims SMS Cash Cow for Mobile Operators," *Financial Times*, April 29, 2013.

66. "Data Prices," The Lex Column, *Financial Times*, June 19, 2012.

67. ITU, *Confronting the Crisis: Its Impact on the ICT Industry* (Geneva: ITU, February 2009), 11, 37–39, available at at http://www.itu.int/osg/csd/emerging_trends/crisis/report-low-res.pdf (accessed January 10, 2014).

68. Wortham, "Data Networks."

69. For one interesting instance, see Kathrin Hille, "Chinese Telecoms Bow to Regulator," *Financial Times*, December 2, 2011, available at http://www.ft.com/intl/cms/s/0/1260a290 -1cd3-11e1-8daf-00144feabdco.html#axzz1fZTPtYTu (accessed January 10, 2014).

70. ITU, *Trends In Telecommunications Reform 2013*, 3–4. On this see Vincent Mosco, *To the Cloud: Big Data in a Turbulent World* (Boulder, Colo.: Paradigm, 2014).

71. "Verizon Completes 1Gbps GPON Field Trial," *TeleGeography*, CommsUpdate, August 18, 2010; Brian X. Chen and Quentin Hardy, "Verizon Plans to Buy Intel Media Division to Expand Its Television Services," *New York Times*, January 22, 2014.

72. "Key Subscribers Milestones Passed as Telcos and Cablecos Battle It Out," *TeleGeography*, CommsUpdate, September 21, 2011; "IPTV Broadband Penetration Reaches 15 Percent, Growth Prospects Are Patchy," *TeleGeography*, The Feed, June 20, 2012.

73. "Telco Pay-TV Subscribers Approaching 100 Million," *TeleGeography*, CommsUpdate January 23, 2012.

74. Pyungho Kim, "Internet Protocol TV in Perspective: A Matrix of Continuity and Innovation," *Television & New Media* 10, no. 6 (November 2009): 536–45; "Softbank Buys 35% Stake in Chinese Online TV Provider Synacast," *TeleGeography*, CommsUpdate, February 4, 2011.

75. The scale and capacities of their existing networks, and the capital expenditure undertaken by market leaders such as China Telecom in China, or Verizon in the United States—Verizon invested around $17 billion in 2009 and the same in 2010—found no parallel in cable television. Roger Cheng, "Wireless Carriers Sow Confusion Over 4G" *Wall Street Journal*, November 4, 2010.

76. "Key Subscriber Milestones," *TeleGeography*, June 20, 2012.

77. David Gelles and Andrew Edgeclife-Johnson, "Comcast Deal Set to Reshape Media Industry," *Financial Times*, January 20, 2011; Brian Stelter and Tim Arango, "Comcast Spends Big in Pressing for Merger," *New York Times*, September 27, 2010; David Pogue, "Cable TV in Pursuit of Mobility," *New York Times*, March 2, 2011; Cecilia King, "Comcast, Time Warner Cable Agree to Merge in $45 Billion Deal," *Washington Post*, February 12, 2014.

78. Shalini Ramachandran and Thomas Gryta, "Telecoms Selling TV Have Bigger Impact on Cable Firms," *Wall Street Journal*, November 1, 2013.

79. Derek Baldwin, "Telecoms Seek Alternate Income from Global Internet Giants," *Gulfnews.com*, October 5, 2011, available at http://gulfnews.com/business/features/telecoms -seek-alternate-income-from-global-internet-giants-1.885011 (accessed January 10, 2014).

80. Mary Lennighan, "Vertically Challenged," *TotalTelecom*, May 2012, 13.

81. Andrew Parker, "Telecoms Groups in Push for Internet Shake-Up," *Financial Times*, April 27, 2011; Simon Kuper, "Le Self-Made Man: Xavier Niel," *Financial Times*, May 4–5, 2013.

82. Andrew Parker and Stanley Pignal, "Push to End 'Free Lunch' for Content Providers," *Financial Times*, February 14, 2011; Andrew Parker and Tim Bradshaw, "European Telecoms Groups Seeking to Shake-Up Content Charging Models," *Financial Times*, July 12, 2011; Andrew Parker and Stanley Pignal, "EU Warned on Broadband Targets," *Financial Times*, July 14, 2011; Amy Graham, "How Carriers Will Make Money (from you) on 4G," *CNN.com*, November 10, 2011.

83. "Upper House Ratifies Dutch Net Neutrality Law," *TeleGeography*, CommsUpdate, May 10, 2012.

84. For the United States, see FCC 10 201, GN Docket 09–191, WC Docket 07–52, "In the Matter of Preserving the Open Internet Broadband Industry Practices," report and order released December 23, 2010.

85. Sascha D. Meinrath, James W. Losey, and Victor W. Pickard, "Digital Feudalism: Enclosures and Erasures from Digital Rights Management to the Digital Divide," *CommLaw Conspectus* 19, no. 2 (2011), 435–37.

86. Marguerite Reardon, "Verizon to FCC: Free Speech Trumps Net Neutrality Rules," *C/Net*, July 3, 2012, available at http://news.cnet.com/8301-13578_3-57465695-38/verizon -to-fcc-free-speech-trumps-net-neutrality-rules (accessed January 10, 2014); Steve Musil, "Senate Confirms Tom Wheeler as FCC's New Chairman," *C/Net*, October 29, 2013, available at http://news.cnet.com/8301-1035_3-57609923-94/senate-confirms-tom -wheeler-as-fccs-new-chairman (accessed January 10, 2014).

87. Sam Gustin, "'Net Neutrality' Ruling Paves the Way For Internet 'Fast Lanes,'" *Time*, January 15, 2014; and, for the circuit court ruling, see http://www.cadc.uscourts.gov/ internet/opinions.nsf/3AF8B4D938CDEEA685257C6000532062/$file/1355-1474943. pdf (accessed February 1, 2014).

88. Marvin Ammori, "Is the Internet Closing?" *Weekly Wonk*, January 16, 2014, available at http://weeklywonk.newamerica.net/articles/net-neutrality/ (accessed February 2, 2014); Edward Wyatt, "Industry and Congress Await the F.C.C. Chairman's Next Moves on Internet Rules," *New York Times*, February 10, 2014.

89. Edward Wyatt and Noam Cohen, "Comcast and Netflix Reach Deal on Service," *New York Times*, February 24, 2014.

90. Henry L. Hu, "The Political Economy of Governing ISPs in China: Perspectives of Net Neutrality and Vertical Integration," *China Quarterly* 207 (September 2011): 523–40, at 538 and 539. For a review of the different forms of technical censorship, see "China," in *Access Controlled: The Shaping of Power, Rights, and Rule in Cyberspace*, ed. Ronald Deibert, John Palfrey, Rafal Rohozinski, and Jonathan Zittrain, 449–87 (Cambridge, Mass.: MIT Press, 2010). For an analysis of freedom of expression and state censorship within a society structured by social-class relations, see Yuezhi Zhao, *Communication in China* (Lanham, Md.: Rowman and Littlefield, 2008).

91. Hu, "Political Economy," 538, 540; "China Mobile Blames Rivals, OTT Products for Slip in Profits," *TeleGeography*, CommsUpdate, October 22, 2013. For additional studies of the social character of freedom of expression in China and of its changing fault-lines with respect to social networks and other digital services, see the articles collected in "Com-

munication and the Class Divide in China," *Javnost* 19, no. 2 (2012), available at http://javnost-thepublic.org/issue/2012/2 (accessed January 10, 2014).

92. "Net Neutrality," The Lex Column, *Financial Times*, January 5, 2011.

93. Peter Aspden, "Europe Casts Hollywood as the Bad-Guy," *Financial Times*, May 11/12, 2013; Hugh Carnegy, "France Touches on Idea of iTax for Tablets to Help Fund the Arts," *Financial Times*, May 14, 2013; David Jolly, "A Tax to Shore Up French Culture," *International Herald Tribune*, May 15, 2013.

94. Andrew Odlyzko, "Network Neutrality, Search Neutrality, and the Never-Ending Conflict between Efficiency and Fairness in Markets," *Review of Network Economics* 8, no. 1 (March 2009): 41.

95. For an example of politically focused struggle between cable-system operators and over-the-top video services, see Thomas Catan and Amy Schatz, "U.S. Probes Cable for Limits on Net Video," *Wall Street Journal*, June 13, 2012.

96. Jenna Wortham, "Cellphones Now Used More for Data Than for Calls," *New York Times*, May 13, 2010.

97. "14% of Wireless Subs Connected to 3G Networks," *TeleGeography*, CommsUpdate, December 3, 2010.

98. Maija Palmer and Chris Nuttall, "Intel Succumbs to Evolution of 4G," *Financial Times*, August 17, 2010.

99. Owen Fletcher, "Cell Shackles Crumble," *Wall Street Journal*, July 12, 2011.

100. Meinrath, Losey, and Pickard, "Digital Feudalism," 435–37; Michael Calabrese, "Solving the 'Spectrum Crunch': Unlicensed Spectrum on a High-Fiber Diet," Time Warner Cable Research Program on Digital Communications Report Series, Fall 2013, available at http://twcresearchprogram.com (accessed January 10, 2014).

101. See studies reviewed in Meinrath, Losey, and Pickard, "Digital Feudalism," 435.

102. Eli, "Let Them Eat Cellphones"

103. FCC Chairman Julius Genachowski, Remarks as Prepared for Delivery, "The Cloud: Unleashing Global Opportunities," Aspen IDEA Project, Brussels, Belgium, March 24, 2011, 3.

104. Ian Kemp, "Spectrum Spats," *TotalTelecom*, September 2011, 1.

105. Cecilia King, "Tech, Telecom Giants Take Sides as FCC Proposes Large Public WiFi Networks," *Washington Post*, February 3, 2013; Michael Calabrese, "Why the Feds Should Promote Wi-Fi Everywhere," *slate.com*, February 8, 2013.

106. Ronald Coase, "The Federal Communications Commission," *Journal of Law and Economics* 2, no. 2 (1959): 1–40.

107. Executive Office of the President, Council of Economic Advisors, "The Economic Benefits of New Spectrum for Wireless Broadband," February 2012, 18, 5.

108. Jonathan Spalter, "Should Some of Broadcasters' Spectrum Be Auctioned Off to Wireless Carriers?" *Wall Street Journal*, November 15, 2011; Amy Schatz, "Fight for Airwaves Set to Continue," *Wall Street Journal*, November 23, 2011. One LTE-based system, similarly, also made claims on frequencies previously reserved mostly for satellite communications. Paul Taylor, "LightSquared Wins Waiver on 4G network," *Financial Times*, January 27, 2011.

109. "Summary of the Middle Class Tax Relief and Job Creation Act of 2012," U.S. Senate Committee on Finance, available at http://www.finance.senate.gov/newsroom/chairman/release/?id=c42a8c8a-52ad-44af-86b2-4695aaff5378 (accessed January 10, 2014).

110. Cecilia Kang, "For Telecoms, Success Rests in Mobile Web Access," *Washington Post*, March 22, 2011.

111. Wortham, "Cellphones."

112. Kevin J. O'Brien, "Top 1% of Mobile Users Consume Half of World's Bandwidth, and Gap Is Growing," *New York Times*, January 6, 2012.

113. Noam, "Let Them Eat Cellphones."

114. Kevin J. O'Brien, "Getting What You Pay for on the Mobile Internet," *New York Times*, April 18, 2010.

115. Amy Schatz, "AT&T Is Set Back on Qualcomm Proposal," *Wall Street Journal*, August 10, 2011; Andrew Parker and Paul Taylor, "Spectrum at the Heart of AT&T's Audacious Move," *Financial Times*, March 22, 2011; "AT&T Buys Spectrum," The Lex Column, *Financial Times*, December 21, 2010; Associated Press, "Merger and Acquisitions in Telecoms, at a Glance," *Boston.com*, July 12, 2013.

116. Gerrit Weismann and Helen Thomas, "Berlin Fears Grow over T-Mobile's US disposal," *Financial Times*, December 2, 2011.

117. Brian Stelter, "With Verizon's $3.6 Billion Deal, Cable and Wireless Inch Closer," *New York Times*, November 3, 2011; "Verizon Strikes Deal to Acquire AWS Spectrum from US Cellular Affiliate," *TeleGeography*, CommsUpdate October 29, 2013.

118. Paul Taylor, "Sprint Investors Vote for SoftBank Takeover," *Financial Times*, June 26, 2013.

119. Peter Svensson, Associated Press, "Data Caps," *Denver Post*, July 6, 2011; "French Telcos Consider Capping 'Unlimited' Web Access," *TeleGeography*, CommsUpdate, August 22, 2011; Anton Troianovski and Thomas Gryta, "Verizon Overhauls Wireless Plans," *Wall Street Journal*, June 13, 2012.

120. Thanks to Ethan D. Schiller for some of the sources used in this paragraph. JiWire Global WiFiFinder, available at http://v4.jiwire.com/search-hotspot-locations.htm (accessed January 10, 2014).

121. "Broadband Wireless Exchange's 'Top Ten' Wi-Fi Hotspot Operators," available at http://www.bbwexchange.com/top10_wi-fi_hotspot_operators.asp (accessed January 10, 2014).

122. Glen Fleishman, "AT&T Now Biggest Hotspot Provider with Wayport Buy," *Arstechnica*, November 6, 2008, available at http://arstechnica.com/uncategorized/2008/11/atampt-becomes-worlds-largest-wifi-hotspot-provider-with-wayport-acquisition (accessed January 10, 2014).

123. "China Mobile Taps WiFi to Break Bandwidth Bottleneck," *TeleGeography*, Comms Update, June 28, 2013.

124. Tarmo Verki, "Public Wi-Fi Hotspots to Grow 4-fold by 2015: Study," *Reuters*, November 8, 2011, available at http://www.reuters.com/article/2011/11/09/us-internet-hotspots-idUSTRE7A801W20111109 (accessed January 10, 2014); Paul Taylor, "Five Cable Operators to Join Up WiFi Networks," *Financial Times*, May 22, 2012; WBA Industry Report

2011, available at http://www.wballiance.com/resource-centre/global-developments
-wifi-report.html (accessed January 10, 2014).

125. Calabrese, "Solving the 'Spectrum Crunch,'" 5.

126. See Chiehyu Li and Bincy Ninan, New America Foundation, "An International Comparison of Cell Phone Plans and Prices," October 14, 2010, available at http://oti.newamerica
.net/publications/policy/an_international_comparison_of_cell_phone_plans_and
_prices (accessed January 10, 2014).

127. Daniel Thomas and Paul Taylor, "4G Upgrade Signals Threat and Opportunity,"
Financial Times, February 25/26, 2012.

128. Daniel Thomas, "European Operators Ready to Talk Mergers," *Financial Times*,
June 19, 2012.

129. AlixPartners, in Daniel Thomas, "Study Points to Telecoms Default Risks," *Financial
Times*, September 19, 2011.

130. "Leading Telcos' Stellar Performance," *ScreenAfrica*, November 29, 2011, available at
http://www.screenafrica.com/page/news/industry/1112343 (accessed January 10, 2014).

131. Daniel Thomas, "Sawiris Targets Telecoms Buyouts," *Financial Times*, June 13, 2012.

132. Daniel Thomas, "Europeans Telecoms Revenue Fall Accelerates," *Financial Times*,
November 25, 2013.

133. "China Mobile reports 1Q results," *TeleGeography*, CommsUpdate, May 3, 2011;
Owen Fletcher, "Cell Shackles Crumble," *Wall Street Journal*, July 12, 2011; "iPhone, You
Never Do," The Lex Column, *Financial Times*, September 12, 2013. By 2014, China Mobile
claimed 767 million customers. "China Mobile Flexes 3G Muscles As Market Expands
78.8%," *TeleGeography*, CommsUpdate, January 21, 2014.

134. Adam Thomson, "Buzz in the Air as AMX Comes of Age," *Financial Times*, November 23, 2010.

135. Adam Thomson, "America Movil Aims for Extra 100m Mobile Users by 2014,"
Financial Times, November 19, 2010.

136. Haig Simonian and Eric Frey, "America Movil Buys into Telekom Austria," *Financial Times*, June 16/17, 2012; Robert Armstrong and Stuart Kirk, "America Movil," Lex in
Depth, *Financial Times*, February 22, 2013.

137. Robin Wigglesworth and Daniel Thomas, "Hutchison Whampoa Bids Euros2bn
for Bankrupt Eircom," *Financial Times*, May 5/6, 2012.

138. Daniel Thomas, "Sawiris Targets Telecoms Buyouts," *Financial Times*, June 13, 2012.

139. Daniel Obi, "Africom Deepens Insight on Global Telecom Brands on Africa," *Business Day*, November 15, 2011, available at http://mobileentertainmentafrica.com/news-2/
africom-deepens-insight-on-global-telecom-brands-on-africa (accessed January 10, 2014).

140. Andrew Parker, "Upwardly Mobile," *Financial Times*, February 11, 2008; "MTN
Group Notches 150 Million Subscribers," *TeleGeography*, CommsUpdate, June 24, 2011.

141. Mary Watkins, "Bharti Seeks to Streamline Operations with Integration of African
Units," *Financial Times*, June 28, 2011.

142. "Airtel Launches Rwanda's Third Mobile Network," *TeleGeography*, CommsUpdate,
April 2, 2012.

143. Ryan Knutson, Thomas Gryta, and Sam Schechner, "Verizon-Vodafone Impact: 'Colossal,'" *Wall Street Journal*, August 30, 2013; "Can You Hear Me Now?" The Lex Column, *Financial Times*, September 6, 2013; "Verizon Bonds," The Lex Column, *Financial Times*, September 12, 2013.

144. New Millenium Research Council, "Major Milestone for U.S. Cell Phone Consumers: Prepaid to Account for 1 out of 4 Wireless Subscriptions by End of 2011," July 29, 2011.

145. "Brazil mobile base tops 242.2m at end-2011, Anatel says," *TeleGeography*, Comms Update January 17, 2012.

146. Nancy Gohring, "Jobs Wanted Own Network with Unlicensed Spectrum," *Computerworld*, November 15, 2011; and Chris Davies, "Jobs Schemed Apple WiFi Carrier Plot for Original iPhone," available at www.slashgear.com/jobs-schemed-apple-Wi-Fi-carrier-plot-for-original-iphone-16195619 (accessed January 10, 2014).

147. I follow Cheol Gi Bae, "The Transformation of Wireless Telecommunications Policies in Korea: The Interplay between Technology, State, Industry, and Users," July 5, 2012, manuscript in author's possession; Brian X. Chen, Nick Wingfield, James Kanter, and Kevin J. O'Brien, "Europe Weighs iPhone Sale Deals with Carriers for Antitrust Abuse," *New York Times*, March 21, 2013.

148. Paul Taylor and Richard Waters, "Purchase Offers Platform for Consolidation of Hardware and Software Makers," *Financial Times*, August 17, 2011.

149. Marconi/Pacific Viewpoint, "Television Manufacturing Wars of Today and Industry Battles of Tomorrow," March 2010; Chris Nuttall, "TV Makers Seek to Return 3D Revolution," *Financial Times*, January 8–9, 2011.

150. Marconi/Pacific Viewpoint, "Television Manufacturing"; Reuters, "Samsung Faces Weak Outlook on Flat Screens and TVs," *New York Times*, October 6, 2010.

151. "Slow TV Sales to Spur LCD Panel Oversupply," *Cens.com*, September 28, 2010; Hiroko Tabuchi, "TV Prices Still Falling, Sony's Profit Drops 8.6%," *New York Times*, February 3, 2011; Brian X. Chen and Nick Wingfield, "TV Makers Drift to Next Big Thing," *New York Times*, January 6, 2014.

152. Nuttall, "TV Makers."

153. "Asian Electronics," The Lex Column, *Financial Times*, July 26, 2012.

154. Jonathan Soble, "Sony Warns of Grim Picture for TVs," *Financial Times*, December 21, 2010; Jay Alabaster, "Sony Says It Lost $6.4 Billion Last Year, over Twice Earlier Forecast," *ComputerWorld*, April 10, 2012, available at http://www.computerworld.com/s/article/9226018/Sony_says_it_lost_6.4_billion_last_fiscal_year_over_twice_earlier_forecast (accessed January 10, 2014); Jonathan Soble, "Sony Faces Pressure to Pull Plug on TVs," *Financial Times*, August 17, 2011; Jonathan Soble, "Sony's TV Woes Spur Losses of $1.2bn," *Financial Times*, November 3, 2011; Jonathan Soble, "Sony Signals Strategy Shift by Halving TV Sales Target," *Financial Times*, November 5–6, 2011; Jonathan Soble, "Sony Unveils Return to Profit," *Financial Times*, May 10, 2013.

155. Jonathan Soble, "Panasonic Warns It Faces Loss of $5.3bn," *Financial Times*, November 1, 2011; Jonathan Soble, "Sony's TV Woes Spur Losses of $1.2bn," *Financial Times*,

November 3, 2011; Jonathan Soble, "Japanese Pioneers Turn Down the Volume," *Financial Times*, November 3, 2011; Jennifer Thompson and Sarah Mishkin, "Japanese Tech Groups Join the Big TV Switch-Off," *Financial Times*, October 8, 2013.

156. Mariko Yasu, "Foreign Makers Tune in to China's TV Market," *Bloomberg Business Week*, August 12, 2010.

157. Thompson and Mishkin, "Japanese Tech Groups."

158. Tim Bradshaw, "Apple Falls Short of Revolutionary in TV," *Financial Times*, November 29, 2013.

159. David Gelles and Paul Taylor, "Deal Secures Place in US Viewers' Homes," *Financial Times*, August 17, 2011; Daisuke Wakabayashi, "Sony TV Unit Seeks Path to Profitability," *Wall Street Journal*, November 27–28, 2010; Nuttall, "TV Makers"; Chen and Wingfield, "TV Makers Drift."

160. Robert Cyran and Agnes T. Crane, "Ante Is Rising in Game Industry," *New York Times*, November 15, 2010; Ian Sherr, "Developers Defeat Rising Game Costs," *Wall Street Journal*, June 11, 2013.

161. Ben Fritz, "Video Game Sales Rise Only 1% in October," *Los Angeles Times*, November 12, 2011, available at http://articles.latimes.com/2011/nov/12/business/la-fi-ct-game-sales-20111112 (accessed January 10, 2014); "Service Record Call of Duty on Top," *Financial Times*, November 12–13, 2011.

162. Chris Nuttall, "Kinect Controller Helps Xbox Sales Overtake Flagging Wii," *Financial Times*, December 8, 2010.

163. Jonathan Soble, "Nintendo Set to Unveil 3D Console," *Financial Times*, February 26–27, 2011; Mark Hachman, "Nintendo, Sony to Suffer in 2012 as Console Market Plunges," *PC Magazine*, April 30, 2012, available at http://www.pcmag.com/article2/0,2817,2403787,00.asp?google_editors_picks=true (accessed January 10, 2014).

164. Nick Wingfield and Brian Stelter, "Xbox Live Challenges Cable Box," *New York Times*, December 5, 2011.

165. Chris Nuttall, "Life Inside the Video Game," *Financial Times*, June 10, 2011; Nick Wingfield and Daisuke Wakabayashi, "Next Wii to Play Off the Tablet Craze," *Wall Street Journal*, June 8, 2011; Associated Press, "Nintendo Sinks to Loss in April–December Period on Strong Yen, Weak Sales of 3DS and Wii," *Washington Post*, January 26, 2012; "Microsoft and Xbox," The Lex Column, *Financial Times*, March 28, 2012.

166. Ian Sherr, "'Sonic' Gets a Second Chance," and accompanying graphic titled "State of Play," *Wall Street Journal*, June 7, 2012; Nick Wingfield, "Next Xbox Will Face New Array of Rivals," *New York Times*, May 22, 2013; "A Game Controller, and More," *New York Times*, June 13, 2013; Ian Sherr and Drew FitzGerald, "New Xbox One Moves Beyond Games," *Wall Street Journal*, May 22, 2013; Daisuke Wakabayashi, "Nintendo Resists the Lure of Mobile Games," *Wall Street Journal*, June 12, 2013; Ian Sherr and Daisuke Wakabayashi, "Xbox One to Launch at $499," *Wall Street Journal*, June 11, 2013; Ian Sherr, "Microsoft Angers Gamers," *Wall Street Journal*, June 12, 2013; Barney Jopson and Andrea Felsted, "Retailers Seek Gaming Bonanza," *Financial Times*, November 21, 2013.

167. Nick Wingfield, "New Consoles on the Way, but Gaming Isn't the Same," *New York Times*, November 11, 2013.

168. Jonathan Soble, "Sony Loses Face over Theft of PS3 Data," *Financial Times*, April 28, 2011; Ben Fritz, "Video Game Sales Rise Only 1% in October," *Los Angeles Times*, November 12, 2011, available at http://articles.latimes.com/2011/nov/12/business/la-fi-ct -game-sales-20111112 (accessed January 10, 2014).

169. Soble, "Sony Loses Face."

170. Chris Nuttall, "Microsoft Eyes Broader Use of Game Controller," *Financial Times*, October 31, 2011, available at http://www.ft.com/cms/s/2/21a337ca-0303-11e1-899a-00144feabdc0 .html#axzz1cM1B1AdG (accessed January 10, 2014).

171. Mike Snider, "Sony Sells More than 1 Million PlayStation 4s," *USA Today*, November 17, 2013, available at http://www.usatoday.com/story/tech/gaming/2013/11/17/sony-sells -1-million-playstation-4s/3618217 (accessed January 10, 2014); Hannah Kuchler and Richard Waters, "Xbox and Cloud Help Microsoft Ease Fears," *Financial Times*, January 24, 2014.

172. "China's E-Book Market Heats Up," *Seeking Alpha*, January 3, 2012, available at http://seekingalpha.com/article/317149-china-s-e-book-market-heats-up (accessed January 10, 2014).

173. "E-Books Open Up," The Lex Column, *Financial Times*, September 3–4, 2011.

174. David Sarno, "Tablet, E-Reader Ownership Jumps to 19% in the US over the Holidays," *Los Angeles Times*, January 23, 2012, available at http://latimesblogs.latimes.com/ technology/2012/01/tablet-e-reader-ownership-in-us-jumps-to-20-over-the-holidays.html (accessed January 10, 2014).

175. Claire Cain Miller, "E-Books Top Hardcovers at Amazon," *New York Times*, July 20, 2010; Julie Bosman, "E-Readers under Christmas Trees May Help E-Books Take Root," *New York Times*, December 24, 2010; Andrew Edgecliffe-Johnson, "E-Books Overtake Print Sales in US," *Financial Times*, April 15, 2011.

176. Andrew Edgecliffe-Johnson, "Amazon's Electronic Book Sales Beat Print," *Financial Times*, May 20, 2011.

177. Andre Schiffrin, *Words and Money* (London: Verso, 2010), 105.

178. David Gelles and Andrew Edgecliffe-Johnson, "Publishers Sued over E-Book Price 'Collusion,'" *Financial Times*, April 12, 2012.

179. David Streitfeld, "E-Book Ruling Gives Amazon an Advantage," *New York Times*, July 11, 2013.

180. Julie Bosman, "Apple Negotiator Defends Tactics in an E-Book Trial," *New York Times*, June 14, 2013.

181. David Streitfeld, "As New Services Track Habits, the E-Books Are Reading You," *New York Times*, December 25, 2013.

182. Matt Hamblen, "Why the Kindle Fire and Nook Tablet are Wi-Fi Only," *ComputerWorld*, November 9, 2011.

183. Figures from Joseph Mann, "Apple iPad Surge Hits PC Shipments," *Financial Times*, January 13, 2011; compare "Gartner Says Worldwide PC Shipments to Increase 19 Percent in 2010 with Growth Slowing in Second Half of the Year," *Financial Times*, August 31, 2010.

184. Richard Waters, "Strength of Microsoft Sales Eases Wall St. Fears," *Financial Times*, October 29, 2010; Mary Watkins, "Tablets Start to Cause Side Effects for PCs," *Financial*

Times, October 15, 2010; Chris Nuttall, "Computing's Old Guard Faces a Tough Year," *Financial Times*, December 31, 2010; Verne G. Kopytoff and Laurie J. Flynn, "PC Makers Are Seeing a Slowdown," *New York Times*, May 18, 2011; Joseph Menn, "Modest Profit for Microsoft as PC Sales Slow," *Financial Times*, October 21, 2011; Sarah Mishkin and Chris Nuttall, "PC Makers Face Tough Fight to Reignite Sales," *Financial Times*, July 16, 2012.

185. Scott Martin, "PC Market in 2013 Notches Worst Decline in History," *USA Today*, January 9, 2014, available at http://www.usatoday.com/story/tech/2014/01/09/pc-market-in-2013-notches-worst-decline-in-history/4394409 (accessed February 3, 2014).

186. Lorraine Luk, "PC Maker Lenovo Posts 44% Gain in Profit," *Wall Street Journal*, November 11, 2010.

187. Richard Waters, "Dell Cuts Revenue Outlook amid Dwindling Consumer Confidence," *Financial Times*, August 17, 2011; Joseph Menn, "HP Shares Plunge as Investors Take Fright at Scale and Timing of Revamp," *Financial Times*, August 20–21, 2011; Justin Scheck and Joann S. Lublin, "Investors Rebel against H-P Plan," *Wall Street Journal*, August 20–21, 2011; Richard Waters, "Tech Scramble Turns Sector on Its Head," *Financial Times*, August 20–21, 2011; Paul Taylor and Richard Waters, "Purchase Offers Platform for Consolidation of Hardware and Software Makers," *Financial Times*, August 17, 2011; Richard Waters, "Whitman Warns of Long HP Recovery," *Financial Times*, June 7, 2012; Kathrin Hille, "Lenovo in Talks as It Seeks Global Smartphone Expansion," *Financial Times*, June 5, 2013; Eric Pfanner, "Mobile Devices Overtake PC Sales at Lenovo," *New York Times*, August 16, 2013.

188. John Ashcroft, "Apple in the Digital Age from the iPod to the iPad," http://promanchesterceo.typepad.com/files/apple-case-study-2011.pdf, table 16.1, p. 21.

189. Apple, Inc., "Earnings Releases FY 2013," available at http://investor.apple.com/results.cfm (accessed February 3, 2014).

190. Chris Nuttall, "iPod Sales Melt Away but Apple Still Leads a Flagging Field," *Financial Times*, November 4, 2011.

191. Joseph Menn, "Apple iPad Sales Fail to Hit Forecasts," *FT.com*, October 10, 2010; Lorraine Luk and Yukari Iwatani Kane, "Apple Readies New iPhone," *Wall Street Journal*, July 7, 2011; Tim Bradshaw, "Apple Falls Victim to Its Own Success," *Financial Times*, January 25, 2013.

192. Richard Waters, "Mobilised against Mobile," *Financial Times*, May 25, 2012.

193. Daniel Thomas, "Smartphone Sales Outstrip Basic Devices for the First Time," *Financial Times*, August 15, 2013.

194. Pfanner, "Mobile Devices"; Claire Cain Miller and David Gelles, "After Big Bet, Google to Sell Motorola Unit," *New York Times*, January 30, 2014.

195. Eric Pfanner, "Smartphone Leaders, Samsung and Apple, Settle In at Top," *New York Times*, October 30, 2013.

196. Charles Duhigg and Keith Bradsher, "How U.S. Lost Out on iPhone Work," *New York Times*, January 22, 2011; Nuttall, "iPod Sales"; Josh Lowensohn, "Apple's 2013 by the Numbers," *C/Net*, October 28, 2013, available at http://news.cnet.com/8301-13579_3-57609686-37/apples-2013-by-the-numbers-150m-iphones-71m-ipads (accessed February 3, 2014).

197. Paul McDougall, "Apple Now Top PC Maker, Report Says," *Information Week*, January 31, 2012.

198. Mary Watkins "Tablet Demand Set to Bolster IT Spending," *Financial Times*, March 31, 2011; Tim Bradshaw, "Tablets Drive Growth as PC Sales and Upgrades Slow," *Financial Times*, June 25, 2013; Brian X. Chen, "iPhone Sales Set Record For Quarter: 51 Million," *New York Times*, January 28, 2014.

199. Joseph Menn, "iPhone and Mac Sales Help Apple Profits Soar," *Financial Times*, April 21, 2011; "iPad 2 suppliers," The Lex Column, *Financial Times*, March 7, 2011; Ian Sherr, "Tablet War Is an Apple Rout," *Wall Street Journal*, August 12, 2011; Nick Wingfield and Nick Bilton, "The Race in Tablets Heats Up," *New York Times*, July 16, 2012.

200. Chris Nuttall and Sarah Mishkin, "Software Titans Enter the Physical World," *Financial Times*, August 10, 2012.

201. April Dembosky, "iPad 2 Boosts Second-Hand Sales," *Financial Times*, March 12–13, 2011.

202. Kathrin Hille, "Apple Achieves Cult Status with iPad 2 in China," *Financial Times*, August 8, 2011; Tim Bradshaw and Sarah Mishkin, "Apple Seals China Mobile Deal," *Financial Times*, December 23, 2013; Saritha Rai, "Cost of Cool In India? An iPhone," *New York Times*, January 13, 2014.

203. Paul Krugman, "Profits without Production," *New York Times*, June 20, 2013.

204. Jack Linchuan Qiu has studied these workers' communicative practices and potentials for several years. For his initial synthesis, supplemented by a continuing stream of additional research, see Qiu, *Working-Class Network Society* (Cambridge, Mass.: MIT Press, 2009). For a valuable study of manufacturing workers in China's information technology and electronics industry, see Yu Hong, *Labor, Class Formation, and China's Informationized Policy of Economic Development* (Lanham, Md.: Lexington, 2011).

205. Duhigg and Bradsher, "How U.S. Lost Out"; Yuqing Xing and Neal Detert, "How the iPhone Widens the United States Trade Deficit with the People's Republic of China," Asian Development Bank Institute, Working Paper No. 257, December 2010; "Employment: Defending Jobs," *The Economist*, September 12, 2011, available at http://www.economist.com/blogs/dailychart/2011/09/employment (accessed January 10, 2014); Ben Bland and Sarah Mishkin, "Foxconn Feels Strain of Staff Shortages," *Financial Times*, October 8, 2013; Malcolm Moore, "Apple's Child Labour Issues Worsen," *The Telegraph*, February 15, 2011, available at http://www.telegraph.co.uk/technology/apple/8324867/Apples-child-labour-issues-worsen.html (accessed January 10, 2014); Apple Inc., "Apple Supplier Responsibility 2011 Progress Report," available at http://www.apple.com/supplierresponsibility (accessed October 10, 2011).

206. Sarah Mishkin, "Pegatron Takes a Bite out of Hon Hai's Apple," *Financial Times*, May 15, 2013.

207. Duhigg and Bradsher, "How U.S. Lost Out."

208. Jonathan Zittrain, *The Future of the Internet and How To Stop It* (New Haven, Conn.: Yale University Press, 2008).

209. "A Virtual Counter-Revolution," *The Economist*, September 4, 2010.

210. Amir Efrati, "Google Targets Amazon with Cloud Services," *Wall Street Journal,* June 29, 2012.

211. Charles Arthur, "Nokia's Handset Business Bought by Microsoft for Euro 5.44bn," *The Guardian,* September 3, 2013, available at http://www.theguardian.com/technology/2013/sep/03/nokia-handset-bought-microsoft (accessed February 24, 2014).

212. Paul Taylor and Richard Waters, "Google in $12.5bn Motorola Phone Deal," *Financial Times,* August 16, 2011; Richard Waters, "Search Group Puts Faith in Numbers," *Financial Times,* August 17, 2011; Miller and Gelles, "After Big Bet."

213. Google Inc., U.S. SEC Form 10-Q, June 30, 2011, 30, available at http://www.sec.gov/Archives/edgar/data/1288776/000119312511199078/d10q.htm (accessed January 10, 2014).

214. Microsoft Inc., SEC Form 10-K: 9, July 28, 2011, available at http://www.sec.gov/Archives/edgar/data/789019/000119312511200680/d10k.htm (accessed January 10, 2014).

215. Kendra Srivastava, "Samsung to Spend $9.3 Billion on R&D," *Mobiledia,* August 30, 2011.

216. Apple Inc., U.S. SEC Form 10-K, September 24, 2011, 7, available at http://www.sec.gov/Archives/edgar/data/320193/000119312511282113/d220209d10k.htm (accessed January 10, 2014)

217. Amazon spent several billion dollars during the most recent reporting interval on marketing, technology, and content costs—and expected these costs to increase. Amazon.com Inc., SEC 10-Q: 19–21, July 27, 2011, available at http://phx.corporate-ir.net/phoenix.zhtml?c=97664&p=irol-reportsother (accessed March 10, 2014).

218. Steve Lohr, "A Bull Market in Tech Patents," *New York Times,* August 17, 2011.

219. "Google and HP," The Lex Column, *Financial Times,* August 20–21, 2011.

220. Andreas Udo de Haes, "Samsung Seeks Ban of iPhone and iPad in The Netherlands," *ComputerWorld,* September 23, 2011, available at http://www.computerworld.com/s/article/9220230/Samsung_seeks_ban_of_iPhone_and_iPad_in_The_Netherlands (accessed January 10, 2014); Associated Press, "Samsung vs. Apple War Set to Explode," September 23, 2011, available at http://www.foxnews.com/scitech/2011/09/23/samsung-vs-apple-war-hits-high-gear (accessed January 10, 2014); Richard Waters, "Cases with High Risks for All Sides," *Financial Times,* June 15, 2012.

221. Tim Bradshaw, "Google and Samsung Tied Closer Together with Global Patent Deal," *Financial Times,* January 27, 2014.

222. Daniel Thomas, "Samsung Makes Break From Android Dependence," *Financial Times,* February 23, 2014, available at http://www.ft.com/intl/cms/s/0/4073d516-9c7a-11e3-9360-00144feab7de.html?siteedition=intl#axzz2uFRgzdem (accessed February 24, 2014).

223. Gustav Sandstrom, "Cellphone Vendors Face Price Pressure," *Wall Street Journal,* July 30, 2010.

224. Gustav Sandstrom, "Low-Cost Chinese Cellphones Power Handset-Shipment Surge," *Wall Street Journal,* November 11, 2010.

225. Richard Waters, "Android's Momentum Eats into Apples and BlackBerrys," *Financial Times,* August 15, 2013.

226. Mary Watkins, "Google's Android Dents Nokia Smartphone Dominance," *Financial Times*, Nov 11, 2010; Andrew Parker and Andrew Ward, "Downwardly Mobile," *Financial Times*, February 25, 2011; Chris Davies, "Nokia 1 Series Takes Web and Social Cheap for Next Billion," *Slashgear*, May 15, 2012, available at: http://www.slashgear.com/nokia-1-series-takes-web-and-social-cheap-for-next-billion-15228279 (accessed January 10, 2014).

227. "Tech, Tock, Tech, Tock," The Lex Column, *Financial Times*, June 5, 2012; Will Connors, "RIM Delays Phone, Shares Plunge 15%," *Wall Street Journal*, June 29, 2012; Richard Blackden, "Blackberry Job Cuts after $1bn Loss," *Financial Times*, September 21–22, 2013.

228. John Gapper, "Europe Holds a Losing Hand in the High-Stakes Mobile Game," *Financial Times*, September 5, 2013.

229. One market study found that these three companies, with Samsung claiming a commanding lead, accounted for roughly one out of three smartphones sold in China during the first quarter of 2012: 11.3 million of a total of 31.2 million. Paul Mozur, "China Vexes Smartphone Makers," *Wall Street Journal*, June 29, 2012.

230. "Smartphones," The Lex Column, *Financial Times*, January 8–9, 2011.

231. Tim Bradshaw and Sarah Mishkin, "China Joins Apple's Annual Ritual of the iPhone Launch," *Financial Times*, September 21–22, 2013; Tom Mitchell, Song Jung-a, and James Crabtree, "Apple Seeks Leap Forward in Biggest Market," *Financial Times*, September 12, 2013; Kathrin Hille, "Shake-out for China Mobile Makers," *Financial Times*, March 26, 2012; Kathrin Hille, "Smartphone Challenge from China," *Financial Times*, December 20, 2011; Paul Mozur, "China Vexes Smartphone Makers," *Wall Street Journal*, June 29, 2012; Kathrin Hille, "Lenovo in Talks as It Seeks Global Smartphone Expansion," *Financial Times*, June 5, 2013.

232. Robin Kwong, Chris Nuttall, and Paul Taylor, "Low-Tech Starts to Drive Growth in Smartphones," *Financial Times*, March 8, 2012; Mitchell, Song, and Crabtree, "Apple Seeks Leap Forward."

233. Associated Press, "Smart Phones Seen Tripling to 5.6 Billion by 2019," *USA Today*, November 11, 2013, available at http://www.usatoday.com/story/tech/2013/11/11/smartphones-forecast/3496169 (accessed January 10, 2014); Bradshaw and Mishkin, "Apple Seals China Mobile Deal."

234. Larry Copeland, "1 in 4 Surf Web While Behind Wheel," *USA Today*, November 12, 2013.

235. Tim Bradshaw, Sarah Mishkin, and Barney Jopson, "Amazon in Mobile Venture with HTC," *Financial Times*, October 16, 2013.

236. Jon Swartz, "Small Businesses Make Square Deals," *USA Today*, December 9, 2011.

237. Richard Waters, "Apple Set To Draw Battle Lines on Mobile Payments," *Financial Times*, January 30, 2014.

238. Martin Peers, "Phone Firms Make Mobile Payment Contact," *Wall Street Journal*, November 27–28, 2010; Tim Bradshaw and David Gelles, "Google Joins Payments Battle," *Financial Times*, February 17, 2011; Andrew Parker, "Groups Look at Apple and Google with Increasing Alarm," *Financial Times*, January 19, 2011.

239. Tom Standage, "Mobile Marvels," *The Economist*, a special report on telecoms in emerging markets, September 26, 2009; Parselelo Kantai, "Mobiles May Be Future of Banking," *Financial Times*, September 30, 2010; Suzanne Kapner, "Visa Steps Up Push into Mobile Banking," *Financial Times*, June 10, 2011. Late in 2013, Qatari telecoms group Ooredoo announced that it had more than one million mobile money customers in Qatar, Tunisia, and Indonesia. "Ooredoo Reaches 1m Mobile Money Customers," *TeleGeography*, CommsUpdate, November 6, 2013.

240. David Pogue, "No Cards, No Cash. Just a Phone," *New York Times*, September 22, 2011; Chris Nuttall, "Google Launches Wallet Service," *Financial Times*, September 20, 2011; "Google Wallet Opens for Business, Visa Gets On Board," *Los Angeles Times*, September 19, 2011, available at http://latimesblogs.latimes.com/technology/2011/09/google-wallet-opens-for-business-visa-gets-onboard.html (accessed January 10, 2014).

241. Lewis Dowling, "Telcos Can Use Prepaid Top-Ups to Break into M-Commerce—Study," *Total Telecom*, September 27, 2011, available at http://www.totaltele.com/view.aspx?ID=467935 (accessed January 10, 2014).

242. Maija Palmer, "Battle over Mobile Payments Intensifies," *Financial Times*, November 30, 2011, available at http://www.ft.com/intl/cms/s/2/cadb9bec-16cd-11e1-bc1d-00144feabdco.html#axzz1fELZDNb1 (accessed January 10, 2014).

243. Stephanie Clifford and Claire Cain Miller, "A Grip on Hand-Held Shopping," *New York Times*, April 16, 2011; Stephanie Clifford and Claire Cain Miller, "Tablet Apps with That Catalog Feel," *New York Times*, May 30, 2011.

244. Jonathan Birchall, "Shoppers Get a Taste of Geographic Marketing," *Financial Times*, October 15, 2010.

245. Christian Sandvig and Dan Schiller, "Is Google's Spy-Fi about Privacy, or Something More?" *Huffington Post*, November 18, 2010, available at http://www.huffingtonpost.com/christian-sandvig/is-googles-spyfi-about-pr_b_785015.html (accessed January 10, 2014). News that the Android operating system may be being used to collect data on mobile users' every keystroke broke eighteen months before the outcry over Edward Snowden's exposures of U.S. government electronic spying. See Katherine Rushton, "Software on Android Phones 'Tracking Every Keystroke'," *The Telegraph*, November 30, 2011, available at http://www.telegraph.co.uk/technology/mobile-phones/8927164/Software-on-Android-phones-tracking-every-key-stroke.html (accessed January 10, 2014).

246. Quentin Hardy, "Head to Head over Mobile Maps," *New York Times*, June 18, 2012.

247. Amir Efrati and Ben Vox Ruben, "Google Buys Startup Waze to Bolster Its Maps, Block Purchase by Rival," *Wall Street Journal*, June 12, 2013.

248. Matt Steinglass, "TomTom Repositions Itself with Apple Maps Tie-up," *Financial Times*, June 13, 2012.

249. Richard Maxwell and Toby Miller, *Greening the Media* (New York: Oxford University Press, 2012). For a shorter introduction see Richard Maxwell and Toby Miller, "The Environment and Global Media and Communications Policy," in *The Handbook of Global Media and Communication Policy*, ed. R. Mansell and M. Raboy, 467–85 (London: Blackwell, 2011).

250. Katrina Fenlon, "Corporate Mass Digitization and Cultural Heritage: From Public Relations to Content Accumulation," unpublished research paper, Graduate School of Library and Information Science, University of Illinois at Urbana-Champaign, January 2014; Dan Schiller and ShinJoung Yeo, "Powered by Google: Widening Access and Tightening Corporate Control" (New York: Leonardo Electronic Almanac, forthcoming).

251. Thomas O. Barnett, Covington and Burling LLP, Statement before Senate Judiciary Committee, Subcommittee on Antitrust, Competition Policy and Consumer Rights, Hearing on Competition in Online Markets/Internet Search Issues, September 21, 2011; April Dembosky and Richard Waters, "Desperately Seeking Data," *Financial Times*, January 19/20, 2013.

252. Matt Crain, "The Revolution Will Be Commercialized: Finance, Public Policy, and the Construction of Internet Advertising," PhD diss., University of Illinois, Urbana-Champaign, 2013.

253. Robert W. McChesney, *Digital Disconnect: How Capitalism Is Turning the Internet against Democracy* (New York: New Press, 2013).

254. Paul Taylor and Richard Waters, "Purchase Offers Platform for Consolidation of Hardware and Software Makers," *Financial Times*, August 17, 2011.

255. Jessica E. Vascellaro, "Apps Developers Who Are Too Young to Drive," *Wall Street Journal*, June 18, 2012; Richard Waters, "Android's Momentum Eats into Apples and Black-Berrys," *Financial Times*, August 15, 2013.

256. Andrew Edgecliffe-Johnson, "Premium Content to Drive Tablets' Popularity," *Financial Times*, January 8–9, 2011; David Gelles and Joseph Menn, "Publishers Anxious over Apple's Strategy," *Financial Times*, February 2, 2011; Thomas Catan and Nathan Koppel, "Regulators Eye Apple Anew," *Wall Street Journal*, February 18, 2011.

257. Nokia's market capitalization in June 2012 had dropped to less than 3 percent of its peak a decade earlier, when it had been the world's largest handset supplier. Daniel Thomas and Michael Stothard, "Nokia Plans Further 10,000 Job Cuts after Second Profit Warning," *Financial Times*, June 15, 2012.

258. Paul Taylor, "RIM Pays Price of Failing to Lure Customers from Apple and Google," *Financial Times*, September 16, 2011; Richard Waters, "Mobilising against Mobile," *Financial Times*, May 25, 2012; Nick Wingfield, "Microsoft Is Expected to Introduce a Tablet," *New York Times*, June 16, 2012; Richard Waters, "Surface Tensions," *Financial Times*, June 23–24, 2012.

259. Google, Inc., U.S. SEC 10-Q, June 30, 2013, 33.

260. Gustav Sandstrom, "Low-Cost Chinese Cellphones Power Handset-Shipment Surge," *Wall Street Journal*, November 11, 2010.

261. Andrew Parker, "Google's Android Overtakes Nokia in Smartphone Race," *Financial Times*, February 1, 2011; Hiroko Tabuchi, "Japan Phone Makers See Opportunity in Android," *New York Times*, March 1, 2011.

262. Song Jung-a and Joseph Menn, "Samsung Takes Top Slot in Phone Sales," *Financial Times*, October 29–30, 2011.

263. Ken Auletta, *Googled: The End of the World as We Know It* (New York: Penguin, 2009), 294.

264. Anna Eppley, "The Man behind Google's Rise," *Wall Street Journal*, August 1, 2011.

265. Jessica E. Vascellaro, "Developers to Apple: Promote Our Apps!" *Wall Street Journal*, June 13, 2012.

266. Tim Bradshaw and April Dembosky, "Apple keeps iPhone in the Upper Tier of the Market," *Financial Times*, September 11, 2013.

267. Tim Bradshaw, "Google Eats into Apple's app pile," *Financial Times*, December 18, 2013.

268. Richard Waters, "Google Races Higher in Patent League," *Financial Times*, January 13, 2014.

269. Christian Oliver, "S Korea to Develop Mobile Platform," *Financial Times*, August 25, 2011.

270. Financial Times Reporters, "Samsung Scrambles To Meet Chief's Reinvention Challenge," *Financial Times*, January 28, 2014.

271. Richard Waters, "Google Lifted on Android Optimism," *Financial Times*, January 31, 2014.

272. Jonathan Soble, "Sony to Challenge iPad with Tablet S," *Financial Times*, September 16, 2011, available at http://www.ft.com/intl/cms/s/2/4ad21130-e05c-11e0-ba12-00144feabdco.html#axzz1YAWept1W (accessed January 10, 2014).

273. Ben Worthen, Justin Scheck, and Gina Chon, "H-P Explores Quitting Computers as Profits Slide," *Wall Street Journal*, August 19, 2011; Joseph Menn, "HP Bosses Defend Strategy Shift after Shares Fall," *Financial Times*, August 22, 2011; Paul Taylor, "Lenovo to Throw Down iPad Gauntlet," *Financial Times*, August 22, 2011.

274. Peter Bright, "The End of an Era: Internet Explorer Drops below 50% of Web Usage," *Ars Technica*, November 2, 2011, available at http://arstechnica.com/microsoft/news/2011/11/the-end-of-an-era-internet-explorer-drops-below-50-percent-of-web-usage.ars (accessed January 10, 2014).

275. Richard Waters, "Android's Momentum Eats into Apples and BlackBerrys," *Financial Times*, August 15, 2013.

276. An early primer on cloud computing is David Mitchell Smith, Daryl C. Plummer, and David W. Cearley, "The What, Why, and When of Cloud Computing," Gartner Research ID Number G00168582, June 4, 2009. A benchmark treatment will be Vincent Mosco, *To the Cloud: Big Data in a Turbulent World* (Boulder, Colo.: Paradigm, 2014).

277. "The concept of renting computing power goes back decades, to the days when companies would share space on a single mainframe with big spinning tape drives. The technology industry has matured to the point where there is now an emerging mass market for this rental model." Brad Stone and Ashlee Vance, "Companies Slowly Join Cloud-Computing," *New York Times*, April 18, 2010, available at http://www.nytimes.com/2010/04/19/technology/19cloud.html?_r=0 (accessed January 10, 2014).

278. Richard Waters and Chris Nuttall, "Cloud Computing Benefits Apple's Rivals," *FT.com*, May 19, 2011.

279. Stone and Vance, "Companies Slowly Join Cloud-Computing." Less well-known but nevertheless important companies also operated in sections of this market. Equinix, for example, ran ninety-five data centers in thirty-seven countries. "Equinix Expands to South America with Brazil Data Centre Purchase," *TeleGeography*, CommsUpdate, February 23, 2011.

280. The *DataCenter Journal* accords continuing coverage. Retrieved at www.datacenter journal.com.

281. John Letzing, "Facebook Plants Roots in Central Oregon," *MarketWatch*, January 20, 2011. Retrieved at http://www.marketwatch.com/story/facebook-data-center-revitalizes-oregon-town-2011-01-20 (accessed January 10, 2014).

282. John Foley, "Signs Points to Amazon Data Center Expansion," *Information Week*, October 29, 2010, available at http://www.informationweek.com/services/hosted-applications/signs-point-to-amazon-data-center-expans/228000376 (accessed January 10, 2014).

283. Quentin Hardy, "IBM Has Big Plans for Investments in the Cloud," *New York Times*, January 20, 2014.

284. Richard Waters and Chris Nuttall, "Cloud Threatens to End PC's Reign," *Financial Times*, June 11–12, 2011.

285. Google Inc., U.S. SEC 10-Q, June 30, 2013, 33.

286. Miguel Helft, "Apple Unveils a 'Cloud' Storage Service for Music, Photos and Files," *New York Times*, June 7, 2011; Martin Peers, "Apple's Flashy Music Margins," *Wall Street Journal*, June 28, 2011.

287. Richard Waters, "Apple Races to Keep Users Firmly Wrapped in Its Cloud," *Financial Times*, June 9, 2011; Joseph Menn, "Apple's iPhone and iPad Apps Migrate to Mac," *Financial Times*, October 21, 2010; April Dembosky, "Facebook in Challenge to Apple with iPad App," *Financial Times*, October 11, 2011, available at http://www.ft.com/intl/cms/s/2/7b21838e-f38f-11e0-b98c-00144feab49a.html#axzz1aQjfNW3O (accessed January 10, 2014); Andrew Ross Sorkin, "Suggestions for an Apple Shopping List," *New York Times*, July 31, 2012.

288. Tim Bradshaw, "Apple Investors Digest Cash Return but Hunger for Hardware," *Financial Times*, April 25, 2013.

289. Matthew Garrahan, "A Cloud up in the Air," *Financial Times*, August 1, 2011.

Chapter 7. Services and Applications

1. Robert W. McChesney, *Digital Disconnect: How Capitalism Is Turning the Internet against Democracy* (New York: New Press, 2013); John Battelle, "The Internet Big Five by Product Strength," *battellemedia.com*, January 5, 2012.

2. Ben Bagdikian, *The Media Monopoly* (Boston: Beacon, 1983). Six additional editions followed.

3. Tim Bradshaw, "YouTube Reaches 1bn User Milestone," *Financial Times*, March 22, 2013; Matthew Garrahan and Andrew Edgecliffe-Johnson, "YouTube Nears Subscription Service for Its Specialist Channels," *Financial Times*, May 6, 2013.

4. Thomas O. Barnett, Covington & Burling LLP, "The Power of Google: Serving Consumers or Threatening Competition?" Statement before Senate Judiciary Committee, Subcommittee on Antitrust, Competition Policy and Consumer Rights, Hearing on Competition in Online Markets/Internet Search Issues, September 21, 2011, 5, available at http://www.gpo.gov/fdsys/pkg/CHRG-112shrg71471/html/CHRG-112shrg71471.htm (accessed January 10, 2014); Claire Cain Miller "As Web Search Goes Mobile, Apps Chip at Google's Lead," *New York Times*, April 4, 2013.

5. Roger Blitz, "TripAdvisor's Anger at Google Incursion," *Financial Times*, April 1, 2013.

6. Tim Bradshaw, "Android Hits 10bn to Narrow App Gap with Apple," *Financial Times*, December 7, 2011; Dennis K. Berman, "Tin Pan Valley: The Coming Shakeout for App Makers," *Wall Street Journal*, June 13, 2012. See also Chris Nuttall, "Apple and Microsoft Wrestle with App Issues," *Financial Times*, June 11, 2012; Shaun Nichols, "Apple: Wow, Thanks for the $10bn-a-year App Store," *The Register*, January 7, 2014, available at http://www.theregister.co.uk/2014/01/07/apple_app_store_10bn_2013 (accessed February 3, 2014).

7. Tim Bradshaw, "Apple Investors Digest Cash Return but Hunger for Hardware," *Financial Times*, April 25, 2013.

8. Jessica E. Vascellaro, "Developers to Apple: Promote Our Apps!" *Wall Street Journal*, June 13, 2012.

9. U.S. FCC 11 103, WT Docket No. 10–133, "Annual Report and Analysis of Competitive Market Conditions with Respect to Mobile Wireless, Including Commercial Mobile Services," Fifteenth Report, June 27, 2011, 21.

10. ITU, *Trends in Telecommunications Reform 2013*, 3.

11. "comScore Media Metrix Ranks Top 50 U.S. Web Properties for December 2011," *comScore.com*, January 23, 2012.

12. Jin Kim, "The Institutionalization of YouTube: From User-Generated Content to Professionally Generated Content," *Media, Culture and Society* 34, no. 1 (2012): 53–67.

13. Patrick Zelnik, "A Universal-EMI Merger Could Rescue the Music Business," *Financial Times*, July 17, 2012.

14. Erica Orden and Geoffrey A. Fowler, "Hollywood Loses SOPA Story," *Wall Street Journal*, January 19, 2012. In late 2013, a third attempt to pass such legislation took shape, this time by senators supportive of the NSA's mass surveillance programs. "Chair of Senate Intelligence Committee Says CISPA Sister Bill is in the Works," *RT*, September 25, 2013, available at http://rt.com/usa/feinstein-cispa-cyber-security-342 (accessed January 10, 2014).

15. Brooks Barnes, "Web Deals Cheer Hollywood, Despite Drop in Moviegoers," *New York Times*, February 24, 2012, available at http://www.nytimes.com/2012/02/25/business/media/web-deals-cheer-hollywood-despite-a-drop-in-moviegoers.html?google_editors_picks=true (accessed January 10, 2014).

16. Richard Waters, "Profits May Elude Mobile Challengers," *Financial Times*, May 30, 2012, available at http://www.ft.com/intl/cms/s/0/2f3b764e-aa75-11e1-9331-00144feabdc0.html#axzz1wOsWPq5T (accessed January 10, 2014).

17. Facebook, Inc., Form S-1 Registration Statement with the U.S. Securities and Exchange Commission, February 1, 2012.

18. Google, Inc. 2011 10-K Report to the SEC, 10.

19. Robert Budden and Robert Cookson, "Search for Fresh Revenue Stream: Google Looks to Beat Music Rivals," *Financial Times*, February 23–24, 2013.

20. Julie Bosman, "Penguin and Random House Merge, Saying Change Will Come Slowly," *New York Times*, July 1, 2013, available at http://www.nytimes.com/2013/07/02/business/media/merger-of-penguin-and-random-house-is-completed.html?emc=eta1 (accessed January 10, 2104).

21. Statement of Paul Misener, vice president for Global Public Policy, Amazon.com, Hearing before the Senate Committee on Homeland Security and Government Affairs, Subcommittee on Financial Management, Government Information, Federal Services, and International Security; and before the House Committee on Oversight and Government Reform, Subcommittee on Federal Workforce, Postal Service, and District of Columbia, June 23, 2010, 2, available at http://www.gpo.gov/fdsys/pkg/CHRG-111shrg58037/pdf/CHRG-111shrg58037.pdf (accessed January 10, 2014).

22. Claire Cain Miller, "E-Books Top Hardcovers at Amazon," *New York Times*, July 20, 2010; Colin Robinson, "The Trouble with Amazon," *The Nation*, August 2–9, 2010. The trend persisted, as Amazon divulged in 2011 that mystery author Michael Connelly was the seventh writer to sell more than one million Kindle books. Jeffrey A. Trachtenberg, " . . . As New One Is Opening," *Wall Street Journal*, July 20, 2011.

23. Kevin J. O'Brien, "European E-Book Sales Hampered by Tax Structure," *New York Times*, December 1, 2011. An account of this transition is John B. Thompson, *Merchants of Culture: The Publishing Business in the Twenty-First Century*, 2nd ed. (New York: Plume, 2012), 313–76. Thompson offers much lower sales figures, though these are for a selection of U.S.-only trade publishers.

24. Thompson, *Merchants of Culture*, 326.

25. Robert Darnton, *The Case for Books* (New York: Public Affairs, 2009); Ken Auletta, *Googled: The End of the World as We Know It* (New York: Penguin, 2009); Robert Darnton, "Google and the Future of Books," *New York Review of Books* 56, no. 2 (February 12, 2009); Hiroko Tabuchi, "To Win, Beat the Apps," *New York Times*, September 26, 2009.

26. Miguel Helft, "Federal Judge Rejects Google's Negotiated Deal to Digitize Books," *New York Times*, March 23, 2011. See Dan Schiller and ShinJoung Yeo, "Powered by Google: Widening Access and Tightening Corporate Control" (New York: Leonardo Electronic Almanac, forthcoming).

27. Mike Masnick, "Google Gets Total Victory over Authors Guild: Book Scanning Is Fair Use," *Techdirt*, November 14, 2013, available at http://www.techdirt.com/articles/20131114/09561525242/google-gets-total-victory-over-authors-guild-book-scanning-is-fair-use.shtml (accessed January 10, 2014); "Google Books Wins Case against Authors over Putting Books Online," *The Guardian*, November 14, 2013, available at http://www.theguardian.com/books/2013/nov/14/google-books-wins-case-authors-online (accessed January 10, 2014).

28. Thompson, *Merchants of Culture*, 337–39, 368–76.

29. David Streitfeld, "As Competition Wanes, Amazon Cuts Back Discounts," *New York Times*, July 5, 2013.

30. Julie Bosman "Struggling Borders to Meet with Publishers," *New York Times*, January 4, 2011.

31. Mike Spector, "Borders Forced to Close All Its Stores," *Wall Street Journal*, July 19, 2011.

32. Trachtenberg, " . . . As New One Is Opening."

33. Julie Bosman, "A Reading of Relief at Annual Book Show," *New York Times*, June 1, 2013.

34. Associated Press, "Barnes & Noble's Loss More than Doubles," *Wall Street Journal*, June 25, 2013.

35. Julie Bosman, "The Dog-Eared Paperback, Newly Endangered in an E-Book Age," *New York Times*, September 2, 2011.

36. Barney Jopson and Andrew Edgecliffe-Johnson, "Amazon Acquires 450 Children's Titles to Enhance Publishing Role," *Financial Times*, December 7, 2011.

37. Julie Bosman, "Publishers Make a Plan: A 'One Stop' Book Site," *New York Times*, May 7, 2011.

38. Jeffrey A. Trachtenberg, "E-Book Prices Prop Up Print Siblings," *Wall Street Journal*, September 12, 2011, available at at http://online.wsj.com/article/SB10001424053111904875404576532353109995700.html (accessed January 10, 2014).

39. Reuters, "EU Commission in E-Books Antitrust Probe of 5 Publishers, Apple," December 6, 2011, available at http://www.reuters.com/article/2011/12/06/eu-ebooks-idUSB5E7N100H20111206 (accessed January 10, 2014); Brian X. Chen and Julie Bosman, "Trial on E-Book Price-Fixing Puts Apple in the Spotlight," *New York Times*, June 3, 2013.

40. Julie Bosman, "Publishers Tell of Disputes with Apple on E-Book Prices," *New York Times*, June 6, 2013; Brian X. Chen and Julie Bosman, "Apple Loses Antitrust Case on E-Books," *New York Times*, July 11, 2013; David Streitfeld, "E-Book Ruling Gives Amazon an Advantage," July 11, 2013.

41. Thompson, *Merchants of Culture*, 368.

42. Charles C. Mann, "The Heavenly Jukebox," *Atlantic Monthly*, September 2000, 50, in Patrick Burkart and Tom McCourt, *Digital Music Wars: Ownership and Control of the Celestial Jukebox* (Lanham, Md.: Rowman and Littlefield, 2006).

43. Burkart and McCourt, *Digital Music Wars*.

44. Eduardo Porter, "The Perpetual War: Pirates and Creators," *New York Times*, February 5, 2010.

45. "The Web's New Walls," *The Economist*, September 4, 2010; Richard Waters, "Media Will Be Forced to Play by the Internet's Rules," *FT.com*, March 9, 2011.

46. David Gelles and Andrew Edgecliffe-Johnson, "Apple Demands 30% Slice of Subscriptions Sold via Apps," *Financial Times*, February 16, 2011.

47. Miguel Helft, "Apple Gives Publishers Sales Break," *New York Times*, June 10, 2011.

48. Matthew Garrahan, "GE Group Squares Up to Apple in iTunes Case," *Financial Times*, May 23, 2012, available at http://www.ft.com/intl/cms/s/0/5f34ca8c-a4ec-11e1-b421-00144feabdco.html#axzz1vmWCk89W (accessed January 10, 2014).

49. Ben Sisario, "Royalties from Digital Radio Start to Carry Some Weight," *New York Times*, June 18, 2012.

50. Ben Sisario, "A Stream of Music, Not Revenue," *New York Times*, December 13, 2013.

51. Ben Sisario, "Facebook to Offer Path to Media," *New York Times*, September 19, 2011. Also see April Dembosky, "Facebook Eyes Digital Stream of Revenue with Credits System," *Financial Times*, July 20, 2011.

52. Ben Sisario, "Music Service from Google Will Sell and Store Songs," *New York Times*, November 17, 2011.

53. Eduardo Porter, "The Perpetual War: Pirates and Creators," *New York Times*, February 5, 2012.

54. Chloe Albanesius, "Google to Demote Sites with 'High Number' of Copyright Complaints," *PC Magazine*, August 10, 2012; Robert Budden and Robert Cookson, "Search for Fresh Revenue Stream: Google Looks to Beat Music Rivals," *Financial Times*, February 23–24, 2013.

55. Janet Wasko, *Hollywood in the Information Age: Beyond the Silver Screen* (London: Polity, 1994); Toby Miller, Nitin Govil, John McMurria, Richard Maxwell, and Ting Wang, *Global Hollywood 2* (London: British Film Institute, 2005).

56. William Kunz, *Conglomerate Culture: Consolidation in the Motion Picture and Television Industries* (Lanham, Md.: Rowman and Littlefield, 2006).

57. Tim Arango and David Carr, "Netflix's Move onto the Web Stirs Rivalries," *New York Times*, November 25, 2010; Brian Stelter, "Netflix's Profit Rises amid a Rush to On-Demand," *New York Times*, April 26, 2011; Brian Stelter, "Netflix Partner Says Comcast 'Toll' Threatens Online Video Delivery," *New York Times*, Media Decoder, November 29, 2010; "Netflix to Stream Films and TV Abroad," *New York Times*, July 6, 2011; Amy Chozick, "Viacom Strikes an Extensive Deal with Amazon to Stream Children's Shows," *New York Times*, June 5, 2013; Agustino Fontevecchia, "Netflix Banks On 'House of Cards' and 'Orange Is the New Black' to Quadruple Its Profits," *Forbes*, October 21, 2013, available at http://www.forbes.com/sites/afontevecchia/2013/10/21/netflixs-awesome-shows-bring-in-more-subscribers-as-profits-quadruple-in-q3 (accessed January 10, 2014).

58. "Hulu Attracts Wide Range of Initial Bids," *Financial Times*, May 25–26, 2013.

59. Emily Steel, "Digital Drag Forecast on Media Growth," *Financial Times*, June 12, 2012.

60. Michael Cieply and Brooks Barnes, "The Incredible Shrinking Studio," *New York Times*, December 23, 2013.

61. Matt Richtel and Brian Stelter, "In the Living Room, Hooked on Pay TV," *New York Times*, August 23, 2010. For general background: Amanda D. Lotz, *The Television Will Be Revolutionized* (New York: New York University Press, 2007).

62. Matthew Garrahan, "Hulu to Put Original TV Shows on Web," *Financial Times*, May 22, 2012. For background: Kenneth Li and Andrew Edgecliffe-Johnson, "Hulu IPO Nears in Drive for Content," *Financial Times*, August 17, 2010; Jessca E. Vascellaro, "Disney's CEO Says Hulu Will Be Sold," *Wall Street Journal*, July 7, 2011; Jessica E. Vascellaro and Sam Schechner, "Hulu's Owners Weigh Cons of a Possible Sale of the Site," *Wall Street Journal*, June 27, 2011; Brian Stelter, "Hulu Owners Call Off Sale, Instead Pledging to Invest to Take on Rivals," *New York Times*, July 13, 2013.

63. Brooke Barnes, "Disney and YouTube Make a Video Deal," *New York Times*, November 8, 2011; Matthew Garrahan and Andrew Edgecliffe-Johnson, "YouTube Nears Subscription Service for Its Specialist Channels," *Financial Times*, May 6, 2013; Worth Paying For?" *The Economist*, May 11, 2013.

64. Emily Steel, "TV's Grip on Global Ad Spend Set to Slip," *Financial Times*, December 9, 2013.

65. Chris Nuttall, "TV Apps Tune Into Uniformity," *Financial Times*, September 4, 2011, available at http://www.ft.com/intl/cms/s/2/49627f14-d707-11e0-bc73-00144feabdc0.html #axzz1WvrPzPdx, accessed January 10, 2014).

66. "Intel and TV," The Lex Column, *Financial Times*, June 27, 2013. Whether this statistic applies to professionally produced TV programs or, in addition, to user-generated and amateur video, is not specified.

67. Brian Stelter, "Google Said to Weigh Supplying TV Channels," *New York Times*, July 17, 2013; U.S. Government Accountability Office, "Video Marketplace: Competition Is Evolving, and Government Reporting Should Be Reevaluated," GAO-13–576, June 2013, 6–7.

68. Amy Chozick, "Viacom Strikes an Extensive Deal with Amazon to Stream Children's Shows," *New York Times*, June 5, 2013.

69. Brian Stelter, "Comcast Hopes to Promote TV Shows in Twitter Deal," *New York Times*, October 9, 2013, available at http://www.nytimes.com/2013/10/10/business/media/through-twitter-partnership-comcast-hopes-to-encourage-tv-viewing.html?_r=0 (accessed January 10, 2014).

70. Michael Dinan, "Report: Global DVR Homes to Quadruple in Five Years," *TMCnet Cable Spotlight*, October 28, 2008, available at http://cable.tmcnet.com/topics/cable/articles/43825-report-global-dvr-homes-quadruple-five-years.htm (accessed January 10, 2014); Tom Morrod, "Cox and Cisco Launch First US Cable Multi-Room DVR," *IHS Screen Digest*, June 16, 2010, available at http://www.screendigest.com/news/cox-and-cisco-launch-us-cables-first-multi-room-dvr/view.html (accessed January 10, 2014).

71. Brian Stelter, "The TV-Internet Nuptials," *New York Times*, January 10, 2011; Claire Cain Miller and Brian Stelter, "Google TV Announces Its Programming Partners, but the Top Networks Are Absent," *New York Times*, October 4, 2010; Joseph Menn, "Apple Ups the Ante in Digital TV Battle," *Financial Times*, September 2, 2010.

72. Suzanne Vranica, "WPP Automated Ad Buys to Include Latin America," *Wall Street Journal*, June 10, 2013; Emily Steel, "Algorithms Threaten to End 'Mad Men' Era," *Financial Times*, May 14, 2013.

73. Andrew Edgecliffe-Johnson, "Nielsen Revamps Online Ad Ratings to Find Campaigns That Hit Home," *Financial Times*, August 8, 2011.

Chapter 8. The Sponsor System Resurgent

1. Stuart Elliott, "The Impulse to Buy Can Start Anywhere," *New York Times*, December 20, 2010; Andrew Edgecliffe-Johnson, "PwC Foresees Big Changes in Advertising Landscape," *Financial Times*, June 14, 2011.

2. Laurel Wentz and Bradley Johnson, "Top 100 Global Advertisers Heap Their Spending Abroad; Focused 62% of Budgets outside U.S. Last Year, with Much Going to China," *Advertising Age* 80, no. 40 (2009): 1.

3. Publicis, the third-largest advertising group, made twenty-five acquisitions during the eighteen months to July 2013. "Advertising," The Lex Column, *Financial Times*, July 19, 2013.

4. Laurie Burkitt, "In China, Women Begin Splurging," *Wall Street Journal*, June 13, 2011.

5. Kathrin Hille, "Big Companies Face Long Road to Recognition," *Financial Times*, May 19, 2011; Patti Waldmeir, "Chinese Wares Face Struggle for Acceptance," *Financial Times*, May 22, 2012.

6. Kathrin Hille, "Chinese Brands Star in Hollywood Movie," *Financial Times*, July 20, 2011.

7. Wentz and Johnson, "Top 100," 1.

8. Duncan Robinson, "Online Stores Think Local to Grow Global," *Financial Times*, January 25–26, 2014.

9. Tim Bradshaw, "European Ad Spend Off Target," *Financial Times*, June 19, 2012.

10. "Nigeria's Mad Men," *The Economist*, April 30, 2011.

11. Bradshaw, "European Ad."

12. Jonathan Barnard, ZenithOptimedia, in Bradshaw, "European Ad."

13. Robert Cookson, "Facebook Fights to Stay Down with the Kids," *Financial Times*, May 17, 2013.

14. "Twitter over $40," The Lex Column, *Financial Times*, November 10, 2013; also see David Carr, "Marrying Companies and Content," *New York Times*, November 11, 2013.

15. Hannah Kuchler and Emily Steel, "Online Advertisers 'Like' Facebook's Attention to Detail," *Financial Times*, January 31, 2014.

16. Andrew Edgecliffe-Johnson, "As the World Turns, Advertisers Tire of Soap Operas," *Financial Times*, April 21, 2011; Martin Peers, "Mixed Ad Message from Newspapers," *Wall Street Journal*, July 29, 2010.

17. Ben Fenton, "Broadcasters Face Bleak Picture of Advertising Cuts," *Financial Times*, May 10, 2011.

18. Emily Steel, "TV's Grip on Global Ad Spend Set to Slip," *Financial Times*, December 9, 2013.

19. Helga Tawil-Souri, "Arab Television in Academic Scholarship," *Sociology Compass* 2, no. 5 (2008): 1400–1415.

20. Emily Steel, "Super Bowl Advertising Goes into Overdrive," *Financial Times*, February 1–2, 2014.

21. Laura Houston Santhanam and Tom Rosenstiel, "Why US Newspapers Suffer More Than Others," Pew Research Center's Project for Excellence in Journalism: 2011 State of the News Media, available at http://stateofthemedia.org/2011/mobile-survey/international-newspaper-economics (accessed January 10, 2014).

22. Andrew Edgecliffe-Johnson, "Hispanic Dawn Breaks for US," *Financial Times*, October 21, 2010; Stuart Elliott and Tanzina Vega, "TV Steps Up Pitch to Hispanic Market," *New York Times*, May 18, 2011.

23. Bill Carter and Tanzina Vega, "In Shift, Ads Try to Entice Over-55 Set," *New York Times*, May 14, 2011. Robert Reich observed that the top 10 percent of households accounted for 40 percent of spending. Robert B. Reich, *After-Shock: The Next Economy and America's Future* (New York: Vintage, 2011), 36.

24. Tim Bradshaw, "WPP Lifts Forecasts as Ad Spending Rebounds," *Financial Times*, August 25, 2010; Tanzina Vega, "After Two Slow Years, an Industry Rebound Begins," *New York Times*, January 3, 2011; David Gelles, "Networks Vie for $18bn Ad Contracts," *Financial Times*, May 20, 2011.

25. "Ad Years and Good Years," The Lex Column, *Financial Times*, March 2, 2012.

26. Tim Bradshaw and Adam Jones, "WPP Shrugs Off Marketing 'Storm Clouds,'" *Financial Times*, August 25, 2011.

27. Suzanne Vranica, "WPP Automated Ad Buys to Include Latin America," *Wall Street Journal*, June 10, 2013.

28. Vincent Mosco, *Pushbutton Fantasies* (Norwood, N.J: Ablex, 1982); Kevin Robins and Frank Webster, "Cybernetic Capitalism" in *The Political Economy of Information*, ed. Vincent Mosco and Janet Wasko (Madison: University of Wisconsin Press, 1988), 44–75.

29. Suzanne Vranica, "The Case of the Invisible Web Ads," *Wall Street Journal*, June 12, 2013.

30. Ashlee, Vance, "Are Social Networks Gonna Blow?" *Bloomberg BusinessWeek*, April 18–24, 2011.

31. Facebook Inc., Form S-1 Registration Statement with the U.S. Securities and Exchange Commission, February 1, 2012, 4.

32. I draw on Van Couvering, who adapts to the internet not Wallerstein's commodity chain but Michael Porter's value, or supply, chain concept. Elizabeth Van Couvering, "The History of the Internet Search Engine," unpublished diss., University of London, 94; Elizabeth Van Couvering, "Navigational Media: The Political Economy of Online Traffic," in *The Political Economies of the Media*, by Dwayne Winseck and Dal Yong Jin (London: Bloomsbury, 2011), 183–200.

33. Oscar H. Gandy Jr., "The Political Economy of Personal Information," in *The Handbook of Political Economy of Communications*, ed. J. Wasko, G. Murdock, and H. Sousa (Chichester: Wiley-Blackwell, 2011), 436–57; Oscar H. Gandy Jr., *The Panoptic Sort: A Political Economy of Personal Information* (Boulder, Colo.: Westview, 1993).

34. Dan Schiller, *Digital Capitalism* (Cambridge, Mass.: MIT: 1999); Matthew Crain, "The Revolution Will Be Commercialized: Finance, Public Policy, and the Construction of Internet Advertising," PhD diss., University of Illinois, Urbana-Champaign, 2013.

35. Crain, "Revolution." Also see Joseph Turow, *The Daily You* (New Haven, Conn.: Yale University Press, 2011).

36. Jeff Chester, *Digital Destiny: New Media and the Future of Democracy* (New York: New Press, 2007), 127–58. Tim Bradshaw, "Facebook to Tap Into Mobile Ads," *Financial Times*, February 6, 2012; Lori Andrews, "Facebook Is Using You," *New York Times*, February 5, 2012; Turow, *Daily You*; Ted Striphas, *The Late Age of Print: Everyday Book Culture From Consumerism to Control* (New York: Columbia University Press, 2009), confirmed by Alexandra Alter, "Your E-Book Is Reading You," *Wall Street Journal*, June 29, 2012.

37. Adam Tanner, "The Web Cookie Is Dying. Here's The Creepier Technology That Comes Next," *Forbes*, June 17, 2013. Available at http://www.forbes.com/sites/adamtanner/2013/06/17/the-web-cookie-is-dying-heres-the-creepier-technology-that-comes-next (accessed January 10, 2014).

38. Julia Angwin, "Online Tracking Heats Up," *Wall Street Journal*, June 18, 2012.

39. Emily Steel, "Big Pop Seen for Online Ads," *Wall Street Journal*, June 8, 2011.

40. Miguel Helft and Tanzina Vega, "Retargeting Ads Follow Surfers to Other Sites," *New York Times*, August 29, 2010.

41. Turow, *Daily You*; McChesney, *Digital Disconnect: How Capitalism Is Turning the Internet against Democracy* (New York: New Press, 2013).

42. Van Couvering, "Navigational Media." ShinJoung Yeo, "Behind the Search Box: The Political Economy of the Global Search Engine Industry," draft PhD diss., University of Illinois at Urbana-Champaign, enriches our knowledge of search services in general and Google Search in particular.

43. Barnett, Statement before Senate Judiciary Committee, Subcommittee on Antitrust, Competition Policy and Consumer Rights, 4.

44. Siri, introduced in 2011, employed the voice of actor Susan Bennett to speak search results to 100 million people by 2013. Jessica Ravitz, "'I'm the Original Voice of Siri,'" *CNN*, October 4, 2013, available at http://www.cnn.com/2013/10/04/tech/mobile/bennett-siri-iphone-voice (accessed February 7, 2014).

45. Eric Schmidt, Executive Chairman, Google Inc., Testimony before the Senate Committee on the Judiciary, Subcommittee on Antitrust, Competition Policy, and Consumer Rights, September 21, 2011, 3–4, available at http://searchengineland.com/figz/wp-content/seloads/2011/09/Eric-Schmidt-Testimony.pdf (accessed January 10, 2014).

46. Dembosky and Richard Waters, "Desperately Seeking Data," *Financial Times*, January 19/20, 2013.

47. Barnett, Statement, 5.

48. Barnett, Statement, 10.

49. Emily Steel, "Marketers Wary of Branching Out on Twitter," *Financial Times*, October 8, 2013.

50. "Merger Set to Create a Marketing Leviathan," *Financial Times*, July 29, 2013; Andrew Edgecliffe-Johnson and Emily Steel, "Investors Cool over $35bn Publicis-Omnicom Tie-Up," *Financial Times*, July 30, 2013.

51. Ken Auletta, *Googled: The End of the World as We Know It* (New York: Penguin, 2009), 174.

52. Google Inc., "Google, Inc. Announces Third Quarter 2013 Results," *Google.com*, October 17, 2013.

53. Eric Schmidt, "MacTaggart Lecture, MediaGuardian Edinburgh International Television Festival, August 26, 2011, available at http://www.theguardian.com/media/interactive/2011/aug/26/eric-schmidt-mactaggart-lecture-full-text (accessed January 10, 2014).

54. Schmidt, "MacTaggart Lecture," 3.

55. Schmidt, "MacTaggart Lecture."

56. Andre Schiffrin, *Words and Money* (London: Verso, 2010), 74; James Kantor, "Facing Antitrust Fights at Home, Google Tries to Avoid One in Europe," *New York Times*, February 21, 2011.

57. Barnett, Statement, 10. Eric Schmidt, Google's board chairman and past CEO, conceded, "Search is subjective, and there's no 'correct' set of search results. Our scientific process is designed to provide the answers that consumers will find most useful." Schmidt, Testimony, 7. Another defender of Google suggested that "defining what factors may be considered in a 'neutral' search would be an impossible task." Susan A. Creighton, partner, Wilson Sonsini Goodrich and Rosati, P.C., Testimony before the U.S. Senate Committee on the Judiciary Subcommittee on Antitrust, Competition Policy and Consumer Rights, September 21, 2011, available at http://www.gpo.gov/fdsys/pkg/CHRG-112shrg71471/pdf/CHRG-112shrg71471.pdf (accessed January 10, 2014); See Richard Sennett, "Real Progressives Believe in Breaking Up Google," *Financial Times*, June 29, 2013.

58. Alex Barker, "EU Warns Google to Change or Face Fines," *Financial Times*, May 22, 2012.

59. Alex Barker and Richard Waters, "Google Deal Ends Antitrust Fight," *Financial Times*, February 6, 2014.

60. "Google Settlement Is Not the Last Word" (editorial), *Financial Times*, February 6, 2014.

61. Philip Delves Broughton, "Brave New Networked World," *Financial Times*, July 19, 2011.

62. Neal Mohan, in Emily Steel, "Google Wins Omnicom as Ally," *Wall Street Journal*, July 15, 2010.

63. Tim Bradshaw, "Omnicom in Deals to Target Online Ads," *Financial Times*, March 10, 2011.

64. Randall Stross, "YouTube Wants You to Sit and Stay Awhile," *New York Times*, May 28, 2010; Dan Schiller and Christian Sandvig, "Is YouTube the Successor to Television—or to *LIFE* Magazine?" *Huffington Post*, March 12, 2010, available at http://www.huffingtonpost.com/dan-schiller/is-youtube-the-successor_b_497198.html (accessed January 10, 2014).

65. Stuart Elliott, "Marketers Trade Tales about Getting to Know Facebook and Twitter," *New York Times*, October 15, 2010.

66. Richard Waters, "Ad Revenue Rise Overshadowed by Ballooning Costs at Google," *Financial Times*, April 15, 2011.

67. Claire Cain Miller, "Google to Sell Users' Endorsements," *New York Times*, October 11, 2013, available at http://www.nytimes.com/2013/10/12/technology/google-sets-plan-to-sell-users-endorsements.html?_r=0 (accessed January 10, 2014); Cecilia Kang, "Google to Put User Photos, Comments in Online Ads," *Washington Post*, October 11, 2013, available at http://articles.washingtonpost.com/2013-10-11/business/42926754_1_google-and-facebook-google-user-google-policy (accessed January 10, 2014).

68. Emily Steel, "AOL Aims for a Slice of TV Ad Pie," *Financial Times*, May 9, 2013.

69. Barney Jopson, "Amazon Set to Sell $800m of Ads as It Woos Business from Rivals," *Financial Times*, June 5, 2013.

70. Robert Cookson, "WPP and Twitter in Analytics Alliance," *Financial Times,* June 7, 2013.

71. Twitter Inc., Form S-1 Registration Statement, U.S. SEC, October 3, 2013.

72. Hannah Kuchler, Tim Bradshaw, and Emily Steel, "Twitter Looks to Mine User Data to Help Sell Advertising on Other Sites," *Financial Times,* October 15, 2013.

73. Vindu Goel, "Facebook Eases Privacy Rules for Teenagers," *New York Times,* October 17, 2013; Hannah Kuchler, Tim Bradshaw, and Emily Steel, "Facebook Admits That Teens Are Losing Interest," *Financial Times,* November 1, 2013.

74. Tim Bradshaw and Richard Waters, "Big Tech Forced to Answer the Phone," *Financial Times,* August 8, 2012.

75. Richard Waters, "Roaming for a Revenue Revolution," *Financial Times,* August 9, 2012.

76. Joe Nocera, "The Fall of the Wall?" *New York Times,* November 2, 2013.

77. Stuart Elliott, "Brought to You by Mountain Dew," *New York Times,* April 26. 2013; Stuart Elliott, "Content Marketing Beckons to an Executive From a Digital Agency," *New York Times,* May 24, 2013.

78. The Democratic Party platform for the 2012 election singled out "Internet freedom"— an issue considered in part III of this book. The Republican Party platform did mention the Fourth Amendment, but solely in terms of governmental trespasses against individuals.

79. *New York Times* Editorial Board, "States Take on Privacy," November 2, 2013, available at http://www.nytimes.com/2013/11/03/opinion/sunday/states-take-on-privacy.html?_r=0 (accessed January 10, 2014).

80. Lawrence E. Strickling, Assistant Secretary for Communications and Information, NTIA, Testimony before the Committee on Commerce, Science, and Transportation, U.S. Senate, March 16, 2011.

81. The location data transmitted by mobile devices and users' web-surfing histories as they moved from screen to screen became sites of intensive developmental efforts. Richard Waters, "Roaming for a Revenue Revolution," *Financial Times,* August 9, 2012; Emily Steel, "Web Groups Seek New Profiles as Cookie Crumbles," *Financial Times,* September 20, 2013.

82. Miguel Helft, "Phone Data Used to Fill Digital Map," *New York Times,* April 26, 2011.

83. Noam Cohen, "It's Tracking Your Every Move and You May Not Even Know," *New York Times,* March 26, 2011.

84. Joel Stein, "Data Mining: How Companies Now Know Everything about You," *Time,* March 10, 2011; Joseph Menn, "Virtually Insecure," *Financial Times,* July 29, 2010.

85. Richard Waters, "A Binary Goldmine," *Financial Times,* May 6, 2011.

86. Strickling, Testimony.

87. Tanzina Vega, "Web Code Offers New Ways to See What Users Do Online," *New York Times,* October 11, 2010; Steve Lohr, "New Ways to Exploit Raw Data May Bring Surge of Innovation, a Study Says," *New York Times,* May 13, 2011.

88. Strickling, Testimony, 3.

89. "Online Reputations in the Dirt," *The Economist,* April 30, 2011.

90. Richard Waters, "Grand Theft Data," *Financial Times*, April 30–May 1, 2011; Eric Dash, "Citi Data Theft Points Up a Nagging Problem," *New York Times*, June 10, 2011.

91. Hannah Kuchler, "Industries Hit by Leap in Hacking Attacks," *Financial Times*, January 14, 2014.

92. Maija Palmer, "TomTom Apologises to Customers after Selling Driving Data to Police," *Financial Times*, April 29, 2011.

93. Emily Steel and Geoffrey Fowler, "Facebook in Privacy Breach," *Wall Street Journal*, October 18, 2010; Miguel Helft and Jenna Wortham, "Facebook Bows to Pressure over Privacy," *New York Times*, May 27, 2010. For a similar exposure see Joseph Menn, "Virtually Insecure," *Financial Times*, July 29, 2010.

94. Claire Cain Miller, "Google Accused of 'Wiretapping' in Gmail Scans," *New York Times*, October 2, 2013.

95. Ashkan Soltani, Testimony before U.S. Senate, Committee on Commerce, Science, and Transportation, Hearing on the State of Online Consumer Privacy, March 16, 2011, 4, available at http://www.gpo.gov/fdsys/pkg/CHRG-112shrg73308/html/CHRG-112shrg73308.htm (accessed January 10, 2014).

96. Raymond Wacks, *Privacy: A Very Short Introduction* (Oxford: Oxford University Press, 2010), xi.

97. Erich Andersen, Deputy General Counsel, Microsoft Corporation, "The Need for a Comprehensive Approach to Protecting Consumer Privacy," Statement before the Committee on Commerce, Science, and Transportation, U.S. Senate, Hearing on the State of Online Consumer Privacy, March 16, 2011, 3, available at http://www.gpo.gov/fdsys/pkg/CHRG-112shrg73308/html/CHRG-112shrg73308.htm (accessed January 10, 2014).

98. Strickling, Testimony, 5, 6.

99. The White House, "We Can't Wait," February 23, 2012, available at at http://www.whitehouse.gov/the-press-office/2012/02/23/we-can-t-wait-obama-administration-unveils-blueprint-privacy-bill-rights (accessed January 10, 2014).

100. Department of Commerce, Internet Policy Task Force, Commercial Data Privacy and Innovation in the Internet Economy: A Dynamic Policy Framework December 16, 2010, iii, available at http://www.ntia.doc.gov/report/2010/commercial-data-privacy-and-innovation-internet-economy-dynamic-policy-framework (accessed January 10, 2014).

101. Federal Trade Commission, Preliminary Staff Report, "Protecting Consumer Privacy in an Era of Rapid Change: A Proposed Framework for Business and Policymakers," December 1, 2010, 3. Also, Edward Wyatt, "After Adding Online Privacy Protections, F.T.C. Chief Resigns," *New York Times*, February 1, 2013.

102. Andersen, Statement, 3.

103. Lawrence E. Strickling, Assistant Secretary of Commerce for Communications and Information, Keynote Remarks Before Global Internet Governance Academic Network, Washington, D.C., May 5, 2011, 1, available at http://news.dot-nxt.com.

104. Samuel D. Warren and Louis D. Brandeis, "The Right to Privacy," *Harvard Law Review* 4, no. 5 (December 15, 1890): 193.

105. Richard R. John, *Spreading The News: The Postal System from Franklin to Morse* (Cambridge: Harvard University Press, 1995); Colin Agur, "Negotiated Order: The Fourth Amendment, Telephone Surveillance, and Social Interactions, 1878–1968," *Information and Culture* 48, no. 4 (October–December 2013): 419–47.

106. Gandy, "Political Economy," 436–57; Oscar H. Gandy Jr., *The Panoptic Sort: A Political Economy of Personal Information* (Boulder, Colo.: Westview, 1993).

107. Kelly A. Gates, *Our Biometric Future: Facial Recognition Technology and the Culture of Surveillance* (New York: New York University Press, 2011); Mark Andrejevic, *Info-Glut: How Too Much Information Is Changing the Way We Think and Know* (New York: Routledge, 2013).

108. Gates, *Our Biometric Future*.

109. Andersen, Statement, 4.

110. John Montgomery, Chief Operating Officer, North America, GroupM Interaction, Testimony before the Senate Commerce, Science, and Transportation Committee, Hearing on "The State of Online Consumer Privacy," March 16, 2011, available at http://www.gpo.gov/fdsys/pkg/CHRG-112shrg73308/html/CHRG-112shrg73308.htm (accessed January 10, 2014).

111. In Edward Wyatt and Tanzina Vega, "F.T.C. Plan Backs Option to Limit Tracking Online," *New York Times*, December 2, 2010. To its credit, the FTC has continued to be a more vigilant regulator than other U.S. federal agencies. Edward Wyatt, "As Online Ads Look More Like News Articles, F.T.C. Warns against Deception," *New York Times*, December 5, 2013.

112. Kevin J. O'Brien, "Panel to Urge Europe to Bolster Data Rules," *New York Times*, May 16, 2011.

113. Wal-Mart to NTIA, Re: Commercial Data Privacy and Innovation in the Internet Economy: A Dynamic Policy Framework (Docket # 101214614–0615–1), January 27, 2011, 1 available at http://www.ntia.doc.gov/files/ntia/comments/101214614-0614-01/attachments/Walmart%20Comments.pdf (accessed January 10, 2014).

114. GE mentioned the Electronic Communications Privacy Act in this context. Nuala O'Connor Kelly, Chief Privacy Leader and Senior Counsel, Information Governance, General Electric, to NTIA, Internet Policy Task Force, Re: Commercial Data Privacy and Innovation in the Internet Economy: A Dynamic Policy Framework, RIN 0660-XA22, January 28, 2011, 1, 2, 3, 4, available at http://www.ntia.doc.gov/files/ntia/comments/101214614-0614-01/attachments/GE%20comment%20letter.pdf (accessed January 10, 2014).

115. Steven Manzo, Vice President, Government Affairs, Reed Elsevier Inc., to Secretary Gary Locke, NTIA, Comments on "Commercial Data Privacy and Innovation in the Internet Economy: A Dynamic Policy Framework," January 28, 2011, 1, 3, 8, available at http://www.ntia.doc.gov/files/ntia/comments/101214614-0614-01/attachments/Reed%20Elsevier%20Comments%20to%20Department%20of%20Commerce.pdf (accessed January 10, 2014).

116. Manzo, Comments, 9.

117. Strickling, Testimony, 6 (quotes).

118. This series in *The Guardian* may be consulted at http://www.theguardian.com/world/the-nsa-files.

119. Quoted in Julian Borger, "Brazilian President: US Surveillance 'A Breach of International Law,'" *The Guardian*, September 24, 2013, available at http://www.theguardian.com/world/2013/sep/24/brazil-president-un-speech-nsa-surveillance (accessed January 10, 2014).

120. Ben Scott recaps this tradition of socio-legal thought, and contributes to it, in his history of U.S. news workers during the 1930s. Dale Benjamin Scott, "Labor's New Deal for Journalism: The Newspaper Guild in the 1930s," PhD diss., University of Illinois at Urbana-Champaign, 2009.

121. Emily Steel, "Big Pop Seen for Online Ads," *Wall Street Journal*, June 8, 2011; "Q3 '11 Internet Advertising Revenues up 22% from Year Ago, Climb to Nearly $7.9 Billion, According to IAB and PwC," November 30, 2011, available at http://www.iab.net/about_the_iab/recent_press_releases/press_release_archive/press_release/pr-113011 (accessed January 10, 2014).

122. ZenithOptimedia, "ZenithOptimedia forecasts stable ad growth in 2013 will pave way for recovery in 2014 and 2015," September 30, 2013, available at http://www.zenithoptimedia.com/zenithoptimedia-forecasts-stable-ad-growth-in-2013-will-pave-way-for-recovery-in-2014-and-2015 (accessed January 10, 2014). ZenithOptimedia, "Global Adspend Set to Return to Pre-Financial Crisis Growth Rates," April 7, 2014, accessed at http://www.zenithoptimedia.com/global-adspend-set-to-return-to-pre-financial-crisis-growth-rates.

123. James Ball, "Angry Birds Firm Calls for Industry to Respond to NSA Spying Revelations," *The Guardian*, January 28, 2014, available at http://www.theguardian.com/world/2014/jan/28/angry-birds-rovio-respond-nsa-spying-revelations (accessed February 6, 2014).

124. Richard Waters, "Google Eyes Cookie Alternatives in Effort to Give Users Greater Control," *Financial Times*, September 19, 2013.

Chapter 9. Growth amid Depression?

1. U.S. Census, 2011 Information and Communications Technology Survey, table 2a "ICT Expenditures and Percent Change for Companies with Employees by Major Industry Sector: 2011 and 2010 Revised," available at http://www.census.gov/econ/ict/xls/2011/full_report.html (accessed January 10, 2014).

2. U.S. Census Bureau, Annual and Quarterly Services Report, January 29, 2013, table 1 "Estimated Revenue for Employer and Non-Employer Firms: 2007 through 2011," available at http://www.census.gov/services/index.html (accessed January 10, 2014).

3. The number of employees working in the sector concurrently declined, and annual payrolls remained nearly flat. U.S. Census Bureau, County Business Patterns, North American FactFinder, retrieved at http://www.census.gov/econ/cbp/index.html (accessed January 10, 2014).

4. Ethan Smith, "New Blow to Music as Concerts Fizzle," *Wall Street Journal*, December 30, 2010.

5. Matthew Garrahan and Andrew Edgecliffe-Johnson, "Digital Distribution Fails to Offset Fall in DVD Sales," *Financial Times*, January 7, 2011; "IFPI Publishes Digital Music Report 2013," February 26, 2013, available at www.ifpi.org/content/section_resources/dmr2013.html (accessed January 10, 2014).

6. Tim Bradshaw, "Party Is Over for Music Downloads," *Financial Times*, September 26, 2010; "IFPI Publishes Digital Music Report 2013," February 26, 2013 available at http://www.ft.com/cms/s/0/4b5a3c80-c998-11df-b3d6-00144feab49a.html#axzz2quInqFKk (accessed January 10, 2014).

7. Matthew Garrahan, "Fall of 20% in Sales of DVDs Poses Challenge for Hollywood," *Financial Times*, May 3, 2011.

8. Matthew Garrahan and Andrew Edgecliffe-Johnson, "Digital distribution fails to offset fall in DVD sales," *Financial Times*, January 7, 2011.

9. Matthew Garrahan, "Fall of 20% in Sales of DVDs Poses Challenge for Hollywood," *Financial Times*, May 3, 2011.

10. MPAA, Theatrical Market Statistics 2010, 3, 4; MPAA Theatrical Market Statistics 2011, 4; MPAA Theatrical Market Statistics 2012, 4. Available at http://www.mpaa.org (accessed January 10, 2014).

11. Jeffrey A. Trachtenberg, "New Economics Rewrite Book Business," *Wall Street Journal*, August 29, 2011, available at http://online.wsj.com/news/articles/SB10001424053111904875404576532351102200460 (accessed January 10, 2014).

12. David Gelles and Andrew Edgecliffe-Johnson, "Americans Ditch TV in Move to Save Money," *Financial Times*, May 4, 2011; Brian Stelter, "Ownership of TV Sets Falls in U.S.," *New York Times*, May 3, 2011. Credit-Suisse analysts speculated in September 2011 that one in five Americans could one day cancel cable or satellite subscriptions. See Andrew Edgecliffe-Johnson and David Gelles, "Uncertain Outlook Drags on Advertising," *Financial Times*, September 24–25, 2011.

13. Matthew Garrahan, "Viewers Pull Plug on Cable TV," *Financial Times*, November 18, 2010.

14. Brian Stelter, "Cable Is Holding Web TV at Bay, Earnings Show," *New York Times*, October 30, 2011; see also Matt Jarzemsky, "Pay-TV Subscriber Losses Felt at Cablevision, Dish," *Wall Street Journal*, August 10, 2011.

15. Emily Steel, "Comcast Bucks Video Loss Trend," *Financial Times*, January 29, 2014.

16. Stephen J. Blumberg and Julian V. Luke, "Wireless Substitution: Early Release of Estimates from the National Health Interview Survey, July–December 2012," Centers for Disease Control, available at http://www.cdc.gov/nchs/data/nhis/earlyrelease/wireless201306.pdf (accessed January 10, 2014).

17. Russell Adams, "Magazine Sales Fall as Celebrity Titles Fade," *Wall Street Journal*, August 10, 2011; Christine Haughney, "Magazine Sales Decline on Newsstands by 10%," *New York Times*, August 8, 2012; Emily Steel, "Magazine Sales Suffer Sharp Fall in US," *Financial Times*, August 8, 2012.

18. Miriam Gottfried, "Warren Buffett's Cut-Price Community Spirit for Newspapers," *Wall Street Journal*, June 23–24, 2012.

19. Pew Research Center, Project for Excellence in Journalism, "The State of the News Media 2013," available at http://stateofthemedia.org (accessed January 10, 2014).

20. U.S. Department of Commerce, Statistical Abstract of the United States, table 1102, "Media Usage and Consumer Spending 1996 to 2005," available at http://www.census.gov/prod/2003pubs/02statab/infocom.pdf, p. 698, (accessed January 10, 2014).

21. U.S. Department of Commerce, Statistical Abstract of the United States, table 1130, "Media Usage and Consumer Spending 2003 to 2009," available at http://www.census.gov/prod/2011pubs/11statab/infocomm.pdf, p. 711 (accessed January 10, 2014).

22. ShinJoung Yeo, "The Mirage of Silicon Valley: Laboring in the Age of the 'New' Economy," presentation, Union for Democratic Communication, San Francisco, November 1, 2013; ShinJoung Yeo, "Behind the Search Box: The Political Economy of the Global Search Engine Industry," draft PhD diss., University of Illinois at Urbana-Champaign, 2013.

23. Conor Dougherty, "Holding Off on a Haircut To to Buy a New Car," *Wall Street Journal*, 25 November 25, 2011. In 2008, total U.S. media spending had increased by 2.3 percent, to $882.6 billion. Stephanie Clifford, "A Look Ahead at the Money in the Communications Industry," *New York Times*, August 4, 2009.

24. Floyd Norris, "Technology Dividends Outpacing All Others," *New York Times*, January 12, 2013.

25. Organisation for Economic Cooperation and Development, "The Future of the Internet Economy: A Statistical Profile, June 2011 Update," 28.

26. World Information Technology and Services and Alliance (WITSA), "Digital Planet 2010: Executive Summary," October 2010, p. 15, fig. 5, available at http://www.witsa.org/v2/media_center/pdf/DP2010_ExecSumm_Final_LoRes.pdf (accessed January 10, 2014).

27. Bede McCarthy, "IT Spending Expected to Grow by 4% amid Uncertain Climate," *Financial Times*, January 4, 2013.

28. Don Clark, "'Internet of Things' in Reach," *Wall Street Journal*, January 6, 2014.

29. Bob Violino, "'Digital Industrial Economy' Combines Physical World and Virtual," *Information Management* 8 (October 2013); "New Devices Drive Global Information Technology Spending," *DenverPost.com*, October 8, 2013.

30. Organisation for Economic Co-operation and Development, "The Internet Economy on the Rise: Progress since the Seoul Declaration," OECD Publishing, 2013, available at http://www.keepeek.com/Digital-Asset-Management/oecd/science-and-technology/the-internet-economy-on-the-rise_9789264201545-en#page3 (accessed January 10, 2014).

31. Quentin Hardy, "Growth Returns to Tech, but Profits Will Not Be So Easy," *New York Times*, January 6, 2014.

32. Organization for Economic Cooperation and Development, "The Internet Economy on the Rise: Progress since the Seoul Declaration" (OECD, September 2013), available at http://www.oecd.org/sti/ieconomy/internet-economy-on-the-rise.htm (accessed February 8, 2014).

33. WITSA, Digital Planet 2010, 14, Figure 3.

34. WITSA, Digital Planet 2010, 14; Daniel Thomas, "Asian Groups Set the Pace in IT Investment," *Financial Times*, January 29, 2013; Andrew Edgecliffe-Johnson, "Brics Set to Eclipse Western Digital Appetite," *Financial Times*, June 5, 2013.

35. "Fibre in New Homes to Be Compulsory," *TeleGeography*, CommsUpdate, January 16, 2013.

36. "China Sets New Targets for Broadband," *TeleGeography*, CommsUpdate, August 19, 2013; "News Analysis: Broadband Blueprint to Facilitate China's Economic Restructuring," *Xinhuanet.com*, August 19, 2013, available at www.xinhuanet.com/english/indepth/2013-08/19/c_1326439 (accessed January 10, 2014).

37. Michael Cieply, "U.S. Box Office Heroes Proving Mortal in China," *New York Times*, April 22, 2013.

38. Benno Teschke, "The Fetish of Geopolitics," *New Left Review* 69 (May–June 2011): 90.

Chapter 10. A Struggle for Growth

1. "Cyberspace" encompasses a greater range of computer-enabled systems than those associated with the open internet, including those used in industrial control processes and private networks of different kinds. This is because, typically, industrial control systems are not in fact kept completely separate operationally from corporate information networks. I will use the two interchangeably throughout the discussion that follows. See Richard Waters, "Industrial Control Systems Offer Open Door to Cyber Attacks," *Financial Times*, July 27, 2012.

2. Steve Lohr, "I.B.M. Posts a Strong Quarter Despite Softness in Revenue," *New York Times*, July 19, 2012.

3. Total Telecom, "The Global 100," October 24, 2013, available at http://totaltele.com.

4. Catherine L. Mann with Jacob F. Kirkegaard, *Accelerating the Globalization of America: The Role for Information Technology* (Washington, D.C.: Institute for International Economics, June 2006), 1; James W. Cortada, *The Digital Hand*, 3 vols. (New York: Oxford University Press, 2004–2008); David Moschella, *Customer-Driven IT: How Users Are Shaping Technology Industry Growth* (Boston: Harvard Business School Press, 2003).

5. Laura DeNardis, *The Global War for Internet Governance* (New Haven, Conn.: Yale University Press, 2014).

6. Daniel Eran Dilger, "Apple Now Adding 500,000 iTunes Accounts Per Day," *Apple Insider*, June 13, 2013, available at http://appleinsider.com/articles/13/06/14/apple-now-adding-500000-new-itunes-accounts-per-day (accessed February 7, 2014).

7. David Gelles, "Skype Begins Move to List on Nasdaq," *Financial Times*, August 10, 2010; "Skype's Share of the Long-Distance Pie on the Increase," *TeleGeography*, Comms Update, March 24, 2009.

8. Richard Waters, "Facebook on Course to Reach 1bn Users," *Financial Times*, July 22, 2010.

9. Waters, "Facebook on Course."

10. Jessica F. Vascellaro, "Google Agonizes on Privacy as Ad World Vaults Ahead," *Wall Street Journal*, August 10, 2010.

11. Twitter, Inc., Form S-1 before the U.S. Securities and Exchange Commission, Registration Statement 3, October 2013, 1, 22.

12. John D. Negroponte, Samuel J. Palmisano, and Adam Segal, *Defending an Open, Global, Secure, and Resilient Internet* (New York: Council on Foreign Relations, June 2013), Independent Task Force Report no. 70, p.9.

13. The United Nations Commission on Trade and Development's (UNCTAD) annual World Investment Reports are the definitive data sources.

14. UNCTAD, *World Investment Report 2013* (New York and Geneva: United Nations, 2013), 2.

15. "The Global Internet is Decentralising," TeleGeography's Global Internet Geography, *TeleGeography*, September 14, 2011.

16. "Europe Emerges as Global Internet Hub," *TeleGeography*, CommsUpdate, September 18, 2013; "Middle East Operators Plot a New Path to Europe," *TeleGeography*, CommsUpdate, October 2, 2013; "Asia's Connectivity Patterns Shift as Carriers Become Less Dependent on US," *TeleGeography*, CommsUpdate, October 17, 2013.

17. Stan Beer, "Global Internet No Longer US Centric," *ITWire*, September 14, 2011, available at www.itwire.com/it-industry-news/market/49749-global-internet-no-longer-US-centric (accessed January 10, 2014).

18. Aaron Ricadela, "Amazon Looks to Widen Lead in Cloud Computing," *Bloomberg Business Week*, April 28, 2010, available at http://www.businessweek.com/technology/content/apr2010/tc20100428_085106.htm (accessed January 10, 2014).

19. Janet Abbate, *Inventing the Internet* (Cambridge, Mass.: MIT Press, 1999), 208.

20. Jack Goldsmith and Tim Wu, *Who Controls The Internet? Illusions of a Borderless World* (New York: Oxford University Press, 2006).

21. Ronald Deibert, John Palfrey, Rafal Rohozinski, Jonathan Zittrain, eds., *Access Controlled: The Shaping of Power, Rights, and Rule in Cyberspace* (Cambridge, Mass.: MIT Press, 2010).

22. "The Global War for Internet Governance: Dr. Laura DeNardis," June 13, 2013, available at http://www.youtube.com/watch?v=tpChBW-3yL0 (accessed January 10, 2014).

23. Ronda Hauben, "The Internet: On Its International Origins and Collaborative Vision (A Work in Progress)," *Amateur Computerist* 12, no. 2 (Spring 2004).

24. Daniel R. Headrick, *The Tentacles of Progress: Technology Transfer in the Age of Imperialism, 1850–1940* (New York: Oxford University Press, 1988), 97–144; Daniel R. Headrick, *The Invisible Weapon: Telecommunications and International Politics 1851–1945* (New York: Oxford University Press, 1991); Jill Hills, *The Struggle for Control of Global Communication: The Formative Century* (Urbana: University of Illinois Press, 2002); Jill Hills, *Telecommunications and Empire* (Urbana: University of Illinois Press, 2007); Dan Schiller, "Geopolitical-Economic Conflict and Network Infrastructures" *Chinese Journal of Communication* 4, no. 1 (2011): 90–107; Dwayne R. Winseck and Robert M. Pike, *Communication and Empire: Media, Markets, and Globalization, 1860–1930* (Durham, N.C.: Duke University Press, 2007).

25. Vijay Prashad, *The Poorer Nations: A Possible History of the Global South* (New York: Verso, 2012).

26. Useful texts are: William J. Drake, "WATTC-88: Restructuring the International Telecommunications Regulations," *Telecommunications Policy* 12, no. 3 (1988): 217–33; Peter Cowhey and Jonathan D. Aronson, "The ITU in Transition," *Telecommunication Policy* 15, no. 4 (1991): 298–310; Richard Hill, *The New International Telecommunication Regulations and the Internet: A Commentary and Legislative History* (Zurich: Schultess, 2013).

27. Dan Schiller, *Telematics and Government* (Norwood, N.J.: Ablex, 1982); Dan Schiller, *Digital Capitalism* (Cambridge, Mass.: MIT Press, 1999), 71–72.

28. Schiller, *Digital Capitalism*, 74–75.

29. The White House, "The Framework for Global Electronic Commerce," July 1, 1997, in Schiller, *Digital Capitalism*, 88.

30. Schiller, *Digital Capitalism*, 75.

31. Milton L. Mueller, *Networks and States: The Global Politics of Internet Governance* (Cambridge, Mass.: MIT Press, 2010), 77.

32. Mueller, *Networks and States*, 78.

33. See, for example, Joseph Mann, "US Unveils International Internet Strategy," *FT.com*, May 17, 2011; Helene Cooper, "U.S. Calls for Global Cybersecurity Strategy," *New York Times*, May 16, 2011, available at http://www.nytimes.com/2011/05/17/us/politics/17cyber.html?_r=0 (accessed January 10, 2014).

34. The White House "International Strategy for Cyberspace: Prosperity, Security, and Openness in a Networked World," May 2011, 23–24 (original emphasis), available at http://www.whitehouse.gov/sites/default/files/rss_viewer/international_strategy_for_cyberspace.pdf (accessed January 10, 2014).

35. White House, "International Strategy for Cyberspace," 24.

Chapter 11. "A New Foreign Policy Imperative"

1. In Cheryl Pellerin, "DOD Expands International Cyber Cooperation, Official Says," American Forces Press Service, April 10, 2012, available at http://www.defense.gov/News/NewsArticle.aspx?ID=67889 (accessed January 10, 2014).

2. Elizabeth Dickinson, "Internet Freedom," *Foreign Policy*, January 21, 2010, available at http://www.foreignpolicy.com/articles/2010/01/21/internet_freedom (accessed February 8, 2014).

3. Wang Jisi, "Understanding Strategic Distrust: The Chinese Side," in Kenneth Lieberthal and Wang Jisi, "Addressing U.S.-China Strategic Distrust," John L. Thornton China Center Monograph Series no. 4, March 2012 (Washington, D.C.: Brookings Institution, 2012), 12. Google, it is important to note, did not withdraw from markets other than search—such as markets for China-based advertising via its Ad Sense programs.

4. The next paragraphs draw on Dan Schiller and Christian Sandvig, "Google v. China: Principled, Brave, or Business as Usual?" *Huffington Post Tech*, April 5, 2010, available at http://

www.huffingtonpost.com/dan-schiller/google-v-china-principled_b_524727.html (accessed January 10, 2014).

5. Nicholas D. Kristof, "Google Takes a Stand," *New York Times*, January 14, 2010, available at http://www.nytimes.com/2010/01/14/opinion/14kristof.html?_r=0 (accessed January 10, 2014); "Google and China," editorial, *New York Times*, March 23, 2010, available at http://www.nytimes.com/2010/03/24/opinion/24wed2.html (accessed January 10, 2014).

6. A video of Secretary Clinton's speech is available at http://www.youtube.com/watch?v=DbwiXRmzKio (accessed February 8, 2014).

7. Rebecca MacKinnon, *Consent of the Networked: The Worldwide Struggle for Internet Freedom* (New York: Basic, 2012), 187–88.

8. George Athan Billias, *American Constitutionalism Heard Round the World, 1776–1989* (New York: New York University Press, 2009), 223.

9. Herbert I. Schiller, "Authentic National Development versus the Free Flow of Information," *Le Monde diplomatique*, December 1974.

10. David E. Sanger, *Confront and Conceal: Obama's Secret Wars and Surprising Use of American Power* (New York: Crown, 2012), 279–80.

11. Mary Beth Sheridan, "U.S. Warns against Blocking Social Media, Elevates Internet Freedom Policies," *Washington Post*, January 28, 2011, available at http://www.washingtonpost.com/wp-dyn/content/article/2011/01/28/AR2011012804554.html (accessed February 8, 2014); Vijay Prashad, *Arab Spring, Libyan Winter* (Oakland, Calif.: AK, 2012), 15, 22. Rebecca MacKinnon, to her credit, makes this point. MacKinnon, *Consent of the Networked*, 192.

12. Schiller, "Authentic National Development"; Herbert I. Schiller, *Communication and Cultural Domination* (White Plains, N.Y.: International Arts & Sciences, 1976).

13. Muhtar Kent, quoted in "Myanmar Is Next Real Thing for Coke," *Financial Times*, June 15, 2012.

14. "Myanmar Is Next Real Thing," 16

15. Joseph S. Nye Jr., *Soft Power: The Means to Success in World Politics* (New York: Public Affairs, 2005).

16. United Nations Centre on Transnational Corporations, "Transborder Data Flows: Access to the International On-line Data-base Market: A Technical Paper," ST/CTC/41 (New York: United Nations, 1983); Karl P. Sauvant, *International Transactions in Services: The Politics of Transborder Data Flows* (Boulder, Colo.: Westview, 1986); Herbert I. Schiller, *Who Knows: Information in the Age of the Fortune 500* (Norwood, N.J.: Ablex, 1981; Herbert I. Schiller, *Information and the Crisis Economy* (Norwood, N.J.: Ablex, 1984); Eileen Marie Mahoney, "Negotiating New Information Technology and National Development: The Role of the Intergovernmental Bureau for Informatics," PhD diss., Temple University, 1987.

17. Rob Kitchin and Martin Dodge, *Code/Space: Software and Everyday Life* (Cambridge, Mass.: MIT Press, 2011).

18. Kitchin and Dodge, *Code/Space*, 47.

19. FCC Chairman Julius Genachowski, "The Cloud: Unleashing Global Opportunities," Aspen IDEA Project, Brussels, Belgium, March 24, 2011, p. 2, available at http://www.fcc.gov/

document/chairman-calls-unleashing-global-opportunities-brussels-speech (accessed January 10, 2014).

20. John Letzing, "Facebook Plants Roots in Central Oregon," *MarketWatch,* January 20, 2011, 2, available at http://www.marketwatch.com/story/facebook-data-center-revitalizes -oregon-town-2011-01-20 (accessed January 10, 2014).

21. Genachowski, "The Cloud," 7.

22. Schiller, *Who Knows,* 79–97; Laura Stein, *Speech Rights in America: The First Amendment, Democracy, and the Media* (Urbana: University of Illinois Press, 2006).

23. *Citizens United v. Federal Election Commission,* 558 U.S. 310 (2010); for discussion of the issues in the context of elections see John Nichols and Robert W. McChesney, *Dollarocracy: How the Money and Media Election Complex Is Destroying America* (New York: Nation, 2013).

24. Adam Liptak, "Court Weighs Whether Corporations Have Personal Privacy Rights," *New York Times,* January 19, 2011, available at http://www.nytimes.com/2011/01/20/ us/20privacy.html (accessed January 10, 2014).

25. Yuezhi Zhao, *Communication in China* (Lanham, Md.: Rowman and Littlefield, 2008).

26. Hillary Rodham Clinton, "Remarks on Internet Freedom," The Newseum, Washington, D.C., U.S. Department of State, January 21, 2010, 2, available at http://www.foreign policy.com/articles/2010/01/21/internet_freedom (accessed January 10, 2014).

27. Clinton, "Internet Freedom," 5.

28. White House, "International Strategy for Cyberspace," 3. For another echo, see Genachowski, "The Cloud," 1.

29. Clinton, "Internet Freedom," 2. This theme was explicated in Evgeny Morozov, *The Net Delusion: The Dark Side of Internet Freedom* (New York: Public Affairs, 2011).

30. Clinton, "Internet Freedom," 3.

31. Clinton, "Internet Freedom," 4; Daniel Lerner, *The Passing of Traditional Society: Modernizing the Middle East* (New York: Macmillan, 1958).

32. Clinton, "Internet Freedom," 7.

33. Hillary Rodham Clinton, "Internet Rights and Wrongs: Choices and Challenges in a Networked World," George Washington University, February 15, 2011, 1, available at http:// blogs.state.gov/stories/2011/02/15/internet-rights-and-wrongs-choices-and-challenges -networked-world (accessed January 10, 2014).

34. Sanger, *Confront and Conceal,* 302–3, 314–15.

35. Clinton, "Internet Freedom," 4 (emphasis added).

36. MacKinnon, *Consent of the Networked,* 188.

37. Clinton, "Internet Rights and Wrongs," 6.

38. MacKinnon, *Consent of the Networked,* 189–91, reviews some of these.

39. Clinton, "Internet Rights and Wrongs," 6.

40. James Glanz and John Markoff, "U.S. Underwrites Internet Detour around Censors," *New York Times,* June 12, 2011.

41. Sanger, *Confront and Conceal,* 297.

42. Scott Shane, "Groups to Help Online Activists in Authoritarian Countries," *New York Times,* June 12, 2012.

43. Condoleezza Rice, *No Higher Honor: A Memoir of My Years in Washington* (New York: Crown, 2011), 305.

44. Eric Schmidt and Jared Cohen, *The New Digital Age: Reshaping the Future of People, Nations and Businesses* (New York: Knopf, 2013), 28.

45. Gerry Shih, "Google Unveils Services Promoting Free Expression," *Reuters,* October 22, 2013, available at http://uk.reuters.com/article/2013/10/22/google-tools-idUKL1 NoIB25B20131022 (accessed January 10, 2014).

Chapter 12. Taking Care of Business

1. Dan Schiller, *Telematics and Government* (Norwood, N.J.: Ablex, 1982).

2. Susan Crawford, *Captive Audience* (New Haven, Conn.: Yale University Press, 2013), 51–62, reviews more recent episodes in this history.

3. U.S. Commerce Department, "Commerce Secretary Locke Announces Public Review of Privacy Policy and Innovation in the Internet Economy, Launches Internet Policy Task Force," press release, April 21, 2010, available at http://www.ntia.doc.gov/press-release/2010/ commerce-secretary-locke-announces-public-review-privacy-policy-and-innovation-in (accessed January 10, 2014).

4. U.S. Department of Commerce, Docket No. 100921457–0457–01, "Global Free Flow of Information on the Internet," *Federal Register* 75, no. 188 (September 29, 2010), 60068.

5. Department of Commerce, "Global Free Flow," 60069. The Seoul Declaration was notably not signed by the Peoples Republic of China.

6. Department of Commerce, "Global Free Flow," 60069.

7. Department of Commerce, "Global Free Flow," 60069.

8. Department of Commerce, "Global Free Flow," 60068.

9. Department of Commerce, "Global Free Flow," 60071.

10. Patrick McGeehan, "White Pages May Go Way of Rotary-Dialed Phone," *New York Times,* May 7, 2010, available at http://www.nytimes.com/2010/05/08/ nyregion/08verizon.html (accessed January 10, 2014); Michael Palm, "Phoning It In: Self-Service, Telecommunications, and New Consumer Labor," PhD diss., New York University, 2010.

11. Richard Waters, "Cloud Control," *Financial Times,* March 26, 2009; Richard Waters, "Tech Rivals in Cloud Computing Clash," *Financial Times,* March 28–29, 2009.

12. If the internet were a country, in one account, "it would be the planet's fifth-biggest consumer of power, ahead of India and Germany." Alex Roslin, "Dirty Data: The Internet's Giant Carbon Footprint," *Montreal Gazette,* June 4, 2011, available at http://albloggedup .blogspot.com/2012/06/dirty-data-internets-giant-carbon.html (accessed January 10, 2014).

13. Richard Waters and Chris Nuttall, "Apple's Rivals Benefit from the New Style of Computing," *Financial Times,* May 19, 2011.

14. Anton Troianovski, "Storage Wars: Web Growth Sparks Data-Center Boom," *Wall Street Journal,* July 7, 2011.

15. Nick Bilton, "Thailand Floods Affect Cloud Computing," *New York Times*, November 4, 2011, available at http://bits.blogs.nytimes.com/2011/11/04/thailand-floods-will-affect-computer-makers-and-web-sites (accessed January 10, 2014).

16. Dave Winer, "US Govt a Big User of Amazon Web Services," December 28, 2010, available at http://scripting.com/stories/2010/12/28/usGovtABigUserOfAmazonWebS.html (accessed January 10, 2014).

17. Via this new privatization drive it hoped to close eight hundred of its existing two thousand data centers (up dramatically from 1998, when it ran a mere 432 of them). Steve Lohr, "U.S. to Close 800 Computer Data Centers," *New York Times*, July 20, 2011.

18. Aaron Ricadela, "Amazon Looks to Widen Lead in Cloud Computing," *Bloomberg Business Week*, April 28, 2010, available at http://www.businessweek.com/technology/content/apr2010/tc20100428_085106.htm (accessed January 10, 2014).

19. Ricadela, "Amazon."

20. ShinJoung Yeo, "From Paper Mill to Google Data Center: The Role of Network Infrastructure and Digital Capitalism," paper presented at the Annual Meeting of the International Association for Media and Communication Research Istanbul, Turkey, July 13–17, 2011, 5.

21. Barney Jopson, "Nasa and Netflix among Users as Expansion Continues at Amazon Cloud Business," *Financial Times*, March 24–25, 2012.

22. Tim Bradshaw, "Apple Investors Digest Cash Return but Hunger for Hardware," *Financial Times*, April 25, 2013.

23. TV programs were an important part of this intended mix, and a coalition of television networks quickly formed to participate in cloud services. David Gelles, "Online Storage Seen as Curbing Piracy," *Financial Times*, June 9, 2011.

24. "Gartner Says Worldwide Cloud Services Revenue Will Grow 21.3 Percent in 2009," March 26, 2009, available at http://www.gartner.com/newsroom/id/920712 (accessed January 10, 2014).

25. Information Technology and Innovation Foundation, "How Much Will PRISM Cost U.S. Cloud Computing Providers?" August 5, 2013, available at http://mpictcenter.blogspot.com/2013/08/itif-how-much-will-prism-cost-us-cloud.html (accessed January 10, 2014).

26. Schiller, *Telematics and Government.*

27. Comments of the Copyright Alliance before the U.S. Department of Commerce, "In the Matter of Global Free Flow of Information on the Internet," Docket No. 100921457–0457–01, November 15, 2010, 7, 4; available at http://www.ntia.doc.gov/files/ntia/comments/100921457-0457-01/attachments/Copyright%20Alliance%20filing%20in%20Commerce%20NoI%20on%20free%20flow%20of%20information%202011%2015%2010.pdf (accessed January 10, 2014).

28. Copyright Alliance, "Global Free Flow," 11–12.

29. David T. Hirschmann, Global Intellectual Property Center, to The Honorable Gary Locke, Secretary of Commerce, Re: Global Free Flow of Information on the Internet, November 15, 2010, 3, available at http://www.ntia.doc.gov/files/ntia/comments/100921457-0457-01/attachments/GIPC%20Comments%20-%20Free%20Flow%20of%20Information%20FRN.pdf (accessed January 10, 2014).

30. A. Robert Pisano, President, Motion Picture Association of America, to Office of the Secretary, U.S. Department of Commerce, Re: Global Free Flow of Information on the Internet, December 6, 2010: 2 (quote), 12, available at http://www.ntia.doc.gov/files/ntia/comments/100921457-0457-01/attachments/international%20filingMPAA.pdf (accessed January 10, 2014).

31. United States Council for International Business, Response to Notice of Inquiry on Global Free Flow of Information on the Internet, December 6, 2010, available at http://www.ntia.doc.gov/files/ntia/comments/100921457-0457-01/attachments/final%20draft%20USCIB%20FREE%20FLOW%20OF%20INFO%20NOI.pdf (accessed January 10, 2014).

32. TechAmerica Submission, Notice of Inquiry on Global Free Flow of Information on the Internet, December 6, 2010: 1–2.

33. TechAmerica Submission, Notice of Inquiry on Global Free Flow of Information on the Internet, December 6, 2010: 2 (root), 3–4 (law enforcement).

34. Useful documentation and commentary are provided in David Moon, Patrick Ruffini, and David Segal, eds., *Hacking Politics: How Geeks, Progressives, the Tea Party, Gamers, Anarchists and Suits Teamed Up to Defeat SOPA and Save the Internet* (New York: OR, 2013).

35. Dan Schiller, "Whose Internet?" *Le Monde diplomatique*, October 2013, available at http://mondediplo.com/2013/10/09surveillance (accessed January 10, 2014).

36. TechAmerica Submission, Notice of Inquiry on Global Free Flow of Information on the Internet, December 6, 2010, 7, available at http://www.ntia.doc.gov/files/ntia/comments/100921457-0457-01/attachments/TechAmericaResponse_DOCNOI_Global FreeFlowInformation_6Dec2010. FINALpdf.pdf (accessed January 10, 2014).

37. TechAmerica Submission, Global Free Flow, 2.

38. Robert W. Holleyman, II, President and CEO, Business Software Alliance, to The Honorable Gary Locke, Secretary of Commerce, Re: Inquiry on the Global Free Flow of Information on the Internet, December 6, 2010, p. 1, 2, available at http://www.ntia.doc.gov/files/ntia/comments/100921457-0457-01/attachments/BSA%20NOI%20Submission%20-%20Commerce%20Global%20Free%20Flow%20of%20Information%20FINAL%20%283%29.pdf (accessed January 10, 2014).

39. *Harper & Row Publishers Inc. v. Nation Enters*, 471 U.S. 539 (1985), in Holleyman, "Re: Inquiry," 3.

40. Holleyman, "Re: Inquiry," 6–7.

41. Comments of Microsoft Corporation, before the United States Department of Commerce, Global Free Flow of Information on the Internet Notice of Inquiry, December 6, 2010: 1, available at http://www.ntia.doc.gov/files/ntia/comments/100921457-0457-01/attachments/Microsoft%20-%20Comments%20on%20the%20Free%20Flow%20of%20Information%20on%20the%20Internet%20-%20Dec%206%202010.pdf (accessed January 10, 2014).

42. Microsoft, "Global Free Flow," 2.

43. Microsoft, "Global Free Flow," 3–4.

44. Microsoft, "Global Free Flow," 4.

45. Microsoft, "Global Free Flow," 5–6.

46. ShinJoung Yeo, "Behind the Search Box: The Political Economy of the Global Search Engine Industry," PhD diss. draft, University of Illinois at Urbana-Champaign, 2014.

47. Google, Comments to the Department of Commerce, Notice of Inquiry on the Global Free Flow of Information on the Internet, 1, available at http://www.ntia.doc.gov/files/ntia/comments/100921457-0457-01/attachments/CommerceFreeExpressionNOI.pdf (accessed January 10, 2014).

48. Google, "Comments," 2.

49. Google, "Comments," 3.

50. Google, "Comments," 3–4.

51. Google, "Comments," 8. The article was "Beijing's Foreign Internet Purge," *Foreign Policy*, January 15, 2010, available at http://www.foreignpolicy.com/articles/2010/01/14/chinas_foreign-internet_purge.

52. Google, "Comments," 5.

53. Google, "Comments," 5–6.

54. Google Inc., Form 10-Q, U.S. Securities and Exchange Commission, for the Quarterly Period Ended June 30, 2013, 36.

55. Google, "Comments," 7.

56. Google, "Comments," 13–14. On this free trade agreement, see Martin Hart-Landsberg, *Capitalist Globalization: Consequences, Resistance, and Alternatives* (New York: Monthly Review, 2013), pp. 90–130.

57. Google, "Comments," 15.

58. Comments of the Entertainment Software Association before the U.S. Department of Commerce, in the Matter of the Notice of Inquiry on 'Global Free Flow of Information on the Internet,' December 6, 2010, 3, 7, available at http://www.ntia.doc.gov/files/ntia/comments/100921457-0457-01/attachments/Global%20Flow%20NOI%20-%20ESA%20comments%2012-6-10%20%28FINAL%29.pdf (accessed January 10, 2014).

59. Heidi Salow and Kate Lucente, Internet Commerce Coalition, to U.S. Department of Commerce, Re: Global Free Flow of Information on the Internet, December 6, 2010, 1, available at http://www.ntia.doc.gov/files/ntia/comments/100921457-0457-01/attachments/ICC%20Letter%20to%20DOC%20re_%20Free%20Flow%20of%20Information%20on%20the%20Global%20Internet.pdf (accessed January 10, 2014).

60. Comments of Computer & Communications Industry Association [CCIA] before the Department of Commerce, In Re: Global Free Flow of Information on the Internet, December 6, 2010, 2, 22–3, available at http://www.ccianet.org/wp-content/uploads/library/NTIA%20Global%20Free%20Flow%20of%20Information%20Comments.pdf (accessed January 10, 2014).

61. Comments of CCIA, 10.

62. Comments of CCIA, 21.

63. Comments of CCIA, 21.

64. Comments of CCIA, 23.

65. For an overview, Glenn Greenwald, "As Europe Erupts over U.S. Spying, NSA Chief Says Government Must Stop Media," *The Guardian*, October 25, 2013, available at

http://www.theguardian.com/commentisfree/2013/oct/25/europe-erupts-nsa-spying
-chief-government (accessed January 10, 2014).

66. Comments of Verizon and Verizon Wireless, before the Department of Commerce, Global Free Flow of Information on the Internet, December 6, 2010, 1, 2, available at http://www.ntia.doc.gov/files/ntia/comments/100921457-0457-01/attachments/12%2006%2010%20VZ,%20VZW%20comments_Global%20Internet.pdf (accessed January 10, 2014).

67. Verizon, "Comments," 2, 4.

68. Verizon, "Comments," 19–20.

69. Verizon, "Comments," 5.

70. Verizon, "Comments," 10.

71. Comments of eBay Inc., before the Department of Commerce Internet Policy Task Force, in the Matter of Global Free Flow of Information on the Internet, December 6, 2010, no pagination, available at http://www.ntia.doc.gov/files/ntia/comments/100921457-0457-01/attachments/eBay%20submission%20to%20DOC%20Free%20Flow%20NOI.pdf (accessed January 10, 2014).

72. For another example, Open Internet Advisory Committee, U.S. Federal Communications Commission, 2013 Annual Report, available at http://www.fcc.gov/encyclopedia/open-internet-advisory-committee (accessed January 10, 2014).

73. Brian Kahin, "Patently Geopolitical: The New Frontier of Government and Market Interaction," Intellectual Property Watch, August 26, 2013, available at http://www.ip-watch.org/2013/08/26/patently-geopolitical-the-new-frontier-of-government-and-market-interaction-2 (accessed January 10, 2014).

Chapter 13. Beyond a U.S.-centric Internet?

1. A history of the DNS is provided in Milton L. Mueller, *Ruling the Root* (Cambridge, Mass.: MIT Press, 2002).

2. U.S. Department of Commerce, "Request for Comments on the Internet Assigned Numbers Authority (IANA) Functions," Docket No. 110207099–1099–01, *Federal Register* 76, no. 38, February 25, 2011, 10569, available at http://www.ntia.doc.gov/files/ntia/publications/fr_ianafunctionsnoi_02252011.pdf (accessed January 10, 2014).

3. Harold Kwalwasser, "Internet Governance," in *Cyberpower and National Security*, ed. Franklin D. Kramer, Stuart H. Starr, and Larry K. Wentz (Washington, D.C.: National Defense University Press and Potomac Press, 2009), 506, 613n55, 508 (quote).

4. Kwalwasser, "Internet Governance," 508.

5. Kwalwasser, "Internet Governance," 501.

6. J. Mathiason, *Internet Governance: The New Frontier of Global Institutions* (New York: Routledge, 2008), 36.

7. Kwalwasser, "Internet Governance," 493–509; the relations between these three organizations are briefly sketched in Department of Commerce, "IANA Functions," 10570; Milton L. Mueller, *Networks and States: The Global Politics of Internet Governance* (Cambridge, Mass.: MIT Press, 2010), 62–63; Laura DeNardis, *The Global War for Internet Governance* (New Haven, Conn.: Yale University Press, 2014), 47–55.

8. Kwalwasser, "Internet Governance," 497; DeNardis, *Global War*, 49–51.

9. Department of Commerce, "IANA Functions," 10569.

10. Hans Klein, "Private Governance for Global Communications: Technology, Contracts, and the Internet," in *The Emergent Global Information Policy Regime*, ed. Sandra Braman (New York: Palgrave Macmillan, 2004), 179–202.

11. Mueller, *Networks and States*, 60–61.

12. Mueller, *Networks and States*, 61.

13. Klein, "Private Governance for Global Communications."

14. R. Austein and B. Wijnen, "Structure of the IETF Administrative Support Activity," RFC 4071, Network Working Group, The Internet Society, April 2005, available at http://www.ietf.org/rfc/rfc4071.txt (accessed January 10, 2014).

15. Mueller, *Networks and States*, 10, 61.

16. Dan Schiller, *How to Think about Information* (Urbana: University of Illinois Press, 2007), 56, 137–39.

17. Mueller, *Networks and States*, 62.

18. Dan Schiller, "Geopolitical-Economic Conflict and Network Infrastructures," *Chinese Journal of Communication* 4, no. 1 (2011): 90–107.

19. Mueller, *Networks and States*, 55–125, quote at 64; Abu Jafar Md. Shafiul Alam Bhuiyan, "Postcolonial States and Internet Governance: Possibilities of a Counter-Hegemonic Bloc?" PhD diss., Simon Fraser University, 2010; Cees J. Hamelink, "Did WSIS Achieve Anything at All?" *Gazette: The International Journal for Communication Study* 66, no. 3–4 (2004): 281–90; Victor Pickard, "Neoliberal Visions and Revisions in Global Communications Policy from NWICO to WSIS," *Journal of Communication Inquiry* 31, no. 2 (2007), 118–39.

20. p. 56.

21. Bobbie Johnson, "US Relinquishes Control of the Internet," *The Guardian*, October 1, 2009 at *guardian.co.uk*. See the official document at http://www.icann.org/en/announcements/announcement-30sep09-en.htm#affirmation (accessed January 10, 2014).

22. Rebecca MacKinnon, *Consent of the Networked: The Worldwide Struggle for Internet Freedom* (New York: Basic, 2012), 204, 210.

23. Marina Ottaway, "Corporatism Goes Global: International Organizations, Nongovernmental Organization Networks, and Transnational Business," *Global Governance* 7, no. 3 (July–September 2001): 15 (original emphasis). Mueller suggests that ICANN's multi-stakeholderism may attest a loose form of corporatism.

24. Ottaway, "Corporatism Goes Global," 16.

25. Mueller, *Networks and States*, 8.

26. I borrow from Mueller, *Networks and States*, 264.

27. The White House, "International Strategy for Cyberspace: Prosperity, Security, and Openness in a Networked World," 10, 12.

28. U.S. Department of Commerce, National Telecommunications and Information Administration, "NTIA Announces Intent to Transition Key Internet Domain Name Functions," March 14, 2014, accessed at http://www.ntia.doc.gov/press-release/2014/ntia-announces-intent-to-transition-key-internet-domain-name-functions.

29. Scott Shane, "Groups to Help Online Activists in Authoritarian Countries," *New York Times*, June 12, 2012.

30. Eric Schmidt and Jared Cohen, "The Digital Disruption," *Foreign Affairs* 89, no. 6 (November–December 2010): 80.

31. Schmidt and Cohen, "Digital Disruption," 75.

32. John D. Negroponte, Samuel J. Palmisano, and Adam Segal, *Defending an Open, Global, Secure, and Resilient Internet* (New York: Council on Foreign Relations, June 2013), Independent Task Force Report no. 70, 66.

33. Big corporations also gained formal status within multilateral organizations such as the UNESCO and the ITU. Viva Leye, "UNESCO, ICT Corporations and the Passion of ICT for Development: Modernization Resurrected," *Media, Culture and Society* 29, no. 6 (November 2007): 972–93; Dan Schiller, "The Legacy of Robert A. Brady: Antifascist Origins of the Political Economy of Communication," *Journal of Media Economics* 12, no. 2 (1999): 89–101.

34. United States Council for International Business to Fiona Alexander, Associate Administrator, Office of International Affairs, National Telecommunications and Information Administration, Re: NTIA Notice of Inquiry, Request for Comments on the Internet Assigned Numbers Authority (IANA) Functions, March 31, 2011: 1, 2, available at http://www.ntia.doc.gov/files/ntia/comments/110207099-1099-01/attachments/FINAL%20USCIB%20comments%20on%20IANA%20NOI%20-%203-31-11.pdf (accessed January 10, 2014).

35. Cisco Systems, Inc., to Ms. Fiona Alexander, Associate Administrator, Office of International Affairs, National Telecommunications and Information Administration, Re: NTIA Notice of Inquiry, Request for Comments on the Internet Assigned Numbers Authority (IANA) Functions, March 28, 2011: 1–2, available at http://www.ntia.doc.gov/files/ntia/comments/110207099-1099-01/attachments/Cisco.pdf (accessed January 10, 2014).

36. Vint Cerf, Chief Internet Evangelist, Google, Inc., to Fiona Alexander, Associate Administrator, Office of International Affairs, National Telecommunications and Information Administration, Re: NTIA Notice of Inquiry, Request for Comments on the Internet Assigned Numbers Authority (IANA) Functions, March 31, 2011: 1, available at http://www.ntia.doc.gov/files/ntia/comments/110207099-1099-01/attachments/20110331093955130.pdf (accessed January 10, 2014).

37. Cerf, "NTIA Notice," 5.

38. Cerf, "NTIA Notice," 1.

39. Cerf, "NTIA Notice," 2.

40. International Telecommunication Union, IANA NOI Response, Subject: Response to Request for Comments on the Internet Assigned Numbers Authority (IANA) Functions; National Telecommunications and Information Administration, docket no. 110207099–1099–01, RIN 0660–XA23, March 30, 2011, 1–4, available at http://www.ntia.doc.gov/files/ntia/comments/110207099-1099-01/attachments/ITU_E910_IANA%20NOI%20response_30-03-2011_final.pdf (accessed January 10, 2014).

41. Thanks to Richard Hill for this formulation.

42. MacKinnon, *Consent of the Networked*, 203.

43. Comments by Kenya on the Notice of Inquiry/Request for Comments on the Internet Assigned Numbers Authority (IANA) Functions by the National Telecommunications and Information Administration, U.S. Department of Commerce, 1, 2, 3, available at http://www.ntia.doc.gov/files/ntia/comments/110207099-1099-01/attachments/Kenya%20comments%20on%20Notice%20of%20Inquiry%20by%20NTIA%20on%20IANA%20Contract%20v4.pdf (accessed January 10, 2014).

44. Kwalwasser, "Internet Governance," 508.

45. Government of India, Department of Information Technology, Sub: Request for Comments on the Internet Assigned Numbers Authority Functions—GoI Comments, available at http://www.ntia.doc.gov/federal-register-notices/2011/request-comments-internet-assigned-numbers-authority-iana-functions#comment-28931 (accessed January 10, 2014).

46. Manal Ismail Egypt GAC Representative Director, International Technical Coordination National Telecom Regulatory Authority, to Fiona M. Alexander, Associate Administrator, Office of International Affairs National Telecommunications and Information Administration, U.S. Department of Commerce, March 31, 2011, 1–4, available at https://web.archive.org/web/20120925231524/http://www.ntia.doc.gov/files/ntia/comments/110207099-1099-01/attachments/Egypt%20Response%20to%20NTIA%20NoI%20on%20IANA%20Functions.pdf (accessed January 10, 2014).

47. Omar Charfen Tommasi, El Director General Ajunto, Secretaria de Comunicaciones y Transportes, Estados Unidos Mexicanos, to Sra. Fiona Alexander, Associate Administrator, Office of International Affairs, National Telecommunications and Information Administration, Annex 2–1, available at http://www.ntia.doc.gov/federal-register-notices/2011/request-comments-internet-assigned-numbers-authority-iana-functions#comment-28931 (accessed January 10, 2014).

48. Ian Bremmer, "Democracy in Cyberspace," *Foreign Affairs* 89 no. 6 (November–December 2010): 90.

49. Hong Shen, "Road to Cyber-Sovereigntism? China's Policy toward Global Internet Governance: From WSIS to WCIT-12," unpublished research paper, University of Illinois at Urbana-Champaign, August 2013.

50. Xiaodong Lee, Deputy Director General and Chief Technology Officer, CNNIC, March 31, 2011, Request for Comments on the Internet Assigned Numbers Authority (IANA) Functions, docket no. 110207099-1099-01, p. 2–3, available at http://www.ntia.doc.gov/files/ntia/comments/110207099-1099-01/attachments/CNNIC%20comments%20on%20IANA%20Funcionts.pdf (accessed January 10, 2014).

51. Xiaodong Lee, "Request for Comments."

52. Wang Chen, Minister of the State Internet Information Office, China, "Promote Internet Development and Safeguard Internet Security," Keynote Speech at the 4th UK-China Internet Roundtable, September 29, 2011, Beijing, *ChinaDaily.com.cn*, available at http://www.chinadaily.com.cn/china/2011-09/29/content_13818671.htm (accessed January 10, 2104).

53. Internet Society of China Comments on the IANA Functions, available at http://www.ntia.doc.gov/files/ntia/internet_society_of_china_comments_on_the_sow_draft_en.pdf (accessed January 10, 2014); and China Organizational Name Administration Center, to Fiona M. Alexander, Associate Administrator, Office of International Affairs, National Telecommunications and Information Administration, U.S. Department of Commerce, March 31, 2011, available at http://www.ntia.doc.gov/files/ntia/comments/110207099-1099-01/attachments/CONAC%27s%20response%20to%20NOI.pdf

54. China Organizational Name Administration Center, to U.S. Department of Commerce: 1, 3, 4.

55. Comments of the Internet Governance Project on the NTIA's "Request for Comments on the Internet Assigned Numbers Authority (IANA) Functions," March 31, 2011, available at http://www.ntia.doc.gov/federal-register-notices/2011/request-comments-internet-assigned-numbers-authority-iana-functions#comment-28973 (accessed January 10, 2014).

56. Vijay Prashad, *The Poorer Nations: A Possible History of the Global South* (London: Verso, 2012).

57. Lawrence E. Strickling, Keynote Remarks before the Global Internet Governance Academic Network, Washington, D.C., May 5, 2011, 3 (quote), 4 (quote), available at http://www.ntia.doc.gov/speechtestimony/2011/remarks-assistant-secretary-strickling-american-universitys-giganet-conference (accessed January 10, 2014).

58. MacKinnon, *Consent of the Networked*, 197.

59. "'e-G-8' Summit Split on Policing Internet," *China Post*, May 26, 2011, available at http://www.chinapost.com.tw/international/2011/05/26/303835/e-G-8-summit.htm (accessed January 10, 2014).

60. G8 Declaration, "Renewed Commitment for Freedom and Democracy," G8 Summit of Deauville, May 26–27, 2011, available at http://www.nato.int/nato_static/assets/pdf/pdf_2011_05/20110926_110526-G8-Summit-Deauville.pdf (accessed January 10, 2014).

61. G8 Declaration, "Renewed Commitment."

62. "Communiqué on Principles for Internet Policy-Making," OECD High-Level Meeting on "The Internet Economy: Generating Innovation and Growth," June 28–29, 2011, Paris, France, available at http://www.oecd.org/internet/innovation/48289796.pdf.

63. The Internet Governance Project commented that the IANA contract "must not become . . . a mechanism by which the U.S. government attempts to influence or second-guess the policies developed by ICANN." "Comments of the Internet Governance Project (IGP) on the Further Notice of Inquiry on the Internet Assigned Numbers Authority Functions," July 28, 2011, available at http://www.internetgovernance.org/wordpress/wp-content/uploads/iana-contract-fnoi-igpcomments.pdf (accessed January 10, 2014).

64. China Internet Network Information Center (CNNIC), Re: Further Notice Inquiry on the IANA Functions, July 28, 2011, available at http://www.ntia.doc.gov/files/ntia/cnnic_comments_on_fnoi.pdf (accessed January 10, 2014).

65. Internet Society of China Comments on the SOW Draft, Eng., July 28, 2011; "Internet Society of China Comments on the SOW Draft," available at http://www.ntia.doc.gov/

files/ntia/internet_society_of_china_comments_on_the_sow_draft_en.pdf (accessed January 10, 2014).

66. "MIIT of China Response to the Further Notice of Inquiry on the IANA Functions," July 28, 2011, available at http://www.ntia.doc.gov/files/ntia/miitcomments_on_iana _functions.pdf (accessed January 10, 2014).

67. Department of Commerce, National Telecommunications and Information Administration (IANA), docket no. 11207099–1319–02, RIN 0660-XA23, "The Internet Assigned Numbers Authority (IANA) Functions," *Federal Register* 76, no. 114 (June 14, 2011), 34660.

68. Department of Commerce, "IANA Functions," 34660.

69. Lawrence E. Strickling, "What Kind of Internet Do You Want?" Keynote Remarks before Internet Society's INET Series, New York, June 14, 2011, available at http://www .ntia.doc.gov/speechtestimony/2011/keynote-remarks-assistant-secretary-strickling -internet-societys-inet-conference (accessed February 18, 2014).

70. Mark MacCarthy, "SIAA Joins Call for U.S. Action to Promote Cross-Border Data Flows," November 3, 2011, available at http://www.siia.net/blog/index.php/2011/11/siia -joins-call-for-u-s-action-to-promote-cross-border-data-flows (accessed January 10, 2014).

71. SIAA, "Promoting Cross-Border Data Flows: Priorities for the Business Community," 1, available at http://www.nftc.org/default/Innovation/PromotingCrossBorder DataFlowsNFTC.pdf (accessed January 10, 2014).

72. NTIA, "Notice—Cancelled IANA Functions—Request for Proposal SA1301-12-RP-IANA," March 10, 2012, available at http://www.ntia.doc.gov/other-publication/2012/ notice-internet-assigned-numbers-authority-iana-functions-request-proposal-rf (accessed January 10, 2014).

73. Might the Commerce Department have been channeling unhappiness expressed earlier by a politically influential business group? The Association of National Advertisers, a trade association whose four-hundred-odd member companies represented more than ten thousand global brands and spent $250 billion annually on marketing, communications, and advertising, wrote to the Commerce Department to express "the deep and abiding concerns of ANA and its members regarding the fashion in which ICANN has executed certain of its existing responsibilities, particularly with respect to consideration and adoption of the generic top level domain ("gTLD") program that ICANN approved on June 20, 2011." By authorizing the establishment of a potentially infinite number of new top-level domain names, ICANN had established the feasibility of new domains (literally!) of accumulation—and struck a blow against the entrenched Web properties belonging to transnational corporate trademark owners. ANA responded forcefully: "ICANN's arbitrary decision to move forward with the Program even though it has failed to establish that the benefits of the Program outweigh its costs and even though the Program is likely to promote consumer confusion, dilution, cybersquatting, violations of online security, privacy, and a host of other malicious conduct, raises questions about ICANN's fitness to make key policy decisions and to continue to perform the IANA functions, at least without a system of appropriate checks and balances on what increasingly seems to be ICANN's unbridled power." Robert Liodice, President and CEO, Association of National

Advertisers, to Fiona M. Alexander, Associate Administrator, Office of International Affairs, NTIA, "Re: Further Notice of Inquiry on the Internet Assigned Numbers Authority Functions Docket No. 110207099–1319–02 RIN 0660-XA23," July 29, 2011. Letter marked "Privileged and Confidential: Subject to Attorney-Client and Work Product Privileges." Available at http://www.ntia.doc.gov/files/ntia/ana_sub_correction.pdf (accessed January 10, 2014).

74. NTIA, "Commerce Department Awards Contract for Management of Key Internet Functions to ICANN," July 2, 2012, available at http://www.ntia.doc.gov/press-release/2012/commerce-department-awards-contract-management-key-internet-functions-icann (accessed January 10, 2014).

75. DNS Extension for Autonomous Internet (AIP) draft-diao-aip-dns-00.txt IETF proposal, June 13, 2012 at https://tools.ietf.org/html/draft-diao-aip-dns-00 (accessed January 10, 2014). The proposal was submitted again in June 2013.

76. Milton Mueller, "Proposed New IETF Standard Would Create a Nationally Partitioned 'Internet,'" Internet Governance Project, June 18, 2012, available at http://www.internetgovernance.org/2012/06/18/proposed-new-ietf-standard-would-create-a-nationally-partitioned-internet (accessed January 10, 2014). See also Andrew Sullivan, "ICANN 44: Examining the AIP Draft Proposal," available at http://dyn.com/blog/icann-44-preview-examining-the-aip-internet-draft-proposal (accessed January 10, 2014).

77. Thanks to Shen Hong for this formulation.

78. I follow Anders, "Who Controls the Internet?" *TechnoLlama*, June 1 2012, at www.technollama.co.uk.

79. "Opening Session Remarks by Lawrence E. Strickling," Internet Governance Forum, Nairobi, Kenya, September 27, 2011, available at http://www.ntia.doc.gov/headlines/2011/opening-session-remarks-assistant-secretary-strickling-internet-governance-forum (accessed February 22, 2014); "Remarks by Lawrence E. Strickling," PLI/FCBA Telecommunications Policy and Regulation Institute, Washington, D.C., December 8, 2011, available at http://www.ntia.doc.gov/speechtestimony/2011/remarks-assistant-secretary-strickling-practising-law-institutes-29th-annual-te (accessed February 22, 2014); "Remarks by Lawrence E. Strickling," Brookings Institution Center for Technology Innovation Meeting on "Principles of Internet Governance: An Agenda for Economic Growth and Innovation," Washington, D.C., January 11, 2012, available at http://www.ntia.doc.gov/speechtestimony/2012/remarks-assistant-secretary-strickling-brookings-institutions-center-technology (accessed February 22, 2014).

80. Robert M. McDowell, "The U.N. Threat to Internet Freedom," *Wall Street Journal*, February 2, 2012, available at http://online.wsj.com/news/articles/SB10001424052970204792404577229074023195322 (accessed January 10, 2014).

81. U.S. Congress, House of Representatives, 112th Cong., 2d Sess. H. Con. Res, May 30, 2012, House Energy and Commerce Committee, "Bipartisan Leaders of the Committee Introduce Resolution to Preserve and Protect a Global Internet Free from Government Control," press release, May 30, 2012 at www.energycommerce.house.gov/press-release/bipartisan-leaders-committee-introduce-resolution-preserve-and-protect-global-internet (accessed January 10, 2014).

82. See Testimony of Ambassador Philip Verveer, Deputy Assistant Secretary of State and United States Coordinator for International Communications and Information Policy; and Statement of Commissioner Robert M. McDowell, Federal Communications Commission, before the U.S. House of Representatives, Committee on Energy and Commerce, Subcommittee on Communications and Technology, Hearing on International Proposals to Regulate the Internet, May 31, 2012.

83. Rachel Sanderson and Daniel Thomas, "US Accused of Telecoms Pact Propaganda," *FT.com*, December 16, 2013, available at http://www.ft.com/cms/s/0/86d4baf4-4774 -11e2-8c34-00144feab49a.html#axzz2r3C4tlb1; for details, including discussion of how the ITU's constitution prioritizes freedom of speech, see Richard Hill, *The New International Telecommunication Regulations and the Internet: A Commentary and Legislative History* (Zurich: Schulthess, 2013).

84. For what follows, see Dan Schiller, "Masters of the Internet," *Le Monde diplomatique*, February 2013, 6, also available at http://www.counterpunch.org/2013/02/07/masters-of -the-internet (accessed January 10, 2014). For a factual recounting of the results of these deliberations, see Richard Hill, "WCIT: Failure or Success, Impasse or Way Forward?" *International Journal of Law and Information Technology* 21, no. 3 (Autumn 2013): 313–28.

85. International Telecommunication Union, "Final Acts World Conference on International Telecommunications (Dubai, 2012)," resolution 3, "To foster an enabling environment for the greater growth of the Internet," 20, available at http://www.itu.int/ pub/S-CONF-WCIT-2012/en (accessed January 10, 2014); see Hill, "WCIT: failure or success, impasse or way forward," 313.

86. Eric Pfanner, "Message, If Murky, from U.S. to World," *New York Times*, December 15, 2012.

87. Hill, "New International."

88. Dwayne Winseck, "Big New Global Threat to the Internet or Paper Tiger? The ITU and Global Internet Regulation," parts 1–4, June 10–19, 2012, available at https://dwmw .wordpress.com/2012/06/10/big-new-global-threat-to-the-internet-or-paper-tiger-the-itu -and-global-internet-regulation-part-i (accessed January 10, 2014).

89. "The Foreign Ministry of India," in one account, "has taken a classically sovereigntist line on most Internet governance issues, but pressure from Indian [civil society organizations] and the private sector pushed India to vote against the WCIT treaty." Milton Mueller and Ben Wagner, "Finding a Formula for Brazil: Representation and Legitimacy in Internet Governance" (Philadelphia: Annenberg School for Communication Center for Global Communication Studies Internet Policy Observatory, 2014), 4.

90. L. Gordon Crovitz, "America's First Big Digital Defeat," *Wall Street Journal*, December 17, 2012.

91. PIR Center (Russian Center for Policy Studies), "Global Internet Governance after Dubai," June 10, 2013. Release available at http://www.pircenter.org/en/news/6466- global-internet-governance-after-dubai-summit (accessed January 10, 2014).

92. PIR Center, Program for "Internet Governance after WCIT-2012: Mapping Key Global Trends and Assessing Russia's National Interests," available at http://www .pircenter.org/en/events/1809-pir-centers-international-seminar-internet-governance

-after-wcit2012-mapping-key-global-trends-and-assessing-russia-s-national-interests (accessed January 10, 2014).

93. PIR Center, "Global Internet Governance after Dubai."

94. World Information Technology and Services Alliance (WITSA), "Special Report on ITU WCIT-2012," January 2013, available at http://www.witsa.org/v2/media_center/ pdf/ITU_Dubai_WCIT12_outcome_report_Final.pdf (accessed January 10, 2014).

95. Lawrence E. Strickling, Keynote Address, Conference on the Future of Internet Governance after Dubai, Columbia University Institute of Tele-Information, New York, June 20, 2013. The program is publicized at http://www8.gsb.columbia.edu/citi/thefuture oftheinternet.

96. Negroponte, Palmisano, and Segal, "Defending," 13, 67.

97. Mueller and Wagner, "Finding a Formula," 1.

98. James Bamford, "They Know Much More Than You Think," *New York Review of Books* 60, no. 13 (August 15, 2013), 4; Alfred M. McCoy, "Imperial Illusions: Information Infrastructure and the Future of U.S. Global Power," in *Endless Empire: Spain's Retreat, Europe's Eclipse, America's Decline,* ed. Alfred W. McCoy, Josep M. Fradera, and Stephen Jacobson (Madison: University of Wisconsin Press, 2012), 360–86.

99. Perry Anderson, "American Foreign Policy and Its Thinkers," *New Left Review* 83 (September/October 2013): 23.

100. This is recounted in the relevant Wikipedia entry "ECHELON," http:// en.wikipedia.org/wiki/ECHELON. For a sustained analysis, see James Bamford, *Body of Secrets* (New York: Anchor, 2002).

101. James Bamford, "The NSA Is Building the Country's Biggest Spy Center (Watch What You Say)," *Wired,* March 15, 2012, available at http://www.wired.com/threatlevel/ 2012/03/ff_nsadatacenter/all/1 (accessed January 10, 2014).

102. Leonard Downie Jr., "The Obama Administration and the Press," Committee to Protect Journalists, October 10, 2013, available at http://cpj.org/reports/2013/10/obama-and -the-press-us-leaks-surveillance-post-911.php (accessed January 10, 2014).

103. Scott Shane, "No Morsel Too Miniscule for All-Consuming N.S.A.," *New York Times,* November 3, 2013.

104. George Parker and Richard McGregor, "Brussels Furious at Ally Spying Claim," *Financial Times,* December 21/22, 2013.

105. James Risen and Laura Poitras, "N.S.A. Report Outlined Goals for More Power," *New York Times,* November 23, 2013; Jason Healey, ed., *A Fierce Domain: Conflict in Cyberspace, 1986 to 2012* (Vienna, Va.: Cyber Conflict Studies Association and Atlantic Council, 2013), 87.

106. Bamford, "They Know Much More Than You Think," 6; Craig Timberg and Barton Gellman, "NSA Paying U.S. Companies for Access to Communications Networks," *Washington Post,* August 29, 2013, available at http://www.washingtonpost.com/world/ national-security/nsa-paying-us-companies-for-access-to-communications-networks/ 2013/08/29/5641a4b6-10c2-11e3-bdf6-e4fc677d94a1_story.html (accessed January 10, 2014); Ed Pilkington, "Phone Companies Remain Silent over Legality of NSA Data Collec-

tion," *The Guardian*, September 18, 2013, available at http://www.theguardian.com/world/2013/sep/18/phone-companies-silent-nsa-data-collection (accessed January 10, 2014).

107. CBS/AP, "German Magazine: NSA Spied on United Nations," August 26, 2013, available at http://www.cbsnews.com/news/german-magazine-nsa-spied-on-united-nations (accessed January 10, 2014).

108. Barton Gellman and Ashkan Soltani, "NSA Collects Millions of E-mail Address Books Globally," *Washington Post*, October 14, 2013, available at http://www.washingtonpost.com/world/national-security/nsa-collects-millions-of-e-mail-address-books-globally/2013/10/14/8e58b5be-34f9-11e3-80c6-7e6dd8d22d8f_story.html (accessed January 10, 2014).

109. Mark Mazzetti and Justin Elliott, "Spies Infiltrate a Fantasy Realm of Online Games," *New York Times*, December 10, 2013; James Glanz, Jeff Larson, and Andrew W. Lehren, "Spy Agencies Tap Data Streaming from Phone Apps," *New York Times*, January 28, 2014.

110. Risen and Poitras, "N.S.A. Report."

111. It was reported that, overall, the NSA maintained "eavesdropping posts" in eighty U.S. embassies and consulates worldwide. CBS/AP, "NSA Spied."

112. CBS/AP, "NSA Spied."

113. Julian Assange, *Cypherpunks: Freedom and the Future of the Internet*. (New York: O/R, 2012).

114. Alfred McCoy, "Surveillance Blowback: The Making of the U.S. Surveillance State, 1898–2020," *Popular Resistance*, July 15, 2013, available at http://www.popularresistance.org/surveillance-blowback-the-making-of-the-us-surveillance-state-1898-2020 (accessed January 10, 2014).

115. Benjamin Dangl, "U.S. Spying and Resistance in Latin America," *CounterPunch*, July 19–21, 2013, available at http://www.counterpunch.org/2013/07/19/us-spying-and-resistance-in-latin-america (accessed January 10, 2014).

116. Quentin Peel, "Europe Calls for Strict Europe-Wide Law on Protecting Personal Data," *Financial Times*, July 15, 2013.

117. James Fontanella-Khan and James Politi, "Data Scandal Clouds Trade Talks," *Financial Times*, June 10, 2013; Hugh Carnegy, "France Expands Digital Spying," *Financial Times*, December 12, 2013; Gregor Peter Schmitz, "SWIFT Suspension? EU Parliament Furious about NSA Bank Spying," *Spiegel Online*, September 18, 2013, available at http://www.spiegel.de/international/europe/nsa-spying-european-parliamentarians-call-for-swift-suspension-a-922920.html (accessed January 10, 2014).

118. BBC News Europe, "Snowden Leaks: France Summons U.S. Envoy over Spying Claims," *BBC*, October 21, 2013, available at http://www.bbc.co.uk/news/world-europe-24607880 (accessed January 10, 2014); Paul Lewis and Angelique Chrisafis, "Barack Obama Calls Francois Hollande Following NSA Revelations in France," *The Guardian*, October 21, 2013, available at http://www.theguardian.com/world/2013/oct/21/us-french-surveillance-legitimate-questions (accessed January 10, 2014); Jens Glüsing, Laura Poitras, Marcel Rosenbach and Holger Stark, "Fresh Leak on US Spying: NSA Accessed Mexican President's Email," *Spiegel Online*, October 20, 2013, available at www.spiegel.de/

international/world/nsa-hacked-email-account-of-mexican-president-a-928817.html (accessed January 10, 2014).

119. Matthew Taylor, Nick Hopkins, and Jemima Kiss, "NSA Surveillance May Cause Break-Up of the Internet, Experts Warn," *The Guardian*, November 1, 2013, available at http://www.theguardian.com/world/2013/nov/01/nsa-surveillance-cause-internet-breakup-edward-snowden (accessed January 10, 2014); Ian Traynor, "Internet Governance Too US-centric, Says European Commission," *The Guardian*, February 12, 2014, available at http://www.theguardian.com/technology/2014/feb/12/internet-governance-us-european-commission (accessed February 18, 2014); European Commission, "Communication from the Commission to the European Parliament, the Council, the European Economic and Social Committee and the Committee of the Regions, Internet Policy and Governance Europe's Role in Shaping the Future of Internet Governance" (Brussels, COM (2014) 72/4), available at http://ec.europa.eu/information_society/newsroom/cf/dae/document.cfm?doc_id=4453 (accessed February 18, 2014).

120. "Germany, Brazil Work on Draft UN Resolution to End Excessive Spying," Global Post, October 26, 2013, available at www.globalpost.com/dispatch/news/regions/europe/131026/germany-brazil-US-draft-un-resolution-spying (accessed January 10, 2014); Nick Hopkins and Matthew Taylor, "Edward Snowden Revelations Prompt UN Investigation into Surveillance," *The Guardian*, December 2, 2013, available at http://www.theguardian.com/world/2013/dec/02/edward-snowden-un-investigation-surveillance (accessed February 18, 2014).

121. Taylor, Hopkins, and Kiss, "NSA Surveillance."

122. Sandeep Joshi, "India to Push for Freeing Internet from U.S. Control," *The Hindu*, December 7, 2013, available at http://www.thehindu.com/sci-tech/technology/internet/india-to-push-for-freeing-internet-from-us-control/article5434095.ece (accessed February 24, 2014).

123. Joe Leahy, "Rousseff Attacks Foreign Spying and Calls for Code to Protect Internet Privacy," *Financial Times*, September 25, 2013; "Latin America Demands Answers from U.S. on Spying," Agence France-Press, July 11, 2013, available at http://www.rawstory.com/rs/2013/07/11/latin-america-demands-answers-from-u-s-on-spying; Julian Borger, "Brazilian President: US Surveillance a 'Breach of International Law,'" *The Guardian*, September 24, 2013, available at http://www.theguardian.com/world/2013/sep/24/brazil-president-un-speech-nsa-surveillance (accessed January 10, 2014); "UN vs. NSA: 21 Nations Discuss Resolutions Restraining US Spying," *Voice of Russia*, October 26, 2013, available at http://voiceofrussia.com/news/2013_10_26/UN-against-NSA-21-nations-discuss-resolution-restraining-US-spying-6298 (accessed January 10, 2014).

124. Geoff Dyer, "Feinstein Urges 'Total Review' of Intelligence," *Financial Times*, October 29, 2013; Spencer Ackerman, "Feinstein Promotes Bill to Strengthen NSA's Hand on Warrantless Searches," *The Guardian*, November 15, 2013, available at http://www.theguardian.com/world/2013/nov/15/feinstein-bill-nsa-warrantless-searches-surveillance (accessed January 10, 2014).

125. Saeed Kamali Dehghan, Nicholas Watt, Alan Travis, and Nick Hopkins, "Hillary Clinton: We Need to Talk Sensibly about Spying," *The Guardian*, October 11, 2013, available at http://www.theguardian.com/world/2013/oct/11/hillary-clinton-spying (accessed January 10, 2014).

126. Spencer Ackerman, "Cyber-Attacks Eclipsing Terrorism as Gravest Domestic Threat—FBI," *The Guardian*, November 14, 2013, available at http://www.theguardian.com/world/2013/nov/14/cyber-attacks-terrorism-domestic-threat-fbi (accessed January 10, 2014).

127. Reuters/Ipsos poll, reported in Alessandra Prentice and Steve Gutterman, "Snowden Still at Airport, Ecuador Asylum Decision Could Take Months," *Reuters*, June 26, 2013, available at http://uk.reuters.com/article/2013/06/26/uk-usa-security-snowden-idUKBRE95P0H820130626 (accessed January 10, 2014).

128. Ezra Klein, "Edward Snowden, Patriot," *Washington Post*, August 9, 2013, available at http://www.washingtonpost.com/blogs/wonkblog/wp/2013/08/09/edward-snowden-patriot (accessed January 10, 2014); Bruce Joffe, "Letter: Let's Honor Snowden as a Hero," *Salt Lake Tribune*, November 16, 2013, available at http://www.sltrib.com/sltrib/opinion/57119133-82/hero-snowden-nsa-accusations.html.csp (accessed January 10, 2014).

129. "Edward Snowden, Whistle-Blower," *New York Times*, January 2, 2014.

130. Associated Press, "European Parliament Invites Edward Snowden to Testify via Video," *The Guardian*, January 9, 2014, available at http://www.theguardian.com/world/2014/jan/09/edward-snowden-invited-testify-video-european-parliament-nsa-surveillance (accessed February 18, 2014).

131. BBC News Europe, "Snowden Leaks"; Glusing, Poitras, Rosenbach, and Stark, "Fresh Leak."

132. Borger, "Brazilian President"; "UN vs. NSA."

133. Associated Press, "Asian Countries Demand Answers over Reports of Spying from Embassies," *The Globe and Mail*, October 31, 2013, available at http://www.ottawastar.com/asian-countries-demand-answers-over-reports-of-spying-from-embassies (accessed January 10, 2014); Glenn Greenwald and Shobhan Saxena, "India among Top Targets of Spying by NSA," *The Hindu*, September 23, 2013, available at http://www.thehindu.com/news/national/india-among-top-targets-of-spying-by-nsa/article5157526.ece (accessed January 10, 2014).Thanks to Manjunath Pendakur for this reference.

134. Tamara Pearson, "Venezuela and Mercosur Discuss Mechanisms to Prevent US Government Spying," *Venezuelanalysis.com*, September 18, 2013, available at http://venezuelanalysis.com/news/10030 (accessed January 10, 2014); Amar Toor, "Cutting the Cord: Brazil's Bold Plan to Combat the NSA," *The Verge*, September 25, 2013, available at http://www.theverge.com/2013/9/25/4769534/brazil-to-build-internet-cable-to-avoid-us-nsa-spying (accessed January 10, 2014); "Brazil Plans to Go Offline from US-centric Internet," *The Hindu*, September 17, 2013, available at www.thehindu.com/news/international/world/brazil-plans-to-go-offline-from-US-centric-Internet/article5137689.ece (accessed January 10, 2014); Sreeram Chaulia, "Snowden Fallout: India's Meow, Brazil's Roar," *RT*, September 29, 2013, available at http://rt.com/op-edge/india-brazil

-china-nsa-fallout-448 (accessed January 10, 2014); Robert Muggah, "After NSA Scandal, Will Brazil Try to Unravel the Internet?" *The Globe and Mail*, September 19, 2013, available at http://www.theglobeandmail.com/globe-debate/after-nsa-scandal-will-brazil-try-to-unravel-the-internet/article14407678 (accessed January 10, 2014); Walker Simon, "South America Studies How to Curb U.S. 'Spying': Ecuador," *Reuters*, September 25, 2013, http://www.reuters.com/article/2013/09/26/us-ecuador-spying-id USBRE98P01P20130926 (accessed January 10, 2014).

135. Bill Woodcock, "On Internet, Brazil Is Beating US at Its Own Game," *Al Jazeera America*, September 20, 2013, available at http://america.aljazeera.com/articles/2013/9/20/brazil-internet-dilmarousseffnsa.html (accessed January 10, 2014); "SACS Angola-Brazil Cable Ready Mid-2015; Telebras Onboard, Shelves US Link," *TeleGeography*, Comms Update, November 15, 2013.

136. Karis Hustad, "In Light of NSA Spying, Brazil May Take a Step Back from World Wide Web," *CSMonitor.com*, November 12, 2013, available at http://www.csmonitor.com/Innovation/2013/1112/In-light-of-NSA-spying-Brazil-may-take-a-step-back-from-World-Wide-Web (accessed January 10, 2014).

137. Amanda Holpuch, "Brazil's Controversial Plan to Extricate the Internet from US Control," *The Guardian*, September 20, 2013, available at http://www.theguardian.com/world/2013/sep/20/brazil-dilma-rousseff-internet-us-control (accessed January 10, 2014). Also see "Canadian Spies Targeted Brazil's Mines and Energy Ministry: Report," *The Globe and Mail*, October 6, 2013, available at http://www.brazilsun.com/index.php/sid/217563656/scat/24437442923341f1 (accessed January 10, 2014).

138. Michael Birnbaum, "Germany Looks at Keeping its Internet, E-mail Traffic Inside Its Borders," *Washington Post*, November 1, 2013, available at http://www.washingtonpost.com/world/europe/germany-looks-at-keeping-its-internet-e-mail-traffic-inside-its-borders/2013/10/31/981104fe-424f-11e3-a751-f032898f2dbc_story.html?wpisrc=emailtoafriend (accessed January 10, 2014).

139. Stefan Wagstyl, Jeevan Vasagar, and James Fontanella-Khan, "German Spy Backlash Threatens EU-US Pact," *Financial Times*, November 4, 2013; Sam Schechner, "Oceans Apart over Privacy," *Wall Street Journal*, January 9, 2014.

140. Alison Smale, "Merkel Backs Plan to Keep European Data in Europe," *New York Times*, February 16, 2014.

141. European Commission, "Internet Policy and Governance," 5.

142. In Geoff Dyer and Richard Waters, "Spying Threatens Internet, Say Experts," *Financial Times*, November 1, 2013.

143. Rita A. Widiadana, "Surveillance Takes Center Stage as IGF Ends," *Jakarta Post*, October 26, 2013, available at http://www.thejakartapost.com/news/2013/10/26/surveillance-takes-center-stage-igf-ends.html (accessed January 10, 2014).

144. Ayee Macaraig, "Distrust and the Post-Snowden Internet," *Rappler*, October 27, 2013, available at http://www.rappler.com/world/regions/asia-pacific/42326-internet-governance-forum-wrap (accessed January 10, 2014).

145. ICANN, "Montevideo Statement on the Future of Internet Cooperation," October 7, 2013, available at http://www.icann.org/en/news/announcements/announcement-07oct13 -en.htm (accessed January 10, 2014).

146. Claire Cain Miller, "Angry over U.S. Surveillance, Tech Giants Bolster Defenses," *New York Times*, November 1, 2013.

147. Monika Bauerlein and Clara Jeffery, "Where Does Facebook Stop and the NSA Begin?" *Mother Jones*, October 31, 2013, available at http://www.motherjones.com/media/ 2013/10/facebook-personal-data-online-privacy-social-norm (accessed January 10, 2014).

148. Rory Carroll, "Google Chairman: NSA Spying on Our Data Centres 'Outrageous,'" *The Guardian*, November 4, 2013, available at http://www.theguardian.com/technology/2013/ nov/04/eric-schmidt-nsa-spying-data-centres-outrageous (accessed January 10, 2014).

149. Ambassador Daniel A. Sepulveda, Deputy Assistant Secretary of State and U.S. Coordinator for International Communications and Information Policy, "Internet Governance 2020: Geopolitics and the Future of the Internet," Center for Strategic and International Studies, Washington, D.C., January 23, 2014, available at http://translations .state.gov/st/english/texttrans/2014/01/20140125291640.html#axzz2tyInxSuz (accessed February 21, 2014).

150. Mueller and Wagner, "Finding a Formula for Brazil"; Ryan Cox, "We Have 18 Months to Find New Governance for a Single Internet, Says ICANN," *Silicon Angle*, January 10, 2014, available at http://siliconangle.com/blog/2014/01/10/icanns-fadi-chehade-says -we-have-18-months-to-find-new-governance-for-a-single-internet-or-else/ (accessed February 21, 2014); Internet Governance Project, "US Cautiously Encourages IANA Reform, Brazil Meeting," January 26, 2014, available at http://www.internetgovernance. org/2014/01/26/us-cautiously-encourages-iana-reform-brazil-meeting/ (accessed February 21, 2014); Richard Hill, "The Future of Internet Governance: Dystopia, Utopia, or Realpolitik?" in *Global Internet Governance in Transition*, ed. Lorenzo Pupillo (Berlin: Springer, forthcoming).

151. Amanda Holpuch, "Google's Eric Schmidt Says Government Spying Is 'The Nature of Our Society,'" *The Guardian*, September 13, 2013, available at http://www.theguardian.com/ world/2013/sep/13/eric-schmidt-google-nsa-surveillance.

152. Matthew J. Schwartz, "NSA Surveillance Fallout Costs IT Industry Billions," *Information Week*, November 27, 2013, available at http://www.informationweek.com/security/ security-monitoring/nsa-surveillance-fallout-costs-it-industry-billions/d/d-id/1112838 (accessed February 18, 2014); Jim Sensenbrenner, "The NSA Overreach Poses a Serious Threat to Our Economy," *The Guardian*, November 20, 2013, available at http://www.theguardian .com/commentisfree/2013/nov/20/jim-sensenbrenner-nsa-overreach-hurts-business (accessed February 18, 2014); Richard McGregor and Richard Waters, "Tech Groups Demand Limits on Spy Sweeps," *Financial Times*, December 9, 2013; Claire Cain Miller, "Angry Over U.S. Surveillance, Tech Giants Bolster Defenses," *New York Times*, November 1, 2013.

153. James Fontanella-Khan and Richard Waters, "Microsoft to Shield Foreign Users' Data," *Financial Times*, January 23, 2014.

154. Spencer Ackerman, "NSA: Six Out of 10 Americans Want Reform of Data Collection, Says Poll," *The Guardian*, January 16, 2014, available at http://www.theguardian.com/world/2014/jan/16/nsa-americans-reform-data-collection (accessed February 18, 2014); Richard Waters, "Obama Drags Tech Companies Deeper into Mire of Surveillance," *Financial Times*, January 21, 2014.

Chapter 14. Accumulation and Repression

1. The best, most up-to-date appraisal is Jason Healey, ed., *A Fierce Domain: Conflict in Cyberspace, 1986 to 2012* (Vienna, Va.: Cyber Conflict Studies Association and Atlantic Council, 2013).

2. Julian E. Barnes, "Pentagon Digs In on Cyberwar Front," *Wall Street Journal*, July 6, 2012.

3. Geoff Dyer and Joseph Menn, "Chinese and Russian Cyberspies Threaten US, Say Intelligence Chiefs," *Financial Times*, November 4, 2011; Joseph Menn and Geoff Dyer, "US Goes Public with Spying Frustrations," *Financial Times*, November 4, 2011.

4. Siobhan Gorman, "Electricity Grid in U.S. Penetrated by Spies," *Wall Street Journal*, April 8, 2009, available at http://online.wsj.com/news/articles/SB123914805204099085 (accessed January 10, 2014).

5. Kenneth Lieberthal, "Understanding Strategic Distrust: The U.S. Side," in *Addressing U.S.-China Strategic Distrust*, by Kenneth Lieberthal and Wang Jisi, 27 (Washington, D.C.: John L. Thorton China Center at Brookings), monograph series 4 (March 2012), 27; for a more extensive tally, see Bryan Krekel, Patton Adams, and George Bakos, "Occupying the Information High Ground: Chinese Capabilities for Computer Network Operations and Cyber-Espionage," prepared for the U.S.-China Economic and Security Review Commission by Northrop Grumman, March 7, 2012; and James Andrew Lewis, Center for Strategic and International Studies, "Significant Cyber Events Since 2006," available at http://csis.org/publication/cyber-events-2006 (accessed January 10, 2014).

6. Richard A. Clarke and Robert K. Knake, *Cyber War: The Next Threat to National Security and What to Do About It* (New York: HarperCollins, 2010), 233.

7. Clarke and Knake, *Cyber War*.

8. Healey, *Fierce Domain*, 41, 77.

9. National Security Presidential Directives, Department of Defense Roadmap and quote in William A. Owens, Kenneth W. Dam, and Herbert S. Lin, eds., Committee on Offensive Information Warfare, National Research Council, *Technologies, Policy, Law, and Ethics Regarding U.S. Acquisition and Use of Cyberattack Capabilities* (Washington, D.C.: National Academies Press, 2009), 10, 216.

10. Healey, *Fierce Domain*, 45, 65, 113; Nicholas Weaver, "Our Government Has Weaponized the Internet: Here's How They Did It," *Wired.com*, November 13, 2013, available at http://www.wired.com/opinion/2013/11/this-is-how-the-internet-backbone-has-been-turned-into-a-weapon (accessed February 4, 2014).

11. Clarke and Knake, *Cyber War*, 228.

12. Owens, Dam, and Lin, *Technologies, Policy, Law, and Ethics Regarding U.S. Acquisition and Use of Cyberattack Capabilities*, viii, 25; David E. Sanger, John Markoff, and Thom Shanker, "U.S. Steps Up Effort on Digital Defenses," *New York Times*, April 28, 2009, available at http://www.nytimes.com/2009/04/28/us/28cyber.html?pagewanted=all&_r=0 (accessed January 10, 2014).

13. The White House, "Cyberspace Policy Review: Assuring a Trusted and Resilient Information and Communications Infrastructure," iii, i, available at http://www.whitehouse .gov/assets/documents/Cyberspace_Policy_Review_final.pdf (accessed January 10, 2014).

14. Owens, Dam, and Lin, *Technologies*, 5.

15. Owens, Dam, and Lin, *Technologies*, 28, 58–59.

16. Christopher Drew, "Military Is Said to Make Progress in Modernizing," *New York Times*, October 28, 2011.

17. William J. Lynn III, "Defending a New Domain," *Foreign Affairs* 89, no. 5 (September–October 2010), 98.

18. John Ribeiro, "US Defense Department Approves Apple's iOS Devices for Its Networks," *IDG News Service*, April 19, 2013, available at http://www.pcworld.idg.com.au/article/462295/us_defense_department_approves_apple_ios_devices_its_networks (accessed January 10, 2014).

19. Booz Allen Hamilton, "RightIT: A Proven Approach to Achieve Cost-Effective IT Capabilities" available at http://www.boozallen.com/media/file/RightIT_Factsheet. pdf (accessed January 10, 2014).

20. Pam Benson, "Utah Will Be Site of Huge Cyber Protection Facility," *CNN*, January 12, 2011, available at http://www.cnn.com/2011/POLITICS/01/12/cyber.defense.center (accessed January 10, 2014); James Bamford, "The Black Box," *Wired*, April 2012, 78–85+.

21. Christopher Drew and John Markoff, "Contractors Vie for Plum Work, Hacking for U.S.," *New York Times*, May 31, 2009, available at http://www.nytimes.com/2009/05/31/us/31cyber.html?pagewanted=all (accessed January 10, 2014); Joseph Menn, "Defence Trains Sights on Threat to Internet," *Financial Times*, October 11, 2011.

22. U.S. House of Representatives, 112th Cong., 1st Sess., "Cyber Intelligence Sharing and Protection Act of 2011," H.R. 3523, November 30, 2011.

23. Dan Schiller, *How To Think about Information* (Urbana: University of Illinois Press, 2007), 53–54.

24. Menn, "Defence."

25. Menn, "Defence." Military cyberwarfare training programs also grew rapidly; the Navy's Center for Information Dominance alone trained twenty-four thousand people each year. Julian E. Barnes, "Pentagon Digs In on Cyberwar Front," *Wall Street Journal*, July 6, 2012.

26. John Markoff and Thom Shanker, "Halted '03 Iraq Plan Illustrates U.S. Fear of Cyberwar Risk," *New York Times*, August 1, 2009, available at http://www.nytimes.com/2009/08/02/us/politics/02cyber.html?_r=0 (accessed January 10, 2014). Earlier precedents also were known. As far back as the late 1990s, the same news story revealed, an

American assault on a Serbian telecommunications network had accidentally disrupted Intelsat communications.

27. Eric Schmitt and Thom Shanker, "U.S. Weighed Use of Cyberattacks to Weaken Libya," *New York Times,* October 18, 2012.

28. Barton Gellman and Ellen Nakashima, "The Black Budget: U.S. Spy Agencies Mounted 231 Offensive Cyber-Operations in 2011, Documents Show," *Washington Post,* August 30, 2013, available at http://www.washingtonpost.com/world/national-security/us-spy-agencies-mounted-231-offensive-cyber-operations-in-2011-documents-show/2013/08/30/d090a6ae-119e-11e3-b4cb-fd7ce041d814_story.html (accessed January 10, 2014).

29. In Nick Hopkins, "Militarisation of Cyberspace: How the Global Power Struggle Moved Online," *The Guardian,* April 16, 2012, available at http://www.theguardian.com/technology/2012/apr/16/militarisation-of-cyberspace-power-struggle (accessed January 10, 2014); also, Nicholas Weaver, "Our Government Has Weaponized the Internet. Here's How They Did It," *Wired,* November 13, 2013, available at http://www.wired.com/opinion/2013/11/this-is-how-the-internet-backbone-has-been-turned-into-a-weapon (accessed January 10, 2014).

30. Jamie Shea, in Carola Hoyos, "Fresh Enemy Emerges in the Battle against Cyberattacks," *Financial Times,* March 12, 2012.

31. "Telling the Truth about Cyberwarfare," editorial, *Financial Times,* June 27, 2012.

32. David E. Sanger, "Obama Order Set Off Wave of Cyberattacks against Iran," *New York Times,* June 1, 2012; David E. Sanger, *Confront and Conceal: Obama's Secret Wars and Surprising Use of American Power* (New York: Crown, 2012), 203–5.

33. Sanger, *Confront and Conceal,* 190.

34. Sanger stated in his news story that "parts" of this effort "continue to this day," adding in his book that "there is no reason to believe that America's cyber wars have ceased." Sanger, "Obama Order"; and Sanger, *Confront and Conceal,* 207, 188–225.

35. "Telling the Truth."

36. Barton Gellman and Ellen Nakashima, "U.S. Spy Agencies Mounted 231 Offensive Cyber-Operations in 2011, Documents Show," *Washington Post,* August 30, 2013, available at http://www.washingtonpost.com/world/national-security/us-spy-agencies-mounted-231-offensive-cyber-operations-in-2011-documents-show/2013/08/30/d090a6ae-119e-11e3-b4cb-fd7ce041d814_story.html (accessed January 10, 2014); Healey, *Fierce Domain,* 64–87.

37. Sanger, *Confront and Conceal,* xvi.

38. Sanger, *Confront and Conceal.*

39. Sanger, *Confront and Conceal,* 420, 243, 355. Largely implicit, this theme imparts a somewhat melancholy tone to portions of Henry Kissinger, *On China* (New York: Penguin, 2011).

40. Sanger, *Confront and Conceal,* 244–45.

41. A. T. Mahan, *The Influence of Sea Power Upon History, 1660–1783* (London, 1890), 87, quoted in Perry Anderson, "American Foreign Policy and Its Thinkers," *New Left Review* 83 (September/October 2013): 9.

42. Clarke and Knake, *Cyber War*, 260, 259; also see Weaver, "Our Government."

43. White House, "Cyberspace Policy Review"; Clarke and Knake, *Cyber War*; Joseph Menn, "Power Grid Looks Exposed to Assault," *Financial Times*, October 12, 2011.

44. Misha Glenny, "We Will Rue the Cavalier Deployment of Stuxnet," *Financial Times*, June 7, 2012.

45. Sanger, *Confront and Conceal*, 247.

46. White House, "Cyberspace Policy Review," iii.

47. White House, "Cyberspace Policy Review," iii.

48. U.S. Government Accountability Office (GAO), "Internet Infrastructure: Challenges in Developing a Public/Private Recovery Plan," September 13, 2006, available at www.gao.gov/cgi-bin/getrpt?GAO-06-1100T (accessed January 10, 2014); U.S. GAO, "Coordination of Federal Cyber Security Research and Development," September 2006, GAO-06–811; U.S. GAO, "DHS Leadership Needed to Enhance Cybersecurity," September 13, 2006, GAO 06–1087T; U.S. GAO, "CyberSecurity: Continued Attention Needed to Protect Our Nation's Critical Infrastructure." GAO 11–865T, July 26, 2011; Menn, "Power Grid"; Executive Order 13636, "Improving Critical Infrastructure Cyber-Security," *Federal Register*, February 19, 2013, available at https://www.federalregister.gov/articles/2013/02/19/2013-03915/improving-critical-infrastructure-cybersecurity (accessed January 10, 2014).

49. "Senators Spar with Power Industry: Is It Safe from Cyber-Attack?" *CSMonitor.com*, July 17, 2012, available at http://www.csmonitor.com/USA/2012/0717/Senators-spar-with-power-industry-Is-it-safe-from-cyberattack (accessed January 10, 2014).

50. David Talbot, "The Internet Is Broken," *MIT Technology Review*, February 15, 2006, available at http://www.technologyreview.com/news/405318/the-internet-is-broken (accessed January 10, 2014).

51. U.S. Department of Commerce, docket no. 110527305-1303-02, "Cybersecurity, Innovation, and the Internet Economy," *Federal Register* 76, no. 115 (Wednesday, June 15, 2011): 34965–67, available at http://www.ntia.doc.gov/federal-register-notice/2011/cybersecurity-innovation-and-internet-economy (accessed January 10, 2014).

52. Cheryl Pellerin, "DOD, Partners Better Prepared for Cyber Attacks," *American Forces Press Service*, October 18, 2011, available at http://www.defense.gov/News/NewsArticle.aspx?ID=65709 (accessed January 10, 2014).

53. Cheryl Pellerin, "White House Launches U.S. International Cyber Strategy," *American Forces Press Service*, May 17, 2011, available at http://www.defense.gov/news/newsarticle.aspx?id=63966 (accessed January 10, 2014).

54. Carola Hoyos, "Fresh Enemy Emerges in the Battle against Cyberattacks," *Financial Times*, March 12, 2012.

55. Cheryl Pellerin, "DOD Expands International Cyber Cooperation, Official Says," *American Forces Press Service*, April 10, 2012, available at http://www.defense.gov/News/NewsArticle.aspx?ID=67889 (accessed January 10, 2014).

56. Clarke and Knake, *Cyber War*, 178.

57. Clarke and Knake, *Cyber War*, 243.

58. Mahan, "American Foreign Policy" 9.

59. Anthony G. Oettinger, "Information Resources: Knowledge and Power in the 21st Century," *Science*, July 4, 1980: 197.

60. Clarke and Knake, *Cyber War*, xi, xiii.

61. Healey, *Fierce Domain*, 85, 21.

62. Clarke and Knake, *Cyber War*, 149.

63. Richard Hill, *The New International Telecommunication Regulations and the Internet: A Commentary and Legislative History* (Zurich: Schulthess, 2013).

64. Herbert I. Schiller, *Information and the Crisis Economy* (Norwood, N.J.: Ablex, 1984), 15–26; Armand Mattelart, *The Globalization of Surveillance* (Cambridge: Polity, 2010), 3.

65. Clarke and Knake, *Cyber War*, 226.

66. Healey, *Fierce Domain*, 49–50.

67. Eric Lichtblau, "Cell Carriers Called On More in Surveillance," *New York Times*, July 9, 2012.

68. "NSA Inspector General Report on Email and Internet Data Collection under Stellar Wind—Full Document," *The Guardian*, June 27, 2013, available at http://www.guardian.co.uk/world/interactive/2013/jun/27/nsa-inspector-general-report-document-data-collection (accessed January 10, 2014); Glenn Greenwald and Spencer Ackerman, "NSA Collected Americans' Email Records in Bulk for Two Years under Obama," *The Guardian*, June 27, 2013, available at http://www.guardian.co.uk/world/2013/jun/27/nsa-data-mining-authorised-obama (accessed January 10, 2014); "The NSA Files," *The Guardian*, available at http://www.guardian.co.uk/world/the-nsa-files (accessed January 10, 2014); Ian Traynor and Dan Roberts, ""Barack Obama Seeks to Limit EU Fallout over US Spying Claims," *The Guardian*, July 1, 2013, available at http://www.theguardian.com/world/2013/jul/01/barack-obama-eu-fallout-us-spying-claims (accessed January 10, 2014).

69. Craig Timberg and Ellen Nakashima, "Agreements with Private Companies Protect U.S. Access to Cables' Data for Surveillance," *Washington Post*, July 7, 2013, http://www.washingtonpost.com/business/technology/agreements-with-private-companies-protect-us-access-to-cables-data-for-surveillance/2013/07/06/aa5d017a-df77-11e2-b2d4-ea6d8f477a01_story.html (accessed January 10, 2014); Tom Engelhardt, "How to Be a Rogue Super-Power," *TomDispatch.com*, July 16, 2013, available at http://www.tomdispatch.com/blog/175725/tomgram%3A_engelhardt%2C_can_edward_snowden_be_deterred (accessed January 10, 2014).

70. Clarke and Knake, 95; see also U.S. GAO, "DOD Supply Chain: Preliminary Observations Indicate That Counterfeit Electronic Parts Can Be Found on Internet Purchasing Platforms," GAO 12–213T, November 8, 2011, available at http://www.gao.gov/products/GAO-12-213T (accessed January 10, 2014).

71. John Markoff, "Old Trick Threatens the Newest Weapons," *New York Times*, October 27, 2009, available at http://www.nytimes.com/2009/10/27/science/27trojan.html?pagewanted=all (accessed January 10, 2014).

72. Executive Office of the President, "The Comprehensive National Cybersecurity Initiative," September 1, 2010, Objective 11, 5, available at http://www.whitehouse.gov/sites/default/files/cybersecurity.pdf (accessed January 10, 2014).

73. Executive Office of the President, "Comprehensive." John Markoff, "U.S. to Reveal Rules on Internet Security," *New York Times*, March 2, 2010, available at http://www.nytimes.com/2010/03/02/science/02cyber.html (accessed January 10, 2014).

74. John Markoff, "A Stronger Net Security System Is Deployed," *New York Times*, June 25, 2011.

75. S. Kent and K. Seo, BBN Technologies, "Security Architecture for the Internet Protocol," Network Working Group RFC 4301, IETF, December 2005. "Because the Internet changes continuously, as systems fail or are replaced or new systems are added, routing tables must be updated constantly. BGP is the protocol that serves this purpose for the global Internet. When BGP fails, portions of the Internet may become unusable for a period of time ranging from minutes to hours." Rick Kuhn, Kotikalapudi Sriram, and Doug Montgomery, "Border Gateway Protocol Security: Recommendations of the National Institute of Standards and Technology," NIST Special Publication 800–54, July 2007, I-1. Also see U.S. Department of Commerce, Internet Policy Task Force, "Cyber Security, Innovation and the Internet Economy," June 2011, "Appendix B: Widely Recognized Security Standards and Practices," 54–64 (hereinafter DoC, "CyberSecurity"), available at http://www.nist.gov/itl/upload/Cybersecurity_Green-Paper_FinalVersion.pdf (accessed January 10, 2014); and Clarke and Knake, *Cyber War*, 74–101.

76. Clarke and Knake, *Cyber War*, 83.

77. Department of Commerce, "CyberSecurity," Appendix C: "Notice of Inquiry Respondents."

78. The White House, "International Strategy for Cyberspace: Prosperity, Security, and Openness in a Networked World," May 2011, available at http://www.whitehouse.gov/sites/default/files/rss_viewer/international_strategy_for_cyberspace.pdf (accessed January 10, 2014); Department of Commerce, "CyberSecurity."

79. DoC, "CyberSecurity," 14.

80. David E. Sanger and Eric Schmitt, "Rise Is Seen in Cyberattacks Targeting U.S. Infrastructure," *New York Times*, July 27, 2012.

81. DoC, "CyberSecurity," 18.

82. DoC, "CyberSecurity," iv–v, 30.

83. Matthew Crain, "The Revolution Will Be Commercialized: Finance, Public Policy, and the Construction of Internet Advertising," PhD diss., University of Illinois Urbana-Champaign, 2013; DoC, "CyberSecurity," 39, 40.

84. U.S. Executive Office of the President, "Cybersecurity Initiative," 1.

85. DoC, "CyberSecurity, 61–62; NIST's statutory responsibilities in this area were codified by the Federal Information Security Management Act (FISMA) of 2002, Public Law 107–347.

86. This widely used figure is cited, for example, in Menn, "Defence."

87. Clarke and Knake, *Cyber War*, 146.

88. Michael S. Schmidt, "New Revisions Weaken Senate Cybersecurity Bill," *New York Times*, July 28, 2012.

89. Schmidt, "New Revisions Weaken Senate Cybersecurity Bill"; 112th Congress, 2d Session, U.S. Senate, Committee on Homeland Security and Governmental Affairs, Testimony

of James A. Lewis, Center for Strategic and International Studies, on "Securing America's Future: The Cybersecurity Act of 2012," February 16, 2012, available at http://www.hsgac .senate.gov/hearings/securing-americas-future-the-cybersecurity-act-of-2012 (accessed January 10, 2014).

90. David Moon, Patrick Ruffini, and David Segal, *Hacking Politics: How Geeks, Progressives, the Tea Party, Gamers, Anarchists and Suits Teamed Up to Defeat SOPA and Save the Internet* (New York: O/R, 2013).

91. 112th Congress, 2d Session, U.S. Senate Committee on Homeland Security and Governmental Affairs, "Press Conference: Co-sponsors Discuss Revised Cyber-Security Act S. 3414," July 24, 2012, available at http://www.hsgac.senate.gov/issues/cybersecurity (accessed January 10, 2014).

92. Barack Obama, "Taking the Cyberattack Threat Seriously," *Wall Street Journal,* July 19, 2012, available at http://online.wsj.com/news/articles/SB10000872396390444433090 4577535492693044650 (accessed January 10, 2014).

93. Siobhan Gorman, "Cyber Bill Relies on Voluntary Security," *Wall Street Journal,* July 25, 2012.

94. Gerry Smith, "Senate Won't Vote On CISPA, Deals Blow to Controversial Cyber Bill," *Huffington Post,* April 25, 2013, available at http://www.huffingtonpost.com/2013/ 04/25/cispa-cyber-bill_n_3158221.html (accessed January 10, 2014).

95. DoC, "CyberSecurity," v, vi; and Testimony of Fiona M. Alexander, Associate Administrator, Office of International Affairs, National Telecommunications and Information Administration, U.S. Department of Commerce, before the Committee on Energy and Commerce, Subcommittee on Communications and Technology, United States House of Representatives, Hearing on "Cybersecurity: Threats to Communications Networks and Public-Sector Responses," March 28, 2012, 1, available at http://www.ntia.doc.gov/ speechtestimony/2012/testimony-associate-administrator-alexander-cybersecurity -threats-communication (accessed January 10, 2014); White House, "International Strategy for Cyberspace."

96. DoC, "CyberSecurity," 44 and n154.

97. White House, "International Strategy for Cyberspace," 11.

98. Messaging Anti-Abuse Working Group, "Comment," 7, in DoC, "CyberSecurity," 45, available at http://www.nist.gov/itl/upload/MAAWG_DoC_Internet_Task_Force-2011 -08.pdf (accessed January 10, 2014).

99. DoC, "CyberSecurity," 45.

100. White House, "International Strategy for Cyberspace," 14.

101. Bradley R. Simpson, *Economists with Guns: Authoritarian Development and U.S.- Indonesian Relations, 1960–1968* (Stanford, Calif.: Stanford University Press, 2008); for the overall U.S.-guided discourse of "development," see Michael E. Latham, *Modernization as Ideology: American Social Science and "Nation Building" in the Kennedy Era* (Durham: University of North Carolina Press, 2000).

102. White House, "International Strategy for Cyberspace," 13.

103. White House, "International Strategy for Cyberspace," 18, 21.

104. "Meridian 2011 Summary," *Meridian Newsletter* 6, no. 1 (January 31, 2012), 2, available at http://www.meridian.org.

105. White House, "International Strategy for Cyberspace," 18.

106. White House, "International Strategy for Cyberspace," 19.

107. Joseph Menn, "Founding Father Wants Secure 'Internet 2,'" *FT.com*, October 11, 2011, available at http://www.ft.com/intl/cms/s/2/9b28f1ec-eaa9-11e0-aeca-00144feab 49a.html#axzz2kpB5vznV (accessed January 10, 2014).

108. American Civil Liberties Union, "Administration Seeks Easy Access to Americans' Private Online Communications," September 27, 2010, available at https://www.aclu .org/technology-and-liberty/administration-seeks-easy-access-americans-private-online -communications (accessed January 10, 2014). See also Electronic Privacy Information Center, at www.epig.org; Thom Shanker and David E. Sanger, "Privacy May Be a Victim in Cyberdefense Plan," *New York Times*, June 13, 2009, available at http://www.nytimes.com/ 2009/06/13/us/politics/13cyber.html?pagewanted=all (accessed January 10, 2014).

109. Clarke and Knake, *Cyber War*, 146.

110. Greg Oslan at Boeing's Narus unit, in Joseph Menn, "Online Privacy Risks Becoming an Early Casualty," *Financial Times*, October 11, 2011.

111. Menn, "Online Privacy."

112. Clarke and Knake, *Cyber War*, 276.

113. Ian Bremmer, "Democracy in Cyberspace," *Foreign Affairs* 89, no. 6 (November–December 2010), 92.

114. White House, "International Strategy," 3, 8 (fragmented) and generally.

115. John D. Negroponte, Samuel J. Palmisano, and Adam Segal, "Defending an Open, Global, Secure, and Resilient Internet," May 2011, 13, 67, available at http://www.whitehouse .gov/sites/default/files/rss_viewer/international_strategy_for_cyberspace.pdf (accessed January 10, 2014). Emphasis in original.

116. Information Technology and Innovation Foundation, "The Impact of PRISM on Digital Trade Policy," July 24, 2013, Washington, D.C., announcement available at http:// www.itif.org/events/impact-prism-digital-trade-policy (accessed January 10, 2014).

117. Information Technology and Innovation Foundation, "How Much Will PRISM Cost U.S. Cloud Computing Providers?" August 5, 2013, available at http://mpictcenter.blogspot .com/2013/08/itif-how-much-will-prism-cost-us-cloud.html (accessed January 10, 2014).

118. Richard Waters, "Cisco Cites EM Backlash over NSA Leaks as It Warns on Sales," *Financial Times*, November 14, 2013.

119. "The Future of Internet Governance after Dubai: Are We Heading to a Federated Internet?" Columbia University Institute for Tele-Information, June 20, 2013.

Chapter 15. From Geopolitics to Social and Political Struggle

1. David Harvey, *The Enigma of Capital* (New York: Oxford University Press, 2010), 215–16.

2. Martin Wolf, "The West No Longer Holds All the Cards," *Financial Times* Special Report "G20 in Pittsburgh," September 24, 2009; Edward Luce, "Tensions over IMF

Threaten to Mar G20," *Financial Times*, September 25, 2009; Krishna Guha, Edward Luce, Chris Giles, and Gideon Rachman, "Scepticism over G20 Pledge of New Era," *Financial Times*, September 26–27, 2009: 1.

3. International Monetary Fund, "Factsheet: IMF Quotas," March 31, 2013, available at http://www.imf.org/external/np/exr/facts/quotas.htm (accessed January 10, 2014).

4. Vijay Prashad, *The Poorer Nations: A Possible History of the Global South* (London: Verso, 2012), 189–91.

5. Claire Jones, "Power Structures: Emerging Nations Seek Better Balance," *Financial Times*, June 18, 2012.

6. Scott Shane, "Global Forecast by American Intelligence Expects Al Qaeda's Appeal to Falter," *New York Times*, November 21, 2008; National Intelligence Council, "Global Trends 2025: A Transformed World," available at http://www.aicpa.org/research/cpahorizons2025/globalforces/downloadabledocuments/globaltrends.pdf (accessed January 10, 2014).

7. Claire Jones, "Power Structures: Emerging Nations Seek Better Balance," *Financial Times*, June 18, 2012.

8. Doug Palmer, "U.S. Seeks Expanded Information-Technology Pact," *Politico*, November 11, 2013, available at http://www.politico.com/story/2013/11/us-pact-trade-info-technology-99631.html (accessed January 10, 2014).

9. Alex Hern and Dominic Rushe, "WikiLeaks Publishes Secret Draft Chapter of Trans-Pacific Partnership," *The Guardian*, November 13, 2013, available at http://www.theguardian.com/media/2013/nov/13/wikileaks-trans-pacific-partnership-chapter-secret (accessed January 10, 2014).

10. Peter Nolan and Jin Zhang, "Global Competition after the Financial Crisis," *New Left Review* 64 (July–August 2010): 97–108. In 2013, symptomatically, three great global industries—steel, petroleum refining, and, as we saw in part 1, auto—all faced massive overcapacity. "An Inferno of Unprofitability," *The Economist*, July 6, 2013; Guy Chazan and Ed Crooks, "Refining Overcapacity Hits Shell, Total and ExxonMobil," *Financial Times*, November 1, 2013.

11. Lin Chun, *China and Global Capitalism: Reflections on Marxism, History, and Contemporary Politics* (New York: Palgrave, 2013).

12. Michael Pettis, *The Great Rebalancing: Trade, Conflict, and the Perilous Road Ahead for the World Economy* (Princeton, N.J.: Princeton University Press, 2013); Peter Nolan, *Is China Buying the World?* (London: Polity, 2012).

13. For a prior formulation, see Dan Schiller, *How To Think about Information* (Urbana: University of Illinois Press, 2007), 177–97.

14. Yu Hong, "Information Society with Chinese Characteristics—Discursive Construction of the Neo-industrialization Strategy in the People's Daily," *Javnost—The Public* 15, no. 3 (2008): 3, 23–38, available at http://www.javnost-thepublic.org/article/2008/3/2/ (accessed February 21, 2014); Yu Hong, *Labor, Class Formation, and China's Informationized Policy of Economic Development* (Lanham, Md.: Rowman and Littlefield, 2011).

15. Yuezhi Zhao, "China's Pursuits of Indigenous Innovations in Information Technology Developments: Hopes, Follies, and Uncertainties," *Chinese Journal of Communication* 3, no. 3 (September 2010): 266–89.

16. "Lenovo," The Lex Column, *Financial Times*, August 20, 2010.

17. Chris Nuttall and Maija Palmer, "Ailing HP Takes $8bn Writedown," *Financial Times*, August 9, 2012.

18. Dan Schiller and Christian Sandvig, "Google v. China: Principled, Brave, or Business as Usual?" *Huffington Post*, April 5, 2010, available at http://www.huffingtonpost.com/dan-schiller/google-v-china-principled_b_524727.html (accessed January 10, 2014); Kathrin Hille and Tom Mitchell, "News Corp Admits Defeat in China with Sale of TV Channels," *Financial Times*, August 10, 2010; Kathrin Hille, "Functionality Remains Top Priority for Chinese Group," *Financial Times*, September 2, 2010; David Barboza, "New China Search Engine Will Be State-Controlled," *New York Times*, August 14, 2010.

19. Facebook, Inc., Form 10-Q, U.S. Securities and Exchange Commission, June 30, 2013, 48.

20. Kathy Chu and William Launder, "U.S. Media Firms Stymied in China," *Wall Street Journal*, December 7–8, 2013.

21. Sarah Mishkin, "$10bn Xiaomi Beats Apple in China," *Financial Times*, August 24, 2013.

22. ShinJoung Yeo, "Behind the Search Box: The Political Economy of the Global Search Engine Industry," draft PhD diss., University of Illinois, Urbana-Champaign, 2013.

23. Brian Deagon, "Alibaba IPO Looms: Inside China's eBay-Amazon-Google," *Investors.com*, January 31, 2014, available at http://news.investors.com/technology/013114-688253-alibaba-group-humongous-ipo-looms-amid-rapid-growth.htm?ref=mp (accessed February 22, 2014); Paul J. Davies, "Alibaba Board Wrestles over Listed Future," *Financial Times*, September 9, 2013.

24. Tom Mitchell, Song Jung-a, and James Crabtree, "Apple Seeks Leap Forward in Biggest Market," *Financial Times*, September 12, 2013; Gregg Keizer, "China Mobile-Apple iPhone Pact 'Very Big Deal,'" *Computerworld*, December 5, 2013, available at http://www.computerworld.com/s/article/9244557/China_Mobile_Apple_iPhone_pact_very_big_deal (accessed February 22, 2014).

25. Nolan, *Is China Buying the World?*, 118.

26. Leigh Ann Ragland et al., Center for Intelligence Research and Analysis, "Red Cloud Rising: Cloud Computing in China," Research Report Prepared on Behalf of the U.S.-China Economic and Security Review Commission, September 5, 2013: 47.

27. Toby Miller et al., *Global Hollywood II* (London: BFI, 2005).

28. Michael Cieply, "U.S. Box Office Heroes Proving Mortal in China," *New York Times*, April 22, 2013; Matthew Garrahan, "China Reels in Hollywood as Multiplex Screens Thrive," *Financial Times*, April 25, 2013.

29. Yu Hong, "Reading the Twelfth Five-Year Plan: China's Communication-Driven Mode of Economic Restructuring," *International Journal of Communication* 5 (2011): 1045–57; Yu Hong, "Between Corporate Development and Public Service: The Cultural System Reform in the Chinese Media Sector," *Media, Culture and Society*, 2014 (forthcoming); Yu Hong, Francois Bar, and Zheng An, "Chinese Telecommunications on the Threshold of Convergence: Contexts, Possibilities and Limitations of Forging a Nation-Centric Growth Model," *Telecommunications Policy* 36, no. 10–11 (November–December 2012):

914–28; Yuezhi Zhao, *Communication in China* (Lanham, Md.: Rowman and Littlefield, 2008).

30. Perhaps unreliable official figures set the worth of China's "cultural industry" alone at $120 billion in 2009. "The 10 Most Important Business Policies of the Year," *China Daily*, December 23, 2010, available at http://www.chinadaily.com.cn/bizchina/2010-12/23/content_11746341.htm (accessed January 10, 2014); Chen Limin, "Cultural Industry Likely to Flourish under State Plans," *China Daily*, December 16, 2010; Yu Hong, "Corporate Development."

31. "China to Shell Out USD325bn on Broadband Development," *TeleGeography*, CommsUpdate, September 19, 2013; "China Sets New Targets for Broadband," *TeleGeography*, CommsUpdate, August 19, 2013; "Fiber in New Homes to be Compulsory," *TeleGeography*, CommsUpdate, January 16, 2013; "China Telecom's LTE Spending to Pass USD7bn in 2014," *TeleGeography*, CommsUpdate, November 26, 2013; "China Hands over TD-LTE Concessions Paving the Way for China Mobile Launch," *TeleGeography*, CommsUpdate, December 4, 2013.

32. Ragland et al., "Red Cloud Rising," 13, 49.

33. Hu Yong et al., "Mapping Digital Media: China," Open Society Foundations, October 2012, available at http://www.opensocietyfoundations.org/reports/mapping-digital-media-china (accessed February 22, 2014).

34. Simon Montlake, "Chinese Leaders Knock On Internet Giants' Doors As Transition Unfolds," *Forbes*, December 13, 2013, available at http://www.forbes.com/sites/simonmontlake/2012/12/13/chinese-leaders-knock-on-internet-giants-doors-as-transition-unfolds/ (accessed February 22, 2014).

35. For one well-publicized U.S. parallel, see "Huawei Sees Resolution of U.S. Security Concern Taking a Decade," *Bloomberg.com*, October 17, 2013, available at http://www.bloomberg.com/news/2013-10-18/huawei-sees-resolution-of-u-s-security-concern-taking-a-decade.html (accessed February 22, 2014).

36. For Microsoft, Clarke and Knake, *Cyber-War*; for Apple, Ronald J. Deibert, *Black Code: Inside the Battle for Cyberspace* (Toronto: Signal [McLelland and Stewart], 2013), 79.

37. Paul Mozur, "China Mobile Calls on Its Clout for 4G Standards," *Wall Street Journal*, August 16, 2013.

38. Supantha Mukherjee and Neha Alawadhi, "China Probe May Be Aimed at Qualcomm's 4G Royalties," *Reuters*, November 26, 2013, available at http://www.reuters.com/article/2013/11/26/us-qualcomm-china-idUSBRE9AO0E820131126 (accessed February 22, 2014).

39. Hasso Plattner, quoted in Chris Bryant, "NSA Claims Put German Business on Guard," *Financial Times*, November 1, 2013.

40. Shira Ovide, "SAP to Have One CEO, an American," *Wall Street Journal*, July 22, 2013.

41. Richard Milne, "Nokia Faces Fresh Test of Endurance," *Financial Times*, September 4, 2013; Adam Thomson, "Combes Seizes Alcatel's Last Chance," *Financial Times*, October 9, 2013.

42. Marie Anchordoguy, *Computers, Inc.: Japan's Challenge To IBM*, Harvard East Asian Monograph 144 (Cambridge: Council on East Asian Studies of Harvard University, and Harvard University Press, 1989).

43. Vijay Prashad, *The Darker Nations* (New York: New Press, 2007); Dan Schiller, *How To Think about Information*, 36–57.

44. Bill Vlasic, Hiroko Tabuchi, and Charles Duhigg, "An American Model for Tech Jobs?" *New York Times*, August 5, 2012. Brazil did not so much capitulate to transnational capital as reintegrate with it on more favorable terms than were available to smaller economies.

45. Sara Schoonmaker, *High-Tech Trade Wars: U.S.-Brazilian Conflicts in the Global Economy* (Pittsburgh: University of Pittsburgh Press, 2002); Bill Woodcock, "On Internet, Brazil Is Beating US at Its Own Game," *Al Jazeera America*, September 20, 2013, available at http://america.aljazeera.com/articles/2013/9/20/brazil-internet-dilmarousseffnsa.html (accessed January 10, 2014).

46. Vivek Chibber, *Locked In Place: State-Building and Late Industrialization in India* (Princeton, N.J.: Princeton University Press, 2003); Jyoti Saraswati, *Dot.Compradors: Power and Policy in the Development of the Indian Software Industry* (London: Pluto, 2012); and Pradip Ninan Thomas, *Digital India: Understanding Information, Communication and Social Change* (New Delhi: Sage, 2012). India continues to promote local production of ICTs on a selective basis. "India to Pay Out INR100bn to Local Vendors," *TeleGeography*, CommsUpdate, October 28, 2013.

47. Dal Yong Jin, *Korea's Online Gaming Empire* (Cambridge, Mass.: MIT Press, 2010); Dal Yong Jin, *Hands On/Hands Off: The Korean State and the Market Liberalization of the Communication Industry* (Cresskill, N.J.: Hampton, 2010); Kwang-Suk Lee, "A Final Flowering of the Developmental State: The IT Policy Experiment of the Korean Information Infrastructure, 1995–2005," University of Wollongong Research Online, 2009, available at http://ro.uow.edu.au/cgi/viewcontent.cgi?article=1247&context=artspapers (accessed February 22, 2014); Kwang-Suk Lee, *IT Development in Korea: A Broadband Nirvana?* (London: Routledge, 2012); Cheol Gi Bae, "The Transformation of the Korean Wireless Telecommunications Policy: Interplays Between the State, Transnational Forces, Business, and Networked Users," PhD diss., University of Illinois at Urbana-Champaign, 2013.

48. "After the Personal Computer," *The Economist*, July 6, 2013; "Chips," The Lex Column, *Financial Times*, July 19, 2013.

49. Eric Pfanner, "Taiwan Chip Industry Powers the Tech World, but Struggles for Status," *New York Times*, September 16, 2013.

50. Valentin Makarov, Stefan Schandera, and Jean-Paul Simon, "The ICT Landscape in BRICS Countries: 5. Russian Federation," *Digiworld Economic Journal* 87 (2012), 163, available at http://is.jrc.ec.europa.eu/pages/documents/CS87_Feat_SIMON_et_al.pdf (accessed January 10, 2014).

51. Jack Linchuan Qiu, "China's Network Society: A Three-Phase Trajectory—Asteroids, Bees, Coliseums," Presentation to Centre for the Study of Global Media and Democracy, Goldsmiths, University of London, May 29, 2013.

52. Jeremy Page, "China Deepens Xi's Powers with New Security Plan," *Wall Street Journal*, November 12, 2013, available at http://online.wsj.com/news/articles/SB20001 4240527023046441045791939212242308990 (accessed January 10, 2014); Sui-Lee Wee and Ben Blanchard, "China to Revamp Security in Face of Threats at Home, Abroad," *Reuters*, November 12, 2013, available at http://uk.reuters.com/article/2013/11/12/uk-china -reform-politics-idUKBRE9AB0Q420131112 (accessed January 10, 2014).

53. Nolan, *Is China Buying The World?*, 59–60; Michael Specter, "The Gene Factory," *New Yorker*, January 6, 2014, 34–43.

54. Hillary Clinton, "America's Pacific Century," *Foreign Policy* (November 2011): 60, available at http://www.foreignpolicy.com/articles/2011/10/11/americas_pacific_century (accessed January 10, 2014).

55. Adrian Wan, "Chinese Software Pioneer Red Flag Bites the Dust," *South China Morning Post*, February 14, 2014, available at http://www.scmp.com/business/china-business/ article/1427823/chinese-software-pioneer-red-flag-bites-dust (accessed February 22, 2014). Thanks to Tang Min for this reference.

56. Simon Rabinovitch and Leslie Hook, "Chinese Groups Step Up Push for Global Deals," *Financial Times*, December 11, 2012.

57. Kathrin Hille, "China's ZTE Seals E200m Mobile Deal with Telenor," *Financial Times*, August 23, 2010.

58. Charles Clover, "Lenovo to Buy IBM's x86," *Financial Times*, January 24, 2014; Richard Waters and Charles Clover, "Lenovo Dials into US Market," *Financial Times*, January 31, 2014.

59. Joe Leahy, "China Telecom Moves to Secure Foothold in Brazil," *Financial Times*, June 14, 2012.

60. Kathrin Hille, "China Telecom Gains Access to AT&T's Networks," *Financial Times*, November 30, 2011, available at http://www.ft.com/intl/cms/s/0/b5f1e728-1b6d -11e1-85f8-00144feabdco.html#axzz1ffP3fhLZ (accessed January 14, 2014).

61. Juro Osawa, "China's WeChat App Targets U.S. Users," *WSJ.com*, January 27, 2014, available at http://blogs.wsj.com/digits/2014/01/27/chinas-wechat-app-targets-u-s-users/ (accessed February 22, 2014).

62. Keith Bradsher, "Chinese Titan Takes Aim At Hollywood," *New York Times*, September 23, 2013.

63. Broadly, I follow Nolan, *Is China Buying The World?*

64. "US Introduces Cyber-Espionage Clause to Funding Law to Lock Out Chinese Vendors," *TeleGeography*, CommsUpdate, March 28, 2013; Richard McGregor, "Huawei Deal With S. Korea Is Threat to US-Seoul Defence Ties, Warn Senators," *Financial Times*, December 4, 2013.

65. State Department cable, February 28, 2009, classified "Confidential," in David E. Sanger, *Confront and Conceal* (New York: Crown, 2012), 369.

66. Another writer noted that "owing more than a trillion dollars to China has clearly placed the United States in the distinctly uncomfortable position of being seen as a financial supplicant to its principal competitor." Alan Dupont, "An Asian Security Standoff,"

The National Interest, May/June 2012, 56. This said, however, as Peter Nolan emphasizes, at $1.2 trillion in June 2011, China's share of U.S. government debt—the largest share by any foreign holder—amounted to about 12 percent of the total. Nolan, *Is China Buying the World?*, 4, and n4.

67. David E. Sanger, "Differences on Cybertheft Complicate China Talks," *New York Times*, July 13, 2013.

68. Andrew Parker, "Huawei Eyes Deals Worth $30 Billion," *Financial Times*, March 9, 2009; Amol Sharma and Sara Silver, "Huawei Tries to Crack U.S. Market," *Wall Street Journal*, March 26, 2009; Kevin J. O'Brien, "Upstart Chinese Telecom Company Rattles Industry as It Rises to No. 2," *New York Times*, November 30, 2009; David Barboza, "Scrutiny for Chinese Telecom Bid," *New York Times*, August 23, 2010; Stephanie Kirchgaessner, "Challenge to Huawei's US ambitions," *Financial Times*, August 22, 2010: 9; "Huawei Sees Resolution of U.S. Security Concern Taking a Decade." *Bloomberg News*, October 17, 2013. Also see Peter Nolan, *Is China Buying the World?*

69. Also see John Bellamy Foster and Robert W. McChesney, *The Endless Crisis: How Monopoly-Finance Capital Produces Stagnation and Upheaval from the USA to China* (New York: Monthly Review Press, 2012), 155–83.

70. Nolan and Zhang, "Global Competition"; Nolan, *Is China Buying The World?*

71. Richard Milne and Anousha Sakoui, "Rivers of Riches," *Financial Times*, May 23, 2011.

72. John Authers, "Corporate America Cannot Cut Its Way to Prosperity," *Financial Times*, July 23, 2012.

73. Tony Jackson "Cash-Hoarding Companies Seem Unable to Splash Out," *Financial Times*, March 12, 2012: 14; Anousha Sakoui, "Concentrated Cash Pile Puts Recovery in Hands of the Few," *Financial Times*, January 22, 2014; Ed Crooks, "'Animal Spirits' of Spending Jostle for Release," *Financial Times*, January 24, 2014.

74. Jenna Wortham and Evelyn M. Rusli, "Silicon Valley Showing Signs of New Bubble," *New York Times*, December 4, 2010.

75. Jessica E. Vascellaro and Ian Sherr, "Rare Miss for Apple as iPhone Sales Cool," *Wall Street Journal*, July 25, 2012; Anousha Sakoui, "Pressure Builds for Groups to Put Their Cash Hoards to Work," *Financial Times*, January 22, 2014. Midway through 2013, just six companies—Apple, Microsoft, Google, Cisco, Oracle, and Qualcomm—held more than one-quarter of the $1.5 trillion hoard possessed by U.S. nonfinancial corporations. Richard Waters, "Tech Sector Still Sitting on a Mountain of Wealth," *Financial Times*, January 22, 2014.

76. Sakoui, "Pressure Builds."

77. Hannah Kuchler and Tim Bradshaw, "WhatsApp Pushes Tech Deal Total to $50bn," *Financial Times*, February 21, 2014.

78. Reported in Milne and Sakoui, "Rivers of Riches."

79. Nick Wingfield, "Amazon's Profit Falls as It Spends Heavily on Projects," *New York Times*, April 26, 2013.

80. Henny Sender, "Pessimism over US and the Dollar Will be Shortlived," *Financial Times*, November 2–3, 2013.

81. Ed Crooks, "US Capital Spending Set to Slow to Four-Year Low in Sign of Caution," *Financial Times*, January 24, 2014; "America's Corporate Investment Drought" (editorial), *Financial Times*, January 24, 2014.

82. "Cisco," The Lex Column, *Financial Times*, March 16, 2012.

83. "Apple/Icahn," The Lex Column, *Financial Times*, December 6, 2013.

84. Kevin J. O'Brien, "Microsoft and Huawei of China to Unite to Sell Low-Cost Windows Smartphones in Africa," *New York Times*, February 5, 2013.

85. Pettis, *Great Rebalancing*.

86. Francis Fukuyama, "Conservatives Must Fall Back in Love with the State," *Financial Times*, July 21–22, 2012.

87. Dominique Strauss-Kahn, "Saving the Lost Generation," *IMF Direct*, September 14, 2010, available at http://blog-imfdirect.imf.org/2010/09/14/saving-the-lost-generation (accessed January 10, 2014).

88. David Harvey, *Rebel Cities: From the Right to the City to the Urban Revolution* (London: Verso, 2012), 159.

89. Quoted in Joe Leahy and Chris Giles, "IMF Warns on Growing Global Risks," *FT.com*, June 17, 2011, available at http://www.ft.com/intl/cms/s/0/a2a1834a-98cd-11e0-bd66 -00144feab49a.html#axzz1PYLWMMOs (accessed January 10, 2014).

90. "General Strike against Cuts Brings Greece to a Halt," *BBC News Europe*, November 6, 2013, available at http://www.bbc.co.uk/news/world-europe-24832847 (accessed January 10, 2014).

91. James Mackintosh, "The World Is Halfway through a Lost Decade," *Financial Times*, August 12, 2012.

92. Lawrence H. Summers, "Technological Opportunities, Job Creation, and Economic Growth," Remarks at the New America Foundation on the President's Spectrum Initiative, June 28, 2010, 3.

93. Ursula Huws, "Crisis as Capitalist Opportunity: New Accumulation through Public Service Commodification," in Leo Panitch, Greg Albo, and Vivek Chibber, eds., *The Crisis and the Left, Socialist Register 2012* (Pontypool, Wales: Merlin, 2011), 64–84.

94. Michael Perelman, *The Invention of Capitalism: Classical Political Economy and the Secret History of Primitive Accumulation* (Durham, N.C.: Duke University Press, 2000); Harvey, *Enigma of Capital*.

95. D. Alpert and D. Bitzer, "Advances in Computer-Based Education: A Progress Report on the PLATO Program," University of Illinois, Computer-based Education Research Laboratory CERL Report X-10, Urbana, July 1969.

96. Anna Vigna, "Mexico's Teleschools," *Le Monde diplomatique*, March 2012, 12.

97. Dan Schiller, *Digital Capitalism: Networking the Global Market System* (Cambridge, Mass.: MIT Press, 1999), 143–202.

98. Paulo Trevisani, "Brazil Welcomes For-Profit Schools as Aspiring Professionals Seek Skills," *Wall Street Journal*, June 27, 2011. For discussion in the context of U.S.-Mexico relations, see Lora E. Taub and Dan Schiller, "Networking the North American Higher Education Industry," in *Continental Order? Integrating North America for Cyber-Capitalism*, ed. Vincent Mosco and Dan Schiller (Lanham, Md.: Rowman and Littlefield, 2001), 163–88.

99. "Protests for Expansion of Public Higher Education in Sri Lanka," *Inside Higher Ed*, March 13, 2013, available at http://www.insidehighered.com/quicktakes/2013/03/13/protests-expansion-public-higher-ed-sri-lanka (accessed January 10, 2014).

100. Andrew England, "Parents Race to Enroll Children as Low Cost Private Schools Boom in S. Africa," *Financial Times*, February 15, 2012; Joe Leahy, "Private Education Offers Lucrative Pickings in Brazil," *Financial Times*, September 29, 2011.

101. Aisha Labi, "Europe's Austerity Measures Take Their Toll on Academe," *Chronicle of Higher Education*, April 29, 2012, available at http://chronicle.com/article/Europes-Austerity-Measures/131739 (accessed January 10, 2014).

102. Motoko Rich, "Private Preschools See More Public Funds as Classes Grow," *New York Times*, June 24, 2013.

103. Steven Yaccino and Motoko Rich, "Chicago Makes It Official, with 54 Schools to Be Closed," *New York Times*, March 22, 2013; Steven Yaccino, "Protests Fail to Deter Chicago from Shutting 49 Schools," *New York Times*, May 23, 2013.

104. Anton Troianovski, "The Web-Deprived Study at McDonald's," *Wall Street Journal*, January 29, 2013.

105. David Leonhardt, "Through Enrolling More Poor Students, 2-Year Colleges Get Less of Federal Pie," *New York Times*, May 23, 2013.

106. Robert Lindsey, "California Weighs End of Free College Education," *New York Times*, December 28, 1982.

107. Ariel Kaminer, "College Ends Free Tuition, and an Era," *New York Times*, April 24, 2013.

108. About 5 percent of students at the two hundred elite four-year colleges came from the bottom economic quartile in 2006. Leonhardt, "Poor Students."

109. Noam Chomsky, "The Assault on Public Education," *Truthout*, April 4, 2012, available at http://truth-out.org/opinion/item/8305-the-assault-on-public-education (accessed January 10, 2014). Chomsky cites Josh Bivens, *Failure by Design* (Washington, D.C., Economic Policy Institute, 2011), available at http://www.epi.org/publication/failure-by-design (accessed January 10, 2014).

110. Floyd Norris, "Colleges for Profit Are Growing, with U.S. Aid," *New York Times*, May 25, 2012.

111. Tamar Lewin, "For-Profit College Group Sued As U.S. Portrays Wide Fraud," *New York Times*, August 9, 2011.

112. U.S. Senate, 112th Cong., 2d Sess., Committee on Health, Education, Labor and Pensions, *For-Profit Higher Education: The Failure to Safeguard the Federal Investment and Ensure Student Success*, Committee Print S 112–37, 4 vols. (Washington, D.C.: GPO, July 2012).

113. Melissa Korn, "For-Profit Schools Increasingly Find the Party Is Over," *Wall Street Journal*, August 23, 2011.

114. John Markoff, "Online Education Venture Lures Cash Infusion and Deals with 5 Top Universities," *New York Times*, April 18, 2012.

115. For a belated exception, see Edward Luce, "Moocs Are No Magic Bullet for Educating Americans," *Financial Times*, November 25, 2013.

116. Tamar Lewin, "Universities Team with Online Course Provider," *New York Times*, May 30, 2013.

117. Ki Mae Heussner, "A New Blackboard? 4 Ways the Ed Tech Giant's New CEO Hopes to Win Back Market Share," *CNN Money.com*, July 12, 2013, available at http://gigaom.com/2013/07/12/a-new-blackboard-4-ways-the-ed-tech-giants-new-ceo-hopes-to-win-back-market-share (accessed January 10, 2014).

118. Trevisani, "Brazil," B6.

119. Richard Garner, "Chalk Talk: Impressive Results in the Far East—A 'Shadow' over Plans to Improve Our Schools?" *The Independent*, February 5, 2014, available at http://www.independent.co.uk/news/education/schools/chalk-talk-impressive-results-in-the-far-east—a-shadow-over-plans-to-improve-our-schools-9110187.html (accessed February 23, 2014).

120. April Dembosky, "US Online Learning Groups Seek to Push Borders," *Financial Times*, August 5, 2013.

121. Andrew Edgcliffe-Johnson, "Apple Opens New Era in Digital Learning," *Financial Times*, January 20, 2012.

122. Amy Chozick, "News Corp. Has a Tablet for Schools," *New York Times*, March 6, 2013, available at http://www.nytimes.com/2013/03/06/business/media/news-corp-has-a-tablet-for-schools.html?pagewanted=all&_r=0 (accessed January 10, 2014).

123. Amy Chozick, "News Corp. Brands Unit for Education as Amplify," *New York Times*, July 24, 2012.

124. Steve Kolowich, "Harvard Professors Call for Greater Oversight of MOOCs," *Chronicle of Higher Education*, May 24, 2013, available at http://chronicle.com/blogs/wiredcampus/harvard-professors-call-for-greater-oversight-of-moocs/43953 (accessed January 10, 2014).

125. For a progress report see Alexei Barrionuevo, "With Kiss-Ins and Dances, Young Chileans Push for Reform," *New York Times*, August 5, 2011; for Quebec, Matthew Brett, "The Student Movement: Radical Priorities," *The Bullet*, Socialist Project E-Bulletin No. 619, April 19, 2012.

126. Associated Press, "Policy Proposals of Top Two Candidates in Chile's Presidential Vote," December 16, 2013, available at http://article.wn.com/view/2013/11/17/Policy_proposals_of_top_2_candidates_in_Chile_s_presidential/#/video (accessed January 10, 2014).

127. Richard Seymour, "Quebec's Students Provide a Lesson in Protest Politics," *The Guardian*, September 7, 2012, available at http://www.guardian.co.uk/commentisfree/2012/sep/07/quebec-students-lesson-protest-politics (accessed January 10, 2014); Xavier Lafrance and Alan Sears, "Campus Fightbacks in the Age of Austerity: Learning from Quebec Students," *The Bullet*, Socialist Project E-Bulletin No. 771, February 9, 2013.

128. Gill Plimmer, "It's Back to the 1980s as Privatization Fever Takes a Grip," *Financial Times*, June 27, 2011.

129. Lydia Polgreen, "Scanning 2.4 Billion Eyes, India Tries to Connect Poor to Growth," *New York Times*, September 2, 2011. For e-government in India see Thomas, *Digital India*.

130. Clive Cookson, "Industry Braced for Information Deluge," *Financial Times*, Health Life Sciences Special Report, June 27, 2011.

131. Nicholas Timmins, "Only the Bare Bones," *Financial Times*, May 17, 2011.

132. Steve Lohr, "Digital Records May Not Cut Health Costs, Study Cautions," *New York Times*, March 6, 2012.

133. Duff Wilson, "Medical Industry Ties Often Undisclosed in Journals," *New York Times*, September 14, 2010; Abigail Zuger, "A Drumbeat on Profit Takers," *New York Times*, March 20, 2012. In 2012, a dozen drug companies paid U.S. doctors more than $1 billion in efforts to influence them to prescribe specific drugs. Andrew Jack, "US Doctors Paid $1bn Last Year by Drugs Groups," *Financial Times*, May 23, 2013.

134. Kevin Sack, "Medical Data of Thousands Posted Online," *New York Times*, September 9, 2011.

135. Amy Harmon and Andrew Pollack, "Battle Brewing over Labeling of Genetically Modified Food," *New York Times*, May 25, 2012.

136. Jennifer Howard, "Google Begins to Scale Back Its Scanning of Books from University Libraries," *Chronicle of Higher Education*, March 9, 2012, available at http://chronicle.com/article/Google-Begins-to-Scale-Back/131109 (accessed January 10, 2014).

137. Katrina Fenlon, "Corporate Mass Digitization and Cultural Heritage: From Public Relations to Content Accumulation," unpublished research paper, Graduate School of Library and Information Science, University of Illinois at Urbana-Champaign, October 2013.

138. U.S. Department of Commerce, Bureau of Economic Analysis and National Endowment for the Arts, "U.S. Bureau of Economic Analysis and National Endowment for the Arts Release Preliminary Report on Impact of Arts and Culture on U.S. Economy," BEA-13–58, December 5, 2013, available at http://arts.gov/news/2013/us-bureau-economic-analysis-and-national-endowment-arts-release-preliminary-report-impact (accessed February 23, 2014).

139. Alasdair Roberts, *Blacked Out: Government Secrecy in the Information Age* (New York: Cambridge University Press, 2006); Pradip Ninan Thomas, *Political Economy of Communications in India: The Good, the Bad and the Ugly* (New Delhi: Sage, 2010); Pradip Ninan Thomas and Jan Servaes, eds., *Intellectual Property Rights and Communications in Asia: Conflicting Traditions* (New Delhi: Sage, 2006); Gaelle Krikorian and Amy Kapczynski, eds., *Access to Knowledge in the Age of Intellectual Property* (Cambridge, Mass.: MIT Press, 2010).

140. Fred Magdoff, "21st Century Land Grabs: Accumulation by Agricultural Dispossession," *Monthly Review* 65, no. 6 (November 2013): 1–18.

141. Jamil Anderlini, "Milestone Passed as More Chinese Live in Cities than in Countryside," *Financial Times*, January 18, 2012; Zhou Xin and Koh Gui Qing, "China City Dwellers Exceed Villagers for First Time," *Reuters*, January 17, 2012, available at http://www.reuters.com/article/2012/01/17/us-china-population-idUSTRE80G0DB20120117 (accessed January 10, 2014); Chandran Nair, "Reverse the Urbanization Policies That Empty Asia's Countryside," *Financial Times*, March 22, 2013.

142. Ed Hammond and Jamil Anderlini, "China Builds Way to Top of Construction League," *FT.com*, March 2, 2011, available at http://www.ft.com/intl/cms/s/0/f9c3e0ca-44ed-11e0-80e7-00144feab49a.html#axzz2kvAKqOQQ (accessed January 10, 2014).

143. Merryn Somerset Webb, "The Caustic Soda Connection," House and Home, *Financial Times*, July 29, 2012.

144. Martin Wolf, "Risks of a Hard Landing for China," *Financial Times*, July 3, 2013.

145. Edwin Heathcote, "Visions Differ as World Cities Build for the Future," *Financial Times*, September 14, 2011.

146. Simon Rabinovitch, "Chinese City Starts Projects to Fuel Growth," *Financial Times*, August 7, 2012.

147. Rebecca MacKinnon, *Consent of the Networked: The Worldwide Struggle for Internet Freedom* (New York: Basic, 2012), 170; also see Yuezhi Zhao, "The Struggle for Socialism in China: The Bo Xilai Saga and Beyond," *Monthly Review*, 64, no. 5 (2012), available at http://monthlyreview.org/author/yuezhizhao (accessed January 10, 2014).

148. Ed Hammond and Jamil Anderlini, "China Builds Way to Top of Construction League," *Financial Times*, March 2, 2011.

149. David Harvey, *Rebel Cities: From the Right to the City to the Urban Revolution* (London: Verso, 2012), 42, 60.

150. Elizabeth Economy, "China's Land Grab Epidemic Is Causing More Wukan-Style Protests," *The Atlantic*, February 8, 2012, available at http://www.theatlantic.com/international/archive/2012/02/chinas-land-grab-epidemic-is-causing-more-wukan-style-protests/252757 (accessed January 10, 2014); "Police Fire Teargas on Chinese Village after Land Grab Protest," *Reuters*, March 10, 2013, available at http://www.reuters.com/article/2013/03/10/us-china-unrest-idUSBRE92909F20130310 (accessed January 10, 2014).

151. Harvey, Rebel Cities, 115–53.

152. Lin Chun, *China and Global Capitalism: Reflections on Marxism, History, and Contemporary Politics* (New York: Palgrave, 2013).

153. Gregg Shotwell, *Autoworkers under the Gun* (Chicago: Haymarket, 2011), 101.

Index

Electronic Data Systems (EDS), 34, 35, 66, 75
email, 22–23
emerging investor countries, 30
energy use by internet, 173, 312n12
enterprise networks, 88
Entertainment Software Association (ESA), 181
environmental damage, 109
Ericsson, 234
Eurodollars, 45, 47
European Union, Data Protection Directive, 178
exchange rates, 43–44, 45, 50–51
Exxon, 75

Facebook: and advertising, 127, 128, 134; and China, 231; data collection, 136; number of users, 153; patent warfare, 106; profit strategy, 116; streaming music, 121
Federal Reserve Bank: austerity policy, 34, 42, 45; and currency trading, 50–51; and electronic finances, 48; response to 2008 crisis, 52, 53
federated internet, 227–28
Fiat, 50
Fields, Gary, 74
film industry, 76, 121–22, 143, 175, 232, 236–37
financial crises: characteristics, 2–3; Great Depression, 1, 2, 3, 46; recession of 1970s, 13–15, 45, 74; of 2008, 1–2, 3–4, 51–52
financial institutions: accountability, 53; debt held, 51; Federal Reserve bailout, 52; and ICT, 47–50; New Deal reforms, 44, 46; postwar stability, 44; product innovations, 46–47; profits, 47; ties with U.S. government, 44, 47, 52, 53, 264n70; transnationalized, 48–49
financialization: of ICT, 84–88; of online companies, 134; U.S. domination, 54. *See also* networked financialization
Flame computer virus, 216
flash crash (2010), 56
Ford Motor Company, 38, 260n95
foreign direct investment (FDI): by China, 29–30; in China, 154, 231–32, 233; and destabilization of fixed-exchange rate, 43–44; flow in 2010, 154; and free-flow

doctrine, 163; free-trade agreements, 29; in ICT, 85; sources, 29–30; by U.S. corporations, 27–29
France, 206, 214, 233
freedom of expression, 140, 162, 165, 202
free-flow policy: in China, 94; and cloud computing, 165, 177–79, 183; Commerce Department inquiry, 171–72, 174–84; and commodity chains, 163–64, 172; and copyright issues, 174–75, 177; and economic recovery, 171; internet intermediaries challenges, 93–94; Obama administration, 159–62, 163, 166–68; and political economy, 94–95, 162–68, 171–72, 174–84; at WCIT-12, 203; in Western Europe, 94–95
free-trade agreements, 29, 180, 181–82

game consoles, 101–2
gaming, 101–2
Gandy, Oscar, 138
Gates, Kelly A., 138
Gates, Robert, 68
Genachowski, Julius, 164, 165
General Agreement on Tariffs and Trade (GATT), 44
General Electric: as ICT supplier, 75; non-production employees, 18; and privacy, 139
General Motors (GM): bailout by government, 38; design process, 25; and ICT, 34–35, 41, 75; profits, 39; as TNC, 35, 37
geofencing, 108
Germany, 206, 207–8, 233
Gifford, Walter, 59
gigantism: movement away from, 61–63, 77, 85–86; movement toward, 53, 76, 79, 80, 264n79
Gindin, Sam, 51
Glanz, James, 167–68
Global Crossing, 86
global factories, 30–31
Global Hollywood, 232
Global Information Grid (GIG), 65–66
Global Intellectual Property Center, 174–75
Global Network Initiative, 178, 182
Global 100, 126
Global Positioning System, 66

Time Inc., 134
Time-Warner, 80
T-Mobile, 97
Toffler, Alvin, 26
TomTom, 136
"Too Big To Fail," 53, 264n79
Toure, Hamadoun, 203
Tower Records, 76
trade, 29, 30, 180, 181–82
transnational corporations (TNCs): adver-
    tising expenditures, 126–27, 297n3; as-
    sets outside U.S., 45; and China, 230–32,
    235–36; and commodity chains, 7,
    249n37; and cyber-confict, 219, 224, 226;
    and destabilization of fixed-exchange
    rate, 43–44; extent, 29; and federated
    internet, 227–28; of financial institutions,
    48–49; and global factories and trade,
    30–31; GM as, 35, 37; and government
    policies, 33; ICANN as, 187–88; and ICT
    networks, 79; internet as instrument of,
    33; and internet governance, 191, 197–98,
    200, 203, 209, 321n73; internet trade,
    183–84; and labor in poor countries, 36;
    media industry, 75–76, 118, 120, 121–22;
    and privacy, 139; U.S. capital investment,
    27–29; U.S. internet intermediaries as,
    154; U.S. internet leaders, 152–53; and
    U.S. military, 221
Twitter, 133–34, 153

Udemy, 243
unilateral globalism. *See* U.S.–centric in-
    ternet
unions: and GM bailout, 38; and New Deal
    reforms, 57; postwar gains, 14; telecom-
    munications workers, 89; and wage-earn-
    ing class, 37, 42
United Auto Workers, 37
United Kingdom, 127, 208, 214, 215, 233, 244
United States: corporate share of interna-
    tional profits, 254n1; debt held by China,
    237, 342n66; global military supremacy
    commitment, 216–17; industrialization,
    17–18; as market for exports, 28–29;
    percent of Americans living in poverty,
    2; policy of containment, 45; postwar fi-
    nancial stability, 44; trade relations with
    China, 236, 238–39. *See also* Defense De-

partment (DoD); specific departments
    and agencies
United States Council for International
    Business (USCIB), 175, 191
U.S.–centric internet: agencies responsible,
    170–71, 176; challenged, 158–60, 188, 193–
    97, 201–3, 207–10, 227–28; global internet
    use, 154–55; multi-stakeholderism, 187,
    189–200; origins, 185–88; role of capital,
    152–54; Snowden revelations, 204–7
U.S. Chamber of Commerce, 174
U.S. Defense Advanced Research Projects
    Agency (DARPA), 22

value chains, 7
VeriSign, 186, 187, 188, 189, 192
Verizon: bundled services, 92; in China,
    233; free-flow policy, 94, 182–83; spec-
    trum holdings, 97; transnational net-
    works, 79; union workers, 89
vertical markets, 92–95, 106
Viacom, 123
video game industry, 101–2, 181
Vietnam War, 45, 59, 60
Viñals, José, 240
Vodafone, 99, 233
Volcker, Paul, 34, 45

Wacks, Raymond, 136
wage-earning class: and austerity policies,
    45, 55, 69, 239–40; and automation, 24,
    34, 47–48, 49–50; and consumption of
    goods, 38–39, 43; and economic inequal-
    ity, 13, 240; educational opportunities,
    241–43, 345n108; in Europe, 39–40;
    global growth, 35–37; and GM bailout,
    38; in information industry, 18–19, 142,
    304n3; labor systems as weapon against,
    36–37; and New Deal reforms, 57, 60;
    and recession of 1970s, 14; social unrest,
    239–40, 243; and unions, 37, 42; on ur-
    banization, 245–46
wage repression, 36–37, 42, 43, 89
Wallerstein, Immanuel, 8, 250n46
Wal-Mart, 76, 118, 139
Wang Chen, 195–96
war supply industry, 59–60, 61
Washington Consensus, 230
Waters, Richard, 108

DAN SCHILLER is a professor in the Graduate School of Library and Information Science and the Department of Communication at the University of Illinois at Urbana-Champaign. He is the author of *How to Think About Information* and *Digital Capitalism: Networking the Global Market System.*

The University of Illinois Press
is a founding member of the
Association of American University Presses.

———————————————————

Composed in 10.75/13 Arno Pro
by Lisa Connery
at the University of Illinois Press
Manufactured by Cushing-Malloy, Inc.

University of Illinois Press
1325 South Oak Street
Champaign, IL 61820-6903
www.press.uillinois.edu